Support Any Friend

Support Any Friend

*Kennedy's Middle East and the
Making of the U.S.–Israel Alliance*

WARREN BASS

A Council on Foreign Relations Book

OXFORD
UNIVERSITY PRESS
2003

OXFORD
UNIVERSITY PRESS

Oxford   New York
Auckland   Bangkok   Buenos Aires   Cape Town   Chennai
Dar es Salaam   Delhi   Hong Kong   Istanbul   Karachi   Kolkata
Kuala Lumpur   Madrid   Melbourne   Mexico City   Mumbai   Nairobi
São Paulo   Shanghai   Taipei   Tokyo   Toronto

Copyright © 2003 by Warren Bass

Published by Oxford University Press, Inc.
198 Madison Avenue, New York, New York 10016

www.oup.com

Oxford is a registered trademark of Oxford University Press

Library of Congress Cataloging-in-Publication Data
Bass, Warren
Support any friend: Kennedy's Middle East and the making of the
U.S.–Israel alliance / Warren Bass.
p. cm.
Includes bibliographical references (p.   ) and index.
ISBN 0-19-516580-2
1. United States—Foreign relations—Israel.
2. Israel—Foreign relations—United States.
3. Arab-Israeli conflict.
4. United States—Foreign relations—Middle East.
5. Middle East—Foreign relations—United States.
6. United States—Foreign relations—1961–1963.
7. Kennedy, John F. (John Fitzgerald), 1917–1963.
I. Title
E183.8.I75B37   2003
327.73056/09/046 21   13042615

1 3 5 7 9 8 6 4 2

Printed in the United States of America
on acid-free paper

To my grandparents

Nate Basserabie
Gert Basserabie
Joe (Chona) Bobrow

May their memories be for a blessing

and Bess Bobrow

And to the memory of Yitzhak Rabin
"O Captain! my Captain!"

Contents

List of Abbreviations

American Israel Public Affairs Committee, AIPAC
Atomic Energy Commission, AEC
Displaced Person, DP
Front de Liberation Nationale, FLN
International Atomic Energy Agency, IAEA
International Monetary Fund, IMF
Intelligence and Research, INR
Israel Defense Forces, IDF
Jewish National Fund, JNF
Joint Chiefs of Staff, JCS
National Security Agency, NSA
National Security Council, NSC
Near East Affairs, NEA
North Atlantic Treaty Organization, NATO
Palestine Liberation Organization, PLO
Surface-to-air missile, SAM
Surface-to-surface missile, SSM
United Arab Republic, UAR
U.N. Palestine Conciliation Commission, PCC
U.N. Relief and Works Agency, UNRWA
U.N. Special Committee on Palestine, UNSCOP
U.S. Agency for International Development, USAID
U.S. Air Force, USAF
Yemen Arab Republic, YAR

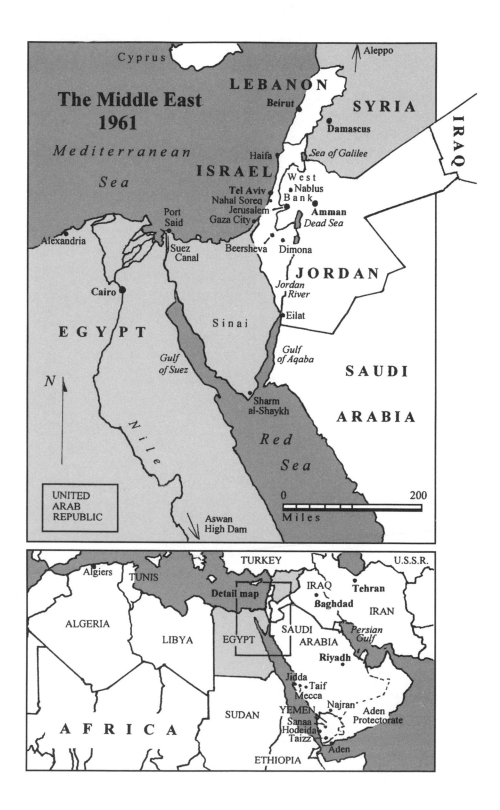

The Middle East
1961

Oh, well, just think of what we'll pass on to the poor fellow who comes after me.

—John F. Kennedy

Support Any Friend

A Time to Fish

The New Frontier and the Middle East

O N A COLD JANUARY DAY, the young president took the inaugural podium without an overcoat, top hat cast aside, eyes squinting, puffs of vapor escaping from his mouth as his hand chopped the frigid air. "Let every nation know," he declared in his clipped New England tones, "whether it wishes us well or ill, that we shall pay any price, bear any burden, meet any hardship, support any friend, oppose any foe, to assure the survival and the success of liberty."

Among those taking note of John F. Kennedy's first presidential performance was a wizened old man an ocean away, with a flat, shovel nose and a riot of white hair sprouting above cabbage ears. Despite his grandfatherly mien and diminutive stature, David Ben-Gurion towered over Israeli politics like a Jewish Gladstone. Israel's founding father was humorless, visionary, indomitable, and ornery enough that even his own admiring biographer sometimes refers to him as "the fighting dwarf."[1] Ben-Gurion had been watching American presidents for decades, and not out of idle interest; Israel's prime minister was determined to forge a strategic alliance with the leading nation of the democratic West. Kennedy spoke of offering support to friends, not allies, but Ben-Gurion was willing to start as the former in hopes of eventually becoming the latter. As Ben-Gurion saw things, the survival and the success of *Israeli* liberty depended on it. Even so, he did not hold out any particularly great expectations for Kennedy. "He looked to me like a twenty-five-year-old boy," Ben-Gurion recalled. "I asked myself: how can a man so young be elected president? At first, I did not take him seriously."[2] For all his initial condescension, however, Ben-Gurion was glad to see a new occupant in the Oval Office—largely because Israel's "Old Man" was eager see another old man, Dwight D. Eisenhower, leave office. Ben-Gurion had repeatedly butted heads with Ike, who had never been overly sympathetic to Ben-Gurion's

1

view of Israel's security dilemmas. Perhaps the Jewish state could make more headway with the new president and the New Frontier.

Also paying heed to JFK's speech from afar in January 1961 was a man much closer to Kennedy's age, himself also charismatic, handsome, and headstrong. With his flashing smile, ink-dark hair, and aquiline features, Jamal Abd al-Nasser too was an activist, gallant young president; but there the similarities with Kennedy ended.[3] Under the leadership of Nasser's Free Officers, Egypt was authoritarian, revolutionary, pledged to pan-Arabism — the quest to unite the Arabs in a single state — and poised as a major neutral power between the Soviet Union and the United States.

That meant Egypt might be in play in the Cold War. "To those new states whom we welcome to the ranks of the free, we pledge our word that one form of colonial control shall not have passed away merely to be re-placed by a far greater iron tyranny," Kennedy said from the inaugural po-dium. "We shall not always expect to find them supporting our view. But we shall always hope to find them strongly supporting their own freedom — and to remember that, in the past, those who foolishly sought power by riding the back of the tiger ended up inside." Nasser and his fellow neutralists paid attention as the new American president tried to avoid being identified with the forces of reaction. Hearing Kennedy's pitch for friendship in the Third World, the most prominent nationalist in the Arab world could not help speculating on what the new season in Washington would bring. Nasser's arsenal — the largest in the Arab world and the spine of the Arab challenge to Israel — came from Moscow, but perhaps he could now make more head-way with Washington. Indeed, perhaps Kennedy's definition of friendship could include the Arab world's greatest nationalist.

During Kennedy's presidency, both Israel and Egypt — the main an-tagonists in one of the Cold War's most dangerous conflicts — tested the limits of what American friendship meant. Of course, when we think of Kennedy's inaugural and his administration, we tend not to think of Ben-Gurion, Nasser, and the other leaders of the Middle East. Indeed, Kennedy's thousand days are remembered mostly for the terrors of the Cuban mis-sile crisis, the parting waters of the civil rights movement, the makings of the Vietnam quagmire, the glitter of Camelot, and the shattering loss of that dreadful November day in Dallas. But while all these things remain central to the public and even the historical memory of the New Frontier, Kennedy's often surprising Middle Eastern policy deserves its own place in U.S. diplomatic history.[4]

Books on U.S.–Israel relations often glide past the Kennedy period, treating it as a place-marker between Suez and the Six Day War, between the martial frostiness of Dwight Eisenhower and the Texan warmth of Lyndon Johnson. But the increasingly complete documentary record on

America's Middle East decisions from 1961 to 1963 tells a complicated tale that reveals much about both the Arab-Israeli conflict and American diplomacy at the height of the Cold War. The Kennedy administration, we can now see, constitutes the pivotal presidency in U.S.–Israel relations, the hinge that swung decisively away from the chilly association of the 1950s and toward the full-blown alliance we know today. Kennedy was the first president to break the arms embargo blocking U.S. sales of major weaponry to Israel; after his term, Washington was deciding *which* arms to sell the Jewish state, not *whether* to sell any arms in the first place. By expanding the limits of what was thinkable with Israel and reaching the limits of what was doable with Egypt, Kennedy set the parameters for America's Middle Eastern policy for decades to come. The Kennedy administration marks not only the end of America's last serious pre–Camp David attempt to court Egypt but also the true origin of America's alliance with the Jewish state.

JFK did not make such moves out of altruism. In his inaugural, he avoided the term "ally," suggesting instead an association that was more than kind but less than kin. Kennedy was not seeking friendship for friendship's sake; he sought compatriots to advance his wider Cold War strategy—ensuring, as he put it, "the survival and the success of liberty."

In the Middle East of 1961, such success seemed far from assured. Kennedy inherited a weakened, uncertain posture in one of the Cold War's key theaters. After the high drama of the 1956 Suez crisis, in which Israel secretly joined forces with Britain and France in an ill-fated bid to topple Nasser, the United States was left off balance. America's ties with Israel were strained by the Eisenhower administration's lingering qualms about the reliability of an American friend that had chosen such a hair-raising gamble as Suez; America's ties with Egypt were strained by mounting U.S. suspicions that Nasser was a communist stalking horse. That left America with few regional friends except the increasingly besieged conservative Arab rulers in Saudi Arabia, Jordan, and Lebanon, who worried about both the Arab-Israeli crisis and Nasser's calls for their overthrow.

So by 1960, Eisenhower was still mending fences in the Middle East—to the voluble scorn of the Kennedy-Johnson campaign. It is important not to underestimate the Kennedy team's contempt for its predecessors' supposed lassitude and complacency. When JFK accepted his party's nomination at the Democratic National Convention in Los Angeles on July 15, 1960, he dismissed the entire Eisenhower administration as "eight years of drugged and fitful sleep." Under Ike, America's freedom of maneuver in the region had been dwindling; Kennedy was convinced that he could do better. The New Frontiersmen moved briskly to widen America's range of options—actively pursuing a rapprochement with Nasser, the key revolutionary leader of the Arab world, and sealing America's first major arms deal with the Jewish state.

The innovations that the New Frontier brought to the Middle East remain inadequately appreciated, even though they have helped guide American policy for decades. JFK's abortive attempt to establish friendly ties with Nasserite Egypt badly startled America's traditional Arab friends — especially Saudi Arabia, which railed against the Nasser initiative with enough vehemence to both help scuttle the U.S.–Egyptian rapprochement and reinforce the centrality of the House of Saud to American diplomacy. JFK's Israel decisions were even more historic. The August 1962 decision to sell Hawk surface-to-air missiles to the Jewish state, which told Defense Secretary Robert McNamara's advisers that it faced a dangerous arms imbalance against Nasser and its other Arab foes, marked the end of the embargo on major arms sales to Israel that had begun under Harry Truman. The Hawk sale constitutes an insufficiently acknowledged watershed in Middle Eastern history, and the U.S.–Israeli diplomacy that produced it sheds light on Israel's strategic thinking in the run-up to the Six Day War of 1967.

Inevitably, discussions of Arab-Israeli policy include consideration of U.S. domestic politics, and some readers will ask whether the Israel lobby had anything to do with the fact that, by the end of Kennedy's life in 1963, U.S.–Israel relations were far warmer and U.S.–Egypt relations were far cooler. On balance, the evidence does not support such conclusions. There is little in the record to show that domestic politics forced Kennedy's hand, and the events described herein are easier to explain through the prism of foreign policy than that of domestic shilling. Simply put, Israel was better able to take advantage of what Kennedy offered; Egypt was too much the captive of its regional constraints. JFK's Nasser initiative foundered not over Israel but over the complicated politics of an ugly showdown in Yemen—the key symbol of inter-Arab political rivalry in the early 1960s and the site of a nasty civil and proxy war between the Arab kings and the radicals who hoped to topple them. Nasser was, in the end, the prisoner of his regional strategy.

As Nasser missed his moment, however, Ben-Gurion seized his. Israel's prime minister avidly sought ever-closer ties with the United States, which he ultimately considered a more suitable and reliable senior partner than Israel's previous great-power patron, the fading imperialist metropole of France. Ben-Gurion had made the support of a great power the central pillar of Israeli foreign policy, and his first choice had virtually always been the United States. For Ben-Gurion, America was an aspiration, France a consolation. Unlike Nasser, the Israeli leader had far fewer local temptations to distract him from the pursuit of American patronage. Unlike

Chaim Weizmann, Israel's first president, who urged the Zionist movement to rely on Great Britain, and unlike the leaders of the leftist Mapam Party, who put their trust in the Soviet Union, Ben-Gurion had long placed his bet on the United States. Ben-Gurion visited America almost annually and even lived there for nearly two years starting in 1940. The more he saw, the more he liked. "What he really wanted was America in his corner," argues Shabtai Teveth, Ben-Gurion's leading biographer.[5]

Still, it was hardly foreordained that the U.S.–Israel friendship would strengthen so appreciably on Kennedy's watch — especially since much of the presidential time spent on the Middle East was devoted to an often acrimonious struggle over what Kennedy, showing marked personal attention, correctly suspected was an Israeli quest to acquire nuclear weapons. Ultimately, however, Kennedy's atomic diplomacy ameliorated the thorniest problem in U.S.–Israel relations — even though, at the time, both Israeli and American diplomats feared their countries were on a collision course over the bomb. In the event, the flexibility of Levi Eshkol, Israel's unjustly underrated third prime minister, helped Washington and Jerusalem work out a regime of limited American inspections of Israel's secretly built nuclear reactor near the unassuming Negev town of Dimona. Mollifying Washington — while not abandoning Dimona — cleared away the most immediate roadblock to an ever more special U.S.–Israel relationship.

There was a larger obstacle to closer U.S.–Israel ties, of course: Arab hostility, and Washington's Cold War fears that the Arab-Israeli dispute would deliver the Arab states to Moscow. However unintentionally, the New Frontier's attempt to court Nasser also wound up doing much to clear these worries away; after all, Kennedy had tried to moderate the foremost Arab radical and failed, which meant that risking Nasser's friendship over a deepening American special relationship with Israel was not risking much at all. Kennedy's failure to dissuade Nasser from his provocative regional course — railing against both Israel and the Arab monarchs — meant that the costs to America of drawing closer to Israel dropped significantly. Kennedy had spoken of supporting any friend; in the Middle East, he found takers only in Israel and the Arab kingdoms and emirates. With the arms embargo on Israel broached, the irritant of Israel's bomb cooled, and the regional landscape clarified, Lyndon Johnson, Richard Nixon, and their successors could build upon the foundations laid by John Kennedy.

MYTHS

Writing a study of this sort inevitably poses several problems. One has to contend not only with primary sources and secondary literature but with what we might call tertiary assumptions: with the widespread perception, particularly among American Jews, that the United States and Israel were inevitable and eternal friends and allies. They were not. To be sure, there was a natural affinity between the two republics, but one theme of this study is that the U.S.–Israel alliance we know today is the cumulative product of individual decisions that could have gone another way. Even as Washington and Jerusalem moved closer, sparks flew. In a February 1963 press conference, Kennedy approvingly quoted Churchill, saying, "'The history of any alliance is the history of mutual recrimination among the various people.'"[6] There is plenty of material here for partisans looking to fuel such recriminations; but the work's larger point is that Kennedy helped forge that alliance in the first place.[7]

That said, many readers friendly to Kennedy, Israel, or both may be surprised by much of what they find herein—JFK's insistence on sending U.S. inspectors to Israel's Dimona reactor, the Pentagon's willingness to exclude Jewish soldiers from the American mission to defend Saudi Arabia, the frequent exasperation of the White House with Ben-Gurion and Israeli Foreign Minister Golda Meir, the commitment by both Kennedy's State Department and his National Security Council to trying to improve relations with Israel's nemesis in Cairo, and so on. Kennedy himself is an unlikely father for America's alliance with the Jewish state—the son of an anti-Semite, a youth who wrote approvingly of British restrictions to bar from Palestine Jews fleeing Nazi Europe, and as determined a foe of Israel's nuclear arms program as has ever lived in the White House. We have grown used to the idea of eternal U.S.–Israeli friendship, even if historically speaking, it simply was not so.

Indeed, the clout of the Israel lobby in U.S. Middle East policy-making today ("Pander, pander, pander," one high-ranking White House official recently advised a speechwriter preparing an address to a pro-Israel group) may reasonably cause many readers to assume that the American Israel Public Affairs Committee (AIPAC) and its siblings played a similar role in Kennedy's day.[8] They did not. The Israel lobby was far less of a force in the 1950s and early 1960s. It had some real influence in Congress, but it did not matter much in presidential decision making. To be sure, Israel considered American Jewry an important asset. "The Almighty placed massive oil deposits under Arab soil," an Israeli diplomat once told a State Department official. "It is our good fortune that God placed five million Jews in America."[9] But both Eisenhower and Kennedy often considered the Israel lobby more nuisance than titan.

Still, unlike Eisenhower, Kennedy was unapologetic about considering domestic political factors in his Middle East policy-making. He also appointed a staffer—Deputy White House Counsel Myer ("Mike") Feldman—

as de facto ambassador to the American Jewish community. Of course, Nasser would have killed for a Mike Feldman of his own. Moreover, as a product of Congress himself and a politician to his fingertips, Kennedy had internalized at least some tendency to weigh the political consequences of Middle East policy. Nevertheless, there is scant evidence in the documentary record that the hunt for Jewish votes ever seriously drove Kennedy's Arab-Israeli diplomacy. That may simply be because the president did not believe American Jewry would truly desert the Democratic coalition that Franklin Delano Roosevelt so lovingly built, or because post-Holocaust, pre–Six Day War American Jews were not yet comfortable throwing their weight around, or because the Israel lobby was locked out of such key issues as Dimona and the Hawk sales, or because Kennedy knew he could appease pro-Israel sentiment with a few blandishments and make the real policy calls as he chose. In the event, domestic politics had a voice, not a veto.

On a related front, the basic affinity between the two fellow democracies proved to be an important element in the deepening special relationship. One factory worker in Tel Aviv, who gave birth the day that John Glenn first orbited the earth, so identified with America that she excitedly named her son John.[10] Moreover, in the early 1960s, progressive, democratic Israel was still widely popular in liberal circles. In a 1962 speech on international development at Rutgers University, Kennedy's civil rights aide Harris Wofford called such Israeli institutions as the kibbutz, the Histadrut labor union, and the Jewish Agency "models and teachers for the peoples seeking freedom in the developing world." Wofford added, "Pericles said that Athens was the school of Hellas. I have suggested that Israel and Gandhi's India are schools of the developing world."[11] Kennedy's supporters often saw Israel as a bastion of liberty and liberalism. But the course of true alliance typically did not run so smooth. The U.S.–Israel bond was forged in the smithy of Middle Eastern hostilities, not born in a parlor of amity.

Beyond pat assumptions about the inevitability of U.S.–Israel friendship, the historian also has to grapple with a certain glamour factor. For an administration known for (or perhaps obsessed with) style, it is worth noting that the key changes that Kennedy and his men brought to America's Middle East posture had little to do with manners or form. Kennedy could be testy in his dealings with both Israel and Egypt, and the sort of syrupy rhetoric that is *de rigueur* today in discussing the special bond between Washington and Jerusalem was almost entirely absent from Kennedy's policy deliberations. He could be conciliatory to Israel in public even as he was being tough as nails in private. Nasser got even less warmth. Jack Kennedy was not a sentimental man.

Nevertheless, Americans are sentimental about Jack Kennedy. Writing about the New Frontier is seriously complicated by stubborn and ardent public perceptions of the period. Kennedy's thousand days are more shrouded in mythology—the name Camelot says it all—than any other modern presidency. While most historians agree that the truly great American presidents were Washington, Lincoln, and FDR—men who helped define both the office and the nation—Kennedy's name perennially appears near the top of the list whenever the public is asked to list its greatest commanders-in-chief. (At least one comedian has unkindly suggested that Kennedy would rank similarly high when the public is asked to *name* a president.) Indelibly, Kennedy remains our image of the modern president. Even Josiah Bartlet, the liberal fantasy president of television's *The West Wing*, whom many consider an idealized version of Bill Clinton, is actually modeled on JFK—right down to the New England inflections, Catholic patrician upbringing, detested Texan ex-senator running mate, dazzling policy versatility, and duplicitously concealed illness. Saying that aspirants to national office look presidential often means only that they remind us, however faintly, of Kennedy—or, to be precise, remind us of our idealized memories of Kennedy. "I still have difficulty seeing John F. Kennedy clear," wrote Theodore H. White.[12] So do we.

Faced with this veneration for a martyred prince, scholars have been tempted to either beat 'em or join 'em. As the historian Alan Brinkley has suggested, writing about Kennedy is often tantamount to sitting in judgment on American liberalism. As such, works on JFK have tended to fall into the categories of either hagiography or gleeful revisionism. The two classic memoir-histories of the New Frontier, Theodore C. Sorensen's *Kennedy* and Arthur Schlesinger, Jr.'s, *A Thousand Days*, are still essential sources; while some of their substance has been overtaken by the release of new documents and the digging of more skeptical scholars, much remains useful, and their elegance remains undimmed. The early anti-Kennedy myth-shattering of a Victor Lasky no longer seems shocking; Seymour Hersh's salacious recent exposé, succinctly entitled *The Dark Side of Camelot*, epitomizes the way Kennedy has been hauled down from his martyr's pedestal. More seriously, a younger generation of Cold War scholars have laid aside the Sorensen-Schlesinger narrative of a president growing into his powers after the Bay of Pigs fiasco until his apotheosis in the Cuban missile crisis; instead, they have found Kennedy to be a consistent Cold War hawk, and a rather sharp-taloned one at that. Meanwhile, a fuller picture of the administration's deliberations has continued to emerge, helped importantly by the release in 2001 of reams of transcripts from the Oval Office tape recordings that Kennedy was secretly making long before Rose Mary Woods had her 15 minutes—or 18½ minutes—of fame.

This book should alter our picture of Kennedy's foreign policy by pointing out the frequently surprising innovations of his Middle Eastern policies, which are hard to square with the revisionist portrait of Kennedy as an inflexible cold warrior. Moreover, it turns out that the reason Kennedy did not make greater inroads with the most interesting Arab leader, Nasser, had more to do with Nasser's lack of imagination than Kennedy's lack of effort—a modest corrective to revisionists prone to blaming Kennedy for a series of other, more genuine Third World blunders.

There is also good reason to consider Kennedy, if hardly a great president, then surely a truly talented commander-in-chief. Beyond his genuine strategic creativity in the Middle East, Kennedy's much-ballyhooed skills often turn out to have been significantly as advertised. Kennedy's interventions in discussions of policy on the Middle East—not, it should be stated frankly, an item consistently at the top of his agenda—were consistently crisp, savvy, and skillful. Of course, his administration's blunders, especially on Vietnam, still do not look any better; that the best and the brightest were able to warn Nasser off his own quagmire in Yemen even as they sank deeper into Indochina does not bespeak overwhelming clarity of vision. Too often, the Kennedy administration reacted to events rather than shaping them. Nevertheless, after more than 40 years, the more we know about JFK as a crisis manager, the more he seems to have been the real thing: cool, salty, and probing. "You're in a pretty bad fix," Air Force Chief of Staff Curtis LeMay sneered to Kennedy during the Cuban missile crisis. "You're in there with me," Kennedy shot back.[13] Hawk he may have been; cad he almost certainly was; but Kennedy's raw talent, agility, and policy mastery remain impressive.

While I remain wary of using history as a primer for policymakers, these pages should be of particular interest to those following the current agonies of the Middle East. *Support Any Friend* is designed to be read with profit by the specialist and with pleasure by the general reader. I have long felt deeply involved—perhaps more involved than I would like—in the fate of the Middle East, and I hope that sense of engagement has helped speed this work along. In *David Copperfield*, Dickens writes, "there is a subtlety of perception in real attachment." Even so, *Support Any Friend* remains a work rooted in archival research and evidence, not presuppositions or speculations. This is not a book about either the saint or the sinner, the martyr or the malefactor; it is a book about a president who was both politician and policymaker, about a talented commander-in-chief directing a talented staff in the pursuit of elusive foreign policy objectives, and about the way that pursuit changed America's Middle East posture.

For greater clarity, this book briefly traces the pre-1960 historical background of U.S. policy toward the Arab-Israeli conflict and the evolution of

Kennedy's own pre-presidential thinking on the Middle East. It then explores the Kennedy administration by chronologically tracing each of its major Middle East policy strands—sometimes doubling back to examine the administration's thinking on, above all, three key issues: Egypt policy and the war in Yemen, the Hawk sale, and the atomic diplomacy related to Israel's Dimona reactor. (To help readers further see how the strands wove together, a chronology is provided.) This book remains a study of Washington decision making, not a work about how Ben-Gurion and Nasser made their decisions about Kennedy; I look eagerly forward to seeing other scholars shed more light on those questions. (This work also touches only glancingly on such fascinating policy questions as Kennedy's handling of other Middle East states, such as Iran, Iraq, and Turkey, that were less directly entangled in the Arab-Israeli snare.) On balance, Kennedy receives a favorable grade in these pages—a solid A for innovation and somewhere south of a B-minus for implementation. He gets it, however, not for being glamorous or eloquent, but for heading an often quarrelsome but indisputably bright team grappling with dizzyingly complex foreign policy problems. America's Middle East policies are serious business; they deserve serious study.

ALL OUR FRIENDS

While this work is devoted to considerations of policy, personality has its place. Indeed, it is almost impossible to immerse oneself in the documentary record and not feel the New Frontiersmen's characters stepping out of the pages, arguing, sniping, gesticulating, trying to best one another in displays of mordant Kennedyesque wit, working late into the night; and it is also almost impossible not to think of how different those documents might have looked if different people had drafted them. As such, I have attempted throughout to provide some of the flavor of the dramatis personae, in the hopes of reminding readers that the policies under discussion were made by men, not machines. The outcomes were the farthest thing from foreordained.

Understanding this means grappling with the protagonists' personalities. Indeed, the characters drew me to this project in the first place. "We cannot learn men from books," Disraeli insisted; but even if we cannot get people entire, we can still get much of them. The charismatic Nasser could be proud, rash, stubborn, self-pitying, or gallant. The pan-Arabist firebrand combined courtesy and steady nerves with genuine radicalism and a conspiratorial, sometimes paranoid view of the world. Nasser's adversary, Ben-Gurion, was fully the Egyptian leader's match in obstinacy. "I am a quarrelsome, obstreperous man," Ben-Gurion himself conceded. He was as brave as he was combative, and he valued both youth and guts; when Israel was seized with "parachute fever," the Old Man made up his mind to take a paratrooper training course until finally being dissuaded by Moshe Dayan.[14] But Ben-Gurion "had no sense of humor whatsoever," sighed Walworth Barbour, Kennedy's ambassador to Israel.[15] In contrast, Ben-Gurion's heir, Levi Eshkol, was perhaps Israel's only funny prime minister, with a gentle manner and a droll, mordant wit. (It is a not entirely appealing testament to the durability of Israel's ruling class that every Labor Party prime minister to date except Ehud Barak—Ben-Gurion, Eshkol, Meir, Moshe Sharett, Yitzhak Rabin, and Shimon Peres—makes their way through this story.)

Chief among the personalities is, of course, Kennedy. With the signal exception of the nuclear issues related to Dimona, the president was only occasionally directly involved in Middle East policy. As one would expect in any White House, issues would be batted around at a staff level and only wind up from time to time on the presidential desk. But Kennedy also dipped in and out. He was an engaged, activist chief executive who presided over a somewhat chaotic White House in which staffers spoke more of such virtues as speed, crispness, and tough-mindedness than of such niceties as process, tidiness, and form. Kennedy was also genuinely, deeply, and sometimes single-mindedly interested in foreign policy—a far cry from such recent presidents as Bill Clinton, who took office with only a passing knowledge of the outside world and a voracious intellect, and George W. Bush, who took office with less than even that and wound up presiding over one of the most shocking crises in the history of the republic. In the 1960s, the height of the Cold War, the American electorate knew what it came to forget in the 1990s: that it could not afford ill-preparedness in its commander-in-chief. As has often been noted by historians, the only mention of domestic policy in Kennedy's famous inaugural address was the hastily added insertion of the two words "at home"—a civil rights reference—in a passage talking about American support for human rights abroad. Indeed, JFK once remarked, "Domestic policy can defeat me, but foreign policy can kill all of us."[16]

On the other side of the terrorist attacks of September 11, 2001, it is easier for younger readers to feel in their bones the tensions of a cold war—"a long twilight struggle" requiring a lasting American strategic commitment abroad. But when looking at Kennedy's own Cold War in the Middle East, it is striking to note the way in which his deepening friendship with Israel did not preclude outreach to Arab progressives, his attempts to avoid signaling that America stood reflexively with the Arab world's reactionaries, and his hope that modernization in the Levant could improve both the Arabs' lot and the West's standing. Progressivism did not contradict principle. Kennedy was capable of deploring French colonialism in Algeria and of denouncing terrorism by those who sought to end it, of trying to help Egypt modernize and of trying to force Saudi Arabia to ban slavery, of befriending Israel and of exploring ways to alleviate the misery of Palestinian refugees. In the Middle East, America has not always steered as well.

Nor, for that matter, as creatively. It is hard to avoid being struck by the pluralism of Kennedy's Middle East policy. After all, how can one explain an administration that reached out to both Israel and to Israel's nemesis? How to explain an administration that tried to befriend both Nasser and Saudi Crown Prince Faysal? How to explain an administration that sold Hawks to Israel to assuage Ben-Gurion's fears of Nasser and sent arms inspectors to Dimona to assuage Nasser's fears of Israel?

The answer may simply be that Kennedy was determined to give himself a wider range of Middle Eastern options than those available to Eisenhower, who had opened major rifts with both Nasser and Ben-Gurion. Kennedy, not himself a particularly devout Catholic, once both alarmed and amused his far more religious wife, Jacqueline, by reciting one of his favorite biblical passages—Ecclesiastes's litany of "a time to be born and a time to die"—and, ever the pol, adding, "A time to fish and a time to cut bait."[17] For JFK's Middle East policy, 1961–62 was a time to fish, a time to hurl a wide net out into the waters of the Middle East and see what would come back in it. The constant quest for alternatives, the dislike for cramped corridors of action, the ongoing search for the middle ground—all were hallmarks of the Kennedy style. So Kennedy was willing to experiment, even if that meant managing the anxiety of the Arab monarchs who were the West's traditional regional colleagues and riding herd on a wary, pro-Israel Congress. But by 1963, the outcomes of the overtures to both Nasser and Israel were ever more visible. By the time of Kennedy's assassination that November, his administration was drawing ever nearer to the time to cut bait.

The New Frontiersmen felt it particularly acutely in May 1963, in the wake of a nerve-fraying week in which the administration had faced the twin specters of a coup in the indispensable regional bulwark of Jordan and a third Arab-Israeli war. Amid the tension, Kennedy sent the latest in a series of letters—once bracingly frank, now downright testy—to Nasser, the chief regional troublemaker. "We want to steer an even course with *all our friends*," Kennedy wrote pointedly, "and we hope it will not be made unduly difficult for us."[18]

Finding such a path was proving difficult indeed for the Kennedy administration—but not unduly so. For while Kennedy and his Middle East staffers hoped to steer an even course with all their friends, the blunt regional reality was that America's friends were either one another's rivals or, increasingly, one another's enemies. The pan-Arabist Nasser was seen as a clear and present danger not only by Israel but also by the conservative Arab states—Jordan, the Gulf emirates, and above all Saudi Arabia— that comprised the keystone of America's traditional Middle East policies. There was no easy way to simultaneously be on all sides of the Arab-Israeli conflict and the inter-Arab cold war. Therein lay much of the originality and many of the limitations of JFK's Middle East policy.

And much of its complexity, too. It is far too neat to say that Kennedy rushed to befriend Israel. Rather, he wound up setting important precedents on U.S.–Israel relations—not because he was a single-minded Zionist or a shill for Jewish votes but because his propensity to avoid extreme alternatives guided him toward decisions that were moderate but still lastingly important. Indeed, Kennedy's penchant for seeking the middle ground on policy questions runs throughout his Arab-Israeli policies. (The lone exception here is Dimona, which spoke to Kennedy's central strategic preoccupations in a way unrivaled by any other Middle Eastern issue.) The Hawk sale, for instance, was an attempt to find a compromise between a State Department that was dead set against any arms sales to Israel and a government of Israel determined to turn America into its main arms dealer. On the Nasser initiative, too, Kennedy chose repeated attempts to sound Nasser out over either cutting him off entirely or wooing him unreservedly. Kennedy often sought maximum flexibility, not maximum decisiveness. But as the 1960s wore on, such flexibility was increasingly hard to come by. Arabs and Israelis alike were either making or being driven into making their Cold War choices—into a time to cut bait.

The fact that Israel's relationship with the United States expanded so significantly under Kennedy may tempt some to argue that he simply had an Israel policy—a straightforward program of reaching out to the Jewish state. In fact, he had an *Arab-Israel* policy, which entailed a careful balancing of regional rivalries and American ambitions. JFK was playing chess in the Middle East, not checkers. Kennedy's Israel decisions came in the context of his Egypt decisions; his Egypt decisions came in the context of his Israel decisions; and both of these came in the context of the Cold War. Above all, the administration's goal was barring Soviet penetration of the Middle East. Its other interests included keeping the Suez Canal open; ensuring that the oil needed to create a prosperous, noncommunist Western Europe continued to flow freely; keeping Arab-Israeli tensions contained so as not to offer any opportunities to Moscow; preventing nuclear proliferation; and retaining a "reasonable degree of rapport with [the] Arab world as well as with Israel."[19] That mandated a nuanced overall Arab-

Israeli policy, with much in it to offend both sides. But only the Israelis were able to make the most of what was offered them and lay the groundwork for their subsequent full-blown alliance. Nasser was too much the prisoner of the Arab cold war to be the beneficiary of the superpower Cold War.

The origins of the U.S.–Israel bond as we know it, then, lie not in one simple shift of presidential will but amid the diplomatic triangle between Kennedy, Nasser, and Ben-Gurion. In effect, JFK opened doors to both Israel and Egypt; one door slammed shut in Nasser's face, but Ben-Gurion jammed his foot in the other. "Oh, well," Kennedy said at one National Security Council meeting, "just think of what we'll pass on to the poor fellow who comes after me."[20] Among other things, he passed on the foundations of the U.S.–Israel alliance.

CHAPTER ONE

Kennedy's Inheritance

America and the Arab-Israeli Conflict, 1917–1960

I N NOVEMBER 1953, Eddie Jacobson, a Jewish Kansas City haberdasher
who had the good fortune to pick as his business partner a scrappy
young man named Harry S. Truman, was asked to introduce his old
friend to an audience at the Jewish Theological Seminary in New York.
Before an eager crowd at the intellectual home of America's largest Jewish denomination, nestled in Morningside Heights in Manhattan, Jacobson
tried to give the former president an introduction that rose to the occasion. "This is the man," Jacobson declared, "who helped create the state
of Israel."

"What do you mean, 'helped create'?" asked Truman. With some feeling, he gave his own view of his role: "I am Cyrus. I am Cyrus."[1]

Truman was a self-taught history buff, so it is perhaps unsurprising that
he could identify with the ancient Persian monarch who liberated the
Jews from their exilic bondage in Babylon. It is also not surprising that he
chose in hindsight to romanticize the cutting of a Gordian policy knot.
Still, Truman's assessment of his own importance has sometimes come to
overshadow the reality of his administration's muddled approach to the
Palestine question—and of the muddled and highly contingent American
relationship with the young state of Israel. In fact, it had never been as
simple as Truman liked to make it sound in retrospect.

America's Middle East policies throughout both world wars and the
early Cold War were produced by a complex intersection of interests and
actors. Throughout, sympathizers with Zionism had to grapple with opponents convinced that U.S. friendship with a Jewish state would hurt
America's posture in the region. Moreover, U.S. Middle East policy was
buffeted by wider trends in world politics: the collapse of the Ottoman
Empire, the rise of Nazism in Germany and communism in Russia, the
devastation of World War II and the Holocaust, the rise of nationalism

and the fall of the great European empires, the indispensability of oil to Western economies, and the superpower jousting of the Cold War. The instinctive modern assumption of deep and abiding friendship between the United States and Israel rings tinny when one looks back at the presidencies that shaped America's encounter with the Middle East. Those White Houses found Middle East policy-making agonizing, and the policies they produced came not from neat ideological certainties but from painstaking attempts to balance U.S. interests and values.

Not least in importance was the administration of John F. Kennedy, who received a complicated inheritance in the Middle East. Woodrow Wilson bequeathed to Kennedy a liberal emphasis on the importance of nationalism; Franklin Roosevelt dissembled and underscored the importance of Saudi oil; Harry Truman demonstrated the difficulty of integrating support for Israel into U.S. Cold War strategy; and Dwight Eisenhower left a region with American influence on the wane and nationalism on the rise. To understand Kennedy's Middle East policies, we must understand what he inherited.

THE HOLY LAND AND THE PRIEST

Woodrow Wilson set the stage for America's policies toward the Arab-Israeli conflict—largely by expressing a value-driven American sympathy for nationalism, including the Jewish desire for self-rule. Temperamentally, it is hard to imagine two men farther apart than the gregarious Truman and the priggish Wilson. Still, they did have at least one thing in common: neither thought much of his State Department. Wilson trusted his secretary of state, Robert Lansing, no farther than the president—no Olympic athlete—could throw him. He relied instead on a series of advisers, including his all-purpose fixer, confidant, and occasional alter ego, the omnipresent Colonel Edward House. Wilson relied, too, on several distinguished American Jews who had managed to become establishment fixtures, including Henry Morgenthau—later named ambassador to the Ottoman Empire—and the man Wilson appointed as a Supreme Court justice, Louis Brandeis.

Brandeis was then America's most influential Zionist. To be sure, this was not saying much in absolute terms—the American Zionist movement was, in the century's first decade, something to be sneezed at—but Brandeis's quiet clout was considerable. While Wilson's Princeton milieu was shot through with the anti-Semitism of its day, it seems not to have rubbed off; the president respected Brandeis, who wound up undertaking an array of missions that today would be bizarre tasks for a sitting member of the highest court in the land.[2]

In 1917, the Zionist movement's center of intellectual gravity was located in London, home of Chaim Weizmann, the urbane, dapper chemist turned nationalist who would 31 years later become the ceremonial head of the new Jewish state. Weizmann, with the help of the sympathetic British Prime Minister David Lloyd George, was trying to succeed where even Theodor Herzl had failed: winning the support of a great imperial power for the Zionist enterprise. With the Allies at war with the crumbling Ottoman Empire, Palestine and much of the rest of the Middle East might soon fall into the hands of the British, who might in turn offer a home for Jewish nationalism. By the spring of 1917, with the world still mired in the muck of the Great War's trenches and Britain increasingly eager to enlist the support of world Jewry in hopes of breaking the stalemate, Weizmann was tantalizingly close to winning British patronage — expressed in the form of the famous Balfour Declaration, in which Britain expressed support for a Jewish national home in Palestine. So one of Weizmann's colleagues, James de Rothschild, asked Brandeis a favor: would he sound Wilson out about the idea of a postwar Holy Land that would be both Jewish and under the protection of Great Britain?

Wilson's response was in some doubt. Wilson saw himself as the tribune of a new politics.[3] The Great War's key causes were, as Wilson saw it, essentially European: the Metternich-style system of shifting alliances and balances of power, the jingoistic legacy of warmongering in general and German belligerence in particular, and the disease of imperialism. Instead of the ruinous old statecraft, Wilson proposed disarmament, a system of collective security rooted in the League of Nations, and self-determination for small peoples. That made Rothschild's proposal something less than a perfect Wilsonian fit. On the one hand, the idea of a Jewish national home jibed neatly with the president's push for self-determination. On the other, Jewish self-rule under the aegis of Britain would come in imperialist wrapping. But on May 4, Brandeis lunched at the White House with Wilson and found the president willing to live with that tension — and accept a British protectorate for the Jews in Palestine.[4]

Both Lansing and House objected. The secretary of state pointed out that America was not yet at war with Palestine's Ottoman masters. Moreover, Lansing wrote, "many Christian sects and individuals would undoubtedly resent turning the Holy Land over to the absolute control of the race credited with the death of Christ."[5] Lansing also feared that Wilson's zeal for self-determination would put the United States on a slippery slope and put "ideas into the minds of certain races."[6] In December 1918, Lansing asked, "Will not the Mohammedans of Syria and Palestine and possibly of Morocco and Tripoli rely on [Wilson's promise of self-determination]? How can it be harmonized with Zionism, to which the president is practically committed? The phrase is simply loaded with dynamite."[7]

Ultimately, however, Wilson's disdain for Lansing kept the State Department out of the loop. Yet House—who often *was* the loop—also urged Wilson to hold off. The colonel fretted that London was plotting some sort of imperialist con game to use Washington to help it snatch up the choice bits of the Turks' collapsing empire. Nonetheless, Wilson's attraction to Zionism overrode his suspicion of Britain. The president "was fascinated with the idea that a democratic Zionism might replace Ottoman despotism and create a haven for oppressed Jews in Palestine."[8] For one thing, the notion appealed to Wilson's messianic side, which was never terribly repressed. For another, there was a political upside. If he opposed the Balfour Declaration, Wilson risked getting outflanked on both the left and the right: Samuel Gompers' American Federation of Labor backed Zionism for fear that the alternative was a massive influx of Jewish immigrants, which could flood the U.S. labor market and depress wages; and both the Republicans and Theodore Roosevelt were also tilting toward Zionism. Moreover, some key satellites in Wilson's orbit—above all Brandeis, but also Rabbi Stephen S. Wise of New York and Brandeis's protégé, Felix Frankfurter—were also wooing him. Finally, Wilson proved willing to tolerate a continued great-power role in the Middle East, paving the way for the League of Nations Mandates that would place Palestine in British custody and let Britain and France divvy up much of the Middle East.[9]

Ultimately, Wilson overruled Lansing and House and told Britain that he would back the Balfour Declaration.[10] In America's earliest encounter with Zionism, the decision-making circle was actually a dot. The U.S. decision to bless the Balfour Declaration was made by the president alone.[11] As Peter Grose has argued, Wilson's Zionism was casual and unreflective, rather than the result of a carefully weighed assessment. He followed his idealistic predilections, his chums, and his views of political prudence. "To think," Wilson mused, "that I, the son of the manse, should be able to help restore the Holy Land to its people."[12]

THE JUGGLER

Another American son of the manse played an even more important and complex role during the second part of U.S.–Zionist relations' early act. Franklin Delano Roosevelt replaced Wilson's elitism with beaming cheer and a sure common touch. "Above all," as Isaiah Berlin has noted, "he was absolutely fearless."[13] Roosevelt was blessed with an invincible certainty that everything—the shipwreck of capitalism, the rise of fascism and communism, and quite simply the largest and most savage war ever—would turn out all right. When he told the American people that they were entitled to freedom from fear, he was merely inviting them to share in his natural state of mind.

Oliver Wendell Holmes famously reckoned that FDR had a second-rate intellect but a first-rate temperament; as it happened, America's longest-serving president proved far wilier than his foes. Indeed, if the yardstick for intelligence is F. Scott Fitzgerald's proverbial ability to retain opposing ideas simultaneously and still function, Roosevelt's second-rate intellect starts to look more like genius. Nowhere was that clearer than on Palestine, where the man whom the historian Warren Kimball calls "the sly squire of Hyde Park" strewed in his wake the flotsam and jetsam of contradictory promises, commitments, and impressions. FDR stands as a lasting reminder that American sympathy for Zionism came with strings attached—that Wilsonian idealism was not nearly enough in a world of cruel choices and unyielding interests. "You know I am a juggler, and I never let my right hand know what my left hand does," said Roosevelt on May 15, 1942. "I may be entirely inconsistent, and furthermore, I am perfectly willing to mislead and tell untruths if it will help win the war."[14] So he was; so it did.

If Wilson's response to the Palestine problem was a casual Zionism, FDR's was by turns fanciful, hard-headed, duplicitous, and pragmatic. The common link was that neither man saw Zionism as a front-burner issue. With a shudder at FDR's easygoing improvisation, one key White House aide, David Niles—who would later become one of Zionism's most strategically placed proponents during the Truman administration—noted that there were "serious doubts" in his mind "that Israel would have come into being if Roosevelt had lived."[15]

A staggering 92 percent of U.S. Jews voted to give FDR a fourth term in 1942.[16] In turn, the president made them one of the building blocks of the New Deal coalition. Like Wilson, FDR seems to have been largely unaffected by the anti-Semitism of his class. (The young Eleanor, however, was not above the odd anti-Semitic jibe; and for all his anticolonialism, Roosevelt's correspondence and chats on Middle East affairs betray a less liberal attitude toward Arabs and Muslims, whom he lumped in with the large parts of the planet he assumed to be lamentably backward.) He was annoyed that his domestic reforms were sometimes sneeringly called the "Jew Deal," and many of his best aides were Jewish. As for Palestine itself, FDR's interest was somewhat limited, although he was fascinated with the Holy Land's geography. (En route to the Tehran summit in 1943, he ordered his pilot to swoop over Palestine as he picked out sites below.

"We've seen it all, from Beersheva to Dan!" he enthused. "You know this country as though you were raised here," an adviser commented. "So I do!" Roosevelt replied.)[17] The president, however, was not much of a Zionist. After 1941, his ideology, such as it was, did not extend much farther than doing whatever it took to win the war.

Roosevelt was lobbied more intensively on Palestine than his predecessors. The American Zionist movement grew dramatically after the Great War, even as Zionism's geopolitical position began eroding. As Nazism rose and as Britain's Balfour enthusiasm cooled, frosted, and then froze over, America's Zionists became increasingly worried. The largest mainstream Zionist groups were Hadassah (for women) and Brandeis's Zionist Organization of America (for men). Their combined membership rose steadily, in some grim symmetry with the rise of Adolf Hitler. In 1935, Hadassah and the ZOA had a total of 50,000 members; in 1939, they had 110,000; in 1945, 280,000; and by the time Israel was born in 1948, fully half a million.[18] For the most part, however, the movement was not a mass one, preferring to leave its lobbying to Roosevelt intimates—particularly Rabbi Stephen Wise, who was a veteran New York Democratic activist and Roosevelt sycophant. More hard-line Zionists preferred Rabbi Abba Hillel Silver of Cleveland, a fiery orator with close ties to Ohio's Republican Senator Robert A. Taft and scant inclination to shield the administration from his rhetorical wrath.

The Zionists at first sought to win Roosevelt over by using *shtadlanim*, or emissaries, to intercede discreetly on the movement's behalf, in much the same way Brandeis so effectively nudged Wilson along. It did not go well. In February 1940, FDR met for the first time with Weizmann. "What about the Arabs?" Roosevelt inquired. "Can't that be settled with a little *baksheesh?*"[19]

Needless to say, it could not. There is no real way of knowing whether FDR appreciated the excruciating intricacy of the Arab-Jewish clash in the British-ruled Palestine Mandate and chose to ignore it, or whether he hoped to glide glibly by the problem. Roosevelt's instincts were often whimsical; he quite liked the idea of simply moving Palestine's Arabs to Iraq, and he flirted with a series of exotic alternative locales for a possible Jewish national home—Rhodesia, Kenya, South America's Orinoco Valley, Tanganyika, and Libya—that made Britain's turn-of-the-century offer of Uganda seem downright pragmatic by comparison.[20] More to the point, FDR was caught in pitiless constraints. Jarring the U.S. public out of its isolationist habits took all the president's considerable ingenuity.[21] The fight against Hitler and Tojo left him little running room, and Great Britain—under both the unsympathetic Neville Chamberlain and the friendlier Winston Churchill—was firmly set against further Jewish immigration into its Palestine Mandate lest this drive the Arabs into the Axis's arms, sever the Allies's oil supplies, and cut India off from its imperial mother. The War and State Departments added that America's Middle Eastern bases could also be threatened.

On the other side of the ledger was an American Zionist lobby that was by turns galvanized and petrified. Under Silver, the movement got out into the streets and cloakrooms, holding rallies and goading Congress into pressuring the administration. Since the Balfour Declaration, the Zionists had clung to the diplomatic ambiguity inherent in the phrase "Jewish national home"; by 1942, they were desperate enough to rip away the shroud and, at New York's Biltmore Hotel, dedicate the movement forthrightly to turning the Yishuv (the Jewish community in Palestine) into nothing less than a state.

For their part, Palestine's Arabs were led by the British-appointed mufti of Jerusalem, al-Hajj Amin al-Husayni. An Axis enthusiast, the mufti fled the Mandate after widespread Arab rioting began in 1936—going to ground in Lebanon, Iraq, and Italy before winding up in Berlin with a British price on his head.[22] Meanwhile, the situation on the ground in Palestine deteriorated, beginning a depressing cycle wherein Arab riots were followed by British commissions of inquiry whose recommendations were hooted down by at least one and often both of the Mandate's warring ethnic groups. And Churchill, whose imperialism was more consistent than his Zionism, showed no sign of overturning the 1939 White Paper barring Jewish immigration and every sign of wishing the Americans would keep their neo-Wilsonian noses out of his putative postwar empire.

Faced with these opposing demands, Roosevelt beamed goodwill at everyone, overpromised, and improvised. The results were bleakest when it came to the Jewish refugees trying to escape the Holocaust. Since 1939, fearing Arab opposition to Jewish immigration, Britain had barred Palestine's door, and FDR largely went along. Roosevelt's failure to help Europe's Jews elude their Nazi pursuers remains an indelible stain on his presidency, and on his country's conscience.[23] There was little American public enthusiasm for a humane refugee policy, and FDR left America's stingy immigration quotas guarded by the State Department bureaucrat Breckinridge Long, an inveterate anti-Semite. As the historian David Kennedy has noted, "The Depression had helped to reinforce an isolationism of the spirit, a kind of moral numbness, that checked American humanitarianism as tightly as political isolationism straitjacketed American diplomacy."[24] On March 1, 1943, Wise told a rally at Madison Square Garden, "When the historian of the future assembles the black record of our days, he will find two things unbelievable: first, the crime itself; second, the reaction of the world to that crime."[25] When Romania halfheartedly suggested ransoming 70,000 of its Jews, the State Department killed the proposal because it assumed they would wind up in Palestine, preferring instead to risk having them wind up in Birkenau. Aides to Treasury Secretary Henry Morgenthau caught wind of the subterfuge and drafted a raging memo with the bitterly unbureaucratic title "Report to the Secretary on the Acquiescence by This Government in the Murder of the Jews."[26] Only in the last year of the war did Washington try seriously to stanch the bleeding of European Jewry, but the admirable exertions of the War Refugee Board, founded in January 1945, were simply too late.

ON GREAT BITTER LAKE

The Roosevelt administration also faced a gap between rhetoric and results on Palestine itself. The Zionists, recognizing that FDR's plans to house the refugees in the earth's proverbial vast uninhabited spaces bespoke a president unwilling to override Britain's determination to keep the refugees out of Palestine, did their best to raise the heat. With little influence over the executive branch, they focused instead on Congress; in 1944, 77 senators and 318 representatives urged FDR to push for Zionism.[27] In that year's elections, Roosevelt was pressed into promising to support a Jewish commonwealth in Palestine; the next day, he promptly approved the usual State Department blandishments to the Arabs to assure them he meant nothing serious. "Public pro-Zionist statements after pressure balanced by secret assurances to Arab leaders constituted the pattern of the later Roosevelt years," the political scientist Steven Spiegel has noted. "At the very least, these contradictory promises to the two sides misled both."[28]

Roosevelt's Soviet diplomacy has frequently been criticized—especially by foes of Yalta—for relying on charm at the expense of consistency. His Middle East diplomacy sometimes suffered from the same failing. On the way home from Yalta, FDR stopped the U.S.S. *Quincy* near the aptly named Great Bitter Lake in the Suez Canal to meet with Ibn Saud, the leader of the Persian Gulf's key oil state, Saudi Arabia. (The ailing president might have had a shorter trip had his original suggestion for a venue for the Big Three summit—Jerusalem—been adopted, but Stalin refused to leave Soviet turf.)[29] Roosevelt hoped to sway Ibn Saud away from his opposition to Jewish statehood and immigration while keeping Saudi oil flowing. For his part, Ibn Saud figured that without U.S. support, the Yishuv was doomed. He was unmoved by FDR's charm offensive, even though the president, ever a believer in atmospherics, went so far as to sneak away for his habitual cigarettes so as not to offend Ibn Saud's Wahhabi puritanism. But Ibn Saud had Roosevelt, as it were, over a barrel. The Saudi king warned Roosevelt that he would not countenance letting more Jews flee-ing Nazism enter Palestine. Roosevelt wound up promising not to "adopt a policy hostile to the Arabs."[30] In March 1945, a visibly exhausted FDR departed from his prepared text during a joint session of Congress to ad lib, "I learned more about the whole problem of Arabia—the Moslems—the Jewish problem—by talking to Ibn Saud for five minutes than I could have learned in the exchange of two or three dozen letters."[31] This brought the predictable howls of Zionist protest, but at a subsequent meeting, Roosevelt assured Wise that his position had not changed.

The trick, of course, was knowing what that position was. FDR never gave much more than lip service to Zionist pleas and basically sided with the State Department and the British, who argued that caution on Palestine made more sense for the Allies. But Roosevelt never went all the way over to full-blown anti-Zionism, either. His welter of contradictory assurances can be explained quite simply: there was a war on, and Roosevelt had bigger problems. Like so many other issues about the postwar world's disposition, the buck did not stop with him. On April 12, 1945, at about 1:45 P.M., FDR was working at a card table at his "Little White House" in Warm Springs, Georgia, when he was struck by an excruciating headache. The president died two hours later of a cerebral hemorrhage, at the age of 63.

A HOUSE DIVIDED

Harry S. Truman's 1948 nominating convention was something less than triumphal. Having held the White House since 1932, most Democratic pols were busily bracing themselves to have their winning streak broken by Thomas Dewey, the starchy Republican governor of New York. "I'm Just Mild About Harry," read one convention placard. Some wags tried to be philo-sophical about the president's limitations: "To err," they said, "is Truman."[32]

On Palestine, that jibe was apt. The Truman administration was a house divided against itself, and the whole farrago gave Truman fits of frustra-tion. The president's initial personal inclinations toward humanitarian-ism soon were submerged in a riptide of improvisation, intra-administration warfare, and vacillation.

Truman inherited Roosevelt's Palestine legacy: a determined Arab world; a nigh-frantic Zionist lobby; a pro-Zionist Congress; the relentless murder of most of European Jewry; thousands of Jewish displaced persons (DPs) languishing in miserable refugee camps; a strikingly united foreign policy bureaucracy dead-set against Jewish statehood; and firm anti-Zionism for varying reasons from some of America's most important allies, including British Prime Minister Clement Attlee and Ibn Saud.

The way Truman muddled his way through this morass has left scholars divided on his motivations. It has often been alleged that Truman's Palestine decisions were driven by crass ethnic pandering. The accusation that Truman was shilling for Jewish votes was leveled first by Attlee's foreign minister, Ernest Bevin, and most cuttingly by his American counterpart, Secretary of State George Marshall. The whiff of inappropriate politicking at the expense of the national interest has hung over U.S.–Israel relations ever since. The charge is not entirely unfair; only a naïf would deny that Truman and his White House advisers understood the political benefits of a tilt toward Zionism. In 1946, a delegation of U.S. diplomats handling Middle Eastern affairs met with Truman to warn him that coziness with Jewish nationalism was wrecking America's position in the region. "I am sorry, gentlemen," the president replied, "but I have to answer to hundreds of thousands who are anxious for the success of Zionism; I do not have hundreds of thousands of Arabs among my constituents."[33]

And yet, for all the blatant opportunism of that remark, Truman often resisted the blandishments of the Zionist lobby. His humanitarian impulses and sympathy for the underdog never made him an ideological advocate of Jewish statehood. Virtually all of the pressure from Congress and interest groups pushed Truman to back Zionism; virtually all of the pressure from within his foreign policy bureaucracy pushed him to thwart it. His attempts to find a middle path left almost everyone angry at him. True, his wavering policies and haphazard process drove his anti-Zionist State Department to distraction, but it also drove at least one of his best Jewish friends, Eddie Jacobson, quite literally to tears.[34]

Throughout, Truman never lost sight of considerations of national interest, reality both political and geopolitical, the situation on the ground in Palestine, and the claims of humanitarianism. That is considerably more than can be said of the antagonists warring for the president's ear and mind: the State Department remained frostily unmoved by the misery of the DPs, and Zionist advocates were deaf to the strategic risks Washington would run by backing Jewish statehood. Truman faced an agonizing series of decisions, and while he did not make them elegantly, he made them with considerable common sense and a refreshing lack of rigid ideological prejudices. Even so, in his attempt to thread the needle, he gave his fingers a few good jabs.

THE WISE MEN

The most important Zionist in the Truman White House was the seemingly omnipresent Clark Clifford, the president's counsel and often the hub of White House policy-making. Crucially, Clifford worked in the White House itself, not in the foreign policy bureaucracy, which gave him the advantages of access and proximity as well as the drawback of seeming—in a time before the metastasis of the White House staff—as if he was meddling in the diplomats' preserve. From outside came Jewish leaders such as Rabbis Wise and Silver; Zionist emissaries including Weizmann and the de facto Zionist ambassador to Washington, Eliahu Epstein; Truman's old friend Eddie Jacobson, who proved an expert opener of the Oval Office door; and such important public figures as Eleanor Roosevelt and the theologian Reinhold Niebuhr.

Against them was arrayed the most formidable bench of foreign policy expertise of the postwar era. Clifford and his allies were up against no less than the Wise Men, the pillars of rectitude who helped create the Cold War world: the nation's first secretary of defense, James Forrestal; two forbidding undersecretaries of state, first the imperious Dean Acheson and then Robert Lovett; Loy Henderson, the head of the State Department's Near East affairs division (known as NEA); George Kennan, the sensitive and brilliant Sovietologist who headed the newly founded Policy Planning Staff; and Secretary of State Marshall himself, the former army chief of staff, nemesis of Nazism, and modern Cincinnatus. (Another diplomat caught up in the drama was the young diplomat heading the State Department's U.N. office, Dean Rusk, Kennedy's future secretary of state.) The foreign policy establishment—and the "e" could well be capitalized—argued that backing a Jewish state could endanger the oil supplies crucial to postwar Europe's recovery, drive the Arabs toward the Soviet Union, and risk rushing U.S. troops to Palestine to save the Jews. "You just don't understand," Clifford remembers being told by Forrestal. "Forty million Arabs are going to push 400,000 Jews into the sea. And that's all there is to it. Oil—that is the side we ought to be on."[35]

Truman disliked being pressured by either side. As the historian Michael Cohen has noted, "It is difficult to determine who irritated Truman more—the Zionists or the State Department."[36] Truman insisted that he was the captive of neither crass domestic politics nor heartless realpolitik. "I don't care about the oil," he once said. "I want to do what's right."[37] While his attitudes toward minorities could be more parochial than the urbane Roosevelt's (he once called Jacobson a "smart Hebrew" in a letter to his wife Bess, and in childhood he referred casually to "kikes"), he was no anti-Semite.[38] Truman took it personally when British Foreign Minister Ernest Bevin accused him of wanting to let more Jews into Palestine because Americans "did not want too many of them in New York."[39]

But Truman was also hardly a Zionist partisan. By 1947, Rabbi Silver had so incensed Truman by thumping the president's desk and raising his voice to the commander in chief that Truman came to hold Silver in roughly the same regard as the radical, rightist Zionist militia known as the Irgun Tzvai Leumi. "Terror and Silver are the causes of some, if not all, of our problems," Truman once complained.[40] The soothing Weizmann had to take over personal contacts with the infuriated president, but Truman's frustration was by no means limited to the overbearing Silver.[41] In 1946, Truman is said to have asked his cabinet, "If Jesus Christ couldn't satisfy them here on earth, how the hell am I supposed to?"[42] During a meeting that year with a congressional delegation from New York, the president interrupted his guests' pro-Zionist presentation. "This is all political," Truman growled. "You are all running for reelection." He was sick, he said, of ethnic demands speaking as parochial blocs rather than simply as "Americans," and kicked the delegation out of his office.[43] Except for its ornery tone, the speech could well have been made by Marshall, Lovett, or Rusk—who, no doubt, would not have been amused by Truman's posture of apolitical propriety.

REFUGEE ZIONISM

Nevertheless, Truman was troubled by the plight of the DPs, and he at various times scowled at the British, the State Department, and the Zionists for not focusing enough on alleviating their suffering. The historian Michael Cohen has aptly called Truman's approach "refugee Zionism." The president was wedded less to the concept of Jewish statehood than to humanitarianism, and he repeatedly declined to endorse Zionism in its own right.

Truman's refugee Zionism was embodied in a push to let 100,000 DPs into Palestine. The magic figure of 100,000 came from Earl Harrison, the dean of the University of Pennsylvania's law school, who led a mission on the DP problem in April 1945. "To anyone who has visited the concentration camps and who has talked with the despairing survivors," Harrison wrote, "it is nothing short of calamitous to contemplate that the gates of Palestine should be soon closed."[44] Moved, the president promptly made the idea his own.

In 1946, a joint Anglo-American Committee of Inquiry on Palestine and the DPs called for turning the Mandate over to the United Nations as a first step toward the creation of a "binational" state in which Arabs and Jews would live side by side. To take out some of the sting for the Zionists, the report proposed easing the 1939 White Paper's restrictions on Jewish land purchases and letting in Truman's 100,000 DPs. Truman liked the document enough that in May 1948, by which time the Anglo-American report had been overtaken by events, he told Judah Magnes, the head of the Hebrew University and a staunch binationalist, that he considered the report a "great document" that he knew almost by heart; Truman showed Magnes his desk copy of it, festooned with tabs to mark off his favorite sections.[45] But the British feared losing both Palestine and Western influence in the Middle East. They played for time by suggesting convening another committee, known as Morrison-Grady, to evaluate the previous committee's report. Truman liked Morrison-Grady's principal recommendations: creating a federal Palestine that was neither Arab nor Jewish; carving out two semiautonomous regions within that state, one for each nationalist group; and, with the Arabs' consent, letting the 100,000 DPs in. The State Department was even more enthusiastic, and neither the White House nor Foggy Bottom minded that the plan did not call for a Jewish state.

But the Arabs refused to give up on the idea of an Arab Palestine. The Zionists also wanted a state of their own, not a canton, but offered to settle for half a loaf: Zionism would now aim to partition the Mandate and establish a Jewish state in its own chunk. Having flirted with two variations on binationalism, Truman gave up. Morrison-Grady was an orphan. On Yom Kippur 1946, Truman tried to preempt Dewey, his presumptive Republican opponent for reelection, by calling yet again for the 100,000 DPs—and formally announcing U.S. support for partition in Palestine.

Truman's reversal here has not escaped critical notices, including accusations of domestic pandering.[46] But given the recalcitrance of the parties on the ground, Truman's continued emphasis on the 100,000 made humanitarian sense. The British insistence that they would take the DPs in only after the parties had agreed on Palestine's ultimate disposition was looking like a diplomatic way of saying "when the cows come home"— since, of course, the parties have still not agreed on Palestine's ultimate disposition as of this writing, more than five decades later. The case for simply doing something to help the refugees was precisely the sort of uncomplicated, pragmatic solution that appealed to Truman's temperament, and it is not hard to see why he clung to that life raft of humanitarian simplicity as his Palestine policy floundered in a sea of diplomatic complexity.

London and Washington differed starkly on the 100,000. British hostility toward the Jewish nationalists was hardly cooled when Menachem Begin's Irgun, the main Revisionist Zionist underground, blew up Britain's Mandatory headquarters in Jerusalem's King David Hotel on July 22, 1946, killing 41. But doing something for the DPs need not have necessarily meant political moves toward partition, particularly since the two most important involved powers—Britain and the United States—were united in their dislike of the idea of Jewish statehood.

As the Anglo-American and Morrison-Grady plans circled the drain, Truman's refugee Zionism went with them. Palestine sunk deeper into civil war, and the British tried to convene Arab-Jewish peace talks in London. When the talks collapsed, a frustrated Bevin kicked the problem to the newly founded United Nations on February 14, 1947, winning cheers in the House of Commons when he blamed the failure on U.S. meddling and the Zionist lobby.[47] The world body empaneled a special committee on Palestine known as the U.N. Special Committee on Palestine (UNSCOP), which, like Britain's 1937 Peel Commission, urged in August 1947 that the General Assembly split the Mandate into two states, one Jewish, one Arab.[48] (A Security Council vote would have been subject to Soviet veto.) Jerusalem was to remain under international control, and the two states were to be bound together for a decade in an economic union. With the Palestine debate now revolving around partition, the strains within the administration were about to be cast into sharp relief.

THE POLITICS OF PARTITION

From the start, the Wise Men were dubious about partition. Middle East oil was the lifeblood of the Marshall Plan, without which postwar Western Europe could be left economically devastated and ripe for communist takeover. If a Jewish state was established and the Arabs turned off the spigot, Defense Secretary Forrestal told an oil executive over breakfast, U.S. car makers "would have to design a four-cylinder automobile."[49] Beyond oil, Washington could lose its regional influence, its military access, and the base at Dhahran, Saudi Arabia. It would run these risks in the name of a partition scheme that was probably unworkable and likely to exacerbate extremism throughout the Muslim world. Such instability would create opportunities for Moscow. And if a new Jewish state was on the verge of being overrun, Washington might have to intervene to save it. Partition should be quietly spurned, Truman's foreign policy bureaucracy concluded. Some began speaking of deferring the issue and turning the Mandate over to an international trusteeship to run Palestine until things calmed down.

Partition was not Truman's preferred outcome, either, but the UNSCOP plan did appeal to his sense of fair play, and it would do something for the DPs. Moreover, supporters of the fledgling United Nations such as Eleanor Roosevelt—now one of America's U.N. delegates—urged Truman not to undercut the world body by discarding UNSCOP's recommendations. And the very same month that UNSCOP delivered its Solomonic message, American public sympathy was galvanized—along with Truman's humanitarian instincts—by the plight of the *Exodus,* a ship full of un-wanted Holocaust survivors wandering wretchedly from port to port.

On October 13, the Soviets startled the United Nations by announcing that they would back partition. To the State Department's dismay, Truman followed suit. Clifford's White House staff began pulling out all the stops to ram the resolution past the General Assembly. Two U.S. Supreme Court justices and 26 U.S. senators urged the president of the Philippines to back partition, and former secretary of state Henry Stettinius badgered Harvey Firestone, the rubber magnate, into badgering in turn the president of Liberia.[50] The Zionists used up most of their chits in Washington, but partition cleared the General Assembly. With the U.S. government confused and divided, the partition resolution passed on November 29, 1947, with 33 votes in favor, 13 against, and 10 abstentions.

Washington was now formally committed to partition, upon which it had staked the newborn United Nations' prestige. But the civil war in Palestine—a nasty clash of both regular troops and guerrillas, fought out among two overlapping ethnic groups scrunched into close quarters, punctuated by terrorism—was not going well for the Yishuv.[51] The State Department pushed through a U.S. arms embargo on the combatants, which it calculated would reduce the chances of all-out war. But the Arab forces were still resupplied by Britain, leaving the Haganah—the mainstream Zionist militia that would become the nucleus for the Israel Defense Forces (IDF)—to rely on captured British arms caches, smuggled American arms provided by Zionist sympathizers, and Soviet weaponry shipped through Czechoslovakia. Outgunned, the Yishuv's leader, David Ben-Gurion, asked the United Nations for a police force to enforce partition.

Instead, the State Department proposed a temporary U.N. trusteeship over Palestine to restore order and defer the question of partition. Truman gave an oral green light to trusteeship. He subsequently claimed that he assumed the State Department would check back in more formally with him before implementing the directive; Secretary of State Marshall figured there was no such need.

The Zionists, losing on the battlefield, now feared they were losing ground at the bargaining table, too. Weizmann, who had crossed the Atlantic to lobby the president, found that not even Truman's old friend Eddie Jacobson could win him entry to the Oval Office. Finally, on March 13, Jacobson broke down in the West Wing when Truman unleashed a blast of resentment at him. The startled Jacobson rallied and gave an emotional if implausible speech comparing the debonair Weizmann to Truman's own hero, Andrew Jackson. Truman paused, swiveled in his chair, and gazed out at the Rose Garden. "You win, you bald-headed son of a bitch," he said. "I will see him."[52] Jacobson left the White House, marched to the closest hotel bar, and gulped back two double bourbons. On March 18, Weizmann met secretly with Truman at the White House, unbeknownst to the Wise Men. He left thinking that the president still backed partition and that the Zionists were back in the game.

The next day, the true degree of confusion in the U.S. policy-making apparatus spilled out into embarrassingly public display. Truman's U.N. ambassador, Warren Austin, told the Security Council that the administration was shelving its support of partition and would push instead to turn Palestine over to the United Nations. The president was fit to be tied. "The State Dept. pulled the rug from under me today," he raged in his diary. "This morning I find that the State Dept. has reversed my Palestine policy. The first I know about it is what I see in the papers! Isn't that hell!" He added, "I am now in the position of a liar and a doublecrosser," and sent a goodwill emissary to assure Weizmann of U.S. support. "There are people on the third and fourth levels of the State Dept. who have always wanted to cut my throat," he scribbled angrily.[53] No other episode so embittered the president against the "striped pants boys," and the resultant bitterness cost the State Department considerable leeway in the Palestine endgame. "I am sorry to say," Truman wrote in his memoirs, "that there were some among [America's Middle East diplomats] who were also inclined to be anti-Semitic."[54] A more likely explanation for the farrago was that Truman, distracted by the worsening situation in Europe, had lost track of the state of play on Palestine.[55]

In April 1948, however, the facts on the ground began to make trusteeship look even less attractive than partition. The battered Haganah rallied, the British left, and the Arab states prepared to invade.[56] With both Arabs and Jews in a confrontational mood, the young Dean Rusk found few U.N. members eager to take charge of Palestine. Forrestal estimated that the American share of the U.N. police force that would have to take control of Palestine would be 50,000 troops, mostly reservists—a deeply unappetizing proposition even without a worsening Cold War and a looming reelection campaign.[57] Truman was souring on trusteeship—which meant a showdown was brewing.

PRESENT AT THE CREATION

With Ben-Gurion likely to declare independence when the British Mandate expired on May 14, the Truman administration now had to decide whether to recognize the new state. A May 12 meeting to resolve the matter degenerated into an astonishing brawl in the White House.[58] At 4 P.M., with Truman seated at his desk behind his famous "THE BUCK STOPS HERE" sign, the participants filed into the Oval Office: Secretary of State Marshall, his deputy Lovett, and other State Department officials, squaring off against the presidential counsel Clifford and two other White House staffers.

Clifford, knowing that Marshall resented his presence, waited for the president to invite him to speak. Trusteeship was a nonstarter, Clifford argued. De facto partition on the ground had already occurred. By recognizing the new Jewish state, Washington would both bow to the inevitable and steal a march on Moscow. Moreover, U.S. security would be enhanced by the presence of a democratic friend in the Middle East.

Marshall prided himself on being unemotional ("I have no feelings," he once told Acheson, "except those I reserve for Mrs. Marshall"), but he went red in the face as Clifford spoke.[59] "Mr. President, I thought this meeting was called to consider an important and complicated problem in foreign policy," Marshall snapped. "I don't even know why Clifford is here. He is a domestic adviser, and this is a foreign policy matter."

"Well, general," Truman replied, "he's here because I asked him to be here."[60]

"These considerations have nothing to do with the issue," the livid secretary of state said, glaring at Clifford. "I fear that the only reason Clifford is here is that he is pressing a political consideration with regard to this issue. I don't think politics should play any part in this."[61]

Lovett, trying to lower the temperature, jumped in. Ben-Gurion's reliance on Czech weaponry and U.S. intelligence reports of communist infiltration of the Yishuv argued for delay lest the new Jewish state tilt toward Moscow. "Mr. President," Lovett said, using a singularly unfortunate idiom, "to recognize the Jewish state prematurely would be buying a pig in a poke."[62]

But Marshall was not done yet, and he jumped in. "If you follow Clifford's advice," he told Truman icily, "and in the election I were to vote, I would vote against you."[63]

The room fell into what Clifford remembers as a dreadful, shocked silence. Marshall was an American icon, and the secretary of state, sitting in the Oval Office, had just accused the president of the United States of being an unworthy hack. The hint of resignation was less than subtle, and Marshall's departure would enrage the unreconstructed GOP anticommunists in Congress and probably doom Truman's reelection bid.

That was quite enough, and Truman knew it. He called the meeting to a close by suggesting they all sleep on it and reassuring Marshall that he was leaning his way. In fact, the reverse was true. After the others filed out, Truman told Clifford, "That was rough as a cob."[64] Marshall not only never spoke to Clifford again, he never even mentioned his name.[65] But the fact that Clifford and Truman were left alone in the Oval Office after the secretary of state and his aides had left gave some sense of where the administration's true center of gravity lay. "Truman did not know how to deal with the conflicting advice that came to him," notes the Cold War historian Melvyn Leffler. "With little knowledge on which to draw, the new president tended to agree with whomever he was talking to."[66] In May 1948, more often than not, Truman was talking to Clifford.

The May 12 showdown marked the nadir of the Truman administration's Palestine confusion. A conciliatory Lovett, rattled by the clash, called Clifford to invite him over for drinks that night. But from then on, events were in the saddle—and so was Clifford. Over bourbon and sherry, Clifford told Lovett that his presentation had been made on Truman's orders and warned the undersecretary of state that he had better get his chief to back down.

During the final sprint to Israeli independence, Clifford acted as a policy entrepreneur, a persistent loner with the gumption and dedication to out-maneuver a stodgy bureaucracy.[67] At 10 A.M. on May 14 itself, Clifford called Eliahu Epstein, the Yishuv's Washington representative, to ask Epstein to arrange to have the new Jewish state ask for U.S. recognition.[68] Epstein was so rushed that he did not even know the new country's name until he heard it over the radio news in his cab over to the White House; with no time to retype the letter requesting recognition for an unnamed "Jewish State," he crossed those words out and wrote "State of Israel" in by hand as he screeched toward 1600 Pennsylvania Avenue.[69] In Tel Aviv, Ben-Gurion declared Israel's independence at 6 P.M., Washington time. Truman recognized it at 6:11.

Austin's U.N. delegation was still rounding up votes for a resolution on trusteeship when word of Truman's decision came over the wires. A U.S. diplomat told the General Assembly of Truman's decision by reading off ticker tape pulled from U.N. Secretary-General Trygve Lie's garbage can. This last reversal from the vacillating superpower enraged many U.N. del-egates; the Cuban envoy stormed toward the rostrum to announce that his country was pulling out of the United Nations, and he had to be physi-cally restrained by American diplomats.[70] Rusk was told later that one en-terprising civil servant actually sat on the Cuban's lap. Still, many of the Cuban emissary's interceptors could empathize. After the vote, Marshall put Rusk on a plane to New York to keep America's U.N. delegation from resigning en masse.[71]

They were not alone in their consternation. When asked later how he got Marshall to go along with Truman's decision, a weary Lovett replied, "I told him it was the president's choice."[72] Some of Marshall's friends who did not see it quite that way urged the secretary of state to quit on principle, Rusk later learned. Marshall is said to have told them "that one did not resign because the President, who had a constitutional right to make a decision, had made one."[73]

In the end, Truman won his 1948 election, and Israel won its 1948 war. The issue receded, especially after war broke out in Korea in 1950. Truman, however, was notably aggravated over Ben-Gurion's refusal to return any land or take back many of the 700,000 or so Palestinians who fled the Arab-Israeli war. Fearing an Arab fifth column, Israel was prepared to offer only to reunite some families and compensate those who had lost their homes.[74] "I am rather disgusted with the manner in which the Jews are approaching the refugee problem," complained Truman, his old humanitarian sympathies again engaged.[75] In 1950, Congress began pressing Truman to sell arms to the Jewish state, but America's reluctant European allies, Britain and France, instead got the administration to join them in the so-called Tripartite Declaration, which demanded limits on arms sales to the Middle East to try to fend off an arms race.

The end of the Truman administration hardly meant the end of arguments about U.S. policy in 1948. Clifford could not have known how durable the charge of election-minded impropriety would prove. But American Jews were not a particularly prominent feature in the Truman campaign's 1948 strategy. In 1948, 65 percent of U.S. Jews lived in New York, Pennsylvania, and Illinois.[76] Truman carried only Illinois, and even then only barely. Clifford blamed the loss of New York (and Maryland and Michigan, for that matter) not on insufficient Zionist zeal but on the Progressive nominee, former vice president Henry Wallace, who ran to Truman's left. And Truman himself never thought Israel had anything to do with his triumph. "Labor did it," explained the president, who was also the only person in the Truman administration who had thought he stood a chance.[77]

Ultimately, a plausible national security case can be made for Truman's policies, up to and including the still-controversial decision to recognize Israel. For starters, the risk of an oil embargo was probably overstated. The Saudis repeatedly told Truman that they could not afford a conflict with the United States over Palestine. Moreover, 1948 was not 1973. America was not helplessly dependent on foreign oil in the wake of World War II; it imported only 6 percent of its oil, and only 8.3 percent of that came from Saudi Arabia.[78] Even in a worst-case scenario, the oil-related downside of a special relationship with Israel was less dire than the Wise Men's warnings. By 1948, Truman could reasonably bow to the inevitable. Israel was on the way, the State Department was out of alternatives, and the real risk was not that Palestine might be partitioned but that the Soviet Union might somehow make hay out of the resultant chaos. Recognition offered a useful hedge against such a possibility. To be sure, there was a political upside to it, but in the end, Clifford offered a pragmatic president a chance to do well by doing good.

In 1961, Israeli Prime Minister Ben-Gurion traveled to New York, where he met with President Kennedy—and with the young Democrat's aging predecessor, Truman. Before Truman left Ben-Gurion's hotel suite, the Israeli leader told him that "as a foreigner I could not judge what would be his place in American history; but his helpfulness to us, his constant sympathy with our aims in Israel, his courageous decision to recognize our new state so quickly and his steadfast support since then had given him an immortal place in Jewish history." Truman's eyes welled up, and they were still moist when he took his leave. "I had rarely seen anyone so moved," Ben-Gurion remembered. "I tried to hold him for a few minutes until he had become more composed, for I recalled that the hotel corridors were full of waiting journalists and photographers." When Ben-Gurion left the suite shortly thereafter, a reporter asked him, "Why was President Truman in tears when he left you?"[79]

Truman loved such sentimental exaltation of his role in Israel's birth—but only in retrospect. At the time, his Palestine decision making was more prone to produce tears of frustration than of joy. But most of the elements of America's special relationship with Israel were laid by the time Truman left office in 1952. Even in these early days, the American attachment to Israel melded an affinity of regimes, the backdrop of the Holocaust, domestic politics, and Cold War realpolitik. But the overall relationship had much less to do with moralism or sentimentality than with diplomacy and the U.S. quest for strategic advantage. The U.S.–Israel relationship would go through its chilliest patch after the GOP triumph in the 1952 elections—a reminder that America's Middle East policies remained rooted in cold calculations about geopolitics, not warm emotionalism about the bonds between democracies. Truman sometimes spoke as if his most important relationship to independence related to Israel, not Missouri. His nostalgia should not be confused with the historical record. Harry Truman was many things, but he was no Cyrus.

GENERAL DISDAIN

In October 1956, a troubled IDF Chief of Staff Moshe Dayan flew back to Tel Aviv from a secret meeting in Sèvres, France. The one-eyed Israeli general had been helping cement a conspiracy among Britain, France, and Israel to try to remove Egyptian President Jamal Abd al-Nasser, the increasingly powerful Arab nationalist whom all three either loathed or feared. But Dayan did not trust the Middle East's erstwhile colonial rulers. He resorted to collusion with them only because he knew no help was forthcoming from the United States. On the flight home, the uneasy Dayan

doodled a cartoon: a dapper Brit and a French woman saying "After you!"
as they watch a plucky little Israeli make his way into the Sinai Desert.[80]
Uncle Sam was nowhere to be seen.

The 1950s were a decade of strange bedfellows in the Middle East, and
few were stranger than the Israelis, their former and thoroughly unloved
British masters, and the region's other major imperial power, the French.
Wandering into the Sinai beneath the gaze of France and Britain, as
Dayan's doodle had it, was not at all what Israel had hoped for. After the
Jewish state briefly but frighteningly flirted with nonalignment shortly af-
ter independence, Ben-Gurion and his ruling Mapai Party had resolved
never again to be without the support of a Western great power, and their
overwhelming preference was the United States. But the United States
was under new management, and the reservations U.S. foreign policy elites
had held during the Truman period about the wisdom of warm ties to
Israel now found a receptive ear in both the Oval Office and the State
Department. Americans liked Ike, as the campaign jingle had it, because
"Ike was easy to like." But Ike did not find it easy to like Israel.

Unlike Truman, Dwight D. Eisenhower had no hesitations whatsoever
about his foreign policy competence. Nor did one of America's more powerful secretaries of state, the former Dewey adviser John Foster Dulles.
Both thought Israel a headache that would make it harder to box up communism in the Soviet sphere of influence in Eastern Europe. This would
make the Eisenhower era the coldest period in the entire U.S.–Israel relationship—a relationship that was now devoid not only of the warm over-
lays and chaotic policy reverses of the Truman period but also of any
reasonable prospect for an upgrade to a full-blown alliance.

Indeed, the only remotely comparable frosts came under Jimmy Carter
(with his sometimes ill-disguised preference for the debonair Anwar al-
Sadat over the quarrelsome Menachem Begin); Ronald Reagan (with
his brief fit of anger with Begin over the 1982 sacking of West Beirut);
George H. W. Bush (who discovered that Yitzhak Shamir's Israel did not
make it appreciably easier to hold together his 1990–91 anti-Iraq coalition); and Bill Clinton (who, notwithstanding his fondness for Israel,
loathed Binyamin Netanyahu with an intensity roughly comparable to
the way Harry Truman might have felt about Abba Hillel Silver's becoming Israel's prime minister). All these interludes, however, differed from
the Eisenhower period in both kind and context. These were squabbles
between a junior and a senior partner, between client and proxy, between
ally and ally. America's basic bond with Israel—as expressed in massive
foreign aid, arms sales, security guarantees, general underlying coordina-
tion or cooperation on regional strategy, political support, a protective
veto in the U.N. Security Council, sentimental rhetoric, congressional

ardor, a healthy respect for the Israel lobby, and more—was never seriously challenged. Under Ike, all these leading indicators were up for grabs.
"It is difficult," Steven L. Spiegel has argued, "to conceive of two American administrations more different in handling the Arab-Israeli dispute
than those of Truman and Eisenhower."[81]

Ike's early attitudes toward Zionism were hardly unsympathetic, but
the future president was never as susceptible as Truman to Jewish
nationalism's emotional appeal. Nor was he willing to surrender his own
independent strategic and tactical judgments about Zionist or Israeli moves.
Unlike his insecure and inexperienced predecessor, the seasoned and
confident former supreme allied commander in Europe could draw on
an almost unmatched wealth of military and foreign policy experience.
His wartime experiences left him with a lasting horror at the Nazis' handiwork. But he was also less than enthusiastic about Zionist braggadocio. In
1956, with the Suez cataclysm brewing, Eisenhower mused in his diary
about an encounter he had had while army chief of staff with "a couple of
young Israelites [sic] who were anxious to secure arms for Israel" in the
run-up to 1948. Ike tried to talk strategy with the pair, but they "belittled
the Arabs in every way," deriding "their laziness, shiftlessness, lack of spirit,
and low morale." The Haganah envoys "boastfully claimed that Israel
needed nothing but a few defensive arms and they would take care of
themselves forever and without help of any kind from the United States."
Ike tried to dissuade them. Having spoken to "many Arab leaders," he
could assure the young Jews that "they were stirring up a hornet's nest and
if they could solve the initial question peacefully and without doing unnecessary violence to the self-respect and interests of the Arabs, they would
profit immeasurably in the long run." Before getting back to the *Sturm
und Drang* of 1956, Eisenhower added, "I would like to see those young
Israelites today."[82]

Ike might not have had much of a handle on what to call inhabitants of
Israel (which, of course, did not yet exist at the time of his chat with the
cocky "Israelites"). But no president since Ulysses S. Grant could speak
with more authority on warfare and its requirements. Ike may have thought
in 1947 that Israel would need U.S. help, but once in the White House, he
refused to make the United States an Israeli arms conduit. When
Eisenhower made up his mind about what a would-be U.S. ally needed
for its defense, there was no court of appeal.

When Eisenhower left office in 1960, replaced by the dashing Kennedy,
he was generally held in poor odor by pundits and presidential scholars—
dismissed as a passive, dim, inarticulate, affable steward of national drift.
(In 1960, James Reston of *The New York Times* wrote a column in which
he rated past presidents in a chat with a fictional friend. "What about

Eisenhower?" Reston asked his interlocutor. "Wasn't he President?" The friend replied, "We must await the judgment of history on that.")[83] Since then, his star has steadily risen. Such "Eisenhower revisionists" as Fred I. Greenstein and Robert A. Divine have convincingly given the lie to the hoary charge that Secretary of State Dulles actually ran U.S. foreign policy for a doddering president. The old joke was that Dulles carried America's diplomacy around in his hat. But as the Cold War historian John Lewis Gaddis notes, "Dulles never enjoyed the virtually free hand in foreign affairs that Truman had accorded Acheson after 1949."[84] Increasingly, Ike has emerged as a sharp, canny pol as well as an able crisis manager and nimble executive. Eisenhower replaced Truman's "THE BUCK STOPS HERE" sign with a desk-top credo of his own: "*Suaviter in modo, fortirer in re*" — Latin for "Gentle in manner, strong in deed."[85]

THE NEW LOOK

Ike's overall foreign policy—known as the New Look—sought the maximum deterrence of communism for the minimum cost.[86] Ike and (especially) Dulles saw communism—Soviet, Chinese, or Third World—as monolithic, tactically subtle, and above all driven and shaped by Marxist ideology. The most hair-raising part of their strategy was the deliberately vague term "massive retaliation," the veiled threat to use the bomb like any other weapon and thereby deter the communists from aggression. Another hallmark of the New Look was an expanded use of covert operations, including coups, which were also seen as a way of buying security on the cheap (a perspective not entirely shared by many Iranians and Guatemalans).

In practice, the New Look proved more nimble and restrained than Dulles's florid oratory often implied.[87] Unlike Kennedy, for instance, Ike stayed cool about the Soviet launch of Sputnik and the subsequent U.S. fears about a nonexistent ballistic missile gap. The New Look's accomplishments included the end of the Korean War, a refusal to pull France's chestnuts out of the fire after Dien Bien Phu, and a general flair for de-escalation.

The New Look emphasized alliances. In 1954, writing in *Foreign Affairs*, Dulles called regional partnerships "the cornerstone of security for the free nations."[88] While the Truman administration sought to use alliances both to create "a preponderance of power" and to enhance its ability to fight a world war against communism, the New Look saw them as stabilizing deterrents designed less to defeat communism on the battlefield than to keep it out of the area in the first place.[89] Dulles hoped "to encircle the Soviet Union and China with a ring of states aligned with the United States . . . not with any expectation that the countries involved could contribute directly to the defense of the United States, but rather with the hope that an American security 'umbrella' over them would discourage Russian or Chinese attacks."[90] Dulles's unprecedented 1953 trip to the Middle East showed a secretary of state eager to add a Levantine link to the containment chain. The new emphasis on regional alliances — which led some of Dulles's critics to accuse him of "pactomania" — helps explain the frostier tone of U.S.–Israel relations under Ike. The Arab-Israeli conflict repeatedly complicated the attempt to build a Middle East defense structure and led to the greatest crisis of Ike's presidency.

At least some of the new tone had to do with the simple fact that Eisenhower was a Republican. American Jews were a key part of the political equation of the New Deal, but they were much less important to the New Look. As one of Dewey's foreign policy advisers, Dulles himself had been involved with the New York governor's criticism of Truman's Palestine policy, which helped inject the issue into the 1948 campaign. But Ike and his team took pride in casting themselves as impervious to the parochial pulls of ethnic interest groups. In all fairness, talk here was cheap. Zionism's main backers in the 1950s included liberals, organized labor, and Jews — none of them groups heretofore known as Republican hotbeds.

Israel did retain considerable support in Congress, and Eisenhower's new evenhandedness between Arabs and Israelis became an issue in the 1954 congressional elections. Eisenhower could never totally ignore the Israel lobby. But paying attention did not mean paying heed. The Israel lobby achieved none of its major objectives during the Eisenhower years: muting the overall emphasis on regional alliances, convincing the government to sell U.S. arms to Israel, and signing a U.S.–Israel defense pact.[91] In October 1956, with the Suez crisis raging, Dulles called Vice President Richard Nixon to check in with the GOP's right flank. "How do you analyze it politically?" Nixon asked the secretary of state. "You are the political expert," replied Dulles. The vice president was sanguine. "We will lose some Israeli votes," Nixon said, but both men agreed that Israel's partisans would vote Democratic anyway.[92] Similar sentiments were voiced with considerably less delicacy by Secretary of State James A. Baker III in 1992.[93]

Along with this sense of political distance came a sense of wariness about Israeli motives. "It would be easy if the situation were all black and white, but it's not," argued one State Department official in 1955. "Extremists in Israel would like to expand their present boundaries. Arab extremists would still like to drive the million and a half Israelis into the sea."[94] The Eisenhower administration also disapproved of Israeli attempts to handle cross-border attacks — launched by Palestinian militants known as fedayeen—by launching reprisals that held the host country (in the 1950s, usually Jordan or Egypt) responsible for attacks staged from its soil. On March 28, 1954, one such IDF raid on the Jordanian village of Nahalin killed 9 and wounded 19 civilians. In response, Henry Byroade, Dulles's assistant secretary of state for NEA, warned that Israel should "drop the attitude of conqueror and the conviction that force and a policy of retaliatory killings is the only policy that your neighbors will understand. You should make your deeds correspond to your frequent utterances of the desire for peace."[95]

The administration also worried that Ben-Gurion's program of *kibbutz galuyot*—the ingathering of Jews from the Diaspora, one of the key ideological principles of Zionism—would tempt Israel into expansionism. On October 29, 1953, an internal State Department report concluded that unlimited Jewish immigration to Israel had ominous implications: "This unrealistic approach can only lead to further economic and financial difficulties and will probably result in additional pressure to expand Israel's frontiers into the rich lands of the Tigris and Euphrates valleys, and northward into the settled lands of Syria."[96] At NEA, Byroade concurred. The Arabs "should have the right to know the magnitude of this new state," he said in 1954. "Their fears are enhanced by the knowledge that the only limitation imposed by statute on immigration into Israel is, in fact, the total number of those of the Jewish faith in the entire world. They see only one result—future attempt at territorial expansion—and hence warfare of serious proportion."[97]

A WHOLE NEW WORLD

The Eisenhower administration's empathy with Arab concerns about Israel's character was hardly accidental. It saw the Arab-Israeli dispute—along with grumbles over British imperialism, especially in Egypt—as one of the primary hurdles to a pro-American Arab world. In 1953, Dulles complained that the Truman administration had "gone overboard in favor of Israel."[98] He and his boss were determined to right that balance, and then some, by demonstratively rebuffing the Israelis on reprisals, arms sales, and aid requests. In 1953, the Israelis got their first taste of tough love after the U.N. Truce Supervision Organization asked Israel to stop diverting the Jordan River's waters toward a new hydroelectric project. When the Israelis balked, the administration promptly cut off U.S. aid, which resumed after Israel backed down. As the Eisenhower administration saw it, keeping the Soviets out of the Middle East mandated an impartial, friendly attitude to both sides in the Arab-Israeli conflict. But some Middle Eastern states were more equal than others. As Spiegel has noted, "Impartiality did not mean equality: to Eisenhower the Arabs offered assets, while Israel constituted a liability to American interests."[99] Put another way, friendship with the Arab states was useful for containment, while friendship with Israel was not.

This new way of viewing the Middle East soon made itself felt. The most powerful Arab states, Iraq and Egypt, found themselves rivals for Arab leadership after a coup led by Nasser's Free Officers toppled the Egyptian king, Faruq, in July 1952. The State Department was split between proponents of warmer ties to the conservative monarchies—especially Saudi Arabia and Iraq, the latter country then run by the pro-Western King Faysal ibn Ghazi and his prime minister, Nuri al-Said—and those who hoped to do business with progressive nationalists like Nasser. The New Look's emphasis on alliances also led Eisenhower to improve ties with Turkey, which he hoped might become the bulwark of a miniature NATO on the Soviets' southern flank.

But Washington was not the only major Western power in the region. The United States saw Britain's imperial ties to the region as a Cold War asset but worried about Arab resentment and the vacuum that could be left by Britain's postwar exhaustion.[100] In 1955, British Prime Minister Anthony Eden established the Baghdad Pact—a new, pro-Western alliance in the Near East rooted in Britain's favorite regional client, Iraq. At its apogee, the Baghdad Pact's membership included Britain, Iran, Iraq, Pakistan, and Turkey—with Nasserite Egypt, Iraq's chief rival, conspicuously absent. Iraq argued that the Arabs' greatest foe was the Soviet Union; Nasser argued that it was Israel and sulked from the sidelines.[101]

Not wanting to alienate Nasser by identifying the United States with both Egypt's main Arab rival and its erstwhile colonial overlord, Eisenhower kept the United States out of the Baghdad Pact. But the damage to U.S.–Egyptian relations was already done. Nasser felt that he was being drubbed on several fronts: the Baghdad Pact had been signed, the United States would not sell him arms, and France was livid at him for his support for the anticolonialist Front de Liberation Nationale (FLN) rebels in Algeria. Moreover, Egypt repeatedly found itself on the receiving end of Israeli reprisals, including a February 28 raid on the Gaza Strip that killed 36 soldiers and 2 civilians and that Nasser saw as proof of Ben-Gurion's determination to keep Egypt cowed.[102] On June 1, 1955, Nasser warned Byroade that if he could not get weapons from Washington, he would get them elsewhere.

Nasser proved as good as his word. On September 27, the Egyptian president announced that he had turned to Czechoslovakia for arms, starting a strategic tilt toward Moscow that would not end until the 1970s. A

flurry of last-minute U.S. diplomacy—which was not helped when Eisenhower suffered a nigh-fatal heart attack—came too late. Moscow offered
MiG-15 fighters, Ilyushin Il-28 bombers, and T-34 tanks; Washington offered underwhelming aid packages and cultural exchanges, the latter of
which Nasser dismissed as "[a] troupe of jazz musicians."[103]

Frustrated, the administration continued to blame Israel. "We are in
the present jam," Dulles said a month after the Czech arms deal, "because the past administration had always dealt with the Middle East from
a political standpoint and had tried to meet the wishes of the Zionists in
this country."[104]

In the run-up to Nasser's surprise tilt toward Moscow, Eden, Ike, and
Dulles had tried to ease Arab-Israeli tension—and thus their regional dilemmas—by pushing the so-called Alpha peace plan that Dulles described
before the Council on Foreign Relations on August 28, 1955. Alpha called
for major Israeli territorial concessions (including rejiggering borders,
cutting the country in two to provide a "kissing point" between Jordan
and Egypt in the Negev, and splitting sovereignty over a demilitarized
Jerusalem with Jordan); demilitarized border zones; repatriation of 750,000
of the 1948 refugees; international supervision of Jerusalem's holy sites; a
Suez Canal open to Israeli shipping; and an end to the Arab economic
boycott, all accompanied by international guarantees to soothe Israeli
anxieties.[105] The overambitious scheme suffered "from terminal deficiencies of realism and judgment," as the historian David Schoenbaum has
dryly put it, "but there was no denying it a certain wrongheaded dash and
boldness."[106] It promptly died. A subsequent peace shuttle between Cairo
and Jerusalem by Robert Anderson, an Eisenhower confidant and former
high-ranking Pentagon official, withered just as quickly.[107]

A series of Nasserite snubs to the West made matters worse. They included recognizing Maoist China, hosting the Soviet foreign minister,
continuing to back the Algerian rebels, and egging on Nasserite radicals
in Jordan. In response, Eisenhower started a secret new initiative known
as the Omega Plan, designed to drive Nasser away from the Soviet Union
and isolate Egypt within the Arab world until it took a more tractable
stance. In case diplomacy failed, Omega also included one of the hallmarks of the New Look, "the option of a covert operation resembling the
1953 CIA-sponsored coup in Iran."[108]

Eisenhower also tried one last carrot along with the sticks: an appeal to
Nasser's enthusiasm for modernization. His vehicle was the Aswan High
Dam—a massive project to redirect the waters of the Upper Nile, create
more arable land, and double Egypt's production of hydroelectric power.[109]
Funding it was proving difficult; the Kremlin feared that the plan would
prove a money pit, and Nasser was not keen to make himself dependent

on Moscow. So in December 1955, Eisenhower and Eden offered to help finance this symbol par excellence of Nasserite development.

Suspicious of both superpowers, Nasser responded coolly. Meanwhile, anti-Nasser officials within the administration protested. So did the Israel lobby and, more importantly, American southerners who did not want to have to compete with Egypt's cotton farmers. The general chill of the Cold War had made major aid to the nonaligned Nasser a tough sell among anticommunist congressmen, particularly for a project that might be too ambitious for Egypt to finish.[110] Beset by second thoughts, Ike hoped to let the matter quietly drop, but Egypt's pro-American envoy to Washington, Ahmad Husayn, unexpectedly managed to persuade Nasser to accept the offer and give the United States another chance. But Eisenhower and Dulles decided to rescind the dam's financing. On July 19, 1956, Dulles broke the bad news to the devastated Husayn, who asked repeatedly whether the decision was final.[111] It was. So, for all intents and purposes, was the U.S.–Egypt rift. Reluctantly, Moscow eventually stepped in, ultimately financing at least a third of the project.

A furious Nasser saw the Aswan snub as an attempt to topple him. Determined to find another way to fund the dam, he dramatically nationalized the Suez Canal Company, heretofore owned by the British and French, on July 26, 1956. Britain and France were incensed. The West could not live with Nasser's "thumb on our windpipe," Eden declared.[112]

In Jerusalem, Ben-Gurion felt the same way. He feared that the 1955 Czech arms deal would upend the regional balance of power, eroding Israel's qualitative military advantage and triggering a deadly round of border fighting. Moreover, Egypt was blockading the strategically crucial Straits of Tiran, cutting off Israeli shipping. Israel faced no greater strategic threat than Nasser. France was offering the Jewish state major arms sales, while the British officials whom Israel had expelled just eight years earlier murmured about their support. So Ben-Gurion, stalemated in his attempts to forge a closer relationship with the Eisenhower administration, turned instead to the only Western great powers at hand.

THE THREE MUSKETEERS

Neither Britain nor France had much sympathy for uppity nationalists. Both governments, still fresh from the searing experience of World War II, were prone to likening Colonel Nasser (as Eden insisted on calling him) to Corporal Hitler. Eden's chancellor of the exchequer, Harold Macmillan, the British cabinet's foremost hawk, was described by the Tory stalwart Brendan Bracken as bellicose "beyond all description," a man eager "to tear Nasser's scalp off with his fingernails."[113] But Britain's dislike for Nasser paled by comparison to France's. In particular, France was influenced by the "Munich syndrome," but it also blamed Nasser for the nationalist rebellion raging in the French colony of Algeria.[114]

French Prime Minister Guy Mollet convinced Eden that Nasser had to go, but he could not convince Eisenhower. The Eisenhower administration had also had a bellyful of Nasser, but it did not want the empires to strike back. France's activism contrasted sharply with Britain's procrastination and America's prudence. The United States repeatedly and forcefully warned against use of force.[115] Israel had little to do with Eisenhower's reluctance to try to drive Nasser out. Rather, he feared that gunboat diplomacy could open the Arab world to the Soviets.[116] Better, Ike figured, to find a modus vivendi with Nasser than to try to get rid of him by force and risk alienating most of the Middle East. But as Henry Kissinger has noted, "once Eden and Mollet had nailed their flag to the anti-appeasement mast" and likened Nasser to Hitler and Mussolini, "they had moved beyond the possibility of compromise."[117]

For a time, American prudence seemed to have the upper hand. But even as Britain and France sat in at two multinational conferences of Suez Canal–using nations, they began planning to topple Nasser. In the absence of American backing, Ben-Gurion reckoned that he had to follow France's lead for fear of endangering his new arms pipeline.[118] The downside, of course, was the taint of collusion with the Middle East's erstwhile imperial overlords. But Ben-Gurion figured that Israel was already branded throughout the Arab world as a colonial implant, and the prospect of aid from a great power was hard to resist.

Britain and France were convinced that America would stand aside. "I know Ike," said Macmillan. "Ike will lie doggo."[119] But if Eden, Mollet, and Ben-Gurion were willing to run the risks of a Soviet response, Ike was not.[120]

On October 22–24, Britain, France, and Israel met at Sèvres, France, to seal the terms of Operation Musketeer, a complicated scheme to provide Britain and France with a pretext to attack Nasser. The unlikely comrades decided to have Israel invade the Sinai, which would let France and Britain demand that the fighting stop and drop paratroopers onto the Suez Canal, supposedly to keep it safe from the very fighting they had fomented. Meanwhile, Israeli troops would batter Egypt's army and forcibly reopen the Straits of Tiran. On October 27, Ike—who found himself in the hospital for a pre-election checkup—sensed a crisis brewing. To a visiting aide, Eisenhower cracked, "Israel and barium make quite a combination."[121]

On October 29, 1956, the second Arab-Israeli war began as Israeli paratroopers and tanks moved into Sinai. Preoccupied with the final days of Eisenhower's reelection campaign and the mounting threat of a crackdown on anti-Soviet demonstrators in Hungary, the administration was caught by surprise.[122] The night before the invasion, a hapless Dulles was reduced to calling the chairman of the American establishment, John J. McCloy, at an ungodly hour and asking him "to call the heads of every major bank to determine if there was an unexpectedly large flow of funds to Europe or Israel that might signal a buildup for war."[123]

Once the war was on, however, American reaction was blunt. Eisenhower snapped that the three Musketeers could go "boil in their own oil, so to speak." When Britain and France issued their "ultimatum" demanding that Israel withdraw, Dulles called the ruse "about as crude and brutal as anything [I have] ever seen."[124] On October 31, Israel's collaborators began their attack on Egypt. "Bombs, by God," Eisenhower roared. "What does Anthony think he's doing?" Meanwhile, Eisenhower hammered the vulnerable British pound, refusing to prop up the dwindling British reserves of oil and currency.[125] When he got Eden on the phone, Ike dressed down the United States's closest ally angrily enough to leave the British prime minister in tears.[126] He was no gentler to the Israelis, warning them that they risked U.N. opprobrium, Soviet attack, and the termination of all U.S. aid. Eisenhower directed Dulles to tell Ben-Gurion that "goddam it, we're going to apply sanctions, we're going to the United Nations, we're going to do everything that there is so we can stop this thing."[127]

Ike promptly suspended much of America's aid to Israel. Britain and France vetoed a U.N. Security Council resolution demanding a ceasefire, so the administration took the fight to the U.N. General Assembly, which overwhelmingly called for a halt to the fighting—with the approval of the Soviet Union, which was busily crushing Imre Nagy's neutralists in Hungary. The administration's misery was made complete when Dulles, wrung out after his exertions at the United Nations, awoke the night of November 2 with excruciating abdominal pains. The secretary of state was sped to Walter Reed Hospital, where he was diagnosed with terminal cancer.

Eisenhower was alone at the helm, then, when the Soviet Union's Nikolai Bulganin warned on November 5 that Moscow might fire missiles into London and Paris if they did not stop the war. Ike's second electoral showdown with Adlai Stevenson paled by comparison. The president warned that any such Soviet attack could mean World War III.

Finally, Eden's nerve broke. The Commonwealth and his allies at home were deserting him; his bitterly disillusioned protégé and minister of state for foreign affairs, Anthony Nutting, wrote that Britain had taken "part in a cynical act of aggression, dressing ourselves for the part as firemen or policemen, while making sure that our fire-hoses spouted petrol and not water and that we belaboured with our truncheons the assaulted and not the assaulter."[128] But the British prime minister's collapse stemmed both from Soviet bluster and American sanctions; even the bellicose Macmillan abruptly changed his tune after the Bank of England began hemorrhaging. Broken, Eden told Mollet it was all over. After ordering his tommies to pull back, Eden called Eisenhower on November 6—election day—to tell him that he need not find out whether Moscow was bluffing about reducing Big Ben to radioactive rubble. With British good manners, Eden also took the time to ask how the vote was going. "I don't give a darn about the election," growled Eisenhower. "I guess it will be all right."[129]

So it was, but Ike's Suez performance remains an impressive display of political sangfroid. The risks that Eisenhower ran had little to do with the Israel lobby; American Jews would vote loyally for Stevenson. "I gave strict orders to the State Department," Eisenhower told a friend during the crisis, "that they should inform Israel that we would handle our affairs exactly as though we didn't have a Jew in America."[130] The stickier political problem was Eisenhower's own party's right flank. Before Suez, GOP hardliners were livid over Nasser's recognition of communist China and acceptance of Soviet arms.[131] Ike did not much care if they were angry at him for saving Nasser. "If they don't want me," he said, "let them get someone else."[132]

THE EISENHOWER DOCTRINE

As 1957 dawned, Britain and France were long gone from Suez, but Israel still held the Gaza Strip and positions in Sinai overlooking the Straits of Tiran. Eisenhower wanted them out; with anti-Israel economic sanctions wending their way through the United Nations, Eisenhower gave a nationally televised speech demanding an Israeli withdrawal. Dulles trumpeted the administration's immunity to the Israel lobby. "We are doing all we can to avoid sanctions," Dulles griped to *Time's* Henry Luce. "I am aware how almost impossible it is in this country to carry out a foreign policy not approved by the Jews. Marshall and Forrestal learned that. I am going to try to have one."[133] By the end of the month, Canadian Foreign Minister Lester B. Pearson took pride of authorship for a package deal: an Israeli retreat from Gaza and its positions athwart the Straits of Tiran, a U.N. peacekeeping force in the Sinai, and U.S. guarantees of "unrestricted navigation in the Straits."[134] On March 7, the IDF began pulling out of Gaza and Sharm al-Shaykh; on April 10, the Suez Canal reopened.

Surveying the wreckage, Eisenhower and Dulles found little to like. The British-backed Baghdad Pact, never a huge success, was now thoroughly disgraced across the Arab world. Worse, the British and French had left behind a political vacuum in the Middle East. To fill it, on January 5, 1957, the president unveiled to Congress what would become known as the Eisenhower Doctrine: arms sales, military assistance, and foreign aid to friendly Middle East states, as well as a commitment to use force "to protect the territorial integrity and political independence of any Middle Eastern state facing overt armed aggression from a country controlled by international Communism."[135]

In practice, the Eisenhower Doctrine came to mean a concerted American attempt to bolster the Arab forces most likely to resist communism—the conservative monarchies, who were also the Arab forces most likely to resist progressivism, neutralism, nationalism, and pan-Arabism. Increasingly, Washington saw Nasser as a communist stalking horse and a threat to regional order.

The United States was rattled when Syria joined Egypt in 1958 to form the United Arab Republic (UAR), a new high point in Nasser's pan-Arabist quest to unite the Arabs in one state. Later that year, riots broke out in Lebanon after President Camille Chamoun—a member of Lebanon's powerful Maronite Christian minority and a foe of Nasser—sought to tinker with the exquisitely delicate Lebanese constitution, which painstakingly balanced power between Lebanon's sectarian groups, and give himself a second term. Nasserite mobs burst onto Beirut's streets. With their long-standing difficulty differentiating between authentic nationalism and encroaching Marxism, Eisenhower and Dulles, as one scholar has quipped, "saw red."[136]

The riots seemed to be ebbing until July 14, when Western policy in the region suffered a jolt comparable only to the Czech arms deal and Suez: Nasser's main regional rival, King Faysal of Iraq, was toppled in a military coup in which both Faysal and Prime Minister Nuri al-Said were brutally murdered. The coup's leader, General Abd al-Karim Qasim, played up Faysal's failure to help Nasser during Suez.[137] Meanwhile, in Lebanon, civil war erupted between Chamoun's Christian allies and the mostly Muslim admirers of Nasser. Fearing that a series of pro-Western dominoes were about to fall in the Middle East, Eisenhower sent the Marines to prop them up. Their arrival calmed the fighting in Lebanon, which eventually returned to the old power-balancing arrangements.[138] In the meantime, Ike and Dulles scoured the region for hints of communist activity, rushing troops to Jordan (with British help), Kuwait, and Saudi Arabia to keep friendly kings on their thrones. None of the other supposedly wobbly Arab dominoes fell, and by October, the American troops were back home.

With Nasser now looking far worse to Eisenhower, Ben-Gurion looked slightly better.[139] Israel had played a useful (albeit minor) role in the 1958 crisis by letting U.S. and British planes fly through its airspace en route to Jordan. But this warmed ties only slightly. When the Soviet Union demanded that Israel stop the overflights, Ben-Gurion decided not to chance a Soviet intervention and said that the flights would stop forthwith. Dulles called Ben-Gurion's reversal "a surrender to the Soviets, a violation of a commitment to the United States, and a bad example for countries willing to stand up to Soviet expansionism."[140] Ben-Gurion again felt the back of Washington's hand. "I was therefore shocked to hear . . . [you] say to our Ambassador that Israel had 'caved in' immediately to a Soviet threat, and that a Soviet letter can bring us to submission," a wounded Ben-Gurion wrote Dulles. "We do not have the physical strength which certain great nations possess."[141] After the 1958 crises passed, U.S. economic and technical aid rose somewhat, and U.S.–Israel relations improved slightly— although after the threat of U.N. sanctions, nationally televised presidential reprimands, demands to give back Israel's territorial gains, voluble disdain for the Israel lobby, and accusations of having endangered the West's entire posture in the Middle East, one might think there was nowhere to go but up.

Eisenhower's view of Israel was not helped by the prospect that Israel might get the bomb. In late December 1960, press reports revealed that Israel was secretly building a nuclear reactor near the Negev desert town of Dimona that might be able to produce the fissile material for atomic weapons. In 1955, under the terms of his Atoms for Peace program, Ike had actually given Israel a much smaller research reactor, but Dimona— a heretofore secret fruit of the French-Israeli nexus—troubled Eisenhower's last days in the Oval Office.

Meanwhile, Nasser felt himself hemmed in. To the Egyptian leader's fury, the new junta in Iraq killed scores of Iraqi Nasserites in 1959 in Mosul.[142] Nasser also found his ties to Moscow cooling after he accused his local communist party of plotting his overthrow and cracked down on it. Eisenhower used the new Soviet-Egyptian strain as the pretext to restart the U.S. aid program that had been severed over Suez, but after the interventions of 1956 and 1958, a major rapprochement between Washington and Cairo seemed unlikely anytime soon. Major arms sales to Israel seemed just as implausible; when Ben-Gurion asked the administration for defensive Hawk antiaircraft missiles in 1960, he was rebuffed. It would take John F. Kennedy to change matters.

LEGACIES

Kennedy inherited a mess in the Middle East. The Baghdad Pact had failed, the Aswan overture to Nasser had failed, and the reliance on the British had failed. Eisenhower and Dulles had left America on chilly terms with both Israel and Egypt, and America's conservative Arab friends were still rattled after the fall of Iraq and the 1958 Eisenhower Doctrine interventions.

In particular, Kennedy took over from what was almost certainly the least pro-Israel presidency in American history. While Eisenhower made some sympathetic noises about the embattled Jewish republic, he never shed his fear that Israel might snarl U.S. regional strategy.[143] Eisenhower and Dulles saw the shambles that their Middle East policy had become—Britain useless, Iraq lost, Egypt and Syria falling into the Soviet orbit, the conservative monarchs anxious and exposed, Israel unpredictable and jittery, and the world rattled by threats of nuclear war—and found in it confirmation of their worries that the Arab-Israeli conflict would seriously undercut the West's ability to keep the Soviet Union out of the Middle East. Suez confirmed Ike's direst suspicions about what Israel could mean for the Cold War.[144] "It wasn't passivity," said Walworth Barbour, Kennedy's genial ambassador to Israel, of Eisenhower's attitude toward the Jewish state. "It was antagonism."[145]

Bad as he felt about Israel, Eisenhower felt even worse about Egypt. Eisenhower and Dulles were not out to save Nasser during the Suez crisis; they were out to save containment. Nasser was still a thorn in the American paw, and America's Middle Eastern interventions—first diplomatic and then military—in 1956 and 1958 respectively were undergirded by the need to respond to the pan-Arabism emanating from Cairo. Indeed, America after Suez could sometimes sound like France before Suez. When Egypt and Syria merged to form the United Arab Republic (UAR) in February 1958, Dulles warned that Nasser "whipped up Pan-Arabism much as Hitler whipped up Pan-Germanism as a means of promoting an expansion of his power."[146]

Kennedy's immediate inheritance, then, was a seriously eroded posture in the Middle East. Truman bequeathed him some warmth toward the Jewish state and a lasting Arab suspicion of Democratic presidents. Eisenhower bequeathed a regional shambles, with Egypt and Israel both in Washington's bad graces. Meanwhile, the Soviet Union—while still skeptical about Nasser, who was not much of a communist—was probing for ways to expand its influence, and the Arab conservatives were looking for ways to limit Nasser's. After the second Arab-Israeli war, peace seemed farther off than ever. With casual contempt, Kennedy would conclude that Eisenhower and Dulles had made a hash of things. It was high time, Kennedy thought, that the torch was passed.

CHAPTER TWO

The Making of the President

John F. Kennedy and the Arab-Israeli Conflict,
1917–1960

IN NOVEMBER 1960, Eisenhower's vice president, Richard Nixon, lost an election by what seemed, until the 2000 fiasco in Florida, the most heart-stoppingly narrow of margins. That put the Democrats back in charge of the White House for the first time in eight years—with historic consequences for the Middle East.

For a president whose tenure was so important to U.S.–Israel relations, John F. Kennedy's earliest attitudes toward Israel were sometimes strikingly cool. Kennedy came to the presidency with both a longstanding interest in foreign policy in general and a reasonable background in Middle Eastern affairs, including two trips to the region and an interest in Arab nationalism that far predated his administration's attempt to court Nasser. JFK had his own attitudes toward the Arab-Israeli conflict, shaped by more than book learning—and some of these attitudes make his subsequent record as the pivotal president in U.S.–Israel relations all the more surprising.

Born the year of the Balfour Declaration, the future president did not grow up in a notably philo-Semitic household. Joseph P. Kennedy, the ambitious and resentment-riddled patriarch, was an unreconstructed and unsubtle bigot who put in a memorably wretched performance as U.S. ambassador to London during World War II. His rancor extended to, among others, Jews. Less an isolationist or crypto-fascist than a blinkered anti-communist, the Kennedy patriarch grumbled privately after Munich of "the Jews starting to mess the thing up" and "Jewish propaganda."[1]

Never a great admirer of perfidious Albion, Ambassador Kennedy seems to have made a point of having his sons witness Britain's ignominy in Mandate Palestine firsthand. The young Jack spent nearly a month there in the miserable summer of 1939, also adding a trip to Egypt. Once in Congress, he subsequently pronounced himself "stirred deeply" by the

Zionists' "daring fight" for independence "under the guns of the British and Arabs."[2]

In fact, he seems not to have been stirred very deeply at all. A fascinating letter he wrote at the time to his father showed scant sympathy for the Zionist cause. Indeed, the letter glancingly indulged the old man's prejudices by noting, "you undoubtedly, if I know the Jews, know the 'whole' story." To be sure, Jack might have been trying to please his father, or he might merely have been rattled by the Mandate's violence. On the future president's last night in Jerusalem, he noted, rightist Jewish terrorists had set off 13 bombs in the Old City. Whatever the reasons, the young Kennedy wrote his father that the 1939 British White Paper cutting Jewish immigration "theoretically presents a good solution, but it just *won't* work"—still a reasonably effusive encomium for the document that Ben-Gurion had vowed to fight as if there were no such thing as Nazism. The best answer, Jack concluded, seemed to be Lord Peel's 1937 partition plan. But on "the Jewish side there is the desire for complete domination, with Jerusalem as the capital of their new land of milk and honey, with the right to colonise in Trans-Jordan" as well. Meanwhile, the anxious Arabs had come to realize the Jews' "superiority and fear it." Popular sentiment on the ground "seems to be with the Arabs," and not just because "at least some" of the Yishuv's leaders had "an unfortunately arrogant, uncompromising attitude. . . . After all, Palestine was hardly Britain's to give away." Meanwhile, most Arabs were "heartily sick of the whole business which is playing hell with their economic life. . . ." "I thought Danzig was a tough problem," Jack continued, referring to Hitler's 1938–39 insistence that the Polish port now known as Gdansk be ceded to Nazi Germany, "but I have never seen two groups more unwilling to try and work out a solution that has some hope of success than these two groups."[3] It is a striking note from the young man who would go on to oversee the first major American arms sale to the Jewish state.

The future president's closest adviser, his younger brother Robert, was actually present at the moment of Israel's birth. Amid the chaos of 1948, Bobby drew markedly warmer conclusions than his skeptical older sibling.[4] On Good Friday in March 1948, amid another paternally mandated postcollege trip to see a bit of the world, Bobby ignored his anxious father's orders to steer clear of trouble and flew from Cairo to Lydda, the town outside Tel Aviv that still houses Israel's major airport. On assignment for the *Boston Post*, Bobby interviewed his way across the war-torn Palestine Mandate, visiting Jerusalem, a kibbutz, and Tel Aviv. (As RFK roved around Jerusalem, scribbling down his impressions, he could not have known that, in the mixed Arab-Jewish neighborhood of Musrara, there lived a four-year-old boy named Sirhan Sirhan.)[5]

The spring of 1948 was hardly a safe time in Palestine: according to Bobby's diary, the Jewish convoy from Tel Aviv to Jerusalem that directly followed his was "cut to ribbons," and the future attorney general's stroll around Jerusalem ended with his being arrested, blindfolded, taken to Haganah headquarters, and ordered to keep off the streets. "They are different from any Jews I have ever know[n] or seen," wrote an impressed Bobby. "I just wish [the Arabs] didn't have that oil." On June 3, a few weeks after the Mandate expired, the *Boston Post*'s man in Israel filed a piece bearing, as Arthur Schlesinger, Jr., dryly noted, "a headline guaranteed to sell papers in Boston: BRITISH HATED BY BOTH SIDES."[6] Bobby dismissed talk that the Jewish state might turn communist as being "fantastically absurd." Indeed, America and Britain might soon "be looking to a Jewish state to preserve a toehold in that part of the world."

Some of Bobby's enthusiasm seems to have ultimately rubbed off on Jack, who ran successfully for Congress in 1946. The young congressman applauded Truman's decision to recognize Israel in May 1948.

The Kennedy brothers, along with their sister Patricia, traveled together to Israel in the fall of 1951 as part of a seven-week congressional trip through the Middle and Far East. For all of Kennedy's robust image, his Addison's disease and chronic back pain made foreign trips an ordeal. JFK kept a journal as they traveled, jotting down vignettes and observations in his inimitable (and virtually impenetrable) scrawl.[7] This time, Kennedy's tone, while still skeptical, had more warmth in it. Arriving in Tel Aviv, the young representative was struck by the pace of construction, the dangers of using the roads at night, and the rugged Israelis. "Soldiers tough, rugged, cocky," he wrote.[8] "[Israelis] very aggressive—confident. Arabs fear expansion— say it is inevitable."[9] During their meetings with JFK, Israeli officials bragged of their policy of unlimited aliyah, or Jewish immigration, telling Kennedy that a group of baffled, backward Yemenite immigrants taking their first airplane ride started a fire on board to cook lunch.[10] The U.N. envoy to the region, Ralph Bunche, sounded a less enthusiastic note, remarking that "the greatest mistake of the Jews was their handling of the Arab problem."[11] But Kennedy seemed to like the young country's toughness. "You can feel sense of dedication—especially in young people—willingness to endure hardship . . . ," he scribbled.[12] "Life for people very hard and tough after exhilaration of war," he added, especially for the elderly.[13]

One of the highlights of the trip was dinner with Ben-Gurion at the prime minister's Jerusalem residence, accompanied by several Israeli ministers and some other Americans, including Franklin D. Roosevelt, Jr., then also a young congressman, and Monnett B. Davis, the U.S. ambassador to Israel. A photograph of the dinner shows Kennedy looking particularly boyish, in a trim gray suit, alongside the doughty Ben-Gurion. "B.-G.

very energetic dynamic, very interested in things at home," Kennedy wrote.[14] After Davis's briefing, FDR, Jr., asked Ben-Gurion about the prospects for Arab-Israeli peace. It depended, Ben-Gurion replied, "on the recognition of the liberal elements, responsive to the peoples [*sic*] wishes —present govt not concerned with peace but with protecting own position." When Davis told Ben-Gurion that the Arab states were "genuinely afraid of Israel," the prime minister asked how a country as huge as Egypt could possibly be frightened. Moreover, "we wouldn't want to go back to Egypt again," Ben-Gurion added. "We had enough the first time."[15] Later in the evening, the wife of Israeli President Chaim Weizmann took FDR, Jr., up onto the roof and pointed out the dividing line across Jerusalem, between the darkness lying over the Arab sections and the bright lights of the Jewish zones.

Upon his return, the young representative of Massachusetts's Eleventh Congressional District was considerably more circumspect about Israel than he had been in 1939—which might have had something to do with Bobby's presence, Joe's absence, or his own pending Senate run. "The true enemy of the Arab world is poverty and want," Kennedy said in a November 1951 radio report about the trip. He foreshadowed his attempt to reach out to Nasser by expressing regret that America had not only "made no new friends" but "lost old ones" by siding too often with the Third World's haves over its have-nots.[16] The Arab world's reaction to Israel had been "hurt and vengeful," he added. Kennedy struck a more pro-Israel note on the floor of the House in May 1952, backing a $76 million appropriation to help Israel absorb refugee immigrants and calling the country "a beacon of inspiration to all free men everywhere."[17] Kennedy made no particular secret about his desire to court Jewish voters during his first statewide race, recalled his speechwriter, Ted Sorensen.[18]

In both the House and Senate, Kennedy offered prudent pro-Israel noises to soothe an important constituency while displaying a consistent interest in making headway in the Arab states and the rest of the Third World. Kennedy's keen awareness of political exigency never made him into a habitual panderer on Jewish issues; the lone post–World War II exemplar limned in his 1956 *Profiles in Courage* was Senator Robert Taft, cited not for his fight against isolationism but for his ornery insistence that the Nuremberg tribunals had amounted to a form of ex post facto vengeance that lay beyond the Anglo-American legal tradition—a position that, whatever its admixture of principle and perversity, hardly showed a finely honed sensitivity to Jewish sensibilities.[19] On the other hand, Senator Kennedy condemned Soviet antisemitism, opposed Eisenhower and Dulles's push for U.N. sanctions against Israel over the Suez war, and, in front of a massive, cheering 1956 Israeli Independence Day celebration in Yankee Stadium, vowed not to let Israel fall. (The legendary Israeli diplomat Abba Eban shared an open car at the Yankee Stadium rally with Kennedy and Marilyn Monroe; he later recalled that Kennedy had remarked, "While both of us have great assets, hers are more visible.")[20] In 1956, Kennedy cosponsored a Senate resolution denouncing the Eisenhower administration's quiet decision not to send Jewish troops or diplomats to Saudi Arabia — an issue that Kennedy would face again in 1963 — and wrote Dulles to urge lifting the U.S. embargo on arms sales to Israel. "It seems to me that if the Egyptians and Arab States are going to receive arms from the Soviets and if we continue to embargo shipments to Israel," the Massachusetts senator wrote, "military imbalance against Israel will result."[21]

Kennedy's most famous speech in the Senate was about the Middle East, but it had nothing to do with Israel. In 1957, Kennedy caused a hullabaloo by advocating negotiations leading to independence for the French colony of Algeria, where the nationalist rebels known as the FLN were waging a bloody guerrilla and terrorist campaign to drive France out. Kennedy also blasted the Eisenhower administration's "head-in-the-sand" attitude toward Arab nationalism, which the young senator took seriously rather than deriding it as a disguise for communism.[22] The French were seriously miffed; in hindsight, the senator seems to have been foreshadowing the interest in Third World anticolonialism that undergirded his Nasser initiative. Nevertheless, critics from Dean Acheson to Adlai Stevenson lambasted Kennedy for breaking so openly with a NATO ally. There was "no Algerian vote in this country," Sorensen dryly noted, but Kennedy made a few ripples with the speech just the same. Harris Wofford, a young lawyer at the deeply unimpressed Acheson's firm, was so taken with the address that he eventually joined Kennedy's staff, becoming a top civil rights aide and eventually the senator from Pennsylvania whose campaign provided much of the template for Bill Clinton's 1992 race.[23] Abba Eban, who watched the speech at Kennedy's invitation from the Senate gallery, remembered being told by French Ambassador Hervé Alphand, "It doesn't matter, this young man will never go far in politics."[24] Farther afield, an American reporter visiting an FLN camp later told Kennedy of being eagerly grilled by dusty rebels about the senator's White House chances in 1960.[25]

Kennedy's bids for religious tolerance were often pitched to include Jews. "Are we to say," the first major Catholic presidential candidate asked during the bruising 1960 West Virginia primary, "that a Jew can be elected Mayor of Dublin, a Protestant can be named Foreign Minister of France, a Moslem can sit in the Israeli Parliament but a Catholic cannot be President of the United States?"[26] But Kennedy also bid more blatantly for Jewish votes during his race against Vice President Richard Nixon, as in JFK's August

1960 letter to Rabbi Israel Goldstein of Manhattan's Congregation B'nai Jeshurun. The Democratic nominee called the Arab states' belligerence the "threshold obstacle" to peace, proposed a Middle East conference to end the state of war and start direct Arab-Israeli peace talks, and promised to move quickly to eliminate the discrimination that kept Jewish American troops from serving in Saudi Arabia.[27] To counter, pro-Nixon ads in Jewish newspapers hinted darkly that Joseph Kennedy was an anti-Semite, but Jewish voters remained largely Democratic.[28] In the Bronx, Kennedy was greeted with hand-lettered signs reading "The home of the bagel thinks Big Jack is able" and "The home of the knishes thinks Jack is delicious."[29]

In August, both Kennedy and Nixon were invited to New York to address the Zionist Organization of America's annual conference. Nixon passed.[30] On August 25, in a ballroom of the Statler Hilton bedecked with a banner reading "Zionism for America and Israel," a dark-suited Kennedy won rapturous reviews in the Jewish press for his most pro-Israel remarks to date, praising a country that carried "the shield of democracy" and honored "the sword of freedom." He had recently been attacked, he said, by the Egyptian media for declaring that Israel was "here to stay." The Cairo newspaper *al-Jumhuriyya* had begged to differ, sniping that, "Time will judge between us, Mr. Kennedy." "I agree," Kennedy told the ZOA audience. "Time will judge whether Israel will continue to exist. But I wish I could be as sure of all my prophecies as I am of my flat prediction that Israel is here to stay." The Jewish state was "the child of hope and the home of the brave," and Zionism was no more merely a Jewish cause than Ireland was merely the concern of Kennedy's fellow Irish Americans. "Friendship for Israel is not a partisan matter," Kennedy continued. "It is a national commitment." The Eisenhower administration, Kennedy said, had committed a "series of incredible American blunders which led to the Suez crisis," and punished "champions of democracy and freedom . . . for their virtues." Instead, Kennedy proposed reaffirming the Tripartite Declaration to "guarantee that we will act with whatever force and speed are necessary to halt any aggression by any nation," convening a regional peace conference, and moving toward mutually beneficial economic development. "The Middle East needs water, not war," Kennedy said in a classic Sorensen alliteration, "tractors, not tanks—bread, not bombs."[31] With some chutzpah, the young Democratic nominee even took a Jewish-themed swipe at the age issue, calling Theodor Herzl's founding of the Zionist movement "the classic case of an ancient dream finding a young leader. . . . Perhaps I may be allowed the observation that the Jewish people—ever since David slew Goliath—have never considered youth as a barrier to leadership, or measured experience and maturity by mere length of days."[32] It was bravura, classy pandering.

Such warmth made sense to Sorensen. "Kennedy was at home with Jews," he later said, "and Jews were at home with Kennedy."[33] Considering the Kennedy patriarch's dim view of Jews, among others, that is perhaps surprising. But there is no sign that JFK shared his father's anti-Semitism. When Sorensen felt compelled to mention the fact that all three of his deputies were Jewish—Myer Feldman, Lee White, and Richard Goodwin—Kennedy shrugged, "So what? They tell me this is the first Cabinet with two Jews, too. All I care is whether they can handle it."[34] Indeed, Sorensen himself—arguably the best presidential speechwriter in U.S. history—though raised a Nebraska Unitarian, had a Jewish mother and maternal grandmother, which probably makes him technically Jewish.

But while Kennedy could relate to American Jews, the studiedly sardonic president found it harder to relate the passions of *Israelis*. Kennedy was a cool politician; Ben-Gurion was a hot one. Years later, Feldman remembered discussing Israel's 1961 trial of Adolf Eichmann with Kennedy.[35] On balance, Kennedy concluded, Israel would be better off commuting the Nazi war criminal's death sentence and jailing him for the rest of his life. As Feldman remembers it, Kennedy argued that Israel would thereby show itself as "a humanitarian nation," suffer no real harm, and win some "brownie points with the rest of the world for not being vindictive"—a typically calculating, measured Kennedy response, even in the face of one of the arch-demons of Jewish history. Feldman never asked Kennedy what he would do if *he* were prime minister of Israel, which was probably just as well; one doubts whether JFK could have made the intellectual leap.[36]

THE OVERRATED ISRAEL LOBBY

When Kennedy met Ben-Gurion again in New York at the Waldorf on May 30, 1961, the new president reportedly decided to use his trademark charming frankness. "You know I was elected by the Jews," Kennedy is said to have told the diminutive Israeli prime minister in private. "I was elected by the Jews of New York. I have to do something for them. I will do something for you."[37] As a matter of electoral math, Kennedy had a point; the president received 800,000 votes in Jewish precincts in New York, which he carried by only 384,000 votes. Still, while such man-to-man, pol-to-pol candor generally worked for JFK, the coarse, nakedly political approach stuck in the craw of Israel's founding father.[38] "You must do whatever is good for the free world," Ben-Gurion reportedly told Kennedy.[39] Being treated like "a politician from Brooklyn" offended him. It was beneath both his dignity and Kennedy's. This was not how statesmen behaved.[40] Afterward, Ben-Gurion was withering. "To me, he looks like a politician," he told his aides.[41]

In fact, this episode—if accurate—hardly conveys the subtlety with which Kennedy weighed domestic politics in shaping his Middle East policies. To be sure, as a former congressional Democrat, Kennedy certainly had made pro-Israel noises for political benefit. As president, he also instinctively looked to American Jews as a natural part of his post–New Deal coalition. But while Kennedy was not immune to considering reactions from Congress or pro-Israel Democrats, his Arab-Israeli diplomacy was largely based on Cold War strategy rather than ethnic politics.

That is not to say that he was a purist. Kennedy's assistant secretary of state for Near East affairs (NEA), Phillips Talbot, remembers once pushing a pro-Arab stance "which admittedly would cause pain to Israel." Talbot remarked that it was terribly difficult to handle decisions touching on both foreign policy and "domestic political considerations," and urged the president to let the foreign policy aspect win. "The trouble with you, Phil," Kennedy reportedly replied, "is that you've never had to collect votes to get yourself elected to anything."[42]

Indeed, Kennedy's White House staff often felt misunderstood by the professional diplomats with whom they now had to work. As the Cold War ground on, much of the legwork for containment in the nooks and crannies of the Third World had fallen to a new generation of regional specialists. U.S. Ambassador to Egypt John S. Badeau and America's other Middle East experts came to be known offhandedly as the Arabists—a term that, as former assistant secretary of state for NEA Richard Murphy has noted, "became a pejorative for *he who intellectually sleeps with Arabs.*"[43] The Arabists found that their profession had suffered much the same terminological fate that Albert Hourani noticed about Orientalists: a discipline had become an insult. Truman left office convinced that many of his Arabists were anti-Semites.[44]

The accusation of impropriety in Israel policy was the Wise Men's great gift to the Arabists. Marshall's scorn for Truman's 1948 calculations resonated with the Cold War regionalists trying to make headway in Beirut, Cairo, Damascus, and Jidda. One classic example of the Arabists' disdain came from Armin Meyer, the former NEA hand turned Kennedy's ambassador to Lebanon. "From the breezes which waft across the blue Mediterranean," Meyer sniffed to National Security Adviser McGeorge Bundy in July 1962, "I am reminded that it is again election year at home and the pressures are once again on you denizens of the White House to do this or that for our little protege, Israel." Meyer also sent copies of his argument against a pro-Israel tilt to other White House aides for "use when any of you are talking with Americans pushing Israel's requests such as my old friends Si Kennen [sic] of the America-Israel Public Affairs Committee and Label Katz of Bnai Brith. I've always found that when you lay out the

facts to such responsible citizens they are ready to stand by their country."
Having garbed his dual-loyalty charge in pious fellow feeling, Meyer concluded with sunny solidarity: "Keep the flag flying."[45] Later, Meyer and
Israel's other critics in the U.S. diplomatic corps would account for much
of the opposition to the Hawk sale and for the subsequent mutterings about
impure motives.

In fact, the Arabists seem to have exaggerated both Kennedy's vice and
Eisenhower's virtue. For one thing, Kennedy hated being pushed around.
A few weeks after Kennedy received the Democratic nomination for president, a Jewish businessman closely linked to Adlai Stevenson, Abraham
Feinberg, held a meeting for the candidate at the Hotel Pierre in New
York with a few dozen Jewish businessmen. Feinberg recalled the session
as a triumph, despite some hostile questions about Joseph Kennedy's views
on Hitler. But JFK reportedly later complained angrily to a journalist friend
that the group had crudely offered to swap campaign funding for control
over Middle East policy.[46] If Kennedy was going to fool with domestic
politics, he would do it on his own terms, not others'.

For another, Eisenhower did not quite keep up the Chinese wall that
NEA would have preferred. It is true that the general flouted the Israel
lobby repeatedly. It is also true that domestic politics had basically nothing to do with Eisenhower's 1960 refusal to sell Hawks to Israel; when Ike
held a White House meeting in late September 1960 with the presidents
of B'nai Brith, the American Zionist Council, the American Jewish Congress, and the Union of Orthodox Congregations of America, none of the
Jewish leaders so much as mentioned the Hawk.[47] But for all his avowed
reluctance to let domestic politics enter American foreign policy,
Eisenhower did just that by flouting his apolitical principles when he met
Nasser at the Waldorf that same month. During the Suez crisis, Ike told
Nasser, he had backed the U.N. push for British, French, and Israeli withdrawals despite the looming election and the "Jewish vote."[48] In effect, Ike
took his stance of apolitical rectitude and tried to swap it for Nasser's respect, even if it entailed the airing of domestic ethnic-politics laundry in
front of a foreign head of state. Kennedy was less priggish about playing
ethnic politics, but he, too, tended to stop shy of outright opportunism.

Kennedy did use Myer ("Mike") Feldman, one of Ted Sorensen's deputies, as a de facto ambassador to American Jewry. A Washington lawyer
who had worked for the Senate Banking and Currency Committee, Feldman joined Senator Kennedy's staff in 1958 as a legislative assistant for
domestic affairs. During the 1960 campaign, Feldman headed the research
team that tended the "Nixopedia," the massive compendium of the vice
president's every utterance, gaffe, vote, inconsistency, and potential weakness.[49] Tapping Feldman to handle American Jewry was certainly a sign

that Kennedy wanted to hear American Jewish perspectives. Feldman was a talented operative; when he introduced George McGovern to a group of Jewish potential donors before the 1972 election, one participant marveled that Feldman "was so good I actually believed, for a minute, that McGovern could win."[50] But Feldman had far less clout than had Clark Clifford, who had handled outreach to American Jews for Harry Truman. Indeed, Kennedy and McGeorge Bundy deliberately decided not to give Feldman intelligence clearances lest he leak sensitive material or embed himself too deeply in foreign policy-making. Bundy's staffers remember the formidable national security adviser turning to Feldman from time to time and saying, "Mike, you know, you're just wrong."[51]

Feldman's day job dealing with domestic matters often kept him several steps removed from the foreign policy loop. Nevertheless, at the president's behest, he became a pipeline to Kennedy for American Jewish groups and sometimes the Israeli embassy. Occasionally, the president would use the pipeline in reverse. At staff meetings in the Cabinet Room, Talbot recalls, Kennedy would sometimes tell Feldman, "Mike, we just have to do it this way. Now, you explain this. Calm the people down. Get them off my back."[52] It was a role that, inevitably, left behind some bruised feelings. Robert W. Komer, who handled the Middle East portfolio for the National Security Council, suspected Feldman of leaking information on Israel like a sieve. The administration's chief enforcer, Attorney General Robert Kennedy, also thought Feldman's loyalties sometimes became confused, although it is not clear whether what bothered Bobby was insufficient loyalty to America or insufficient loyalty to his brother. Indeed, the attorney general's ferocity in defending his brother may have led him into an unfortunate slur on Feldman's patriotism. "His [Feldman's] major interest was Israel rather than the United States," RFK reportedly later complained.[53]

The president, true to form, was more ironic about Feldman's role than his glowering brother. When Kennedy met Ben-Gurion at the Waldorf in May 1961, the two leaders' discussion briefly turned to Israel's kibbutzim, or communal farming collectives. "How about Myer Feldman—it would do him no harm to go to a kibbutz," Kennedy breezily suggested. "After all, you want all the Jewish fellows to go over there."

"We want only the best to go," Ben-Gurion replied.

"I think anyway that Feldman should stay here," Kennedy said.

"This is a rather doubtful compliment," Feldman sighed.[54]

But for all Kennedy's ribbing, Feldman often found himself called into situations that were awkward at best. After all, bringing Feldman into the diplomatic loop injected a domestic-politics reality check into the foreign policy–making process—sometimes to the irritation of the State Department. When Feldman told a White House meeting in August 1962 that Israeli Ambassador Avraham Harman "does quiet things down" upon request, an uncharacteristically fuming Secretary of State Dean Rusk—usually the most temperate of men—shot back that it was improper for an Israeli diplomat to call on a political aide like Feldman.[55]

Rusk was not alone in his concerns, or in fearing that Kennedy might represent a marked departure from the policies favored by the Middle East specialists and Arabists who staffed NEA. Indeed, the veteran U.S. diplomat Armin Meyer was worried enough that Kennedy's attitudes toward Israel diverged from NEA's to hold onto a copy of Kennedy's August 1960 ZOA speech. Throughout Kennedy's term, some of his Middle East hands fretted that the exigencies of the campaign would spill over into governance. And worries about JFK's susceptibility to pro-Israeli influence were exacerbated by the fact that he came out of Congress, the bastion of the Israel lobby.

Such fears, however, proved overblown. For example, Kennedy made the academic John Badeau his ambassador to Egypt—notwithstanding Badeau's impeccable Arabist credentials and a long cable that Badeau, then president of the American University in Cairo, had sent Truman in 1948 protesting America's "hasty recognition" of Israel. (Ironically enough, the only hiccup at Badeau's confirmation hearing was Senator J. William Fulbright's ill-founded suspicion that Badeau might be too pro-Zionist.[56]) Nor did Dean Rusk's 1948 opposition to recognizing Israel or Douglas Dillon's 1960 opposition to arming it bar them from the highest reaches of the Kennedy administration.

Why didn't the powerful Israel lobby block such nominations? Perhaps because the Israel lobby was not that powerful. Such American Jewish groups as B'nai Brith and the American Jewish Congress spent the 1950s trying to create Israel-related branches, while the Reform movement struggled to shake off its earlier opposition to Zionism.[57] Meanwhile, the main pro-Israel group, AIPAC, still had only a handful of staff. Shut out almost completely by the end of the Eisenhower administration, AIPAC relied on the relationships that its founder, I. L. Kenen, had painstakingly built on Capitol Hill. For all of the lobby's capacity to influence Congress, its ability to shape White House policy remained limited. On the major Israel decisions made by the Kennedy administration—on arms sales, nuclear inspections, security ties, and wider regional strategy—it is difficult to discern any direct impact left by the Israel lobby. Feldman made sure that Kennedy knew where American Jewry stood, but Kennedy made his own calls from there.

What is easier to find is the lobby's influence over Congress. As we shall see, it helped scuttle a mooted Nasser summit in Washington and put the nail in the coffin of the administration's attempts to court Nasser with foreign aid. The Israel lobby was quite capable of producing congressional resolutions offering Israel rhetorical support or steadily flowing aid—albeit at levels far below the current billions of dollars per year—but it had a harder time changing executive-branch behavior.[58] For one thing, few pro-Israel partisans were eager to return to the hostility of the Eisenhower period, which made it hard for the lobby to really threaten to abandon the new Democratic president. Even so, the perennial need to keep Jewish voters and fundraisers within the New Deal coalition was firmly lodged in the back of Kennedy's deeply political brain, and the specter of Democratic congressional losses also sometimes crossed the president's mind. But the Israel lobby never really tried to play hardball on major personnel and policy choices.

Indeed, perhaps the most telling document about the relative influence of the Israel lobby in the early 1960s—and the anxieties of American Jewry—is an unprompted letter to Kennedy from Jacob Blaustein, the elder statesman of the "uptown" American Jewish establishment, consisting mostly of prosperous, well-established Reform Jews of German descent. On a 1961 trip to Israel, Blaustein told the new president, he and Ben-Gurion had "signed a strong, official reaffirmation" of their 1950 joint statement that America's Jews, "as a community and as individuals, have only one political attachment and that is to the United States of America; they owe no political allegiance to Israel." This reaffirmation, Blaustein assured Kennedy, ensured that "there can never be raised against [American Jews] any question of dual loyalty. American Jews are Americans." He was delighted, Blaustein continued, that "that you will meet with Prime Minister Ben-Gurion on his forthcoming visit to *our* country . . ."[59] It strains credulity to imagine so insecure a community overplaying its hand. Blaustein's preemptive strike on charges of dual loyalty richly evokes an American Jewry that was still seriously uncertain about where the frontiers of American tolerance lay. America's first Catholic president might well have felt a flash of recognition.

THE BEST AND THE BRIGHTEST

Kennedy chose a very different sort of foreign policy team from his predecessor. Disdainful of what he saw as Eisenhower's overreliance on John Foster Dulles, impatient with bureaucratic timidity, and distrustful of his hawkish Joint Chiefs of Staff, Kennedy sought to consolidate U.S. diplomacy closer to the White House. The Middle East staff that he assembled included some exceptional talent—enough, indeed, to remind one that the description of Kennedy's hard-charging advisers as "the best and the brightest" was originally meant as a compliment, not a post-Vietnam insult. This team also had to balance a series of competing factions that shaped Kennedy's foreign policy—liberals, JFK loyalists, Cold Warriors, Arabists, career foreign service officers, and social scientists eager to try out theories of economic development in the Third World.

Kennedy wanted to be his own secretary of state, which may explain his selection of the colorless Dean Rusk. But while Kennedy would have made his presence felt on foreign policy no matter who ran the State Department, Rusk was hardly his first choice. The early front-runner, Senator J. William Fulbright of Arkansas, fell inelegantly out of contention; like most Democrats from the solid South, Fulbright had signed the Southern Manifesto, a pro-segregation document, and opposed many civil rights bills. He had hurt his chances further by making several speeches on the Middle East that the Israel lobby disliked. (Joe Kennedy, figuring that a man disliked by both the Zionists and the NAACP must be doing something right, sent Fulbright a case of Scotch after the senator was passed over.)[60] Over lunch in December at his Georgetown home, Kennedy asked Robert Lovett—George Marshall's deputy in 1948 and one of the 1940s Wise Men—if he'd like to be secretary of state (or, for good measure, secretary of defense or treasury). But Lovett begged off, pleading physical infirmity, and suggested instead Dean Rusk of the Rockefeller Foundation, who eventually wound up with the job. Kennedy's staff did not seem to know that Rusk, as a young State Department aide, had been caught up in the chaos of the 1948 decision making around the birth of Israel.[61] Rusk's State Department would become the most important bureaucratic opponent of rapprochement with Israel and the most enthusiastic bureaucratic advocate of rapprochement with Egypt.

Two prominent liberals were passed over by the New Frontiersmen for being insufficiently tough to be secretary of state. Kennedy's sometime rival, Adlai Stevenson, and Kennedy's sometime ally, former Connecticut governor Chester Bowles, wound up somewhat removed from the action as, respectively, U.N. ambassador and special presidential envoy to Africa, Asia, and Latin America. Among the other key administration players were Robert S. McNamara (the "S" stood, inauspiciously, for Strange) as a commanding secretary of defense and the broadcasting legend Edward R. Murrow as the head of the U.S. Information Agency.

For his assistant secretary of state for NEA, Kennedy chose Phillips Talbot, a genial, smart specialist on the Indian subcontinent and a Bowles associate. In early 1961, Ambassador Ellsworth Bunker in New Delhi handed a shocked Talbot a message asking him to take the post. Talbot had never met Kennedy, was not involved in Democratic politics, and had never served in government before. Bowles left Talbot with the impression that the administration had wanted a South Asia specialist heading up NEA; it seemed unthinkable to name either an Arabist or a Zionist.[62] (Despite Bowles's lasting affection and respect for Talbot, he came to regret the choice; Bowles felt that Talbot too often sided with Pakistan over India.)[63]

For his regional ambassadors, Kennedy turned mostly to career foreign service officers, including sending Parker T. Hart to Saudi Arabia and Walworth Barbour (a portly, cheerful, and widely liked diplomat who had previously served in Moscow, Athens, Cairo, and Baghdad) to Israel. There were two main exceptions.

First, William B. "Butts" Macomber, a former top Dulles aide, longstanding Republican, and Eisenhower Doctrine enthusiast, was sent to Jordan. Macomber first saw JFK in action the day the future president was sworn in as a senator—a ceremony that Macomber attended as the guest of a senator from the other side of the aisle, Prescott Bush of Connecticut, the scion of a Republican dynasty.[64] During Macomber's stint as Dulles's assistant secretary of state for congressional relations, he and Kennedy had struck up a rapport. Macomber fondly remembers the boyish Massachusetts senator, apparently feeling philosophical on his fortieth birthday, thoroughly depressing Senator John Cooper of Kentucky by asking him, "John, what does it feel like to be old?"[65]

Second, John S. Badeau, who spoke Arabic and had lived in the Arab world almost without interruption since 1928, was made ambassador to Egypt. Badeau's unusual prominence made his selection the rough equivalent of sending John Kenneth Galbraith to India or George F. Kennan to Yugoslavia.[66] While Badeau could never rival Galbraith's closeness to Kennedy, he did try to bond early on with the president over their mutual suffering from back pain, noting that he found it helpful to have his grown daughter walk on his back. "Caroline's only three," JFK replied. "She's not big enough."[67] Badeau also set a foot wrong in his first meeting with Nasser, who was leery of Arabists in the first place; the eager ambassador insisted on speaking his American-accented classical Arabic until a confused Nasser finally asked him to switch over to English.[68]

Kennedy used several devices to keep the White House in control of the foreign policy-making process. In addition to his unorthodox use of Feldman, Kennedy added a more lasting new bureaucratic wrinkle by transforming the National Security Council—a backwater under Eisenhower and Dulles—into an assertive interagency body designed to bring together the differing perspectives of the State Department, the Pentagon, the Joint Chiefs of Staff, the Treasury Department, Stevenson's U.N. mission, and diplomats in the field. As McGeorge Bundy—an aggressively brilliant, infinitely confident, off-puttingly arrogant Republican Brahmin and former Harvard dean—himself put it, his job was to be "the traffic cop." The NSC also acted as Kennedy's eyes and ears, ensuring that policies were rooted in real-world pragmatism rather than the sometimes politically tone-deaf, wimpy, or impractical suggestions of the bureaucracy. The rise of what wags frequently called "Bundy's State Department" did little for those who worked at the actual State Department.[69]

Bundy's first deputy, Walt W. Rostow, was an adherent of the so-called Charles River school of economists, which argued that "imaginative aid from the industrial world" could help Third World countries "reach a 'take-off' point from which their development would follow a self-generating path."[70] Nasser liked Rostow's ideas enough to have one of his books, *The Stages of Economic Growth*, translated into Arabic and passed out to the entire UAR cabinet.[71] A layer farther down, where most of the staff work was done, the Middle East portfolio at the NSC fell to the ebullient, indefatigable Robert W. Komer, an old CIA colleague recommended to Mac Bundy by his brother William. With his sharp pen, keen wit, abrasive spirit, and ceaseless energy, it is easy to see how Komer appealed to— and sometimes aggravated—the New Frontiersmen.

For all the young new administration's reputation for what Kennedy's accent rendered as "vigah,"[72] Macomber decided that its Middle East line-up was highly qualified but not terribly fresh; he liked to call it the "old, old Frontier."[73] But it was, if anything, united in its disdain for its predecessors. The New Frontiersmen felt "a basic contempt for the Eisenhower administration," David Halberstam noted. "The Kennedy people looked upon their predecessor as flabby, unaware of a changing world, and far too dependent on military response."[74] Eisenhower's Middle East diplomacy looked to Kennedy's aides a bit like a man slipping down a large sand dune, grabbing at shrugs and brushes as he slides farther, and finding that each plant he grabs comes out at the roots. Confident, ironic, determinedly cool, and proudly decked out with tie clips in the shape of Kennedy's PT-109 patrol boat, the best and the brightest were determined to do better. The Soviets were gaining more influence in Cairo, Damascus, and Baghdad; the Arab kings were jittery over the rise of Nasser; and Israel was still feeling the chill of the Eisenhower administration's suspicion. Jack Kennedy was confident that he understood the Middle East better than his predecessors, that he had a feel for the rising forces of national pride that were transforming the Cold War, and that he could offer support and friendship on attractive, progressive terms to both Arab and Jewish nationalists. For Kennedy's Middle East team, it was time to fish.

CHAPTER THREE

Uncle Sam and Mister Big

A Fragile Overture to Nasser

O N SEPTEMBER 8, 2000, an astonishing collection of world leaders gathered inside an ancient Egyptian temple—located on Manhattan's Upper East Side. President Bill Clinton welcomed about a thousand dignitaries and heads of state attending the United Nations' Millennium Summit to a reception at one of the most striking sites in New York City: the Temple of Dendur, an entire Nubian shrine honoring the goddess Isis, dramatically housed in the Sackler Wing of the Metropolitan Museum of Art in a soaring glass hall looking out over Central Park.[1]

The Temple of Dendur was not only a relic of a long-gone Egypt; it was also a relic of a long-gone Egypt policy. Few in the temple that day remembered how the Met had originally acquired the jewel in its Egyptology crown: as a reciprocal gesture of Egyptian goodwill, a token of gratitude offered in September 1963 after the Kennedy administration had attempted a rapprochement with the largest and most powerful of the Arab states.[2] As Washington weighed and eventually approved $16 million to save the priceless temples at Abu Simbel from flooding by the Aswan High Dam, Cairo offered the Temple of Dendur in return; the temple arrived in 1965 and was awarded to the Met in 1967, the same year as the Six Day War.[3] By then, the overture to Egypt (formally known as the United Arab Republic) had already run aground on the shoals of inter-Arab politics, and today it is all but forgotten. But for about half of JFK's thousand days, the attempt to find common ground with UAR President Jamal Abd al-Nasser—the man whom Kennedy's aides sometimes called the "Mister Big" of the Arab world—was the most innovative prong of America's Middle East policy.

The Eisenhower administration had been far less interested in reaching out to Nasserite Egypt. In the 1950s, such leaders as Indonesia's Sukarno, India's Nehru, and Yugoslavia's Tito sought, each in his own way, to steer a "neutralist" path between the Cold War's antagonists, the Soviet Union and the United States. Nasser claimed to be similarly inclined, but Eisenhower and Secretary of State John Foster Dulles were dubious. After Egypt began receiving arms sales from the Soviet bloc in 1955, Dulles wrote off the Egyptian leader's pan-Arab nationalism—the drive to unite the Arabs in one vast state strong enough to stand up to the superpowers—as a veneer designed to divert attention from Nasser's underlying communist sympathies. In 1958, the dream of a United Arab Republic, heretofore easy to deride, suddenly became flesh as Syria joined a union with Egypt. U.S.–Egyptian relations hit their nadir that same year, when the fall of Hashimite Iraq and the threat of a Nasserite revolution in Lebanon led Eisenhower to send in the Marines. In his waning days in office, Ike relaxed his suspicions of Nasser slightly, but U.S.–Egypt relations remained strained.

Having blasted the GOP during the 1960 campaign for isolating America in the Middle East, Kennedy and his aides were not prepared to leave America's relationship with the pivotal Arab state in such disrepair. JFK's overture to Nasser was the last major American attempt to bring Egypt into the Western orbit until the aftermath of the 1973 Yom Kippur War. The initiative represented a break with the Eisenhower administration's tendency to view Third World nationalists as communist wolves disguised in neutralist sheep's clothing. While Dulles had called Third World neutralism merely "a transitional stage to communism,"[4] Kennedy saw new frontiers for American influence with such independent-minded progressive leaders as Sukarno, Nehru, Nkrumah (of Ghana), Tito—and Nasser. "All over the world, particularly in the newer nations, young men are coming to power—men who are not bound by the traditions of the past—men who are not blinded by the old fears and hates and rivalries—young men who can cast off the old slogans and delusions and suspicions," Kennedy said in his July 1960 speech accepting the Democratic nomination. Laying it on a bit thick, he added, "More energy is released by the awakening of these new nations than by the fission of the atom itself." Beyond the generational kinship that JFK felt with the young nationalists lay an important policy experiment championed by the National Security Council's Walt Rostow and the State Department's Chester Bowles and Adlai Stevenson. Kennedy's advisers were intrigued by the idea of finding a way to wean such neutralists away from Moscow, even if they could not be lured all the way into the Western camp. They hoped that the Third World might find a third way.

But the overture to Nasser represented more than simple continuity with JFK's wider Third World strategy; it represented a sharp break with past U.S. and U.K. policies in the Middle East. America's traditional Middle Eastern friends had been the conservative monarchs who had proven the bulwarks of Britain's imperial grand design east of Suez. By the time Kennedy took office, however, those monarchs were more embattled than ever. Egypt's King Faruq fell to the so-called Free Officers' coup in 1952, which soon propelled Nasser to power. Iraq—heretofore the pillar of Britain's regional strategy, which revolved around installing members of the Hashimite royal family in power in Iraq and Jordan, as well as more briefly in Syria and the Hijaz—was rocked by a nationalist coup in 1958. Increasingly, Nasserism seemed menacing to the monarchs, and Cairo's pan-Arab nationalism a pretext for knocking them off their thrones. Kennedy reached out to Nasser in an attempt to gain a Cold War advantage, but by 1961, the Arabs were plunging into a cold war of their own in which the forces of conservatism—the oil sheikhdoms, the Hashimites, and Lebanon—squared off against the forces of revolution—Nasserite pan-Arabism and the Ba'ath Party.[5] Of course, both Arab camps were rent with dissension and rivalry, but overall, this basic split was becoming the central dynamic of inter-Arab politics.

Both Arab conservatives and Israelis saw Nasser as their worst enemy—and were rattled by Kennedy's attempt to reach out to their nemesis. Even though the president's men argued repeatedly that an American policy that gave the United States more influence over Egyptian behavior would ultimately redound to Israel's benefit, Israeli Prime Minister David Ben-Gurion remained unconvinced (as did his heir, Levi Eshkol). But Ben-Gurion's distaste for Nasser was, at the least, matched by the visceral reactions of King Husayn of Jordan and Saudi Crown Prince Faysal, who became Riyadh's de facto leader on Kennedy's watch. For all the Arab fears that the Kennedy administration would prove helplessly beholden to American Jews, congressional Zionists, and the Israel lobby, the White House proved capable of publicly speaking warmly about Israel while privately moving toward rapprochement with the Jewish state's most dangerous foe. But ultimately, what derailed that rapprochement was not AIPAC's displeasure but Saudi Arabia's. The overture to Nasser collapsed not because of Israel but because of the Arab conservatives and Nasser's rashness. American domestic politics mattered around the margins, but the main reason that Kennedy and Nasser parted company on bitter terms lay far beyond the water's edge.

Kennedy's Nasser overture ran up against the outer limits of the headway that America could make with Arab radicalism. While it is easy to criticize Kennedy's Third World policies—most notably, the zigzags of his Cuba policy and the dangerous inertia of his Indochina policy—as being blind to local subtleties, the New Frontier showed some real creativity in the Arab world. Kennedy was willing to woo an unlikely partner. But Nasser felt himself too hemmed in by his own feud with the

Arab monarchs to take advantage of what Kennedy was offering: a rising edifice of friendlier U.S.–UAR ties, centering around foreign aid, a new diplomatic tone, the dispatch of high-level U.S. envoys, development cooperation, a rich personal correspondence between the two presidents, and even the prospect of a Kennedy-Nasser summit in Washington, DC. But the overture's collapse—hors de combat of Nasser's ill-fated adventure in Yemen—left little of Jack Kennedy's Egypt policy but the Temple of Dendur.

CAIRO'S ECHO OF MARSHALL

One might have expected Nasser to relish the prospect of a change in Washington, especially the rise of a young liberal whose most famous senatorial speech had been the 1957 address that made him Congress's foremost advocate of Algerian independence. Moreover, after the anti-Nasserite Eisenhower Doctrine interventions of 1958 in Lebanon and Jordan, one would have expected Nasser's enthusiasm to be all the keener. As it happened, however, Cairo was wary of Kennedy even before the new president took office. During the 1960 campaign that pitted the Massachusetts senator against Eisenhower's vice president, Richard M. Nixon, the state-run Egyptian press seemed to have a hard time deciding which man it loathed more.

Al-Jumhuriyya, the Cairo daily, ran a typically blistering article on August 19, 1960, that echoed the central charge that George Marshall leveled against Harry Truman: prostituting foreign policy to buy Jewish votes. "No, Mr. Kennedy," ran the paper's banner headline. The Democratic nominee "extends his hand to every Zionist begging for his vote," the paper commented. "Kennedy, who is trying to obtain Jewish votes, bows before everything which is Jewish, upholds Zionist advocations, prays in every Zionist synagogue." *Al-Jumhuriyya* seemed unable to decide whether Kennedy would prove a simple extension of Ike, arguing that Kennedy "thinks like Eisenhower and Truman," "does not use his own brains," and (PT-109 and his Pulitzer Prize winner notwithstanding) "does not know courage." On the other hand, there was nowhere to go but up: "Understand, Mr. Kennedy, you cannot be more stupid than all those who have preceeded [*sic*] you."[6]

Nor was the criticism limited to Egyptian mouthpieces in Cairo. At their only meeting, a September 1960 conversation at New York's Waldorf Astoria Hotel, Nasser is said to have told Eisenhower that "he would find it difficult to decide if he were asked to vote" in the next election—not an overwhelming compliment to Ike's vice president. While he fancied

Kennedy's youth and liberalism, Nasser said, he would probably have voted for Nixon out of gratitude for Eisenhower's support during the 1956 Suez crisis.[7] Nasser would later change his tune. Protests in New York forced him to quit Manhattan and rent a house in Long Island during his 1960 stay, where he spent most of his free time following the presidential race. After watching the famous first Kennedy-Nixon debate on television, the Egyptian leader later claimed to be among the millions who were convinced that Kennedy was the better choice.[8]

Even Mustafa Kamel, the ebullient UAR ambassador to Washington who would become perhaps the most indefatigable advocate of warm U.S.–UAR ties, sent out a press release to make sure that all of Washington knew that the Egyptian press had blasted the Democrats' Middle East plank. The plank called for peace talks, an end to the Arab economic boycott of Israel, "independence for all states" (i.e., Israel), "unrestricted use of the Suez Canal by all nations" (i.e., Israel), and "resettlement of Arab refugees in lands where there is room and opportunity for them" (i.e., not Israel).[9] This, Kamel's press release complained, amounted to "a denial of Arab rights." He cited al-Jumhuriyya again, warning that the platform's endorsement of a solution to the Palestinian refugee problem that would suit Israel "suggests that the Zionists within the Democratic Party played a big role in writing this part of the platform." The paper added that the Democrats' stance confirmed Nasser's view that America had not yet learned that "the Arab people are their own masters."[10]

Meanwhile, some officials within the outgoing Eisenhower administration had their own apprehensions. In July 1960, Assistant Secretary of State for Near East Affairs (NEA) G. Lewis Jones wrote Secretary of State Christian Herter to warn against dragging the Arab-Israeli conflict into the presidential race. "It would be our hope that as occasion permits the influence of the Executive Branch might be discreetly exercised in order to divorce the Arab-Israel question as far as possible from the coming political campaign," Jones wrote. Herter scrawled back his basic assent but added, "However the issue certainly will be in this campaign to some extent."[11]

Herter was right. NEA was particularly irked by Kennedy's friendly 1960 speech before the Zionist Organization of America. "The Kennedy speech is of course an unabashedly partisan appeal for the votes of Zionists and Israeli sympathizers," complained Nicholas Thacher, one of Jones's aides. Kennedy not only "reaffirm[ed] the glory of Israel in grandiloquent terms," he also proposed "a sledge hammer approach to the delicate problems of the Middle East," along the lines of the Democratic platform. "I believe Ben-Gurion himself is aware that a vastly more subtle approach is required if American statesmen are to make a real contribution to peace in the

Middle East," Thacher added. So agitated was Thacher that he, like Jones, offered campaign advice from Foggy Bottom: "I wonder if we cannot persuade the Republicans that a statesman-like speech with a much more balanced approach can perhaps be written in a manner to give it a good deal of appeal to Israel's sympathizers in the U.S."[12]

On August 28, another State Department official tried to jump into the campaign—Armin Meyer, who would serve as Kennedy's deputy assistant secretary of state for NEA until October 1961, when he would become ambassador to Lebanon. The previous evening, Meyer had heard on the radio that the ZOA had blasted Ike's Middle East record. Convinced that "we shouldn't take such calumny lying down," Meyer dashed off a draft letter from Eisenhower himself to the ZOA. "And frankly I don't think Nixon-Lodge would find it anything but helpful," he added. The letter seems never to have been sent. But Meyer still complained bitterly that "it'll get worse and worse as the campaign goes on and we State Department types will be roundly believed to be total incompetents."

But Meyer's wrath that summer was not limited to Kennedy. "Just heard the shocking news of the blow-up of the Jordan Foreign Ministry and death of my friend Haza," he added in a bitter reference to the late Jordanian prime minister, Haza al-Majali. "That devil GAN is going to get his someday."[13] Meyer might have been even angrier had he known how the mistrusted JFK would wind up treating the hated "GAN"—Gamal Abdul Nasser.

COLD WAR OPENERS

The Middle East fell off the radar for the administration's first few months as it reeled from crisis to crisis in Cuba, Laos, and the Congo. Not until the spring of 1961 did the new administration catch its breath enough to try to seize the initiative in the previously neglected Middle East. Indeed, the most effective piece of diplomacy toward Egypt in the administration's earliest days in office may have come from the first lady, who delighted Nasser by taking a personal interest in saving the Abu Simbel temples and sending him a warm thank-you note about an exhibition on King Tut "in her own hand on tiny feminine notepaper."[14]

On February 20, 1961, Nasser sent his first-ever letter to Jacqueline Kennedy's husband. The conduit was G. Frederick Reinhardt, the American ambassador to Cairo; at the time, such correspondence was frequently hand-delivered to American diplomats in the field, who then cabled it back to Washington. The subject lay far from the Middle East, in the Congo, a former Belgian colony that had plunged into dizzying chaos shortly after becoming independent in June 1960. With Belgian troops scurrying back into the Congo and the United States widely blamed for former Congolese prime minister Patrice Lumumba's death at the hands of the new CIA-backed regime led by Colonel Joseph Mobutu, the Congo was becoming a poster-child for decolonization gone awry.[15]

As an African neutral power, Egypt found this hard to take. In Nasser's letter, written about a week after word of Lumumba's death got out, he appealed to Kennedy's oft-invoked anticolonialism. (He also wrote to Soviet leader Nikita Khrushchev and British Prime Minister Harold Macmillan.) Nasser urged Kennedy to back a U.N. commission of inquiry and Security Council resolutions to end the intervention by Congo's old Belgian masters, adding that America should live up to its principled stance against imperialist meddling during the Suez crisis.[16]

Kennedy responded in kind: with reasonably polite but reasonably predictable Cold War rhetoric. Chester Bowles, the liberal former Democratic governor of Connecticut turned State Department envoy to the Third World, called Nasser's letter "broad" and "non-provocative" and suggested JFK try to lure Nasser toward a neutral (rather than pro-Soviet) stance.[17] On March 1, Kennedy wrote back, completing the first exchange of what would become a fascinating extended direct correspondence between the liberal Cold Warrior and the Arab nationalist. JFK wrote that Washington and Cairo agreed that the Cold War should be kept out of the Congo, that "influential uncommitted states" such as Egypt could help the United Nations ease the crisis, and that assassinations, of Lumumba or anyone else, were to be deplored.[18]

Kennedy added that "all assistance outside the United Nations framework to any action in the Congo, whether of men, material or money, should be viewed with the utmost gravity and strictly interdicted." The president clearly had Belgium in mind, but there is no way to know whether this was also an oblique reference to Israel. Mobutu's troops received significant training aid from the Israeli government, which spent much of the 1960s trying to break its regional diplomatic isolation by reaching out to postcolonial Africa. Some two hundred Congolese paratroopers were trained in Israel.[19] If Mobutu was grateful for Israel's help (as one State Department official put it later in the Kennedy administration, "the Congolese have a crush on the Israelis"), Nasser was annoyed.[20]

Kennedy and Nasser, still trying to take each other's measure, exchanged genial telegrams in March on Egypt's national day.[21] The next month, Kennedy sent Nasser a longer letter asking him to meet with Henry Cabot Lodge, the former Republican senator from Massachusetts and Nixon's 1960 running mate, who was planning a private visit to Cairo. Kennedy added a personal touch by passing along Jacqueline Kennedy's regret that the first lady would not be able to take Egypt up on an invitation to see the premiere of the new sound and light spectacular at the Pyramids.[22] The letter went out on April 17—the very day that some 1,400 Cuban rebels landed their boats at the Bay of Pigs.

The resultant fiasco triggered an exchange markedly chillier than that over the Congo. On April 18, Nasser "sent a well-publicized message" to Cuban leader Fidel Castro "expressing solidarity" with the island's communist regime, accusing Washington of imperialist aggression, and comparing the Bay of Pigs to Suez.[23] For good measure, Nasser made similar noises in a joint declaration with Yugoslavia's Marshal Tito. On May 3, goaded by Bowles (whose persistence would come to annoy his White House colleagues), Kennedy fired off a defensive five-page letter on Cuba to Nasser. An irritated Kennedy told Nasser that Washington remained every bit as principled in 1961 as it had been in 1956. JFK pointed to Cuba's human rights abuses and noted, "Genuine nationalist revolutions, such as your own, have prompted no similar distress." And Kennedy added a 1956 analogy of his own. True, there had been meddling in Cuban affairs—but by Moscow, not Washington. In a sharp reference to the Red Army crackdown on the 1956 Hungarian uprising, Kennedy added that he did "not intend to be lectured on 'intervention' by those whose character was stamped for all time on the bloody streets of Budapest."[24]

Nasser took the letter rather calmly. His May 18 response quoted the Prophet Muhammad's dictum: "Your friend is he who is true to you, not he who only believes you." Having met Castro twice, Nasser encouraged Kennedy to rethink his Cuba policy and to stop denying U.S. involvement in the attempted coup. But he added that in sticking up for Castro, "our aim was not to stand against the United States" but to hold true to neutralist principle.[25]

The early JFK-Nasser correspondence was not over the Middle East but frequently alluded to it—as well as the wider Cold War. The choice between anticommunism and support for nationalism was a false choice, Kennedy implicitly argued. For his part, Nasser was concerned about what the New Frontier's prosecution of the Cold War meant for the stability of Third World regimes. But both men spoke of frankness as a virtue—a theme that would become the hallmark of their correspondence.

The early U.S.–UAR wrangling over the Cold War had a wry denouement in the United Nations. Conor Cruise O'Brien, then the Irish envoy to the United Nations, remembers sitting next to Gideon Rafael, the Israeli representative, during the General Assembly debate on the Bay of Pigs. Rafael sat impassively, doodling on his notepad, while U.S. Ambassador Adlai Stevenson trudged unhappily through an overblown text. "I have told you," Stevenson said, "of Castro's crimes against man. But there is even worse: the record of Castro's crimes against *God*." Several delegates squirmed. "Fidel Castro has . . . *circumcised* the freedoms of the Catholics of Cuba," Stevenson continued.

Rafael abruptly turned to O'Brien. "I always knew," the Israeli diplomat said, "that *we* should be blamed for this, sooner or later."[26]

RETHINKING NASSER

The New Frontier's determination to shake off the perceived torpor of the Eisenhower era predisposed the president's aides toward activism, on Egypt as elsewhere. On the staff of the newly invigorated National Security Council led by McGeorge Bundy, Walt Rostow preached the virtues of Third World development. Bundy and Rostow formulated a series of diplomatic nettles for the new administration to grasp. Their Middle East staffer, the unflagging Bob Komer, recalled that among their key suggestions "was the question of reappraising our relations with Nasser and seeing whether we couldn't get back on a better footing with the key actor of the Arab world."[27] It was a project sure to rattle Nasser's foes, the Arab conservatives and the state of Israel. "If you have 'friends' like Col. Nasser," warned Leonard Farbstein, a Democratic congressman from New York, "you don't need any enemies."[28]

Indeed, there certainly seemed room for improvement—as well as bases for progress—during the new administration's first major high-level personal encounter with the UAR: a February 7, 1961, meeting between Rusk and Egypt's ambassador to Washington, Mustafa Kamel. That meeting was the first in a series of interactions with the UAR that prompted the Kennedy team to review America's late-1950s skepticism of Nasser.

Kamel began in sweeping fashion: he told Rusk that Egypt shared the United States's opposition to communism but blamed the chill in U.S.–Egypt ties on the Arab-Israeli conflict. He explained away Egyptian willingness to accept "Soviet help"—a euphemism for massive arms sales—by pointing to Egypt's fears of the Western-backed Israel, which now had the French-built nuclear reactor at Dimona. Kamel then offered a modest proposal: perhaps the Arab-Israeli dispute could be "put in the refrigerator" and taken out of American politics? The Arabs, Kamel warned, were "frankly suspicious" that the Kennedy administration would follow in the path of Truman in 1948. But Kamel assured Rusk that he personally had tried to explain to his bosses in Cairo the differences between "Trumanism" and the Kennedy administration, which he felt was "not unfriendly" to the Arabs. The attempted self-portrait is of a reasonable, cosmopolitan diplomat trying to explain away in advance any future excesses by referring to his hotheaded masters back home. If the United States would "neutralize pressure groups here"—which is to say, the Israel lobby—the UAR "would take similar action against unfriendly elements there." For his part, Rusk assured Kamel that he shared the Arab world's anxiety about the Israeli nuclear program.[29]

Like many ambassadors, Kamel occasionally got ahead of his government. But this time, the Kennedy administration responded with genuine curiosity to his suggestion of finding a way to prevent the Arab-Israeli conflict from interfering in Cairo's relations with Washington. On May 8, Kennedy himself took the unusual step of meeting with Kamel; unfortunately, the minutes of the meeting have been lost.[30]

Having criticized Eisenhower for being reactive, the New Frontier now sought to seize the initiative in the Middle East. A few days after meeting Kamel, Kennedy sent similar letters to six major Arab heads of state— Nasser, Lebanese President Fuad Chehab, Jordan's King Husayn, Iraqi Prime Minister Abd al-Karim Qasim, King Saud, and Imam Ahmad ibn Yahya Nasir al-Din Allah of Yemen. To some degree, Kennedy's hand had been forced; Israeli Prime Minister David Ben-Gurion had let the administration know that he would be in the United States in May, and while the administration made a point of not offering the Israeli leader a formal state visit, JFK did agree to meet Ben-Gurion in New York on May 30 en route to a June 3 summit in Vienna with Khrushchev. The State Department hoped the letters would smooth any ruffled Arab feathers, reassure Arab leaders of the Kennedy administration's "impartiality" in Arab-Israeli affairs, and blunt "the natural fears of the Arabs [that] any new Administration and particularly a Democratic one" might resemble Truman's more than Eisenhower's.[31]

The smooth letter to Nasser was vintage Kennedy—and a degree warmer than their earlier correspondence. Kennedy offered an implicit apology for not having spent more time on the Middle East in his early days in office, which had "perforce been largely occupied with the several international crises of immediate concern"—a delicate way of referring to the Bay of Pigs and crises in Laos and the Congo. Better late than never, JFK reached out to the Arab leaders as "men of good will" and invoked the names of Lincoln, Wilson, and FDR, whose ideas "played so great a part in the emergence of vigorous, independent Arab states, respected as sovereign equals in the international community." With Nasser, Kennedy laid it on thick, mentioning his pride in America's role during "the critical days of 1956." For good measure, Kennedy noted that the U.S. government, "itself the product of a union of several independent states, was pleased to recognize the formation of the United Arab Republic on February 22, 1958, the birthday anniversary of our own first President, Washington."

The underlying emphasis of the letter was placed on economic development. JFK attributed the "relatively tranquil" state of the region over the past three years to "statesmanship" from leaders "who have given priority to constructive programs of economic development."

With his meeting with Ben-Gurion looming, Kennedy had little choice but to refer to the Arab-Israeli conflict, which, he wrote, involved "deep emotion" and defied "easy solution." He offered to help resolve the Palestinian refugee problem by "the principle of repatriation or compensation for properties." The U.S. approach, still left vague, was to be rooted in U.N. General Assembly resolutions on the refugees and would try to revive the Palestine Conciliation Commission (PCC)—the U.N. body established in 1948 to mediate the Arab-Israeli dispute and help repatriate and resettle Palestinian refugees—as its chief vehicle. The letter to Nasser alluded to U.S.–Egyptian strains, but Kennedy also listed some goodwill gestures: asking Congress to join a U.N. campaign to save the Abu Simbel temples and other archeological treasures in Upper Egypt now threatened with flooding by the Soviet-built Aswan High Dam; student exchanges; and compliments for Egyptian industrialization. The peroration spoke of America's "sincere friendship" for the Arabs. "I want to be certain that you and other Arab leaders have no misunderstanding of our attitude towards the Arab people," Kennedy wrote, given "the interdependence of all men who wish to remain free."[32]

It was a clear attempt to break the ice. To create trust, Kennedy offered both concrete measures and flattery. JFK himself "was anxious to use this technique of personal diplomacy," Komer recalled, and his Middle East aides assured him that this was "the way business gets done in the Arab world."[33] Nasser responded in kind; he even took the time to send Kennedy a congratulatory telegram after NASA sent John Glenn on America's first successful manned space flight.[34] (In the interests of neutralism, Khrushchev got a similar note about Yuri Gagarin.)[35]

Even Mike Feldman, Kennedy's in-house interpreter of Israeli sensitivities, thought the administration had a real opportunity on its hands with Nasser. The United States, whatever its disagreements with the Egyptian leader, "must seek a viable relationship [with Nasser] as an alternative to forcing him to rely on the Soviet bloc," Feldman wrote.[36] Still, he warned Kennedy that Ben-Gurion was unlikely to see things that way. The Israeli leader would use his meeting with Kennedy to "contend that Nasser is a Soviet tool seeking domination of the Middle East and Africa," Feldman wrote, and to warn that the Arab boycott and restrictions on Suez blocked regional economic development.

Sure enough, Kennedy found Nasser high atop Ben-Gurion's agenda. When the two leaders sat down in the presidential suite at the Waldorf

Astoria in the late afternoon of May 30, JFK discovered that, if anything, Feldman had downplayed Ben-Gurion's distaste for Nasser. The Israeli prime minister likened Egyptian intentions not to communism but to Nazism. "If they should defeat us," Ben-Gurion warned, "they would do to the Jews what Hitler did." To make matters worse, he added, the Arabs also "do not value human life." While the two leaders covered other topics, the conversation kept looping back to Egypt. "All questions in the Middle East depend upon Nasser," Ben-Gurion said gloomily. Kennedy did not fight his guest on this one. Instead, he reckoned that Israel and the United States "have to assume that Nasser will make our lives as difficult as possible." Ben-Gurion offered no demur.

The Israeli prime minister used his dim view of Egyptian intentions and his fears of Egyptian capabilities to push Kennedy to sell Hawk surface-to-air missiles to Israel. The UAR had 300 fighter planes, Ben-Gurion said, as well as 200 more fighters that the other Arab countries would pitch in; Israel had just ordered 60 Mirages (a French-built supersonic interceptor) to counter. But it still needed to level the playing field.

Perhaps, Ben-Gurion suggested, Kennedy could do some good by dealing with Nasser's Soviet friends. Might the administration use the pending Vienna summit with Khrushchev to issue a joint communiqué affirming the territorial integrity of all Middle Eastern states? Not only would Israel be pleased, Ben-Gurion noted, so would other Arab states who felt threatened by Nasserism. Countries such as Jordan and Iraq "are much more worried than we are," Ben-Gurion said. Kennedy was less enthusiastic, doubting that Khrushchev would want to irritate Nasser or affirm the still-disputed Israel-UAR border. Of course, part of the point of Ben-Gurion's proposal was to try to drive a wedge between Cairo and Moscow. Perhaps mindful of his looming summit in Vienna, JFK replied dryly that Khrushchev was "pressing hard on many issues."

Kennedy put Ben-Gurion on notice about America's renewed push to tackle the Palestinian refugee issue. Again, Ben-Gurion pointed an accusatory finger at Nasser. "They—the UAR and any Arabs—don't care what happens to people," the prime minister warned.

If Ben-Gurion was hoping to get the new president to write off Israel's Egyptian nemesis, he was to be disappointed. Nasser's press had attacked the White House over the Bay of Pigs, JFK noted, but the administration had still sent its May letter to the Egyptian leader—as a way to ensure that the United States could keep up its close ties to Israel while retaining the ability to "be helpful" in the wider region. For his part, Ben-Gurion assured Kennedy that he did not "hate Arabs" and would be glad to see the United States "help them."[37] At 6 P.M., the two leaders parted.

Kennedy and Ben-Gurion's sparring over Nasser at the Waldorf provides some of the best evidence we have about what Kennedy thought of his Egyptian counterpart. Kennedy did not buy Ben-Gurion's portrait of Nasser as an irredeemable tyrant, although the president did agree that Nasser could make serious trouble.

After some politicking in New York, Kennedy left for his Vienna summit, where he received a startling drubbing from Khrushchev on a host of Cold War issues. Returning in a foul mood, troubled by the fear of higher U.S.–Soviet tensions, the president was greeted by a series of acerbic return letters from the very Arab leaders he'd sought to mollify. On July 10, Kennedy sent a testy note to Bundy asking for a report from the State Department about "whose idea it was for me to send the letters to the Middle Eastern Arab leaders. The reaction has been so sour I would like to know whose idea it was, what they hoped to accomplish and what they think we have now accomplished."[38]

Three days later, a defensive response from Dean Rusk appeared on the president's desk. The Arabs still blamed Truman for Israel's creation, Rusk wrote, and they fretted about both the Democrats' return to the White House and some of Kennedy's warm 1960 campaign rhetoric about Israel. Those fears were exacerbated by a few incidents early in the administration, including Israel's display of heavy military equipment in an Independence Day parade in Jerusalem and Congress's voluble discussion of cutting off the U.N. Relief and Works Agency (UNRWA), the U.N. agency providing humanitarian aid for Palestinian refugees, which got 70 percent of its governmental funding from Washington. The timing of Ben-Gurion's visit therefore struck the Arabs as poor, Rusk wrote, but once the decision to host him had been made, the State Department had tried to use the Waldorf meeting as a chance to tell the Arab world about Kennedy's interest in helping ameliorate the Palestinian refugee problem. The letters sought to introduce Kennedy as a reasonable new voice in Middle East affairs with a principled concern for Arab suffering, not a pro-Israel shill.

Moreover, Rusk saw the Arab world's reaction as generally "mild and moderate." The most obdurate of the lot, Iraq's Qasim, simply stayed silent, recognizing that supporting Kennedy's push to resettle or repatriate refugees would implicitly recognize Israel. King Husayn of Jordan kept it "relatively friendly," absent some posturing "to compensate for the political handicap he recently acquired in marrying a British girl." The one genuinely sour note was struck by King Saud, whose reply—drafted, the State Department's Arabists figured, by the Saudi diplomat Ahmed Shuqairi, whom even the understated Rusk called "notoriously venomous"—was "undiplomatic to the point of being insulting." (Shuqairi would go on to found the PLO in 1964 and be replaced four years later by Yasir Arafat, who also thought him a gasbag.) The letters had reaffirmed the State Department's old "desire to be impartial in Arab-Israel matters," Rusk wrote. "Certainly the trend of this past March and April when the Arabs were rapidly concluding that we were hopelessly pro-Israel, has been arrested." And in contrast to the firestorm after Eisenhower's meeting with Ben-Gurion the previous year, Rusk wrote, Kennedy's missives let the Israeli leader's visit pass with "almost unbelievably mild reactions in the Near East."[39] In fact, Rusk was too sanguine; the antagonistic tone of Saudi Arabia's letter hinted that the world's key oil state was wary of the Kennedy administration even before it began reaching out to Saudi Arabia's regional rival, Nasser.

So was it worth extending a hand to Nasser? On June 27, the administration unveiled a new National Intelligence Estimate (NIE)—a formal assessment designed to guide policymakers, culled from the intelligence staffs of the CIA, the State Department, and the military—on "Nasser and the Future of Arab Nationalism."[40] The new analysis represented a sharp departure from the Eisenhower era, in which Third World nationalist movements were often seen as either stalking horses or synonyms for Marxism. While the Kennedy administration's NIE process did not paint Nasserism as akin to communism, it was not terribly enthusiastic about the phenomenon, either. "Militant nationalism will continue to be the most dynamic force in Arab political affairs," the NIE began, "and Nasser is very likely to remain its foremost leader and symbol for the foreseeable future."

Worse, Washington could be backing the wrong side. "The long-term outlook for the conservative and Western-aligned regimes is bleak," the NIE continued. Neutralism, social reform, and pan-Arab unity were the wave of the future; the conservative monarchies risked being swept away. On the other hand, the administration concluded that Nasser's vision of a grand, unified Arab republic was unlikely to go much beyond his already shaky union with Syria. Nasser was not in much of a position to expand his economy without significant help from abroad—be it from East or West. So to keep the UAR's two pieces together, he would have to play the perennial Israel card and exploit Arab fears over Israel's nuclear program and plans to divert the Jordan River for hydroelectric power. The UAR's army, still the only Arab fighting force that stood much of a chance against the IDF, continued to give Nasser "a unique claim to Arab leadership."

In Cold War terms, then, the NIE was subtler than Dulles's Manichean view of the universe. It took Nasser's stance of "positive neutralism" seriously even as it deplored anti-Americanism in Egyptian propaganda. Still,

Cairo's military dependence on Moscow was not buying the Kremlin that much loyalty, the NIE argued. In practice, Nasser tended "to side more often with the [communist] Bloc than with the West," but he still fundamentally believed that either superpower would cheerfully dominate Egypt if given the chance. (The hangover from British occupation is not difficult to discern.) Over the long haul, the administration hoped to be able to exploit "the inherent incompatibility between ultimate Soviet ambitions in the Middle East and the aspirations of Nasser and the Arab nationalists" toward independence and neutralism.

Komer was particularly enthusiastic about the NIE. "Here is the case for our attempting to stay in the game with Nasser," Komer wrote to Rostow, "not trying to outbid the Soviets, not deluding ourselves with any idea that we can bring him into the Western camp but merely that we must live with him and he must live with us." Even so, a "rapprochement along these lines may take years and involve numerous zigs and zags," he warned. So Komer urged the United States to get in the fight for Egypt for the long haul and start trying to buy amity with aid.[41]

Some rethinking was going on in Cairo as well as in Washington. For one thing, while the underlying military relationship was never in peril, Egypt's ties to the Soviet Union were growing increasingly cold. After Qasim came to power in Baghdad in 1958 and trumpeted his closeness with Iraq's communists, Moscow felt compelled to back him, to Nasser's lasting dismay.[42] As the neutralist, pan-Arabist Nasser and the socialist, particularist Qasim jostled for the mantle of Arab revolutionary leadership, a startled Nasser came to resent the Kremlin's pro-Qasim meddling—a resentment that, in turn, caught the White House's attention. Nasser's public statements could sound simultaneously nonaligned and nondemocratic; as he once put it, he barred political parties since if he had three parties, "one would be run by the rich, one by the Soviets, and one by the U.S."[43] When the Soviet Union resumed atomic testing, there was silence from many of the neutralist leaders attending a summit in Belgrade hosted by Yugoslavia's leader, Tito. But Nasser condemned the blasts. "A lot of other people didn't, and the President was very sore, particularly at Tito's equivocal attitude," Komer recalled.[44] At Kennedy's ill-fated Vienna summit with Khrushchev, in which the tough old communist bullied the rattled young president, a passing comment by Khrushchev gave the administration one of the summit's few silver linings. "Nasser, Nehru, Nkrumah, and Sukarno—all of them have said that they want their countries to develop along Socialist lines," Khrushchev snorted. "But what kind of Socialist is Nasser when he keeps Communists in jail?"[45] Nasser himself seemed to have returned the sentiment. When Senator Hubert Humphrey met Nasser during an October 1961 visit to Cairo, the Egyptian leader told the Minne-

sota liberal that he had warned Khrushchev himself that "the Communists were traitors," agitators, and potential conspirators seeking to topple
the Free Officers. "Is this what you mean by coexistence?" Nasser said
that he had asked Khrushchev. The Soviet leader was (reportedly but plausibly) irritated.[46] With his reflexive suspicion of superpower bullying, Nasser
had balked at Dulles; at a minimum, he now bristled at Khrushchev.

In any event, while America's more traditional Middle East friends had
been annoyed by JFK's May letters, it turned out that Nasser had liked
Kennedy's handiwork.[47] On August 30, Egyptian Ambassador Kamel finally delivered Nasser's response, which a State Department analysis called
"extraordinarily warm in tone, mild in language, forthcoming, and hopeful
for the relations of the two countries in the future."[48] Unlike Kings Saud and
Husayn, Nasser expressed "immense satisfaction and appreciation" for
Kennedy's letter. "We have always tried, are still trying and will invariably
insist on trying to extend our hand to the American nation," Nasser wrote.
"I assure you that what hurts us most deeply is the fact that we often find
our hand hanging alone in the air."

The key problem, Nasser insisted, was Palestine. Having tried to guess
JFK's attitude on the Arab-Israel question from reading Kennedy's campaign book, *The Strategy of Peace*, Nasser went on at some length about
Zionist perfidy, Truman's abandonment of principle, and Israeli expansionism. He objected to Wilson's and FDR's unfulfilled promises of self-
determination, as well as to the Baghdad Pact, the withdrawal of Aswan
Dam aid, and the Eisenhower Doctrine. Israeli aggression—as seen in its
1955 raid on Gaza—had driven Egypt away from a pure development
agenda and forced it to acquire Soviet arms in self-defense. As for the
tripartite attack of October 29, 1956, Nasser wrote that "the American people
sympathized with our position through the memories of their experience
at Pearl Harbor." The collapse of the Baghdad Pact posed the questions:
"Why is the American policy reduced to such ruins? . . . Why does the
United States, a country established on foundations of freedom and by
means of a revolution, oppose the call of freedom and revolutionary movements, and line up with reactionary forces and enemies of progress?" Nasser
urged Kennedy to rethink U.S. policy, "calling upon your youth and courage." This letter was "for you and not to be taken for what is termed by
some who profess knowledge as 'local consumption' or 'psychological
mobilization,'" Nasser concluded. He hoped that Kennedy's quest to "'the
New Frontier' – to quote your expression" would inspire the Egyptian
people, "who look to the American nation with love and admiration."[49] To
be sure, real problems divided the sides, but Nasser was clearly interested
in an ongoing engagement. The courting of Nasser seemed to be getting
somewhere.

NEITHER UNITED . . .

As it happened, the Kennedy administration was about to face its first major Middle East crisis—and Nasser was about to face one of the worst humiliations of his career.[50] Syria, Egypt's junior partner in the United Arab Republic that Nasser hoped would pave the way to a still larger state that would unite the Arab nation, was growing restless. When the UAR pushed a sweeping nationalization program in the summer of 1961, Syrian business leaders and some of their allies in the military decided they had had enough. In late September 1961, a new anti-Nasser regime backed by both Syrian conservatives and army officers came to power in Syria—and promptly bolted from the union. The secession, known in Arabic as the *infisal*, was as stinging a humiliation as Nasser had ever faced. Nasser was left with little of the two countries' merger other than the two stars on Egypt's flag.

Pointing to Egypt's large African population, Nasser's Arab rivals japed that the United Arab Republic was now neither united, nor Arab, nor a republic.[51] The White House was less gleeful; it worried that Syria's secession might trigger a regional war, in one of several ways—if an embarrassed Egypt tried to force Syria back into the union, if an exuberant Jordan came to the aid of the anti-Nasser regime in Damascus, or if an expansionist Israel somehow used the chaos as a pretext to seize the West Bank. Kennedy's Middle East staffers scrambled to find Nasser a soft landing.

In fact, Kennedy's foreign policy bureaucracy ultimately found itself presented not with a war but with a potential opportunity: a chastened, more tractable Nasser, dented in the eyes of the Arab world and perhaps inclined to focus on development at home rather than joust for leadership abroad. The Kennedy administration pointedly tried not to worsen Nasser's embarrassment, even warning its traditional regional friends (the Arab conservatives) and its aspiring regional ally (Israel) to contain their enthusiasm over their archenemy's discomfiture. Washington's first task was to sidestep an all-out Middle East war in 1961; its second was to nurture the hope that the new, smaller UAR might turn inward. In fact, Nasser reacted to his loss of prestige with wounded pride, not newfound humility—a response that would ultimately help drive Nasser into his disastrous intervention in Yemen and wreck the Kennedy administration's hopes for a rapprochement with Egypt.

On 7:15 P.M. on September 28, a worried Talbot phoned Rusk to tell him that Syrian military units were attempting a coup in Damascus. NEA figured that the rebels were, by Syrian standards, pro-Western conservatives, but Talbot was more concerned about losing sway with a radical than gaining sway with a conservative. The coup, Talbot argued, put Nasser "in an almost impossible box."[52] If he let the putsch succeed, his prestige in the Arab world would take a body blow; if he tried to crush it, he might well fail, and the idea of Egyptian forces grappling with their Syrian brethren was almost unimaginable to the pan-Arabist faithful. The State Department glumly assumed that any new regime in Syria would be unstable; as Komer paraphrased their reservations, while the "present crew" of conservatives "may seem all right, who will ride in on their coattails?"[53] Worst of all, Talbot also feared that the crisis might spiral out of control—either from Jordan intervening to help the putschists and deal a blow to the conservatives' rival, from Nasser marching his troops into Syria, or from Ben-Gurion sending troops into the West Bank during a UAR-Jordan showdown.

The administration scrambled to react. At 9:15, Komer passed along a report to Bundy warning that Nasser seemed ready to use force to keep Syria within the UAR. But Nasser's military options were unappealing; if the coup leaders now held Damascus, Egypt's troops would have to seize a beachhead around Aleppo, in northeast Syria—no mean feat.

Rather than merely bottling up the conflict, Komer suggested trying to use it for American ends. Unlike Talbot, he was clearly intrigued by the possibility of acquiring a friendly regime in Damascus, but he also realized that one sure way to hamstring the rebels was to let them be tarred as American stooges. So Komer recommended ensuring that Washington "does *nothing* overtly," since publicly backing either side was a losing proposition. The U.S. Sixth Fleet should stay put off of the coast of Rhodes. Meanwhile, Jordan, Turkey, and Iraq should be encouraged to assure the Syrian putschists secretly of their support—both to warn Nasser off of attacking Damascus and to buck the rebels up. Komer agreed with Talbot that a Nasserite intervention could "really put fat in fire" if Egypt invaded Syria, Jordan followed suit, and Israel invaded Jordan. But he took a dim view of Nasser's military options; if the coup was really taking hold, he doubted Nasser could take Aleppo and then march on Damascus. So Washington should place a very quiet bet on the coup. "In sum," Komer wrote, "let not the left hand know what the right is doing."[54]

In a cable at 10:33 to America's regional embassies, the State Department warned them to gear up. In Amman, King Husayn had been caught flat-footed by the coup, and the U.S. ambassador to Jordan, William B. Macomber, was promptly dispatched to warn him to stay out of it. An Egyptian-Jordanian showdown in Syria could spark a conflagration that would consume the Middle East, Macomber's instructions read. America wanted to keep supporting the king, but Husayn should not try to take too much advantage of Nasser's humiliation—although the State Department carefully left that sentiment just shy of an overt threat to sever aid.[55]

Another key source of administration worries was Israel—the country that Kennedy had so praised during the 1960 campaign. But Kennedy's foreign policy bureaucracy worried that the Jewish state might take advantage of the crisis to snatch the West Bank of the Jordan River, which had been held by Jordan since the end of Israel's 1948–49 War of Independence. The West Bank was enormously important to both Israeli security (as a natural trap for invading tanks) and to Jewish history (as the site of most of the Hebrew Bible's key episodes). For both reasons, Ben-Gurion might have been sorely tempted to take the West Bank had it been on offer. But Israel's prime minister was both pragmatist and visionary, and he knew that Israel had enough on its plate without dreaming of larger borders.

Still, the Kennedy administration was taking no chances. The U.S. embassy in Tel Aviv was directed to be ready to meet immediately with Ben-Gurion if Jordanian or Egyptian troops were spotted headed for Syria; such troop movements might give Israel a pretext for a plunge eastward. The Israelis were to be warned not to exacerbate tensions by mouthing off or mobilizing their armed forces.[56]

Over the next 24 tense hours, the State Department later concluded, Nasser blinked. The conservative rebels in Damascus would be able to stay. The State Department told its embassies the day after the coup that Nasser had actually gone ahead and ordered an invasion of Syria but then pulled back, either because of a "change of heart" or the failure of his spearhead force to gain a foothold.[57] Nasser had to move quickly to quell the coup or not at all. As time went by, the junta's grip on Syria strengthened, and for Nasser, the risks within the inter-Arab political arena of attacking his brethren in Syria grew. Within a day or two, the new Syrian leader, Ma'mun Kuzbari, began exchanging barbs with Nasser, and the State Department assumed that Syria's formal secession from the UAR was a question not of whether but of when. Nevertheless, the initial war scare seemed to have passed.

But the situation within Syria remained murky and dangerous. (The State Department was hard-pressed to explain why the otherwise right-leaning junta had named a communist, Adnan Quwatli, as interior minister—unless they were actually dealing with another, less left-wing Syrian politico also named Adnan Quwatli. State Department Executive Secretary Lucius Battle gamely promised to let the White House know which Adnan Quwatli they were dealing with.) Such farce aside, Syria's secession had dealt a body blow to Nasser's prestige, Battle warned, and the pan-Arabist leader's domestic foes were "sharpening their knives in anticipation of the day when his crown falls." Israel sighed with relief at the ebbing of the pan-Arab tide, and such gleeful conservatives as King Saud,

Lebanese President Chehab, and King Husayn could barely contain their schadenfreude. But the State Department was less sanguine. To buck himself up, Nasser might lash out elsewhere—and one likely target was the West. The haste with which King Husayn and the shah of Iran had recognized the new regime in Damascus had lent credence to Nasser's charges that the coup was the fruit of "imperialist machinations." To avoid piling on Nasser, Washington was at pains to let Cairo know that it was pursuing business as usual during the crisis.[58]

Komer was less worried than the State Department's Egypt experts that Nasser's grip on power might be threatened, but he was concerned that the coup had further destabilized a never terribly stable region. Nasser might make a bid for Arab unity by striking out at Israel; or he might try to undermine the Syrian junta; or he might sit in Cairo, sulk, and watch his prestige erode; or, worst of all, he might scurry, humiliated, "back into the arms of Moscow." But not all the scenarios were bad. A chastened Nasser might turn his energies toward development at home. "Now is also the time to be extra nice to Nasser," Komer wrote in a memo to Rostow and Bundy. "Nasser-Moscow relationship seemed to be cooling recently; we don't want to let this trend be reversed by default." So the Kennedy administration should avoid rushing to recognize the new Syrian regime for fear of arousing Nasser's suspicion that America somehow lay behind the coup. The administration should also consider finally extending a formal invitation to Nasser to visit Washington, as well as green-lighting more loans. "In sum," Komer concluded, "my recipe would be public posture of hands off, discreet, indirect encouragement of new regime, and nice noises to Nasser."[59]

Sure enough, on September 30, Egyptian Foreign Minister Mahmud Fawzi met Rusk in New York and asked the United States not to recognize the new regime. Nasser blamed the coup on the jealous Arab kings, later claimed that King Saud had told him of spending £12 million to fund the putsch, and accused the CIA of complicity.[60] Quick recognition, Fawzi complained, would smack of Western meddling in the coup, preempt the nonaligned movement, give a U.S. imprimatur to a regime that might still fall, and help vivisect the UAR. Washington told Egyptian Ambassador Kamel that it liked the Egyptian idea of monitoring the Arab world's reaction; if the majority of Arab states recognized the Damascus junta, Washington surely need not hang back.[61] The same day, King Husayn summoned Ambassador Macomber to urge the Kennedy administration to promptly recognize the new Syrian government. Macomber sternly replied that outside intervention in the UAR crisis might well spark a regional catastrophe "and quite possibly World War III."[62] The Kennedy administration was not going to kick Nasser while he was down.

The crisis seemed to be passing, but the administration's jitters had not quite abated. On the evening of October 3, the State Department warned its Middle East posts that Nasser suddenly seemed to be preparing a thrust against Syria, from both the air and sea.[63] For the next three days, the Sixth Fleet kept a careful eye on Alexandria, watching for either Egyptian support for a counter-coup in Damascus or a full-blown invasion wherein Nasser's navy would take the port of Latakia and his air force the airfield at Aleppo.

At 11 P.M., Rusk added another telegram to Ambassador John Badeau in Cairo. The cable offered a direct message from Kennedy himself to Nasser, praising the Egyptian for his friendly August letter, sympathizing with his postcoup dilemmas in Syria, and thanking him for his "efforts to stabilize the situation by peaceful means." The administration was still sufficiently concerned that the UAR's death rattles might echo beyond Syria's borders that it had finally opted to intervene at the highest level. Kennedy told Nasser that he had been "especially impressed with Nasser's statesman-like address of September 29," which ruled out any shedding of Arab blood to settle the Syrian crisis.[64] Washington, the president noted, had not made up its mind about recognizing the rebels and hoped to consult with Cairo on the matter. In other words, JFK told Nasser that whatever he might be up to in Alexandria, he should let matters lie. Nasser thanked Badeau for the message, for the administration's decision not to demonstratively move the Sixth Fleet around, and for its willingness to move slowly on recognition.[65]

The spike of alarm subsided soon after Kennedy weighed in. The next day, King Husayn told Macomber that Jordan had pulled back most of its troops from the border with Syria. Moreover, the king assured the ambassador, the new regime in Syria was now confident that it could fend off any possible Egyptian countercoup without outside help. Nasser's moment to keep the UAR together, the king concluded, had come and gone. Sure enough, Nasser never tried to roll back the Syrian coup by force.

The new regime in Damascus soon sent Washington a formal request for recognition, leaving the administration in a conundrum: recognizing the new Syrian regime too quickly would irritate Nasser, and recognizing it too slowly would irritate the Arab conservatives. But Nasser let the administration off the hook by having his U.N. ambassador announce that Egypt would not oppose Syrian membership in the world body and the Arab League.[66] With even Nasser reconciled to the coup, the Kennedy administration moved quickly to recognize the new Syrian leadership.[67] In early November, Phil Talbot became the first American diplomat to visit the Kuzbari regime, which pointedly hosted a luncheon for him in the state guest house that had served as Nasser's home in Damascus.[68] To help salve Nasser's pride, JFK personally sent Nasser a courteous message.[69]

Nevertheless, Nasser's nerves were clearly frayed. On October 27, he began arresting army officers and interrogating civilians, including children, for fear that he might suffer the same fate as the regime in Damascus. "The arrests are indicative of the extent to which Nasser's confidence in Egyptian support for his regime has weakened," noted Roger Hilsman of the State Department's Intelligence and Research (INR) bureau.[70] In a longer study a few days later, INR concluded that the "secession of Syria constitutes the greatest setback President Nasser has suffered since he took power."[71]

On October 16, Bundy asked the State Department for policy recommendations toward Cairo and Damascus after the coup.[72] As the formal response wended its way through the bureaucracy, Komer passed along a bullish assessment of his own to his bosses. "I am convinced," he wrote, "that recent events *may* present us with the best opportunity since 1954 for a limited marriage of convenience with the guy who I think is still, and will remain, the Mister Big of the Arab world."[73] Nasser was too important to ignore, but the administration thought it had more to work with now that Mister Big had been cut down to size.

AMITY AND AID

One of the savviest interpreters of U.S.–UAR relations proved to be John Badeau, who struck up cordial relationships with Nasser and many of his aides. The Egyptian leader once urged Badeau to smoke his pipe—an affectation at which the New Frontiersmen back home would have sniffed disdainfully. The grateful ambassador told Nasser that a pipe was a perfect prop for a diplomat; if Egyptian Foreign Minister Fawzi ever asked a difficult question, Badeau could buy a few minutes tamping down the pipe while thinking of an answer. "Tell me," replied Nasser, who did not think much of Fawzi, "has my Foreign Minister ever asked you a direct and difficult question?"[74] Badeau also sometimes tried to shield his hosts from anti-Egypt sentiment in Congress. When one particularly boorish senator visited Cairo, Badeau recalled, the man requested a meeting with Abd al-Moneim Kaissouni, the British-educated Egyptian economics minister, and then asked Badeau if the beautifully fluent Kaissouni spoke any English. His suspicions aroused, Badeau said he would check and interpret if necessary. Sure enough, during the meeting, the senator harangued Kaissouni, bragging of his own importance and warning that Egypt's foreign aid lay in his hands. "Senator, you'd better let me translate that," said an embarrassed Badeau, switching into Arabic to assure the bemused Kaissouni that the uncomprehending senator was suffering from delusions of grandeur. "Please don't apologize," Kaissouni grinned. "We have people just like this in the Egyptian government."[75]

As he grew more comfortable in Cairo, Badeau argued that American relations with the Free Officers' regime had evolved through four phases. "The Honeymoon" ran from 1952 to 1954, when Eisenhower hoped to enlist post-Faruq Egypt in an anti-Soviet regional military pact and ease tensions with Israel. After the Czech arms deal in 1955, which saw the Soviet Union start arming Egypt, Ike and Dulles shifted over to "Direct Opposition," trying to isolate Egypt within the Arab world. The remainder of the Eisenhower period was devoted to the "Cool but Correct" phase, which acknowledged that the hyperactive attempt to quarantine Nasser had flopped. Foreign aid resumed, albeit in modest quantities, and the United States watched with interest as Egypt's ties to the Soviet Union cooled and the union between Egypt and Syria began to fray. In the fourth phase, under Kennedy, Washington shifted to "A Positive Policy"—a "conscious determination . . . made at the highest level of the United States Government to undertake an action program seeking to build a broad and useful relationship with the UAR."[76] Nasser's confidant, Muhammad Hassanein Haykal of the Cairo daily al-Ahram, had his own typology— the period from the Free Officers' coup until the Czech arms deal was Seduction, followed by Punishment until Nasser's 1958 falling-out with Khrushchev, followed by Containment as Kennedy took over.[77] But both Badeau and Haykal agreed that Kennedy opened a new chapter—the most important American attempt yet to reach out to the Arabs' preeminent nationalist, Israel's nemesis, and the Soviets' potential prize.

The principal tool that the New Frontier would use to mold Badeau's "Positive Policy" was foreign aid. The United States had cut off such assistance to Egypt in 1956 over Suez, but the Eisenhower administration renewed the program after it had gotten over the shocks of 1958. Still, aid was doled out on a project-by-project basis, and the pace of U.S. approval for development loans was sluggish—only $15 million in 1960.[78] Kennedy, however, would make foreign aid a staple of his Third World overtures in general and of the outreach to Nasser in particular. As the political scientist Hans Morgenthau put it in 1960, "foreign aid is but the continuation of diplomacy by other means."[79] Under Truman and Eisenhower, Egypt received just $254 million in total aid; under Kennedy, it received $500 million—a significant sum of taxpayer money to spend courting an often truculent and anti-Western autocrat.[80] More than two-thirds of that came from surplus American grain sold under the provisions of Public Law 480 (PL-480), a development assistance program that sold excess American foodstuffs at subsidized rates to needy countries. "The basic strategy of our aid program," an internal administration memo ran, was "to seek to enmesh the UAR with the Western world and to reduce the UAR's reliance on the Soviets."[81]

By the end of May 1961, Talbot saw a sharply improved climate in U.S.–Egypt relations and urged the administration to keep courting Nasser. On May 27, the administration approved the sale of 200,000 more tons of wheat. Cairo noticed, and followed up with a request for even more such assistance for fiscal year 1962. Talbot found that reassuring—a sign that "we are on the right track provided we do not force the pace."[82]

The NSC was even more bullish than the State Department. Komer proposed "a major shift in policy toward Nasser"—using aid as bait to lure Cairo away from Moscow.[83] The State Department, Komer wrote, wanted to dole out aid gradually, "without any fanfare, as an exercise in quiet diplomacy"—including a multiyear PL-480 deal, $72 million in U.S. loans, 350,000 bales of cotton, insecticides, rice, economic advice, and help repairing the temples at Abu Simbel. Why not bundle all that up, Komer asked, and present it to Nasser in a shiny package as a token of a "new chapter in US-Egyptian relations"? McGeorge Bundy's deputy, the development enthusiast Walt Rostow, also advocated boldness. With Nasser chafing on an uncomfortably short Soviet leash, Rostow urged a dramatic step-up in long-term foreign aid, extending beyond PL-480 deals. Moreover, Rostow suggested that the new assistance come with no direct strings attached, which had proved the most effective model in the administration's recent dealings with another prickly neutralist, India's Nehru.[84] And Rostow, for one, thought that the administration's interest in courting Nasser went all the way up the chain of command. "The president is anxious to get closer to this fellow," Rostow said in a June phone call to Undersecretary of State for Economic Affairs George Ball.[85]

The feeling seemed mutual. On December 1, Egyptian Ambassador Kamel told Talbot "with considerable emotion" that he had "wonderful news": he had received orders from Nasser himself that the UAR was to rely on the Kennedy administration for its economic development. That meant accepting Rostow's aid suggestions, including a multinational consortium and high-level advisers to help plot development strategy. The visibly excited Kamel called his new marching orders "the most significant turning point in U.S.–U.A.R. relations since the fiasco of the Aswan Dam."[86]

But while the NSC, the State Department, and the Egyptian embassy were sold on the Nasser initiative, the president was not. Komer's memos to Kennedy, for all their characteristic vim, took on a defensive tone as the administration neared the end of its first year. Even a successful overture would leave Nasser as "a neutralist and nationalist," Komer admitted to JFK in a December 1961 memo. But if Nasser had a "vested interest" in better ties, he would be less likely to make anti-Western mischief across the region. "Thus perhaps our greatest gains would be negative," Komer wrote. Washington "would not get a great deal from Nasser, but at least we might restrain him from doing a lot of things we don't like."

In italics, Komer continued, *"This immediately brings up the Israeli problem."* With a bow toward domestic political reality, he wrote, "One cannot propose a new initiative toward Nasser without assessing its likely impact on Israel and its supporters in the US." Of course, a stronger Egypt could be in a better position to menace Israel, but Ben-Gurion liked the idea of an Egypt focused less on pan-Arab agitation abroad than on economic development at home. American leverage over Egypt would not hurt Israel's position, either, Komer pointed out. If Washington and Cairo were friendlier, he argued, Nasser would be able to more easily accept continued U.S. support for the Jewish state. As Komer put it, "The Arab-Israeli issue is one on which the UAR and US would simply have to agree to disagree." If Nasser remained truculent, Komer concluded, the initiative "could be cut off at any point."[87]

U.S. Agency for International Development (USAID) officials were not so sure, worrying that a multiyear PL-480 deal without strings attached would cost Washington leverage over Nasser.[88] But the State Department and the NSC brushed these objections aside and urged the skeptical Kennedy to go beyond just aid. "How we treat the volatile and sensitive Nasser will be just as important as what we give him," wrote Komer in January 1962.[89] Both the NSC and the State Department agreed that the administration should send an envoy to Cairo to meet Nasser. After considering several names, including Bobby Kennedy, the State Department and the NSC settled on Chester Bowles, the president's main envoy to the Third World, an Adlai Stevenson ally, and a liberal tribune of modernization abroad. Bowles's trip, Rusk wrote Kennedy, would "demonstrate through the presence of one of your close advisers" the depth of the administration's commitment to better relations.[90]

But Kennedy's misgivings about Nasser remained—worsened, perhaps, by a rising backlash from Nasser's foes. Still smarting from Suez, France tried to block International Monetary Fund (IMF) aid to Egypt and blasted Kennedy's attempted rapprochement on its clandestine radio broadcasts.[91] When King Saud met Kennedy on February 13, the Saudi leader called Nasser "a Communist who presents a real danger to the Arab World."[92] Israel's friends also chimed in. Pro-Israel senators tried to attach strings to Nasser's aid,[93] and Mike Feldman, the administration's barometer of American Jewish opinion, wrote Komer that he "struggled to find the substance of the advantage to the United States in our proposed overtures to Nasser . . ."[94] Kennedy told the NSC's Carl Kaysen that

Washington "seemed to be giving too much aid to the UAR."[95] The grumbling president then sat back to hear how Bowles would fare in Cairo.

MISSIONS TO CAIRO, MISSION FROM CAIRO

Bowles's three-day visit in mid-February turned out to be cordial. From the U.S. embassy in Khartoum, Kennedy's envoy wired that his trip had been "more encouraging than I had anticipated. . . . It is clear, for the moment at least, that [the] UAR has made [the] decision to try to improve its relations with us." Better still, Nasser took a pragmatic view of the Cold War: he would take Moscow's arms and alms "when convenient but will tightly restrict Sino-Soviet activities and will vigorously oppose encroachment of communism into the Middle East."[96] Thus encouraged, Bowles urged the administration to forge ahead with the rapprochement by sending an economic expert—the administration had by now settled on Edward Mason, a Harvard economist—to help lay the groundwork for more targeted U.S. development aid and a summit for Nasser in Washington.

A few days later, the traveling Bowles sent along a longer, more reflective cable, this time from the U.S. embassy in Addis Ababa. "[I]f Nasser can gradually be led to forsake the microphone for the bulldozer," Bowles mused, "he may assume a key role in bringing the Middle East peacefully into our modern world." Bowles noted that the Free Officers' regime mixed both the microphone—the hortatory invocations of pan-Arab leadership—with the bulldozer—the sober path of economic development. Still, anti-Zionism was no passing phase in Egypt. "The UAR takes the same view of Israel that the US takes of the USSR," Bowles wrote. "We will make no headway by scorning this evaluation." Nasser and his aides felt that the United States was flatly pro-Israel and were "convinced that our government cannot stand against internal Zionist pressure," Bowles noted. "They believe that the US reaction to the Suez attack was the exception rather than the rule." Having taken power by conspiracy themselves, Bowles wrote, the Free Officers "are in effect human seismographs reacting violently to every adverse wave." Washington should keep its eyes on the prize—a somewhat better relationship with a key neutralist—rather than expecting Nasser to "stop acting like the revolutionary leader that he clearly is."[97]

True to revolutionary form, Nasser made a surly speech a few days later, denouncing "traitors in our midst" and excoriating Jordan, Saudi Arabia, and Syria.[98] On March 27, however, Nasser caught a break: the Syrian army installed a new government, shunting aside Prime Minister Kuzbari and the conservatives who had yanked the country out of the UAR. The next day, the administration's intelligence agencies prepared a new National Intelligence Estimate assessing Nasser's prospects—and underscoring the Cold War logic of courting the agitated Egyptian leader. The document argued that Nasser would continue to glower at the Arab conservatives, Israel, Britain, and France—but would have to keep his ties to both superpowers significantly less hostile "because of his heavy dependence on the US for food and on the USSR for military and development aid."[99]

Kennedy was "was still in [an] anti-Nasser mood," Komer warned Bundy.[100] The wary president personally asked the U.S. Information Agency to monitor the level of anti-American agitprop in the state-run Egyptian media. The agency's director, the broadcasting legend Edward R. Murrow, reported that while America was still being pilloried for colonialism in Africa, dollar diplomacy in Latin America, and favoritism toward Israel and "Arab reactionaries," the attacks were "not as vituperative" as those reserved for Britain, France, Jordan, Saudi Arabia, and Yemen. One sample quote from the Cairo newspaper *al-Akhbar* ("In his efforts to invade Africa, Kennedy relies on four weapons, namely foreign aid, labor unions, the Peace Corps, and the U.N.") was "typical of the whole Egyptian line," Murrow wrote.[101]

Unsurprisingly, Kennedy was lukewarm about offering more taxpayer dollars to a country that called aid an imperialist weapon. Given Kennedy's "hesitations about our policy toward the UAR," Komer urged, Mason should not offer much new.[102] But Egyptian expectations got raised anyway. "While I have stressed on every possible occasion the exploratory nature of the visits from President Kennedy's representatives," wrote Badeau from Cairo, "Nasser and Company would not be human (or Arab) if they did not read something into them."[103]

So it was with some misgivings that the White House finally sent Mason to Egypt to perform the promised economic assessment. Sure enough, Mason's mission—on the heels of visits by Bowles and Food for Peace Director George McGovern[104]—"probably created certain expectations in the UAR," the economist himself admitted. But it also offered U.S. officials a better picture of Egypt's needs, which suggested new ways for the administration to ingratiate itself. Mason spent two weeks touring Egypt and meeting with Nasser and several top Egyptian advisers. After a bad crop failure in 1961, Mason found, Egypt was running a balance-of-payments debt and suffering from stalled national income growth and investment. The IMF had offered to help, but that would still not be enough to take care of the immediate shortfall without slashing Nasser's wider development plans. Still, Mason reckoned that the UAR could, barring another major crop failure, "support a growth rate of four to six percent per annum"—respectable by any economic yardstick. Nor did Mason worry that mismanagement from centralized, state-run industries would hobble Egyptian growth rates—in retrospect, a bad bet.

Mason had four suggestions for next moves. He recommended that PL-480 aid continue on the much-discussed multiyear basis, that the Development Loan Fund double its aid for 1962 to somewhat more than $30 million, that the "present small figure" of $2.5 million for technical assistance also be doubled, and that the administration carry on with its step-by-step approach of rewarding Egypt for improved behavior with economic cooperation.[105]

To follow up, Nasser dispatched his minister of economy, Kaissouni, to Washington in April. The Egyptian minister left town in a fine mood. The administration offered to help out with Egypt's alarming $120 million balance-of-payments crunch, and the IMF pitched in $42.5 million for economic stabilization. For his part, Kaissouni agreed to contact Germany, Britain, Italy, and Japan about forming a consortium to provide more economic help.[106] By May 28, Komer was pleased enough with the new climate to put in Kennedy's pile of weekend reading a lengthy internal State Department paper, ponderously titled "WHITHER UNITED STATES–UNITED ARAB REPUBLIC RELATIONS." The paper called the Nasser overture a valuable long-term way to "imbed the UAR in the Free World."[107] It argued that the administration should not be rocked off course by the provocations that would inevitably emanate from Cairo, even though some of Nasser's actions would wind up "annoying a segment of the American public"—a polite way of saying American Jews. But Israel's friends were not the only ones left unconvinced by the State Department's optimism—or left wondering how bad Egyptian behavior would have to get before the administration reversed course.

RAPPROCHEMENT AND ITS DISCONTENTS

Saudi Arabia and Israel feared that a rise in Nasser's stock would mean a bear market in their own. Both countries, with their very different agendas, did their best throughout 1961 and 1962 to cool any new U.S. enthusiasm for Nasser.

The Saudis were not easy to mollify. As a June 1962 State Department memo warned the White House, "The Saudis now appear to feel our aid to the U.A.R. implies a lessening of U.S. concern for Saudi Arabia."[108] It did not help that the administration's FY 1962 budget offered Egypt a total of $247.5 million in aid and gave only $1.8 million to Saudi Arabia (which, to be fair, was far wealthier).[109] The irked Arab conservatives ratcheted up a nasty propaganda exchange accusing Nasser of selling out Palestine for

American blood money. Radio Amman, seizing upon the Nasser-JFK correspondence, told its listeners that "secret negotiations" between Washington and Cairo were under way "to determine the price which Nasser was to receive from America as wages for his part in the liquidation of the Palestine issue." Front-page articles in the Saudi newspapers *al-Nadwah* and *al-Bilad* sneered that "Nasser's answer to Kennedy makes it clear that the Arab-Israeli dispute is no longer engaging the attention of Egyptian rulers," who were no longer willing to join in "the Arab stand against Zionist plots to eliminate the Palestine issue."[110] The NSC figured that Saudi Arabia and Jordan were accusing Egypt of going wobbly to goad Nasser into becoming more stridently anti-Israel—which would then sour his relations with the United States, stop the administration's overture to Egypt, and restore the Arab monarchs to their previously unchallenged role as America's clients.[111]

The administration hoped to make Nasser's life a little easier here by moving on the Palestinian refugee issue. Kennedy tapped Joseph Johnson, a friend of Secretary of State Rusk, to lead the renewed push—under the auspices of the Palestine Conciliation Commission (PCC), a long-dormant U.N. body—that JFK had advertised in his May 1961 letters to the major Arab leaders. The U.N. envoy began with a round of consultations. Over the course of about a week in Cairo in May 1962, Johnson spent two hours alone with Nasser and many more in meetings with top Egyptian officials, in what he called a "uniformly friendly" atmosphere. That friendliness did not prevent Nasser from giving Johnson an earful about Zionist xenophobia and Ben-Gurion and Moshe Dayan's supposed determination to use force to cow the Arabs. Still, Nasser was reportedly downright wry about recognizing the limits on the numbers of Palestinian refugees that Ben-Gurion would consider accepting back into Israel.[112]

He had a point. Ben-Gurion opposed anything that might produce an influx of Palestinian refugees bitter over 1948, and Foreign Minister Golda Meir quickly developed a strong—and strongly reciprocated—dislike for Johnson.[113] The Johnson mission eventually flopped, but its very existence shows how far off base the worried Arabists of the late Eisenhower State Department were about the Kennedy administration. Moving at all on the 1948 refugees was no way to curry favor with Israel or its friends on Capitol Hill.

Nor was wooing Nasser. Jerusalem feared that closer ties between Washington and Cairo would come at its expense. As the State Department's George Ball told Kennedy, "the UAR request for cotton under P.L. 480 to meet domestic deficiencies was interpreted by Israel as permitting the UAR to use more of its own cotton to purchase Soviet arms" by freeing up more money in Nasser's budget.[114]

Still, Israel's opposition was tempered by pragmatism. If Israel could not halt the Nasser initiative, it could at least try to slow it—or ensure that the Jewish state was compensated for its forbearance. On June 15, the NSC's Carl Kaysen lunched with Israeli Ambassador Avraham Harman, who pointedly asked whether the U.S. overture to Nasser was getting anywhere. Kaysen replied that "it was too soon to tell." Noting Harman's obvious distaste for the Egyptian regime, the New Frontiersman asked what alternative Israel might suggest for handling Nasser, but Harman declined to take the bait. "Remember," Harman said, "if you don't succeed, we will be facing those dogs."[115]

Another reliable measure of Israeli displeasure came from Mike Feldman, who lay outside the formal foreign policy loop but began checking in more frequently in the spring of 1962 in his capacity as de facto Israeli advocate. At one point, he went so far as to ask the State Department to tally up a balance sheet of recent friendly and unfriendly actions by Nasser, which the State Department duly did—giving, unsurprisingly, the Egyptian leader a passing grade.[116] "Mike is certainly beating on State these days with a drumfire of queries," Komer observed to Bundy in late May. "I'm not sure he realizes that our long-term ability to promote steps toward an [Arab-Israeli] settlement depends largely on a sufficiently even-handed attitude toward Arab *and* Israeli to give us leverage with Arabs. As you know, I agree that [the] pendulum has swung sufficiently that compensatory gestures toward Israel [are] desirable, but I believe that: (1) what Israelis really need and want is reaffirmation of our security guarantee; (2) we should use this prospect to get certain concessions from them." Komer also wanted to "remind Arabs that a third round against Israel is futile." (In fact, it turned out to be not so much futile as calamitous.) "We're too cautious," Komer wrote, "about telling Arabs the score."[117]

Israel's friends agreed. The June 25 issue of the influential liberal magazine *The New Republic* featured a cutting unsigned editorial entitled "Courting Nasser." Jordan, Iran, Israel, and Lebanon were all asking the same question, the article said: "Is the United States planning to make Egypt the focus of its interest and concern, and if so why?"[118] Kennedy mentioned the piece to Bundy, who asked State Department Executive Secretary William Brubeck to respond. Brubeck, seemingly worried that the president might have taken the criticism to heart, sharply replied that the piece was attacking a straw man—a "mockery" of the administration's policy.[119] The editorial was indeed filled with errors, but the fact that Kennedy and Bundy were fussed enough to want such a memo written suggests considerable external pressure to halt the Nasser overture.[120]

The issue that crystallized the administration's reservations about its outreach to Egypt was the question of inviting Nasser to visit Washington—an idea that was enthusiastically endorsed by most of Kennedy's advisers but never quite made it past the president himself. In general, the displeasure of the Israel lobby failed to dampen the Nasser overture, but this time, domestic politics weighed heavily on Kennedy's mind. As Komer put it, a summit was "a gesture of statecraft the President was in favor of as long as the domestic political timing was good."[121] Kennedy, a deeply political animal, unapologetically thought through the domestic implications of diplomatic decisions, in stark contrast to the Marshall-Eisenhower line that even weighing such considerations was ipso facto inappropriate. JFK was often willing to buck domestic pressures, but he at least wanted to know what they were.

In the case of a Nasser summit, they were stark. During Nasser's 1960 visit to New York, he had been greeted by large, embarrassing demonstrations.[122] Israel, many American Jews, and much of Congress would protest; Arab conservatives would yowl; and Republicans would accuse the administration of fawning over a communist. Nor was the administration getting much out of the regular visits from another truculent neutralist, Indonesia's Sukarno. Moreover, one anti-Western crack by Nasser—or, worse, an en route stopover in Castro's Cuba—would echo for weeks.

Still, most of the president's men were keen. After all, Eisenhower had gotten away with meeting Nasser in New York around the September 1960 opening of the U.N. General Assembly. Bowles told Kennedy that a state visit would salve Nasser's dignity, offer a cheap way to counterbalance the Soviets' influence, and force the Egyptian leader to watch his tongue both before and after the trip. The NSC concurred. "As a very important wheel in the Arab and neutralist world," Komer wrote, Nasser "too should get the Kennedy treatment."[123] In Cairo, John Badeau rejected the idea of waiting "to determine whether Nasser will be a 'good boy' before bringing him to the States" and urged his colleagues to ignore the Israel lobby.[124] Even Mike Feldman did "not think the domestic political repercussions would be insuperable if we handle them properly"—arranging a businesslike, low-key visit safely away from the midterm congressional elections, with enough lead time to soothe American Jewish leaders.[125]

The State Department, however, was not thinking in low-key terms. It wanted to give Nasser a full-blown state visit, not a quick White House stopover on the way to the U.N. General Assembly or a private chat like Ben-Gurion's 1961 Waldorf meeting with Kennedy. Rusk proposed helicoptering the leader of pan-Arabism to the White House lawn, where he would be greeted with military honors and personally escorted to a suite at Blair House by Kennedy and Rusk. During a two-day stay in Washington, Nasser would be treated to two Oval Office meetings, a state luncheon with Kennedy, a state dinner with Rusk, and a return luncheon with Kennedy. Nasser would then spend a week getting exposed to the glories of the wider United States, ferried about by U.S. government planes and cars. "New York will be avoided," Rusk added.[126]

The prospect of anti-Nasser protests in Manhattan may have done it for the president. Kennedy's political antennae were acute enough to twitch hard at the thought of an administration love-in with a temperamental neutralist who nursed a grudge against Zionism.[127] On February 1, Kennedy decided things had gone far enough. "Call off the idea of a Nasser visit," he told Bundy.[128] The national security adviser, too, felt "that the promise of gain is not worth the certain turmoil."[129]

That did not quite kill the idea, although it did help scare off both Komer and Rusk. But Chet Bowles—still the only senior administration figure to have met Nasser—was persistent enough to try putting his head in the lion's mouth: in May 1962, he tried to persuade an American Jewish Congress audience that a U.S. policy that encouraged Nasser to focus on development would reduce the Egyptian leader's "time and energy" to pursue anti-Israel mischief. Over dinner, Bowles found that many members of the group's board of directors seemed to buy the argument. Bowles later told Bundy that the episode showed that the Israel lobby could be won over to a warmer U.S.–UAR policy and a Nasser summit, adding that "with careful handling and frank explanation our domestic political problem should not present any unmanageable difficulties."[130] This time, Feldman, whose job it was to know such things, disagreed.[131] So did McGeorge Bundy, who thanked Bowles for his "missionary work" at the American Jewish Congress speech but poured cold water on the summit idea. The administration had reached out quite enough to Egypt recently, so why should it "rush in with yet another plum?" And Bundy was less sanguine about the American Jewish and Israeli response to a Nasser visit in the wake of Israel's recent reprisal raids against Syria on the Golan Heights, which had left Israeli partisans feeling "rather bruised." Bundy told a disappointed Bowles that Kennedy should "see a little more of the color of Nasser's money before he sat down to play face-to-face poker with him."[132] A summit would simply have to wait. Kennedy was willing to run political risks in his Middle East policy, but it was not his style to beg for trouble.

THE HIGH-WATER MARK

If any moment marked the apogee of the Nasser overture, it was probably June 21, 1962, when Nasser wrote Kennedy the warmest letter of their entire correspondence. As ever with Nasser, the style was flowery. But this time, he was tossing the sort of bouquet the administration had craved since the overture began. Kaissouni had enjoyed "a general feeling" in Washington "of understanding for the appreciation of the problems of the countries aspiring to progress," Nasser wrote. The Egyptian leader wrote that, when asked at press conferences or by U.S. diplomats what he wanted from Washington, he invariably answered, "All we seek and desire is understanding." Of course, outside forces would continue to cause tensions. "Yet I am positive that mutual understanding will keep those differences between limits that will not be exceeded," Nasser wrote. "Moreover, it affords us a wide scope for cordial, fruitful and constructive relations between us. . . ." This long-sought new understanding, he added, "calls for our deep thanks and has our total support."[133]

While Nasser's letter did double duty as a simple thank-you note after the Kaissouni mission, its unprecedented warmth and subtext delighted the State Department. "For one thing," Brubeck wrote Bundy, "Nasser's statement of sincere gratitude is practically unique in the history of US-UAR relations." In particular, Foggy Bottom liked Nasser's passage about keeping U.S.–UAR squabbles "within limits not to be exceeded"—evidence, the State Department hoped, that Nasser was truly intending to turn inward and away from mischief-making abroad. Some of the credit for Nasser's pragmatic May 21 National Charter, which sought to steer a middle course between communism and capitalism, might well be due to the sound advice of Badeau, Bowles, and Mason, Brubeck wrote.[134] With a hint of glee, the State Department later suggested that the Nasser letter could "probably be put to most effective use" by confidentially disclosing "its contents to influential members of Congress" as necessary if foreign aid to Egypt was ever under attack on Capitol Hill.[135] The NSC was equally enthusiastic. "We've made a score on relations with the key guy in the Arab world," Komer wrote Bundy. "[L]et's keep nurturing it."[136]

Kennedy responded in kind, with as friendly a letter as he would ever write to Nasser. On August 16, JFK told Nasser of his pleasure that "the relations between our two countries have been placed on a fruitful basis of cooperation and understanding" and that "problems between us can always be discussed fully and frankly, quietly and in confidence." He assured Nasser that he did not intend "any alteration in the basis of our cordial and expanding relationship." Secretary Rusk "will be delighted" to welcome Kaissouni back in the fall for another aid mission, Kennedy added. He ended the letter by wishing Nasser "continued success in your great efforts to promote the political, economic and social well-being of your people."[137]

It was a promising beginning for a policy that brought together several disparate portions of Kennedy's foreign policy team. The Nasser initiative united America's longstanding Arabists (such as Badeau), the Stevensonian liberals (such as Bowles), and some of the administration's great enthusiasts, the development advocates of the NSC (such as Rostow and Komer). It was an odd bureaucratic combination, but one powerful enough to steer the administration through a significant policy shift on a key Third World player.

But it was all about to fall apart—not because the New Frontier had failed to offer Nasser a tempting opportunity, but because Nasser would prove incapable of taking full advantage of it. The collapse of Nasser's union with Syria would not drive him to focus demurely on the home front; it was about to drive him to recklessness abroad—into a disastrous, unwinnable war of his own in Yemen.

The Nasser initiative's failure helped warm U.S.–Israel relations; thanks to the Kennedy experiment, the Johnson administration was more dismissive of the chances of ever luring Egypt away from the Kremlin. The knowledge that there were limits on America's ability to make inroads with Nasserism ultimately helped encourage closer U.S. ties with Israel by reducing the downside of friendship with the Jewish state. By the end of the 1960s, Egypt and its fellow Arab revolutionaries increasingly seemed lost, so all that Kennedy's heirs were risking by reaching out to Israel was the friendship of the Arab conservatives—the uneasy monarchs of Jordan, Saudi Arabia, and the Gulf emirates, none of whom could afford to forego American patronage in the first place.

By autumn 1962, Israel and the Arab conservatives were united in bewilderment over the Kennedy administration's enthusiasm for reaching out to Nasser, whom they regarded as a menace to regional order. The New Frontier disagreed—until Nasser blundered into a Vietnam of his own. Nasser would end his career as a tragic figure, and he was about to make one of the worst mistakes of his life—which would mean, among other things, that Uncle Sam had gotten as close as he ever would to Mister Big.

CHAPTER FOUR

Nasser's Vietnam

Yemen, the Arab Cold War, and the Limits of Rapprochement

S HORTLY AFTER THE CUBAN missile crisis, John F. Kennedy retired to his Palm Beach house to spend the Christmas of 1962 on a working vacation. No matter how much the president—perennially plagued by back pain and other ailments—wanted his rest, the press of business would not permit it, and Secretary of State Rusk would visit the Kennedy compound several times to discuss foreign policy problems. One time, Caroline Kennedy, aged five, met Rusk at the door. "Hello, Mr. Secretary," she chirped. "I am very worried about the war in the Yemen. Please tell me what is happening in the Yemen today."

Rusk was taken aback by such an adult question, which struck him as just the sort of thing that Caroline's father would ask. The straight-laced secretary of state was still trying to stammer out an answer when he heard JFK laughing behind a screen.[1]

The Yemen problem seemed the perfect foreign issue with which to tease the Buddha-like Rusk—it was dull, worthy, complicated, obscure. But over the coming year, Kennedy would conclude that Yemen was no laughing matter. After a September 1962 coup by Nasserite revolutionaries toppled Yemen's wheezing, medieval imamate, the country plunged into civil war. A wider war quickly ensued, in which Egypt rushed in to defend the coup and Saudi Arabia rushed in to try to reinstall its fellow royalists. The fractious Arab state on the foot of the Arabian Peninsula—its traditional tribal politics now overlaid with inter-Arab rivalry—became a Third World flashpoint and an arena for Nasserites to confront the Arab conservatives. Not only would the sole major Middle East war on Kennedy's watch roil the region, it would doom the administration's rapprochement with Nasser, reinforcing America's ties to the Arab conservatives and making it easier for the United States to move closer to an all-out alliance with Israel.

The Yemen crisis was particularly dismaying to those New Frontiers-men who had urged the administration to bet on Nasser. In the spring of 1963, Ambassador John Badeau sent a cable to the State Department that would have been considered quirky by most writerly standards—and was downright eccentric by diplomatic ones. After making the embassy rounds in Cairo, the American ambassador to Egypt wrote not about his own activities but about his competitor's: "I suggest USSR Ambassador Erofeev may be sending [a] despatch [*sic*] of [the] following character to the Krem-lin." Badeau's Soviet counterpart would surely be warning his bosses that the Soviet Union had been thrown back on the defensive in the Middle East over the past 18 months, after making such inroads with Nasser be-tween 1955 and 1958. "Beginning in 1959 but more particularly under Kennedy Administration, US has made ominous comeback in UAR, ap-parently with direct support of President Kennedy," Badeau imagined the Soviet ambassador writing. After all, America was giving Egypt enough food aid to make up nearly half of its cereal supply; Washington had pro-vided the Ministry of Education with hundreds of thousands of American textbooks translated into Arabic; and the local media now seldom flailed the United States. The American ambassador had "ready entree" to Nasser and had seen him at least 25 times during 22 months on the job.[2] Mean-while, Nasser was developing his own arms industry to free himself from reliance on the Soviets. The Soviet ambassador's overall 'view' of Nasser was gloomy: a mere "bourgeis [*sic*] national leader with no comprehen-sion of either [the] truth or inevitability of socialist triumph" whose al-leged socialism was "only a facade" to defend a system that denied basic rights to his workers and peasants.[3] Back in Washington, the NSC's Bob Komer called Badeau's foray into fiction "both entertaining and imagina-tive," passed it along to McGeorge Bundy to put in President Kennedy's stack of weekend reading, and even tried out the same sort of pitch on the columnist Rowland Evans.[4]

Badeau's fantasy of driving the Soviets into such a swivet was funda-mentally a display of wishful thinking—a futile attempt to salvage his be-loved Nasser overture, which was by then being dashed against the regional rocks. The telltale absence in Badeau's jeu d'esprit was a gaping hole the size and shape of Yemen. Kennedy's attempted rapprochement with pan-Arabism was important to its proponents in the bureaucracy, but the en-tire administration knew that Yemen's implications were something else entirely.

The central problem was that Nasser's thrust eastward had deeply un-nerved Saudi Arabia. The puritanical, ultraconservative, oil-rich House of Saud already had tremendous influence over U.S. Middle East policy in the early 1960s, and it feared that if Nasserism toppled the Yemeni monarchy, Saudi Arabia might be next. The Saudis' anxiety about Yemen engaged the core national security interests that undergirded America's decision to commit itself to the Middle East in the first place: stability and oil. However much the Kennedy administration might explore the idea of befriending Egypt or Israel, Saudi Arabia would always remain primus inter pares.

The partisans of the Nasser initiative hated to give up on it, but there was increasingly little they could do. The Yemen war had exposed the deepest fault lines in inter-Arab politics, reinforcing all of Kennedy's own hesitations about where his Egypt policy was heading. Suddenly, the overture to Nasser looked less like an innovation than an indulgence—and an unsustainable one at that.

Badeau, Talbot, Komer, and their colleagues clung to Nasser, but by 1963 Nasser was not clinging to them. Nasser did not much care for the cocky new regime in Yemen, but he was convinced that his brand of revolutionary pan-Arab nationalism could not bear the loss of prestige of seeing the coup in Yemen fail—certainly not with the Arab monarchs still crowing over the humiliating 1961 collapse of Nasser's union with Syria. For Cold War advantage, the Kennedy administration had hoped to gain ground with Nasser, but Nasser viewed his room for maneuver through the prism of a small, raw, bitter cold war of his own.

At the time, it was hardly clear that Yemen was the coup de grace that was to end the Nasser overture. For one thing, Nasser and Kennedy remained cordial enough to each other even as their countries' relationship eroded. In August 1962, as the Yemen crisis broke, one of Nasser's intelligence officers used America's chief spymaster, CIA head John McCone, to pass along to the president and first lady several gifts from Nasser: a striking silver tea service, an ivory model of a solar boat, a green brocade, and some fine white Egyptian silk.[5] For another, Yemen seemed terribly insignificant, at least at first. "I don't even know where it is," Kennedy cheerfully told British Prime Minister Harold Macmillan in November 1962.[6] But the mote in Kennedy's eye turned out to be a beam in Nasser's.

Moreover, the overture to Nasser had been designed to produce long-term payoffs rather than immediate dividends. Badeau particularly liked to cite one of Dean Acheson's favorite stories, the one "about the farmer who plowed up his turnip crop every week to see how it was doing and then was disappointed when nothing grew."[7] But with Yemen, the president's patience ran out. The frankness of Kennedy's tone to Nasser, once touted as a virtue, now began to sting. In fact, the New Frontier's overture to Egypt wound up disintegrating so dramatically that within months of the outbreak of civil war in Yemen, the Kennedy administration was actually sending the U.S. Air Force into action above the Saudi border to limit

Nasser's appetites—an operation known sourly to White House wags as "Komer's war."[8] Over one tense weekend in 1963, Kennedy called the NSC's Carl Kaysen three times to warn him to watch Yemen closely. "If we are going in there shooting down Egyptian bombers," Kennedy said, "I want to hear about it before we shoot."[9] America and Egypt had gone from the brink of friendship to the brink of war.

Israel watched the Yemen war with apprehension—and sometimes, in Ben-Gurion's case, with alarm. In fact, Yemen would help the United States make its Cold War choices in the Middle East, which would help give Israel the alliance with America it had long sought. In Yemen, Nasser would reveal himself as the captive of inter-Arab politics, rather than a progressive pragmatist interested in working with the West. With Nasser lost, the United States would rely more on its traditional regional partners, the Arab conservatives, and its would-be regional ally, the Jewish state.

Throughout the Yemen crisis, Kennedy's Middle East aides tried repeatedly to use their supposedly improved relationship with Cairo. The logic of the Nasser initiative dictated that new warmth would grant new leverage, which in turn would help the administration to limit the blowback from Nasser's overreaching. Yemen, in other words, was the key test of whether Kennedy could construct something out of constructive engagement. But as the prisoner of his own competition with the Arab monarchs, Nasser felt that he should no more withdraw from Arabia than the Kennedy administration felt it should withdraw from Indochina. Indeed, if the New Frontiersmen understood the irony of lecturing both Egypt and Saudi Arabia about the futility of attempting to impose their own chosen leaderships on an unruly, divided polity in a far-flung corner of the Third World, they did not let on.

THE MAKING OF A QUAGMIRE

Yemen was never much of a state; its south was at perennial odds with the north, its roiling politics were tribal and dizzyingly complex, and the government in the capital of Sanaa often seemed not to govern much more than Sanaa itself. Indeed, the Kennedy administration's interest in the war in Yemen never had very much to do with Yemen itself. "It made little difference to the American position whether Yemen was ruled by an imam or a president, by Nasser, the Saudis or the British," Badeau noted later.[10] What mattered was the regional fallout. So over the course of the 1960s, leaders who knew or cared little for Yemen would find themselves deeply embroiled there—from Nasser, concerned about his pan-Arab prestige; to Kennedy, concerned about his Cold War position; to the British, concerned about their longstanding colonial influence in southern Yemen and their protectorate in nearby Aden; to the Saudis and Jordanians, concerned about their thrones.

The crisis caught almost everyone by surprise. In July 1962, students in Sanaa rioted, shouting their support for Nasser. Cairo radio aired paeans to their heroic struggle against the oppressive, reactionary ruler of Yemen, Imam Ahmad, who styled himself "protector of God's religion." Ahmad — a qat-chewing, autocratic relic with kohl daubed around his eyes and daggers, beads, and bandoleers dangling from his belt — had infuriated Nasser by cutting ties with Egypt in 1961 after Syria left the UAR and by denouncing Nasser's economic program as un-Islamic.[11] On September 19, the elderly Imam Ahmad died in his sleep, to be replaced by his hapless son, Muhammad al-Badr. On September 26, army tanks shelled the Sanaa building where Badr was working, forcing him to flee. Colonel Abdallah Sallal, having left his old job as head of the palace guard to overthrow the man he was supposed to be protecting, declared the existence of the Yemen Arab Republic (YAR) — an unexpected windfall for Nasser and revolutionary Arab nationalism, and an unexpected body blow for the Arab monarchs. Since Nasser had failed to lure Syria back to the pan-Arab fold after its 1961 departure from the union, a success in Yemen for his brand of nationalism would be all the sweeter.

That seems to have been about all Nasser saw of Yemen's complexities at the start. Sallal promptly asked Nasser for help in driving out Badr's royalists, who had fallen back to the hills of northern Yemen to fight a guerrilla war against their usurpers. Nasser dithered for three days about whether to try to help the rebels; while he considered, he realized that he knew so little about the situation in Yemen that he asked Ambassador Badeau for background on the country.[12] Nasser had scorned Badr since Yemen's then–crown prince had visited the Cairo zoo, spotted a heretofore unnoticed qat tree, climbed it, and sat on a branch happily chewing leaves.[13] With a dim view of his foes and little knowledge of what he was getting into, Nasser took the plunge and sent advisers, arms, and material to Sallal. By October 1962, as the rest of the world watched the Cuban missile crisis, Nasser was flooding some 20,000 Egyptian combat troops into Yemen, bristling with Soviet weaponry. He hoped to extend his sway over the Red Sea, harry the British in Aden, rattle the Saudis, and above all save a pan-Arab revolution whose momentum seemed in danger of becoming "irretrievably lost" after the collapse of the union with Syria.[14]

Badeau, Komer, and the other proponents of the Nasser initiative were loath to admit the inescapable conclusion: the Syrian secession of 1961 had not convinced Nasser to focus his attention meekly inward. Rather, it had left Nasser sufficiently embarrassed within the inter-Arab arena that he was willing to recklessly support a revolution far from his borders. After the collapse of the UAR, as the historian Malcolm H. Kerr puts it, the Egyptian government "reversed the course of moderation that it had cautiously developed since 1959 and assumed the stance of the militant revolutionary, uncompromisingly dedicated to the overthrow of its conservative neighbors."[15]

Those neighbors promptly rang the alarm bell. At the American U.N. mission's suite at the Waldorf in New York, Rusk got an earful about Nasser from Saudi Crown Prince Faysal, who was in town for the opening of the U.N. General Assembly and who feared his country might be next on the chopping block.[16] With the help of the similarly anxious Jordanians, the Saudis began quietly sending funds and weapons to the fleeing Yemeni royalists. Yemen's civil war was no longer just Yemen's.

Egyptian Vice President Anwar al-Sadat—the future commander of the 1973 Yom Kippur War, great shatterer of Arab taboos about talking with Israel, and architect of a U.S.–Egyptian rapprochement far more lasting than Nasser's—met with Badeau on September 27 in Cairo to pass along an ostensibly friendly word of advice: Washington should not back up Prince Hassan, the Yemeni royal who had fled to Saudi Arabia and had become the putative new leader of the monarchy. The administration replied that Yemeni internal politics were none of its concern. But Washington drew a red line: the British outpost in Aden—often used to shoulder heavy imperial lifting in the Gulf—was a "vital interest," and Cairo would do well to work with the republican leaders to ensure the U.K. position there remained intact.[17] Three days later, Sadat warned Badeau that the United States should not let itself "unwittingly be twisted around [the] British finger." But he did add that for all Cairo's bad blood with London, it would not goad the republicans to try to add to Britain's difficulties in Arabia. Sadat also asked Badeau whether, since the United States was staying out of the internal Yemeni succession struggle, it might get Saudi Arabia to follow its example. Badeau gently told Sadat not to get carried away. But the U.S. ambassador did agree to meet with the de facto foreign minister of the new Yemeni regime.[18] That brought a howl of protest from Ahmad Zabarah, the Yemeni monarchy's chargé d'affaires in Washington, who urged the administration not to recognize Sallal's new government. "You are not only letting your friends down, but encouraging your enemies," he passionately told Talcott Seelye, the officer from the State Department's division of Near Eastern Affairs (NEA) handling the Arabian Peninsula.[19]

Those friends—especially Saudi Arabia—felt the letdown keenly. "Unfortunately, the Yemen revolt has brought to a boil all Saudi fears of Nasserism," the NSC's Komer wrote Kennedy on October 4. "[T]he House of Saud well knows it might be next." Nasser was having just that message shouted over Egyptian state radio. Crown Prince Faysal—who was, to the administration's relief, in the process of taking over from his brother, the flagging, unimaginative, and widely scorned King Saud—used his U.S. trip to try to enlist Kennedy to the kingdom's defense.[20]

After complaining about American equivocation at an awkward dinner party in New York thrown by U.N. Ambassador Adlai Stevenson, Faysal flew to Washington for an October 5 working lunch with Kennedy, Talbot, Komer, Seelye, and other Middle East aides.[21] Faysal said that the new Yemeni regime could stand only with outside support, which he warned came "[n]ot only from the UAR but also from the Soviet Union." It was a pitch perhaps better suited to Eisenhower than to Kennedy, but JFK did note dourly that both Moscow and Cairo had already recognized the Yemeni revolutionaries.

Faysal linked the Nasser initiative to the current crisis. American assistance to Egypt, Faysal warned, wound up being used to undermine Nasser's neighbors—especially Saudi Arabia, whose overthrow was obviously Nasser's "sole aim." Kennedy pointed out that U.S. aid to Egypt mostly took the form of food assistance, but Faysal was already in full rhetorical flight, warning that the administration was giving aid and comfort to the enemy.

Kennedy seems to have had enough at this point. He tried to lower the volume by asking Faysal what his administration could usefully do to help Saudi Arabia. Get Nasser to stop undermining Middle Eastern monarchies, Faysal replied. Kennedy said that "he doubted very much that our influence with Nasser or with other recipients of United States aid is as great as it is sometimes thought to be." When the discouraged Faysal asked if he could personally convey to King Saud assurances of American friendship, the president, seeing something he could easily do, firmly replied, "Yes, definitely."

After lunch, the principals headed to the more intimate quarters of the White House's upstairs living room. There, Kennedy urged the Saudis to focus on domestic reforms, which Komer had called the surest antidote to Nasserism. Kennedy also offered a few more reassurances, such as moving a few U.S. Navy destroyers into Saudi ports as a display of friendship and expediting the pending sale of several F-5A fighters. But the president made it clear that American sympathy could be limited by Saudi parochialism. With so much of his time being taken up with civil rights questions, the president touched on one particularly grating irritant: the Saudi refusal to let Jews into the country, including members of the U.S. Congress. Dryly, the president assured the Saudi prince that lifting the anti-Semitic ban would hardly trigger "an onrush of transit passengers through the Dhahran International Airport."[22]

The more immediate onrush was of a distinctly different sort: Egyptian troops flooding into Yemen. "I sent a battalion to raise the siege of Sana'a," Nasser cracked ruefully, "and then I reinforce the battalion with a division."[23] As Washington started getting reports of Egyptian army movement, Badeau was dispatched to warn Cairo against military intervention. When Badeau flashed a diplomatic red light to Sadat on October 6, the Egyptian vice president agreed in principle that outsiders should keep out of Yemen. But he then complained that Saudi Arabia had already sent troops into northern and eastern Yemen and, in a new sign of suspicion, asked Badeau whether the administration was pushing King Husayn of Jordan to back his fellow monarchists in Yemen. Badeau denied any U.S. involvement.[24]

Sadat's complaint proved to be a mirror of the monarchs', who also dreaded the thought that America might be backing the other side. In Riyadh, Saud and Faysal likened the first arrival of Egyptian troops on the Arabian Peninsula in over a century to a Latin American violation of the Monroe Doctrine.[25] In Tehran, the shah of Iran fretted that Nasserism might even ultimately win a Persian Gulf foothold.[26]

By October 1962, Yemen was a witches' brew.[27] The British, worried about their Aden protectorate, had decided to support Prince Hassan covertly; Yemeni tribal leaders were choosing sides; Nasser's troops were already on the ground in Sanaa and the western port town of Hodeida; Saudi troops were massing on the Saudi-Yemeni border; and a Jordanian delegation of pro-Hassan advisers was also on the ground.[28] To make matters worse, about 120 Americans were living in the southwestern Yemeni city of Taizz, and the old imamate had let in some Soviet troops for good measure.

All that put the U.S.–Egyptian rapprochement at risk. The White House brushed past Egyptian protestations of innocence; when Ambassador Kamel insisted to Komer that "the UAR was doing absolutely nothing in Yemen; there was only one Egyptian there," Komer merely smiled sardonically.[29] To make things trickier, Nasser's minister of economy, Kaissouni, was back in town to follow up on his previous round of aid discussions, and the State Department wanted to finally sign an expanded, multiyear PL-480 aid agreement for Egypt just as Yemen was going up in flames. An unhappy Komer advised Kennedy to go ahead. The president did—but reluctantly, and with orders to make "make every effort to insure minimum publicity." Cairo was also told to play it down. In the end, Talbot and Kaissouni signed the new aid package quietly on October 8, without any of the attendant publicity that had once been the core of Komer's view of the overture to Egypt.[30]

If the Kennedy administration fretted that it might have to choose between Saudi Arabia and Egypt, Nasser feared that he might have to choose between Yemen and the United States. On October 10, Nasser's closest confidant and frequent back channel—Muhammad Hassanein Haykal, the editor of Egypt's main newspaper, *al-Ahram*—gave Badeau a personal message from the Egyptian president that sought to explain away Nasser's intervention. The conservatives had started meddling first in Yemen, Haykal complained. Now that the kings were in the game, Haykal said, Cairo could not let the republicans "be driven to [the] wall." But the clearly unhappy Haykal also assured Badeau that Nasser "had no intention of embarrassing" Kennedy with the UAR's Yemen policy. Badeau was left with the impression of a government torn between its fear of being dragged into a bruising fight and its fear of letting the Yemeni revolution fail.[31]

Meanwhile, the Yemeni royalists and their allies were putting the blame squarely on Nasser. In Amman, King Husayn passed along to Macomber a furious message from Imam Badr, on the lam in the Yemeni hinterland, where he was trying to reverse "this mad action." (The king assured Macomber that some of Badr's rhetoric "sounds better in Arabic.") "It pains us to inform you that the President of the UAR supported on its first day this irregular action and is doing so until now," Badr seethed. "We are now convinced that the plan for this disorder was devised in Cairo and we are informing you of this very serious interference in the internal affairs of an independent Arab State."[32]

Yemen was fast becoming a no-win situation, Komer decided. If "we come down on UK/Jordan/Saudi side there goes our new relationship with Nasser; if we come down on other side, we open Pandora's box," he wrote Talbot. "If we do nothing, we offend all our friends." Better to take the bull by the horns, Komer figured, and find a way to protect "our investment in Nasser" while preserving the Aden protectorate and the Saudi monarchy. Komer envisioned brokering a package wherein the new Yemeni regime's permanence would be accepted, Nasser would "call off [his] war against Arab kings" and silence his inflammatory radio broadcasts, both Yemen and Egypt would assure the British that Aden was safe, and ties between Arab radicals and conservatives would be reestablished.[33] The State Department agreed, and Badeau was directed to use Haykal as a back channel for some frank talk. The administration, Badeau told his interlocutor, might well find itself drawn into a "real mess" in Yemen if the current standoff between Egypt and the Saudis dragged in the British and the Soviets. In some ways, Kennedy found the new progressive regime in Sanaa more appealing than its hidebound predecessor, but he also shared the Saudis' fears for their own stability and the British's concerns over Aden. He reasoned that Nasser "must satisfy us, Saudis and UK" that Egypt would refrain from making mischief in Saudi Arabia, Jordan, and Aden.[34] Thus began a long and frustrating American quest for a way out of the Yemen morass, even as Soviet-armed

Egyptian troops fought near the Saudi border. The next few months would make it clear that the administration was already in the middle of the "real mess" that Badeau dreaded.

THE SHOCK OF RECOGNITION

The broad design of the administration's plan to restore order in Yemen remained reasonably consistent: the United States would recognize the new regime, both conservative and Nasserite outsiders would butt out of the civil war, and Yemen's new masters would promise not to menace Aden or Saudi Arabia. But getting that complicated sequence moving proved to be excruciating, largely because both Riyadh and Cairo felt that the stakes in Yemen were too high to step back.

The most immediate question—as sticky in Yemen in 1962 as it had been in Syria in 1961—was whether to recognize the new regime. Recognition was one of the Kennedy administration's hole cards, and one that it did not want to play too soon. An increasingly impatient Sadat told Badeau on October 18 that while his government could understand why the White House was slowly feeling its way on recognition, the Yemeni and Egyptian masses saw only "deliberate delay."[35] Komer was reluctant to move too quickly lest Saudi Arabia and Jordan blame the ultimate defeat of the royalists on U.S. recognition of their usurpers.[36] But some State Department officials thought that promptly recognizing the new government in Sanaa would moderate its behavior.[37]

The administration still needed to ensure that its relative agnosticism about the fate of the Yemeni monarchy was not read in the region as a shrug about who ruled in Riyadh and Amman. The Saudis likened recognition of Sallal's regime to "a hunting license to go after Saudi Arabia."[38] Kennedy himself wrote Faysal to pledge America's "deep and abiding interest" in Saudi stability, but the Saudis were not easily mollified.[39] On November 2, they complained that the Yemeni rebels had used Egyptian aircraft to cross the Saudi frontier and bomb five targets within Saudi Arabia itself. Faysal began demanding that Washington steam several U.S. warships, preferably including an aircraft carrier, toward Saudi ports.[40] The administration declined but offered a few less dramatic shows of force, including a joint military exercise later in the year and visits by U.S. warships and aircraft to the oil kingdom, as well as the loan of a dozen F-86 warplanes.[41]

To the administration's chagrin, it was not the only one flexing its muscles. The White House was particularly annoyed by Jordan's behavior. "We and the British totally subsidize this artificial country," fumed the

NSC's Komer. "If King Hussein is so worried about Nasserism, his best defense against it is to strengthen Jordan's own internal fabric, not try to lick Nasser in Yemen (a fight he can't win)."[42] Nevertheless, the young king went along with a request from King Saud and sent six of his Hawker Hunter jets to Taif to help his brother monarch ward off attacks from Egypt and Yemen, as well as 62 military advisers and a cache of rifles.[43] Husayn told Kennedy that the free world could no more ignore subversion in Yemen than it could ignore missiles in Cuba.

The partner in America's oldest special relationship also watched Yemen with unease. The Middle East's erstwhile colonial overlords, the British, were worried about their old Gulf and Hashimite friends, but they were most immediately concerned about Aden, one of their key redoubts east of Suez. The government of Harold Macmillan—a wry, shrewd Tory who was usually one of the president's favorite foreign leaders—was torn over whether or not to recognize the new Yemen Arab Republic; the Foreign Office was not terribly perturbed by the fall of the wheezing old imamate, but the Colonial Office was eager to give Nasser "a bloody nose."[44] The arrival of Soviet-armed Egyptian troops ominously close to Aden let the Colonial Office carry the day.[45]

When Kennedy sent a letter to the key regional players—the new Yemeni government, the Jordanians, the Egyptians, and the Saudis—spelling out his plan, Washington and London's traditional Middle East friends hissed.[46] "This thing is actually what Nasser wants," Crown Prince Faysal said coldly to U.S. Ambassador Pete Hart. "It therefore means that Nasser's point of view has been adopted and is imposed on us." Neither Jordan nor Saudi Arabia was ready yet to give up on their royalist brethren in Yemen, but the United States seemed to be. "I plead with you not to trust Nasser," Faysal continued, visibly fighting for control of his rage, "and not to accord your recognition [to Sallal's regime] before [the Egyptians] have withdrawn all their forces."[47] Faysal was so furious at the administration for going first to Nasser that he picked up Kennedy's letter in front of Hart and "slammed it down on the table."[48]

But after having been yelled at for over a month, the administration was growing increasingly deaf to Saudi and Jordanian protests. Indeed, Komer hoped that the shock of recognition would force Riyadh and Amman to abandon their doomed and self-destructive quest to restore the Yemeni royalists.[49] Egypt's response to the peace plan—which, after all, did lock in its pan-Arab triumph in Yemen—was less ear-splitting than the Saudi wail of despair.[50] Komer came to entertain visions of luring Nasser, too, away from his own self-destructive folly. "Our hunch is that Nasser is bleeding a bit from his extensive commitment to Yemen," Komer told Kennedy, "and is rather grateful for our offer to help close it out."[51]

Thus began a few weeks of wrangling over the content of the statements from Nasser and Sallal, which had to assuage Saudi, British, and Jordanian anxieties enough to merit U.S. recognition of the new Yemeni regime. By mid-December, the sides had hammered out acceptable language for both Cairo and Sanaa. The former promised to undertake a phased pullout of its troops in Yemen in tandem with a Saudi and Jordanian retreat from the frontier; the latter promised to be bound by the previous regime's treaty commitments, to discourage Yemenis in Aden from rebellion, and generally to refrain from disturbing its neighbors.[52] On December 18, Yemen released its communiqué; on December 19, Egypt followed suit; and around noon that day, the State Department announced that the Kennedy administration had recognized the new republic in Yemen. "We may turn out to be wrong, but we acted with Jordanian and Saudi interests in mind," said Kennedy in a personal message designed to calm down King Husayn.[53] Keeping on good terms with both Arab revolutionaries and conservatives was proving excruciating.

EYEBALL TO EYEBALL

Jack Kennedy, of course, had bigger problems than Yemen. In the fall of 1962, Kennedy's energy was devoted not to the Middle East but to keeping the planet from extinction after U.S. intelligence discovered Soviet missiles in Cuba. As it happened, however, at least some of the Cuban missile crisis itself was influenced by past Middle East traumas. After all, Khrushchev divined a basic lesson from his 1956 nuclear saber-rattling over Suez: "the way to succeed with foreign powers was to rattle rockets in their faces."[54] That did not prove a terribly prudent moral in 1962.

The special Executive Committee (or ExComm) of the NSC that the president convened to manage the crisis actually gave Nasser a walk-on part in the drama. On October 23, during the ExComm's 10 A.M. meeting in the Cabinet Room, the president's advisers—including CIA Director McCone and Llewellyn ("Tommy") Thompson, a veteran Sovietologist brought in to interpret the Kremlin's moves—tried to sort out how Adlai Stevenson should make the U.S. case at the United Nations. As the meeting wound down, McCone suggested showing photos of the Cuban missile sites to noncommunist ambassadors. This bit of show-and-tell would line up support at the United Nations for the American quarantine of Cuba, expose the Kremlin's prevarication, and spare the administration from having to display the photos in public. Over the phone, Stevenson was enthusiastic. "He was going to go ahead with it with a friendly ambassador," McCone told the rest of the ExComm. "He's going to think about the UAR and Romania."

"Well, I wouldn't think about the UAR," replied Thompson, who was not about to classify Nasser as friendly.[55]

Despite Thompson's skepticism, the Egyptian president's reaction to the showdown in Cuba was restrained. On October 22, Nasser was among the world leaders who received letters detailing the White House's stern reaction to Khrushchev's missile gamble. On November 1, with the crisis over, Nasser handed Badeau a brief response to Kennedy in which he declared that the time had passed for wrangling over the nature of both the Cuban missile bases and the American response. Nasser certainly did not endorse the U.S. blockade, and he gave "all parties to the dispute"— Kennedy, Khrushchev, and Castro—credit for "wisdom, sound assessment and sense of responsibility." But he did not hew to Moscow's party line, let alone Havana's. "We deeply appreciate the fact that the American measures—irrespective of our opinion thereon—were carried out in a way devoid of aggressive incitement," Nasser wrote, which pleased Kennedy's aides and must have set Khrushchev's teeth gnashing. "We appreciate your pledge not to invade Cuba militarily," Nasser added, "and we feel that this pledge was a genuine contribution to easing tension." He concluded by noting that America's "might and prestige" gave it more ability to "consolidate peace . . . than any other" country—including, presumably, the Soviet Union.[56]

An appreciative Komer advised Bundy and Kaysen to show Nasser's letter to Kennedy as an "obvious note of congratulations on [his] handling of [the] Cuban crisis . . . however carefully drafted." The letter meant "(a) Nasser hopes we aren't sore at [the] UAR attitude during [the] crisis, which was as good as could be expected; (b) he wants to continue the dialogue with JFK and has seized this chance to do so; (c) he's still anxious about our attitude toward Yemen."[57]

While pushing his luck with Kennedy over Yemen, Nasser clearly did not want to overdo it over Cuba, too. One anonymous, high-ranking Egyptian diplomat let it be known "that he estimated that 90% of the Egyptian people fully understood the reasons for the United States action." Talbot, in response, suggested that Rusk tell Egyptian Deputy Foreign Minister Zulfikar Sabri that one would never know that Egyptians were so understanding from reading the UAR press.[58] The State Department took Nasser's parting words about American uniqueness "to mean that Nasser fully appreciates the relative strength of the US and weakness of the USSR as demonstrated in the recent crisis." They added that Nasser, recalling the Kremlin's inability to help him out during the 1958 crises in Lebanon and Jordan, was now telling his advisers "that he was among the first to recognize the essential weakness of Khrushchev's military position."[59]

There was also an unexpected—and deadly—nexus between Egypt and the Cuban missile crisis. In the spring of 1962, the United States put some 40,000 troops through the paces of what the Pentagon brass euphoniously called "Lantphibex-62," the largest military drill ever carried out in the Caribbean area. In early April, Kennedy and the visiting shah of Iran personally watched 10,000 American soldiers storm from 34 amphibious ships onto a North Carolina beach. When the Kremlin got wind of Lantphibex and "an even larger practice invasion" scheduled off of Puerto Rico's Vieques Island, it began thinking of more ways to soothe the jittery post–Bay of Pigs Castro about his place in Moscow's affections.[60]

Meanwhile, both Castro and Nasser were waiting impatiently for shipments of SA-2 antiaircraft launchers, including V-750 missiles. The overburdened Soviet defense industry simply did not have enough SA-2s to go around. Earlier, Moscow had seen no reason to offend the prickly Nasser by delaying the arrival of his SA-2s "if the security of Castro's regime was not immediately threatened."[61] But now, worried that Kennedy might be tempted into a full-blown U.S. invasion of Cuba, the Soviet Union weighed its priorities differently. On April 12, the Kremlin decided to send the very SA-2s originally earmarked for Nasser to Castro instead. Cuba was now a more pressing Soviet arms priority than Egypt.[62] The snub was yet another irritant in Soviet-Egyptian relations. Without access to Egyptian archives, there is no real way to know whether this particular slight was part of the chain of events that brought the United States and Egypt tantalizingly close to reconciliation, but the missile diversion certainly was part of the chain of events that brought the world ominously close to incineration. On October 27, one of the SA-2s originally intended to wind up in Egypt was fired instead from a Cuban missile base located near Banes, on Cuba's northern coast, with lethal accuracy. It brought down a U-2 spy plane flown by Major Rudolf Anderson—the lone American fatality of the Cuban missile crisis.

THINGS FALL APART

After the missile crisis, the administration continued to adjust uneasily to a newly tense Middle East. The quest for closer ties with Egypt was becoming a long twilight struggle. Still, the State Department remained committed to the overture's underlying logic. But if the State Department was still dangling carrots before Nasser, the White House was increasingly partial to sticks.

On Christmas Eve 1962, Kennedy sent along a message for Badeau to deliver to the Egyptian leader. Washington's "very substantial aid" to Cairo still betokened a desire for better ties, Kennedy told Nasser, but the Yemen morass threatened "our vital interests in Aden, the Persian Gulf area, and throughout the Arabian Peninsula." JFK sternly reminded Nasser that the United States stood "fully behind the integrity of Prince Faysal's regime."[63] When Badeau met with Nasser, the two men's earlier friendly talk of foreign aid, anticommunism, and economic development was replaced with uneasy wrangling about Yemen and the heated rhetoric on Cairo radio.[64]

Meanwhile, a discouraged King Husayn complained to Ambassador Macomber that he and Faysal "stood out like [a] sore thumb" for backing the West. The United States, in particular, "took them for granted while deferring to Nasser," who was now "getting what he wanted" from America despite his massive intervention in Yemen.[65] In a rare angry interview with UPI's Middle East correspondent, the bitter king not only accused the administration of "shattering" regional stability, he actually sharpened his quotes when the reporter read them back to him.[66] Nor was Husayn the only disappointed monarch. "I beg you not to be deceived, as I was by the promises of President Nasser, and only to accept as proof deeds such as you insisted on from Cuba," cabled the erstwhile amir of Yemen, Badr, from his exile in Riyadh.[67]

The year ended on a sour note: a UAR fighter launched an attack on an alleged royalist supply site at Najran, just on the Saudi side of the Saudi-Yemeni border. Ambassador Hart was dispatched to warn Faysal not to stoke the flames by arming the royalists, but the administration's real anger was reserved for Cairo's attempts to cow Riyadh. Nasser protested that the Saudis were using Najran to stockpile arms for the royalists, but an unmoved Rusk sent Badeau to register the administration's strongest protest to date. The White House had obligingly recognized Sallal's regime, Rusk noted, to show its faith in Nasser and Sallal's good intentions. But if "that confidence is now shattered by provocative attacks on Saudi territory," the secretary of state warned, it was hard to see how the "policy of cooperation with [the] UAR to which [the] US attaches [the] highest importance could remain unaffected." And for Badeau's information, Rusk attached an even direr warning: the net effect of Egypt's bombings and radio propaganda was to bring the administration close to scuttling the overture to Nasser.[68]

After the Najran airstrike, the State Department formally told its regional embassies that a Nasser visit was "postponed pending some progress in [the] Yemen situation."[69] The first time Kennedy seriously contemplated a Nasser visit, domestic politics pushed it off; now, the delay was caused by Yemen. In the end, the two men would never meet.

Faced by the prospect of tit-for-tat bombings by Egypt and Saudi Arabia, the NSC now began to push to get tougher with Nasser, over the objections of a reluctant State Department. American frustration was exacerbated by UAR propaganda, such as a New Year's Day broadcast on the Voice of the Arab Nation radio station that urged Arabs to "blow American influence out of [the] Arabian Peninsula."[70] Thus goaded, the U.S. policy turned toward reassuring Faysal and deterring Nasser. "I'd like to see us threaten him a bit," Komer growled. But he did not think Nasser was beyond redemption, so a "few harsh words now may save our Nasser policy rather than wreck it."[71]

In Cairo, an increasingly fretful Badeau also favored sternly warning Nasser but feared that Washington was about to repeat what he saw as the key error of the Eisenhower approach: condescension and the suspension of aid.[72] Linkage between more aid and less mischief seemed virtually inevitable, though, and there was a steely tone to the letter from Kennedy that Badeau was ordered to deliver on January 20. Kennedy repeated his mantra that frank dialogue was one of the gains in U.S.–UAR relations but warned that "misunderstandings" from the Yemen affair could "prejudice our growing rapport." Cairo seemed to suspect that Washington was "pursuing a double policy in Yemen" by failing to ensure that the Saudis lived up to their end of the disengagement bargain. Not so, Kennedy wrote. The administration was pursuing its own Arabian interests, not backing the Saudis' doomed support of the hapless royalists. But the Najran bombings, Kennedy added, had not helped a whit. Nor could Washington force London to recognize the new Yemeni regime when Sallal blustered about menacing Aden. "I see no reason," JFK wrote, why America's interests in Saudi Arabia, Aden, and the wider Gulf "need impede mutually satisfactory relations between us . . . I hope this letter will help clear the air between us." He concluded, "Many people in both of our countries question whether good relations between us are really possible. I think they are wrong, but it is up to us to prove them wrong."[73]

On January 24, Nasser invited Badeau to a 70-minute meeting to respond to Kennedy's letter. Egypt would be able to disengage, Nasser complained, if the Saudis would just stop arming and funding some of Yemen's tribes, who were de facto mercenaries backing the royalists. He was open, he added, to trying disengagement again with an outside mediator.[74] U.N. Secretary-General U Thant wound up naming the veteran Middle East hand Ralph Bunche as his special Yemen emissary.

The administration's attempts to prod Nasser to find a way out of Yemen may have proved too subtle by half. Nasser seems to have been more encouraged by Kennedy's December recognition of the YAR than he was discouraged by Kennedy's January reprimand. One night in early 1963, Nasser used parachutists to drop 108 bundles of arms and ammunition on the Saudi coast north of Jidda; early the next morning, an American special-forces mission on a training flight for Saudi pilots spotted the air-drop and tipped off the livid Saudis, who accusingly displayed the bundles at a nearby barracks.[75] But simple embarrassment over being caught red-handed was not going to end the Egyptian intervention. With the battle-field pendulum now swinging back in the royalists' direction, Nasser seemed to figure that he was stuck. By February 1963, Egypt had some 40,000 troops tied down in Yemen.[76] "Conclusion—this peanut war will be with us a long time yet," Komer resignedly wrote Bundy.[77]

Nasser would not pull back from Yemen, but Kennedy could pull back from Nasser. Increasingly, the administration was being pressed to do just that by a key Middle East player: the barons of the oil industry, who strode confidently through Washington's corridors of power to explain why what-ever was bad for Saudi Arabia's well-being was bad for America's economy and why Kennedy should never have departed from Dulles's old line that Nasser was a menace.[78] Finally, Big Oil and the Israel lobby had found something they could agree on: Nasser's villainy.

To mollify the petroleum industry, Kennedy sent Terry Duce—a former vice president of the Arabian-American Oil Company (Aramco), the giant U.S. firm that held Saudi Arabia's first oil concession—to Saudi Arabia to meet with Faysal on the administration's behalf.[79] Talbot and his aides also met repeatedly with oil executives, including a Yemen briefing for top officials from Aramco, Standard Oil, Texaco, Gulf Oil, and Mobil on January 11. On January 28, Kermit Roosevelt—a top ex-ecutive at Gulf Oil and a man not known for eschewing meddling in the Middle East—dropped by the NSC to see Komer. Roosevelt, whom Komer chummily referred to as Kim, brought a blunt message: Nasser was not a man America could do business with "because our interests and his are simply incompatible." Turning Nasser inward was a fantasy; each time Nasser dwelled on internal development, he "found it so frus-trating" that he "turned back to foreign adventures." Roosevelt also com-plained about "State's failure to keep the oil companies clued in," which was creating misunderstandings. Komer replied that they would "try to do a better job."[80]

Big Oil was hopping mad about the menace Nasser posed to Saudi Arabia—so angry, in fact, that Kennedy himself had begun to keep an eye on the Yemen mess. In an Oval Office meeting on February 25, the presi-dent began by pointing out a blistering column by Joseph Alsop, one of the capitol's leading pundits, that claimed that the State Department was thwarting efforts to head off an Egyptian invasion of Saudi Arabia. Alsop blamed Talbot and the "eminent Middle East do-gooder" Badeau for the hopelessly naïve "be-nice-to-Nasser policy."[81] Alsop's source, Kennedy said, was probably Kim Roosevelt. So what, JFK asked, was Big Oil's beef?

Undersecretary of State for Political Affairs George McGhee replied that "they couldn't abide seeing Nasser win."

The meeting also marked a new nadir for Kennedy's Egypt policy: the attempt to woo Nasser became reduced to an attempt to deter him from waging war on Saudi Arabia. Over Assistant Secretary of Defense for International Security Affairs Paul Nitze's objections, the State Department suggested sending a "plate glass fighter squadron" to Jidda, the Red Sea city that served as the part-time seat of the Saudi government. For Nasser, crossing the Saudi border would then mean engaging the squadron, shattering the glass, and setting off a very angry superpower fire alarm. The Pentagon hated the idea of using a handful of jets as cannon fodder for the entire Egyptian airforce, but the Saudis' unquenchable anxieties about Nasserism made it a risk that might well have to be run. Assuming that Faysal would not stop helping the royalists, the White House might simply have to spook Nasser out of going to war against the House of Saud. Kennedy himself was more sanguine than some of his advisers. He told his aides that he not only thought that Nasser would not invade Saudi Arabia, he thought that Faysal would turn down the offer to harbor American pilots. Just the same, Kennedy decided to send Ellsworth Bunker, a former U.S. ambassador, to ask Faysal if he would swap suspending aid to the royalists for the protection of the fighter tripwire.[82]

With Nasser's planes still bombing Najran, the administration's patience began to wear thin. On March 2, Kennedy sent another personal message to Nasser via the embassy in Cairo. Kennedy's language was tougher this time, and Rusk's covering instructions to Badeau were tougher still. The president himself spoke of a "real risk that events [in Yemen] might lead to a collision involving the interests of our two countries." Egypt seemed not to have gotten the message about America's insistence that Saudi Arabia be left unmolested. Unless Egypt stopped attacking Saudi Arabia, the administration would have to rethink its entire Egypt policy. Nasser needed to weigh which he valued more: harassing Saudi Arabia or warming ties to the West. As it stood, the continued Egyptian attacks on Saudi Arabia were forcing the administration "into choosing Saudi Arabia over the UAR," however reluctantly. The sooner Nasser shaped up, the better. But for now, Rusk warned, "current UAR actions are running US-UAR relations onto [the] rocks."[83]

Nasser did not yet know about the suggestion to use American forces on March 3, when he sent Kennedy a lengthy response. Nasser's letter tried to remain cordial to Washington but seethed at Riyadh and Amman. Arab nationalists fretted that Kennedy's Yemen policy was tied up with the regional reactionaries; Nasser happened to "personally agree" with these doubts, but he was simultaneously (and confusingly) "sure of the soundness of [Kennedy's] aims." Nasser agreed to avoid clashes on the Yemeni borders and denounced "outside intervention in the affairs of Yemen." But Faysal and his fellow Arab reactionaries had started the fight, Nasser complained, so he'd had to respond to Sallal's request for help against the attacks coming from Najran. "God knows how anxious we were to spare every drop of Arab blood," Nasser wrote, but he had to make it clear that Saudi and Jordanian aggression would not "go unpunished."[84]

Kennedy, unmoved, again warned Nasser to show restraint and not threaten Saudi Arabia.[85] On March 4, after Badeau briefed Nasser on the forthcoming mediation efforts by Bunker and Bunche, a thoughtful silence descended. "All right," Nasser finally said, "I will tell Marshal Amr to stop the attacks for the immediate future while we see how the missions get along."[86]

After hearing back from Badeau, Komer concluded that Nasser's response to being read the riot act was "just about as responsive as could be expected. . . . After justifying his bombings as intended merely to cut off Saudi gun-running rather than to overthrow Faysal, he in effect says he'll hold off further attacks for a few weeks to give our mediation efforts a chance."[87] Still, the NSC aide wrote a few days later, "let's not fall all over ourselves to tell Nasser we still love him at this point."[88] Komer seemed concerned that Kennedy, never Nasser's greatest fan, was on the verge of souring on the entire overture, which could set America's position in the Arab world back to the days of Eisenhower and Dulles. "It's one thing to defend [the] Saudis against aggression," Komer noted with, even for him, striking bluntness. "It's another to declare we choose the kings over the bulk of the Arab world; that would be the real way to lose our oil."[89]

The most elegant way to avoid having to make that choice was to make Yemen go away. At 4:30 P.M. on March 11, Kennedy held a meeting on Yemen with several top aides, including Rusk, Talbot, McGhee, Nitze, Bundy, Kaysen, Komer, and the recently returned Bunker. The special emissary reported that Faysal was worried that he was being abandoned by the United States but reckoned that, on balance, disengagement was still doable. But that entailed overriding the Pentagon and sending U.S. planes as a tripwire. Kennedy added that the key seemed to be getting Saudi Arabia to stop bailing out the Yemeni royalists. "[I]f we got Faysal turned off," Kennedy pointed out, "we have got a good line with Nasser."[90] This, of course, would take some doing. Nasser's goal, Faysal had told Bunker, was to "crush him."[91] A weary Komer sighed that the "main thrust of our effort still must be to get Faysal to disengage before he commits suicide."[92]

In early April, the administration tried again, sending Bunker shuttling back to the region for a round of migraine-inducing diplomacy. He carried a personal message from Kennedy for Nasser, pointing out the administration's evenhanded concern for the integrity of both Saudi Arabia and the YAR, for both Aden's security and Egypt's position.[93] On April 3, at 6 P.M., Bunker and Badeau met with Nasser. Their proposal, which had been recalibrated after Bunker's earlier soundings, called for a careful sequence of disengagement moves: the Saudis would cut off aid to the Yemeni royalists, a 20-kilometer demilitarized zone would be set up along the Saudi-Yemeni border, Egypt would start pulling its troops out of Yemen within a fortnight of the Saudi severance, Nasser would press Sallal to treat his neighbors responsibly, and the United Nations or some other mediating body would work with the combatants to oversee the disengagement process.[94] Nasser signed on. On April 6, Bunker met again with Faysal and got the Saudi leader to agree in principle to cut off the Yemeni royalists—provided Nasser stopped attacking the Saudis and began pulling his troops out of Yemen.

Gratified, the administration began planning more training exercises on Saudi soil, as well as looking into sending the U.S. Air Force (USAF) tripwire squadron.[95] It also began selling disengagement to its allies, including the resolutely anti-Nasser Saudis and a Tory government in London slow to trust Cairo. During one phone conversation, Kennedy and Macmillan got into a lengthy wrangle over Yemen until the president got bored, suggested that the British prime minister speak instead to Washington's Yemen expert, and handed the receiver over to a startled Komer. The NSC aide, who had never so much as spoken with Macmillan before, swallowed hard and carried on with the argument. "Is the President still there? I presume he's gone," Macmillan said plaintively after he and Komer had gone around in circles for awhile. "No," replied Komer. "The President is sitting right here." So he was: JFK had listened to the whole exchange, puffing on a cigar and grinning broadly.[96]

The administration found itself caught between Faysal, who thought that U.S. aid to Nasser gave America the leverage to get Egypt out of Yemen, and Nasser, who thought that America's oil-related ties to Saudi Arabia gave it the leverage to get Faysal to stop backing the royalists. In fact, all that Bunker and company could do was keep hectoring both obstinate sides. On April 15, Nasser and Faysal finally agreed to pull their troops out of Yemen simultaneously and make room for a U.N.–supervised demilitarized zone of 20 kilometers on each side of the Saudi-Yemeni border.[97] Three days later, Kennedy wrote Nasser to thank him for his "constructive and statesmanlike approach" to the Bunker shuttle; a similar note was passed along to Faysal. Nasser had told Badeau that he feared that U.S. policy toward Egypt might have shifted over the course of the Yemen crisis. But Kennedy now told Nasser that "United States policy has not changed, nor do I see any *current* reason to change it"—with the clear hint that more bad behavior could mean real trouble.[98]

Even if the Kennedy administration did not yet see Yemen as a sign that the Nasser rapprochement had failed, the Israelis begged to differ. As Sadat would later complain, Israeli diplomats worked determinedly during this period at "creating a rift between the United States and Egypt."[99] Such an Israeli strategy was clear enough during a 75-minute Washington meeting in early April between Undersecretary of State for Political Affairs U. Alexis Johnson and Shimon Peres, the future Israeli prime minister who in April 1963 was a young protégé of Ben-Gurion's and a precocious deputy defense minister. Peres urged the State Department to see Nasser as a regional foe. In the long run, Peres concluded with breathtaking inaccuracy, the "overthrow of Hussein and Saud-Faisal [was] unavoidable," but for now, both Israel and the United States should do what they could to prop the monarchs up. The administration, Peres told Johnson, was "too reluctant" to push Nasser toward the peace table with Israel. Conditions might "not be so propitious five years hence." (This time, Peres got it right: in five years, the region would still be shaking after the earthquake of the Six Day War.) And Nasser was more menacing than the Americans seemed to realize, Peres added. The Israeli government had "definite information" that Egypt had used poison gas during the Yemen war—as searing and traumatic a charge as an Israeli official could make, and one that is now widely thought to have been true.[100]

Peres got to deliver his anti-Nasser message at the highest possible level later during his visit. On April 5, Peres went to the White House to meet Mike Feldman. While strolling through the executive mansion, the pair bumped into President Kennedy. Whether this encounter was impromptu or not—such hallway coincidences are often not entirely coincidental— Kennedy asked Peres if they could meet later in the day. During their chat, Peres called Jordan Israel's "major danger point" and Nasser Israel's greatest foe. Turmoil in Amman, if directly or indirectly backed by Nasser, could well prompt an Israeli intervention. Egypt, Peres told Kennedy, was "the only Arab country that Israel really fears."[101]

Increasingly, America's traditional Middle East friends were starting to know the feeling.

THE COUP FLU

As 1963 wore on, the regional consequences of the showdown in Arabia became dangerous. Over one anxious April weekend, Washington was forced to confront both its biggest Middle Eastern war scare since the collapse of the UAR two years earlier and the prospect of the fall of one of its conservative regional linchpins, Jordan. Ironically, the parties whose rashness the Kennedy administration most feared during the April crisis were those it had done the most to reach out to: Egypt and Israel. Only seven years after Suez, some U.S. officials—including not only State Department Arabists but Kennedy himself—still worried that Israel might solve its security dilemmas by lashing out. By the same token, only five years after the West had intervened to prop up Jordan and Lebanon from Nasserite agitation in 1958, the president's advisers were dramatically less concerned that Nasser was a communist stooge but increasingly dubious about their ability to do business with him.

The fuse began burning on February 8. That day, with ideological ballast provided by the Ba'ath Party—a power-hungry group of self-styled progressives who disdained the doddering Arab kings, jostled with Nasser, and yearned for the chance to try out their own mix of socialism and authoritarianism—Iraqi army units staged a coup in Baghdad. They replaced Qasim with Nasser's old Iraqi champion, Abd al-Salam Arif. Ever since 1958, when Qasim's own coup had toppled the pro-Western Hashimite monarchy that had previously ruled Iraq, Nasser and Qasim had nurtured a genuine dislike for each other. Qasim's own subsequent crackdown on Iraqi Nasserites did not help. Nasser considered Qasim a deviationist rather than a revolutionary fellow traveler, and no tears were shed in Cairo when the Ba'ath finally yanked him off the stage. The Kennedy administration was similarly dry-eyed over the fall of Qasim. "He was a fanatic and we just didn't get along with him," Komer remembered later.[102] At the time, Komer wrote Kennedy that Qasim's fall was "almost certainly a net gain for our side. . . . Nasser is trying to embrace the new crew, but we suspect he's whistling in the wind."[103] The White House quickly decided to recognize the new regime and even proved willing to entertain minor arms sales.

Iraq was not the only Arab state susceptible to the coup flu. Hafiz al-Asad and other Ba'athists in Syria welcomed the news of Qasim's fall.[104] In early March, Syrian army units launched another successful coup in Damascus. The administration's initial read of the new regime pegged it as pan-Arabist and Ba'athist but not communist.

In March and April 1963, the far-left, modernizing, new dictatorships hammered out a tripartite agreement in principle on a new and expanded UAR. An April 18 letter from Kennedy to Nasser ended with an at least mildly disingenuous note of congratulations to Nasser and his "Iraqi and Syrian collaborators" on the previous day's triumphant signing ceremony, but Nasser scarcely needed the encouragement.[105] Nasser bullied his new comrades at the union talks. "They were his clients," noted the historian

Malcolm Kerr, "and he addressed them as such."[106] Nasser gave Michel Aflaq, the Ba'ath's leading intellectual and principal theorist, "a particularly miserable time, dismissing his twenty years of intellectual endeavour as a university don might reject a dull student's research essay," as Kerr put it. Briefly cowed, both Syria and Iraq adopted new flags with three stars to symbolize the new three-part union. But the Egyptian leader's swagger was short-lived: the Syrian Ba'athists began, predictably enough, to tilt toward Baghdad, providing a regional counterpoise to Cairo. Facing a newly invigorated Ba'ath, Nasser began to regret having a huge chunk of his combat-ready troops—between a third and a half, the NSC figured—tied down in Yemen. Sure enough, as the new Ba'athist regimes consolidated power, they proved obsessed with the idea of staying ahead of Nasser.[107]

Jerusalem was thinking something similar, albeit with different motivations. Most Israelis were dismayed to see pan-Arabism cresting again after Syria's 1961 defection, but few were more distressed than the prime minister. An agitated Ben-Gurion sent Kennedy a personal message on April 26, noting with alarm the attempt to reconstitute the late, unlamented UAR. The new union's founding communiqué had spoken of a "military union" to "liberate Palestine," Ben-Gurion noted, but Nasser continued to lap up "large-scale financial aid from the United States and other Western powers." That served "to set Russian arms in action against Israel." Ben-Gurion urged Kennedy to push for a joint U.S.–Soviet statement promising to cut off aid to any Middle Eastern aggressor. While Israel appreciated Kennedy's groundbreaking August 1962 decision to sell the Jewish state defensive Hawk surface-to-air missiles, it now regretfully felt "that in the light of new offensive weapons being prepared by Israel's neighbors, the Hawk alone is not a deterrent."[108] Meanwhile, Israel deployed more troops along its border with Jordan.

In fact, many other Israeli officials—including Avraham Harman, Israel's ambassador to Washington—thought Ben-Gurion was panicking. But the Old Man's anxiety soon became Kennedy's problem. The day that Egypt, Iraq, and Syria signed the tripartite declaration, a wave of unrest broke in Jordan. Pan-Arabist agitation had gone from a rumble to a roar, and Yemen had served as an amplifier: King Husayn's intervention on behalf of the Yemeni imamate had been deeply unpopular among Jordan's largely Palestinian citizenry and the all-important Jordanian army. In mid-November 1962, the commander of the Jordanian air force and two Hawker Hunter pilots had embarrassingly defected to Cairo.[109] Now, student demonstrators on the Jordanian-controlled West Bank cheered the new UAR on, unsettling King Husayn, whose prime minister, Wasfi Tell, had to resign after losing a no-confidence motion.[110] Suddenly, the coup flu looked like it might become an epidemic.

America's man in Amman was William B. Macomber, a former Dulles adviser with an abiding sympathy for moderate Arab monarchs and a friendly relationship with his Democratic boss. During an Oval Office meeting on one of Macomber's trips back to Washington, an amused Kennedy teasingly asked the single Macomber about King Husayn's recent wedding and asked when he was going to follow suit.[111]

But such amusing exchanges were far off in the spring of 1963, when Macomber abruptly found himself on the hot seat. On April 21, Macomber warned his superiors stateside that Jordan was effectively under martial law.[112] Meanwhile, Cairo's Voice of the Arab Nation radio called upon the "free valiant men in Arab Jordan" to topple King Husayn, make Jordan the fourth component of the UAR, and annihilate Israel. The Jordanian people had made Husayn a "laughing stock," crowed the Egyptian announcer. "All that remains is for you to overthrow his throne forever."[113] By late April, the State Department was getting word that the rioting in Jordan could turn into a full-blown, Nasserite coup. At the United Nations, a grim Ralph Bunche warned Adlai Stevenson that he had never seen the Jordanian U.N. ambassador so worried.[114] Meanwhile, Israeli officials tried to prod the United States into backing the embattled king by a campaign of leaks (some of dubious veracity) to the country's ferociously competitive and notoriously scoop-addled media, including an April 25 story in *Ma'ariv* reporting that State Department officials had revealed to Israeli Ambassador Harman that the United States "would stand by Hussein."[115]

On April 27, Undersecretary of State George Ball called Defense Secretary Robert S. McNamara at 8:50 A.M. to ask where to deploy the Sixth Fleet and whether the Pentagon could evacuate American citizens in Jordan. "The situation is that it would appear to be an army or military coup done with the complete knowledge of the UAR," Ball told McNamara over the phone. "It's all a part of that whole business that's been going on in Iraq and Syria. The real problem is whether the Israelis will sit still."

"Suppose they didn't?" McNamara asked.[116]

That, in a nutshell, was the administration's instant new preoccupation. The State Department was seized with anxiety that the sudden appearance of a radical regime on Israel's eastern flank would prod Ben-Gurion to sweep into the West Bank—which could in turn trigger an Arab-Israeli war. Israel "may decide for military action in Jordan or Egypt, or both," the State Department warned its regional ambassadors.[117] Years later, both Macomber and Feldman said that Kennedy might have sent in the Marines to save Husayn.

At 10:15 A.M., in a 45-minute Oval Office meeting, Kennedy and several top aides—including Ball, McNamara, Feldman, Bundy, and Komer—

sprang into crisis-management mode.[118] The rebels, Ball reported, "seemed Baathist but friendly to Nasser." In mere weeks, the UAR had gone from being a sour old fiction to swelling to include not only Egypt, Syria, and Iraq but perhaps a post-Hashimite Jordan as well. Suddenly, Cairo radio's boasts sounded vastly less like hollow braggadocio.

Kennedy's two major immediate worries were Israel and the 500 or so U.S. citizens in the area. The latter problem was reasonably easy to handle: McNamara recommended airlifting the Americans out from some nearby Jerusalem airfields. But the Israelis, Ball said, might either "rectify their lines in the Jerusalem area or take over the entire West Bank." Facing the specter of a Nasserite Jordan on his flank, Ben-Gurion would probably want as much buffer as he could get. Kennedy pointed out that "obviously the UAR would not give Israel any guarantee in return for being allowed to incorporate Jordan in the new UAR." Jordan might become the cockpit of a tussle between Nasser and Ben-Gurion.

The president then jumped to the heart of the wider policy matter. What, he asked his aides, had "we gained from our policy toward Nasser? He was obviously a coming force in the Middle East and we naturally wanted to stay on the right side of him, but what about the growing accusation that our support was helping him pursue expansionist policies?" Kennedy was particularly worried that Israel — or its lobby, or its friends in Congress — would blame a naive administration, arguing that U.S. foreign aid to Nasser had emboldened the pan-Arabists and triggered the current crisis.

In response, James Grant of NEA offered the usual defense for engagement with Nasser, which he said had moderated Nasser's behavior. Komer added that Nasser seemed not to be actively pursuing an anti-Israel policy. But neither justification entirely answered the president's question. The more ground Egypt gained in the inter-Arab arena, the more it alarmed Israel and the Arab conservatives, and the more difficult it became for the administration to defend the efficacy of constructive engagement with Nasser.

In this inflamed climate, Kennedy ruled out two pro-Israel gestures that had been requested by Ben-Gurion: a joint U.S.–Soviet statement affirming regional borders and a Washington visit for Ben-Gurion. The latter, he added, would just add heft to the oft-heard Arab complaint that the administration was too pro-Israel. Kennedy's comment sparked an extraordinary exchange between McNamara and Grant. Pondering the regional balance of forces, the defense secretary mused that Israel might never be secure "until it got the West Bank of the Jordan; this seemed the logical military frontier." Grant countered that "if Israel grabbed the West Bank, it would prolong Arab-Israeli hostility by 15 years." Although conversation swiftly shifted away from such cosmic mulling, McNamara and Grant's ruminations unwittingly touched on what would become the nexus of Israel's political debate from the Six Day War on.

The danger, however, was a third Arab-Israeli round in 1963, let alone 1967. From JFK's point of view, "the real problem now was that the Israelis might move, not the Arabs." Indeed, Ben-Gurion's most recent letter hinted at a land grab. "Israel is really the danger," Kennedy argued, "since it wants to move first if there is a coup in Jordan."

To tamp down the flames, the administration decided to issue stern warnings. Israel would be told to do nothing rash. Nasser would be warned that while the United States had no interest in an Arab-Israeli war, Israel might choose a "preventive war before the Arabs were ready"—the idea being to find a way for the administration to deter Nasser from raising tensions or crowing without making the White House appear to be in Israel's thrall. And the U.S.S. *Saratoga* and U.S.S. *Enterprise* were both sent to the eastern Mediterranean.[119]

But for all of Kennedy and the State Department's alarm about Israeli intentions, the American embassy in Israel seemed unsure what all the fuss was about. "We have no (repeat no) indications" that Israel was girding itself to intervene on the West Bank, cabled Ambassador Walworth Barbour. "High-level IDF contacts appear concerned but not excited."[120]

Barbour then offered a virtuoso exegesis of the central staple of Arab rejectionism: that Israel was expansionist. Indeed, Eisenhower, Dulles, and many Arabist diplomats thought Zionism's commitment to untrammeled Jewish immigration implied revanchism. "Does Israel theoretically want [the] West Bank?" Barbour asked. On balance, he reported, Ben-Gurion's Israel preferred the territorial status quo. True, a land grab would give the IDF more room for maneuver; satisfy the "general yearning for [the] reestablishment [of] 'traditional' Israel, including all Jerusalem (Wailing Wall)"; and boost tourism by giving Israel a monopoly over the Christian holy places. But the first two reasons—the security-minded and nationalist rationales that would after 1967 be offered intermittently by the left-leaning Labor Party and insistently by its rightist Likud rivals—"do not weigh heavily with responsible Israelis." Ben-Gurion felt that Israel could accommodate many more Jewish immigrants within its present borders. Worse, the "West Bank could be [an] economic and demographic liability if [its] present population remained." Most of the West Bank's 700,000 Arab inhabitants were supported by the UNRWA relief agency, and "presumably not all would flee voluntarily under Israeli attack and occupation." Moreover, Israel would have to endure the "political liability" of widespread international opprobrium for an act of aggression. So while the West Bank was on Ben-Gurion's mind, it was not on his plate. Barbour had laid out the central themes of the grand Israeli argument between the forces of territorial compromise and those of territorial maximalism—four years before the 1967 war and a mere 30 years before the Oslo accords.

Turning to the more immediate crisis, Barbour noted that the key condition required for Israel to grab the West Bank was the arrival in Jordan of "dangerously hostile" Arab strike forces, probably under Nasser's command. That would both win support in key Western capitals for Israeli preemption and dramatically narrow the IDF's window for mobilization. As the Labor-affiliated newspaper *Davar* noted, Nasserite militants in Jordan would no more be an internal Jordanian affair than rockets in Cuba had been an internal Cuban affair. "To prevent such [a] contingency, Israelis will do everything feasible to protect [the] king's position," Barbour wrote. But that meant above all deterring Nasser by *threatening* to intervene, not by *actually* intervening.

Barbour then added an analysis of Israel's capabilities and calculus that foreshadowed the Six Day War itself as accurately as his analysis of the pros and cons of seizing the West Bank foreshadowed Israel's post-1967 political debates. What could Washington do about a hypothetical Israeli land grab? Israel would rather not defy the United States, Barbour wrote, but short of a sweeping U.S. guarantee of Jordanian territorial integrity, there probably was little that the United States could do to warn off the Israelis if they truly felt their existence was at stake. "Israel would enthusiastically welcome" a "formal security guarantee" of its own existence, but that might tie America's regional hands. "Nothing will dissuade Israelis from action if [they are] convinced [that the] threat of Arab attack [is] imminent," Barbour warned.[121]

To make sure that Egypt did not give Israel any pretexts, the administration ordered Badeau to speak to Nasser himself. A UAR-backed coup in Jordan would mean Israeli action, the State Department warned, and the administration "cannot count on restraining Israel" when the Jewish state felt itself threatened.[122] But the ambassador was way ahead of Washington; on his own initiative, Badeau passed on his personal alarm and anger over Egypt's inflammatory radio barrages to Nasser's aide-de-camp, Sami Sharaf. Jordanian radio had cackled over the 1961 collapse of the union with Syria, and "they are now getting [it] back," replied Sharaf. He then offered a few pallid reassurances, which even the patient Badeau snappishly dismissed as cold comfort.[123]

Meanwhile, in Amman, Ambassador Macomber headed over to the Defense Ministry at noon. King Husayn, in the middle of a meeting with his generals, halted it to meet the American envoy. Macomber reiterated America's support for "Jordan's continued independence and integrity" under Hashimite rule, and the beleaguered king responded with gratitude. Throughout the crisis, the diminutive Husayn was being excoriated by Nasser and the Ba'ath. A veteran U.S. monitor called one series of Iraqi broadcasts the "'vilest' he has heard from any Arab Radio in 30 years listening." To fan the flames, a Radio Baghdad front calling itself Jordan Republic Radio and claiming to broadcast from Nablus screeched, "Hearken to the Voice of the Republic, you dwarf . . . Oh heroic army, collaborate with the people and smash the puppet King."[124]

Despite Iraq's bluster, a cool Macomber cabled the State Department that the worst seemed to have passed. There were no major riots in the streets anymore, so the "immediate threat" of "internal turbulence may, for [the] time being, be subsiding."[125]

Israel was less sanguine. Ball and a few NEA aides were dragged into the office on Sunday by Harman, the Israeli ambassador, at the personal request of a still-agitated Ben-Gurion—upset both by the Jordan crisis and the inclusion of a promise to destroy Israel in the founding document of the new Egypt-Iraq-Syria union. How, Ben-Gurion asked, could one reconcile such a statement with Egypt's receipt of Soviet weaponry and Western aid and its supposed adherence to the U.N. Charter? The West needed to see Nasser's true colors. If Jordan fell, Israel would insist on a demilitarized West Bank. Anything less would leave hostile troops from Egypt, Iraq, Syria, or Jordan "within 1/2 mile from Israel's capital in Jerusalem and adjacent to the critical Natanya waist [near Tel Aviv] where Israel is only fifteen kilometers wide." UAR troops on the West Bank would leave Israel "in permanent danger and inaction would be tantamount to suicide," Ben-Gurion warned.[126] Still, the IDF's unruffled, professional response to the crisis makes one wonder whether Ben-Gurion really thought the king was about to fall, or if he was simply panicked by the resurrection of pan-Arabism.

Exaggerated or not, Ben-Gurion's anxieties had the administration's attention. At 12:20 P.M. on April 29, Bundy called up Ball to ask, "What are the Jews and Arabs up to?" Ball told the national security adviser about his meeting with Harman, whom Bundy described as "a hard bitten cookie"—by New Frontier standards of toughness, a considerable compliment. "I hope you are as weary about this as Komer and I are," Bundy added. Ball did not demur.

"I don't see the President going to war with Israel to recover the West Bank," Bundy continued. "I wonder if anyone is in a position to say that to the Israelis. The trouble with Mike [Feldman] is that he is an unreliable channel, and the trouble with the rest of us is they don't trust us." Ball agreed. "We are stuck, really," Bundy sighed. "The President is the only man who can say things that they will believe."[127]

The coup threat continued to recede, although suspicion of both Israel and Egypt did not. When Nasser met Badeau, the Egyptian leader denied any knowledge of a coup in Jordan, much less sponsorship. The Egyptian president agreed that an Israeli attack on the West Bank would mean a disastrous Egypt-Israel war. Nasser struck Badeau as "fatigued, sober and concerned," but he also seemed unsure what all the fuss was about: King Husayn, Nasser reckoned, would survive the upheaval.[128]

Syria and Iraq were dressed down even more directly. The American embassies in Baghdad and Damascus sternly told the new regimes that the "clearly nervous" Jewish state was not a "US satellite" and even hinted at a superpower showdown. "Attempted intervention [by] other Arab states could well lead to regional war with unforeseeable repercussions including [the] involvement [of] non-regional powers," the State Department's marching orders read. "Peace and progress must go hand-in-hand; to sow the wind of instability in Jordan is to risk the whirlwind of war that may render difficult or unobtainable the goals toward which all aspire."[129]

The new game, Komer wrote Bundy, was not the increasingly remote chance of a putsch in Amman but the Israeli attempt to make hay out of the coup scare. Ben-Gurion seemed to want either the United States in his corner or quiet "reassurances from us (e.g., joint planning, security commitment)." Feldman had leaped "like a shot" at McNamara's proto-Likudnik suggestion that Israel might take the West Bank, Komer sighed.[130] But Israel's real security problem, Komer argued, was a potential nuclear arms race with Egypt, not a revolutionary Arab army in the West Bank cul-de-sac.

But Israel's friends in Congress saw the April crisis as a warning that Kennedy's Nasser policy was wrongheaded. As usual, the early-1960s Israel lobby elicited more congressional rhetoric than presidential action. At the daily White House staff meeting on May 1, discussion centered around that morning's *New York Times*, which reported an attack by congressional liberals and pro-Israel stalwarts, including Senators Hubert Humphrey (D.-Minn.) and Jacob Javits (R.-N.Y.), on "the administration's allegedly pro-Nasser and pro-Arab policy in the Middle East."[131] For its part, the Egyptian press gave prominent play to Congress's complaint, blasting Javits as "one of Israel's agents in America."[132] With the Jordan crisis, the tilt toward Nasser looked unsustainable. Kennedy's immediate concern was "to take some of the domestic political cutting edge off these Congressional Zionist-inspired attacks." After the May 1 staff meeting, Komer asked the State Department for a memo to refute charges that the outreach to Nasser was coming at Israel's expense.[133] What the doctor ordered was a liberal senator to come to the administration's defense, rather than Israel's. But as the minutes dryly note, "even Arthur Schlesinger could think of no one in this category."

As a further sign that Kennedy was concerned that his Egypt policy was producing problems for him in Congress, the State Department's outgoing cables on Israel and the Arab-Israeli conflict were now being vetted by

Mike Feldman, the de facto White House envoy to American Jewry. On May 11, NEA's Grant wrote to Rusk that the White House was "under steadily mounting domestic political pressure" to take a more pro-Israel stance. "The Israelis are determined to use the period between now and the 1964 Presidential elections to secure a closer, more public security relationship with the United States, notably through a public security guarantee and a cooler, more antagonistic relationship between the United States and the UAR." Kennedy seemed to want to accommodate the Israel lobby without hurting U.S. regional interests. "At best," Grant concluded, echoing the State Department's traditional resentment of political influence over Israel policy, "this would be extremely difficult to accomplish."[134] As with the question of a Nasser summit, the Jordan crisis had opened the door to letting politics at home move policy abroad.

Beyond the reintroduction of precisely the sort of political calculations that would have made Marshall blanch, the Jordan crisis showed how far American Middle East policy had come since the last comparable scare, the 1958 Eisenhower interventions to prop up Jordan and Lebanon. The Israelis saw the 1963 Jordan crisis much as Eisenhower had seen its 1958 predecessor: as a symptom of metastasizing Nasserism. After three radical Arab states had in effect declared war on Israel by declaring its existence illegitimate in the Cairo union document, complained Ben-Gurion, what did anyone expect? Tellingly, however, it was the U.S. response that had changed. This time, rather than panicking and sending in the Marines, the White House worked methodically to tamp down the region's escalatory propensities—even if that meant taking a dim view of both Israeli and Egyptian intentions.

In Amman, Macomber was left fuming. First the White House had emboldened Nasser and embarrassed the monarchs by recognizing the Yemeni coup; now it had ended the crisis by sending the Sixth Fleet toward Jordan, thereby making the already besieged king look like a Western patsy.[135] Macomber, a resolute fan of the "BYK" (Brave Young King), wanted no part of Foggy Bottom's tilt toward Cairo, and with inter-Arab tensions exacerbated by coups in Yemen, Iraq, and Syria and a near-coup in Jordan, Nasser seemed a destabilizing force.[136] That meant more pressure on the administration to buck up its traditional friends—and that, in turn, meant focusing anew on Yemen.

KOMER'S WAR

Thinking back on the experience of working for Kennedy, Bob Komer would remember the embarrassment of having the president ask him about an article in *The New Republic*. "I haven't seen it yet, Mr. President," replied the shamefaced NSC aide. "I'll go take a look and let you know." Komer thumbed through the current issue, but the only article that seemed relevant was a rather bland piece on the administration's China policy. The next day, Komer said, "Mr. President, that article about Communist China seemed to be rather dull. What was it that struck you?"

"Oh, I don't mean that article," Kennedy replied, picking up an advance copy of the next issue. "I was talking about the article on Yemen."[137]

When the Yemen crisis broke, Kennedy had frankly admitted not knowing where on earth it was. Now, his Middle East aides said that their boss "could give an excellent briefing on the Yemen to anybody."[138] Kennedy's Nasser overture would end, with painful irony, with the White House actually putting U.S. pilots in harm's way to prevent Nasser from overreaching. Yemen could scarcely be heard over the *Sturm und Drang* of the wider Cold War, but Kennedy actually ran the modest but real risk of getting bogged down there. In November 1962, after Egypt launched a nigh-daily barrage against Saudi border posts that it alleged were supplying the royalists, U.S. fighters scrambled from the Dhahran airfield to make "demonstrative sorties" over the major Saudi cities, far from the border zones where the clashes were taking place.[139] By January 1963, the administration was weighing answering Egyptian bombings and "piteous Saudi appeals for air support," Komer told Bundy, by "sending some US fighters to scare UAR off. . . . But *there would be risk of US fighters ending up duelling with UAR (or Soviets)*."[140] Tellingly, the only deployment of American troops to the Middle East on Kennedy's watch was to Saudi Arabia. That American intervention—like its vastly larger successor 27 years later, Operation Desert Shield—was designed to protect the world's leading oil producer from the Middle East's leading radical Arab nationalist.[141] But it was also intended to circumscribe the Arab cold war. In a sense, the mission that the Pentagon code-named Operation Hard Surface might just as well have been dubbed Soft Landing.

Military intervention was, as ever, a sure sign that diplomacy alone was reaching its limits.[142] Soviet stalling was forcing the United Nations to move, as Badeau put it, "as slowly as cold molasses"[143] on formally starting overseeing the disengagement process negotiated by Bunker.[144] To speed things up, the administration turned back to JFK's pen-pal diplomacy on May 27, when Kennedy sent Nasser his first letter since the Jordan crisis.[145]

With each passing letter, Kennedy's formulaic invocation of the virtues of frank talk had come to precede blunter and blunter reprimands. That disturbed Badeau, who was increasingly suspected by his bosses back home of having "contracted an acute case of 'localitis'" that made him an unlikely bearer of harsh messages.[146] During a consultation visit back to Washington, an unhappy Badeau remembered watching Kennedy personally toughen up one such letter. "This will not do at all," the president said after a secretary read a draft back to him. "I've got something very direct and slightly unpleasant to say to Nasser in the first paragraph. You didn't say it. You pussyfooted about it. You have something unpleasant to say? Say it."[147]

True to his own dictates, Kennedy wrote sharply that Nasser was playing with fire in Jordan. After another crisis in Jordan, "a major conflict might ensue—and one in which our assessment indicates that the Arab forces might not be at any advantage." As Nasser would discover the hard way in 1967, Kennedy was quite right about the Arab forces' prowess.

America's commitment to Israel's security and integrity had not heretofore "prevented the growth of friendly US-UAR relations," Kennedy wrote, "and I hope it will not do so in the future." The American president also had no problem with "freely chosen Arab unity." After all, in Yemen, the administration had recognized the modernizers over the medievalists. But pan-Arabism must not threaten Israel or the Arab conservatives. Kennedy opposed both Arab aggression against Israel and Israeli aggression against the Arabs. "We showed this in 1956," Kennedy wrote, "and mean it just as much today. . . . We want to steer an even course with all our friends, and we hope it will not be made unduly difficult for us."

Nasser responded by blaming the Saudi and Jordanian monarchies' "active anti-revolutionary policies" in Yemen for their own domestic woes. But he thanked Kennedy for his mediation efforts and hinted at a withdrawal from Yemen.[148h] Meanwhile, Egypt continued to harass the Yemeni royalists' supply lines, often by using a single plane to bomb a Saudi camel caravan or sending a few more planes to strafe a Saudi border post.[149] And on June 7, U.N. Secretary General U Thant finally announced that he was out of patience with a series of Soviet stalls and was sending a U.N. mission to oversee the disengagement from Yemen.

The repeated postponements of the dispatch of the U.N. observer mission had also meant the delay of the dispatch of the oft-promised U.S. Air Force squadron to Saudi Arabia. "Faysal is panting for it," Komer wrote Kennedy.[150] In particular, the Saudi leader had fretted that the November 1962 U.S. overflights, which covered only Riyadh and the other major Saudi cities, had implied that *border* attacks were still "fair game" for Nasser.[151] The Pentagon remained unenthusiastic, warning the State Department that while the squadron "may deter the UAR from air operations over Saudi Arabia, it lacks the military capability to provide an adequate air defense of Saudi Arabia."[152] As many of the top USAF brass saw it, the Saudis' own pilots spent too much time either flying in airshows or, embarrassingly, defecting to Egypt. The Air Force chief of staff, General Curtis LeMay, was said to be particularly apoplectic about the idea of picking up the slack, insisting that he needed the air unit elsewhere and fearing that the fighters would be "sitting ducks for any sufficiently determined MIG pilot."[153] Talbot found the notoriously forbidding LeMay's apprehensions faintly ridiculous—not the first time Kennedy's advisers would clash with a haughty military.[154] Despite the Pentagon's complaints, both Rusk and Komer urged Kennedy to send the U.S. squadron to try to both deter Nasser and soothe Faysal. On June 13, the president signed off on deploying eight F-100D fighters and a large command-and-control transport plane to Jidda. They did not travel light; Pentagon planning for Operation Hard Surface included 560 support personnel and 861.3 tons of equipment.[155]

The USAF pilots' rules of engagement—leaked, to the Pentagon's rage, to some Saudi officials—made it clear that there were barbs on the tripwire. Komer later insisted that Kennedy "only authorized the deployment" after the Saudis had provided a series of undertakings designed to prevent the fighters' combat use.[156] In fact, while the Pentagon sought to portray the Kennedy administration's only military intervention in the Middle East as a "token air defense" mission, a U.S.–Egypt clash was possible, even under rules of engagement deliberately watered down by the White House.[157] The Hard Surface squadron was to scramble within 40 miles of the Saudi-Yemeni border; if Egyptian planes violated Saudi airspace, the U.S. fighters were to intercept them and try to escort the intruders either out of Saudi airspace or to a convenient runway. But if the intruder eventually fired on the Americans or began bombing the Saudis, the F-100Ds were to "destroy the 'intruder.'"[158] The Pentagon, which remained leery about flinging so small a force into Saudi skies, insisted that the fighters be fully combat-ready and armed with Sidewinder missiles.[159]

Before the squadron could scramble, however, a singularly awkward last-minute glitch intruded. Saudi Arabia had long refused to issue visas to American Jews, from ordinary citizens to members of Congress to U.S. troops. The Hard Surface squadron would not need visas, but to avoid any possible Saudi protest, an April 1963 Air Force operations plan began its personnel section thus: "Personnel of Jewish faith or Jewish extraction will not be selected."[160] The State Department considered this discrimination unnecessary but declined to insist on the inclusion of Jewish servicemen. In Riyadh, Ambassador Hart suggested that Jewish troops need not be barred but that the entire deployment receive a sympathetic briefing on Saudi customs, Islam, and the hajj, as well as a warning not to mention Palestine to any locals.[161]

A few weeks later, the Pentagon removed the offending sentence from the operations plan.[162] But word soon got out. On June 10, Emmanuel Celler—the long-serving Democratic representative from Brooklyn who had advised the 1960 Kennedy campaign on civil rights and chaired the

House Judiciary Committee—told the *New York Times* that some Jewish servicemen were actually among the proposed American mission's personnel.[163] Both the State Department and the NSC agreed that the administration should carry on; as Komer groaned, "if we went to Faysal and posed yet another hurdle he might go off the deep end."[164]

Ironically enough, by Saudi standards, Faysal was a relative moderate on civil rights: his first action on taking executive authority from King Saud was to formally abolish slavery.[165] Notwithstanding the House of Saud's bold step into the nineteenth century, the spring of 1963 was an awkward moment for a liberal White House to segregate its own troops. In April, Martin Luther King, Jr., was scratching out a letter from a Birmingham jail cell; in early May, Bull Connor was unleashing snapping dogs and blasting hoses at children; by late May, Governor George Wallace was preparing to make his stand in the schoolhouse door, and King's allies were planning a march on Washington; and on the same June day that Celler went to the *Times*—in the words of the historian Taylor Branch—a "tall, schoolmarmish, and fatefully dignified" Southern Christian Leadership Conference leader named Annell Ponder was being savagely beaten on the floor of a Winona, Alabama, jail by a mob of policemen "cursing the name Bobby Kennedy."[166]

The Saudis did not see such matters as their problem. They threw a diplomatic fit when they got word of the snag, insisting that the administration denounce Celler. But Talbot told Hart to hang tough; civil rights issues were so important that condemning the chairman of the House Judiciary Committee at Saudi Arabia's behest was "totally out of [the] question."[167]

If the Saudis gave the Kennedy administration a hard time about keeping Jewish troops out of the kingdom, American Jewry was far less dogged about trying to get them in. American Jewish groups made little fuss over the anti-Semitic Air Force directive, and they sometimes even helped the administration handle its damage control. The American Jewish Committee's Washington representative obligingly popped over to the State Department and agreed to help discourage journalists from poking around the story.[168]

Nasser responded to the imbroglio with a combination of glee, anger, and pandering to anti-Jewish animus. Cairo's state-run Voice of the Arabs radio station denounced the presence of "Jewish soldiers" as "enemies of God." By late June, the government-controlled press had also taken up the theme, running front-page stories about the arrival on Saudi soil of American aircraft and Jewish troops. Egyptian editorials witheringly noted that the "entry of Jewish American soldiers" into the holiest domains of Islam was powerful proof of the House of Saud's contemptible dependence on foreign backing—a theme that would be echoed decades later by Osama bin Laden.[169]

In Washington, those foreign backers were not happy about the mess either. Nevertheless, the civil rights struggle raging across the American South would have made public acquiescence in Saudi anti-Semitism a serious international embarrassment for Kennedy. "The heart of the question is whether all Americans are to be afforded equal rights and equal opportunities," the president declared in the historic prime-time address he delivered the night after Celler's *Times* story. "We preach freedom around the world," Kennedy added, "and we mean it."[170] And yet he meant it less in Saudi Arabia. On June 27, Faysal finally agreed to a face-saving suggestion from the State Department. The Saudis reaffirmed their anti-Semitic visa policy, the Americans reaffirmed their nondiscriminatory service policy, and the two sides agreed to agree that the inherent tension between the policies fortuitously happened not to have come up this time around. Riyadh did not ask, and Washington did not tell.[171]

Much as Kennedy did not want Operation Hard Surface to cause a civil rights controversy, he wanted even less for it to start a war. To Bundy's amusement and Komer's dismay, Kennedy began to refer to Yemen as "Komer's war" and to ask his mortified aide how it was coming along. Bundy picked up on the theme and quipped, "When it goes well, we call it Komer's war, and when it goes poorly, we call it Talbot's war."[172] But Komer's war was no joke. To give some sense of scale, the only comparable American deployment to Saudi Arabia before 1990's huge Operation Desert Shield was the Carter administration's dispatch of F-15s to the desert kingdom to calm its nerves after the Iranian revolution — and those planes were unarmed.[173] For good measure, Nasser was warned off of further bombing of Saudi Arabia and told that the American pilots were on their way. Kennedy himself was watching grimly, unsure that his more literal-minded military grasped the fundamentally political point of the mission. Kennedy called the NSC's Carl Kaysen three times to grill him on the fighters' rules of engagement, which the president gave one final personal review before the pilots scrambled for the Middle East.[174] As his advisers remember it, Kennedy told them he wanted to "be sure no war starts that I'm not in control of."[175]

On July 2, the NSC asked Kennedy for formal permission to send the Hard Surface fighters to Saudi Arabia. "JFK approved pronto," Komer noted with satisfaction.[176] Hart worked with the still-leery Air Force to set up an irregular pattern of overflights, varying between patrols near Qizan on the Yemeni-Saudi border and flights down the north Saudi coast, to keep the Egyptians guessing about when they might meet an F-100.[177] But the deployment did not stop Egyptian attacks, leading LeMay and other members of the Joint Chiefs to grouse that Hard Surface was ineffectual. But State Department officials downplayed the later Egyptian raids and judged the squadron "an effective deterrent" whose stay should be extended.[178] The NSC cautiously agreed that the squadron had averted an Egyptian-Saudi showdown—at, as Komer wrote, a net cost of "a temporary deployment of 8 jets and 500 men (this sure beats the Congo)."[179] As it turned out, Hard Surface lasted into the Johnson administration.

Kennedy's Saudi deployment was of a piece with "flexible response," the New Frontier doctrine that emphasized "calibration and 'fine tuning'" in implementing the wider Cold War strategy of containment—to the rage of the absolutist LeMay, who disliked seeing a job half done and detested seeing his forces used to underscore a diplomatic point.[180] But much as Hard Surface fit in with Kennedy's overarching Cold War policy, it marked a nadir for his Middle East policy. With American pilots in harm's way over the Arabian Peninsula, the United States had now directly interposed itself between an angry Egypt and an anxious Saudi Arabia—a glum terminus for the attempt to woo Nasser. Indeed, when Hard Surface was first mooted inside the White House, Kennedy's advisers had gloomily noted that it could "mean [the] end of our Nasser policy."[181] So it did.

THE FINAL DAYS

By the summer of 1963, America's relationship with Nasserite Egypt was becoming, quite literally, poisonous. On July 11, when Badeau met with Nasser, the two men had a grim wrangle over reports in the London *Daily Telegraph* accusing Egypt of breaking a major international taboo by using chemical weapons in Yemen. Perhaps, Nasser said, the confusion arose out of his troops' use of "Opal," a version of Napalm, on Yemeni fields and villages. Badeau was unconvinced, having heard ugly reports about substances ranging "from phosphorus to mustard gas." Nasser offered an unconvincing denial, admitting to the use of an Egyptian-made bomb whose "precise chemical content" was unknown to him.[182]

Behind the scenes, the administration made a series of what Komer called "tough private noises" to the Egyptians about the use of poison gas. The NSC did not buy Nasser's denials, but the State Department did not want to make too much out of the issue. If the agent was homegrown, Badeau guessed, it must not be terribly sophisticated. Kennedy was content to let Britain and the United Nations lead the charge on this one. Komer agreed, noting that pushing too hard could wreck what was left of constructive engagement with Cairo.

Still, Komer wearily admitted that the policy was proving a tough slog. He did not wish to sound defensive, Komer wrote Bundy. But did everyone "realize that we've never been in [a] better position in [the] Arab world; we're on reasonably good terms with revolutionary Arabs, yet without losing our old clients. This is right where we want to be, despite pain and strain involved in staying there."[183]

Some of that strain was in evidence on July 19, when Kennedy sat down to an oft-delayed meeting with a delighted Kamel, Nasser's ambassador to Washington. Beforehand, Komer had warned the president that allegations of Egyptian chemical warfare were making the rounds on Capitol Hill. Kamel, too, kept one eye on domestic American politics by including the obligatory plea for the administration to resist Zionist blandishments. But Kamel also laid it on thick for Kennedy: his recent American University speech was nothing less than "immortal in human history." Then he asked for more aid money.

Kennedy was unmoved. After an unenlightening discussion of Yemen, Kamel complained again about Egypt's treatment in the American media. JFK pointed out that he did not control it. But Kamel should not worry; Kennedy, too, was taking lumps for his relationship with Nasserism. Indeed, Kennedy argued, "attacks on UAR here are really attacks against" the White House.[184] JFK then claimed that he was due at another meeting and ducked out on the garrulous ambassador.

Privately, the administration's manners were less refined. In order "to drive home assinity of UAR poison gas gambit," the CIA passed along the "full technical particulars on type of CW they used" to some (presumably Egyptian) interlocutors whose identities still remain secret. "We also quoted to them appropriate extracts from their CW manual on use of this stuff," Komer wrote Bundy, "and reminded them that Saudis, British, and others would no doubt find out what we had already."[185]

By now, the tilt to Nasser was under sharp attack in Congress. The Israel lobby and the oil industry had made little headway with White House officials, but they found a far more receptive audience on Capitol Hill. The increasingly plausible allegations of chemical warfare combined with another odious charge—that Nasser was using Nazi scientists in his rocket program—to paint an ugly portrait of the Egyptian leader. In April, a bipartisan group of six senators, including Jacob Javits and Kenneth Keating of New York, wrote Kennedy, urging him to use his "good offices" to convince West Germany and other European nations to "hold its nationals in line."[186] When Badeau raised the issue with Nasser, the Egyptian leader called the charges "Israeli propaganda." "Are all Germans Nazis?" he asked rhetorically. "Are German scientists working in big countries all Nazis too?" Nasser added that he did not know whether the Germans in the UAR had been members of the Nazi Party but assured Badeau that they "stuck completely to their scientific work" while in Egypt.[187] Later, Komer would deride these reports, speaking of "a couple of fourth rate German scientists who used to work for the French; then the French fired them, and the Egyptians hired them."[188] But while Komer insisted that Egypt's missiles were too primitive to carry chemical weapons, he did not specifically deny that Egypt had used chemical warfare in the first place. Nonproliferation experts now agree that Egypt did use chemical warfare in Yemen—probably mustard gas.

In this sour new atmosphere, Badeau warned Nasser that Egypt would probably take a drubbing during Congress's pending foreign aid debates. Cairo "might tend to disregard these as being only Zionist inspired," Badeau told a visibly exhausted Nasser. But Nasser would do well to study the debates "very carefully . . . with a view to determining what factors in UAR public image caused difficulty in the United States."[189] Chemical warfare in Yemen, unmet disengagement commitments, and virulent radio propaganda all sprang readily to Badeau's mind.

By midsummer of 1963, Nasser was still getting mixed grades from Washington. On the one hand, after much prodding by U Thant and the administration, Nasser finally started moving a few thousand troops out of Yemen in August.[190] On the other, after Syria quashed a late-July coup attempt by local Nasserites, Nasser excoriated his foes, including Israel and especially his erstwhile Ba'athist partners in Syria, whom he denounced on July 22 as "secessionist, inhuman and immoral," and, for good measure, "fascist."[191] Moreover, while disengagement generally seemed to be holding now that U.N. observers were in place, Saudi arms smuggling to the royalists and Egyptian border violations still rumbled on in the background. (Komer told Kennedy about an Egyptian plane's attack on a Yemeni border village: "casualties one camel.")[192] For good measure, the administration brokered a series of secret Saudi-Egyptian talks over Yemen's future.

But many of Egypt's troops were not getting out, and some Saudi aid was still getting in. Along with Defense Secretary McNamara, Kennedy decided to beef up American airpower in the region to help show that Washington was serious about halting the vicious cycle in Yemen. The Pentagon counted 201 USAF planes in the region against 339 Egyptian planes—not great odds. So Kennedy agreed to deploy two fighter squadrons from Europe and a second carrier strike force from the Sixth Fleet to achieve parity with Egypt and demonstrate U.S. commitment to Saudi sovereignty.[193] Kennedy also pre-positioned several B-47 bombers in Spain, after assuring Khrushchev that they were not rigged to carry nuclear arms.[194]

The administration was officially determined to stick with disengagement while it tried to help quietly midwife the birth of a Yemeni regime that both Egypt and Saudi Arabia could accept. The key was the Mister

Big of the Arab world. Disengagement would work only if the U.N. observers stayed in, which would work only if Faysal stayed out, which would work only if Nasser started getting out. To try to start the sequence, the administration finally hit Nasser where it hurt—forging an explicit linkage between Yemen and continued U.S. aid.

Nasser had a lot to lose: in 1963, Washington sent Cairo $2.3 million in technical assistance, a supporting assistance loan of $10 million, $36.3 million in development loans, $125.5 million in PL-480 aid, and $12.5 million from the Export-Import Bank. For 1964, Nasser had already asked for an additional $30 million loan to cover a payments shortfall, in addition to the multiyear PL-480 commitment of about $150 million per year and a projected development loan of between $15 and 25 million.[195] In late September 1963, Kaissouni returned to Washington to hunt for the 1964 dollars. But this time, the Egyptian minister was told that no answer to his request was likely to come during his visit. Not only was the administration concerned that the previous year's IMF stabilization money had been squandered, the cost of Nasser's Yemen misadventure remained "a very high hurdle," as Rusk put it, to more U.S. aid.[196] With the administration balking at even the appearance of underwriting Nasser's Yemen war, Kaissouni assured Rusk that the Egyptian campaign was much cheaper than press reports indicated, and was declining in any event.[197] But Rusk made the linkage clear: further U.S. aid to Egypt was "to a great extent dependent upon satisfactory performance in Yemen."[198] The carrot that Washington had originally offered to lure Egypt out of the Soviet camp had now been turned into a stick to drive Egypt out of Yemen.

Nasser resented being squeezed. When Badeau warned Nasser that his U.S. aid was on the line, the Egyptian leader reacted so angrily that Kennedy told his aides, "Let's lay off these aid threats."[199] On October 21, Badeau sat down with Nasser around noon for a "baldly direct" (a diplomatic euphemism for nerve-frayingly tense) meeting to deliver a tough, Komer-drafted message from Kennedy. JFK blamed Nasser for not living up to his part of the Yemen bargain, while U.S. intelligence estimated that Saudi gunrunning and aid had almost completely halted. "On the other hand," Kennedy wrote, "the UAR has not made phased withdrawals on a scale consistent with our understanding of the spirit of the agreement." The Yemen imbroglio, he added, "is inevitably complicating, not least in the Congress, my own effort to carry forward our policy of friendly collaboration" with Nasser. "If we should let Yemen affect our larger interests in this manner, we would have lost our ability to shape events and have permitted events to dominate us."[200]

It turned out to be Kennedy's last letter to Nasser. The Egyptian leader protested to Badeau that an Egyptian division or so would be enough to keep order in Yemen if the Saudis would just stop meddling. As it was, he claimed to have 28,000 troops in Yemen, down from 32,000.[201] A week later, Nasser told Badeau that Egypt could pull another 5,000 troops out of Yemen by the end of the year.[202]

Badeau's counterpart in Saudi Arabia, Ambassador Hart, meanwhile spent three hours in a "very intense argument" with Faysal. The Saudis did not want to be the ones to pull the plug on the U.N. mission, but Faysal was still not willing to cut loose the Yemeni royalists. Hart warned that "Hard Surface could not remain and become a screen for renewed Saudi help" to the royalists.[203] Faysal shot back that if America would not defend him, he might have to buy other planes and hire mercenaries to fly them. Meanwhile, U Thant was preparing to release a U.N. report announcing that disengagement had been stymied by Saudi recalcitrance. If that happened and the U.N. observer mission expired, the administration warned Faysal, it would "have no alternative but to withdraw Hard Surface aircraft."[204] Finally, Faysal blinked. In the end, the prospect of having the dead cat of the U.N. mission left on his doorstep was too unappealing. Talbot argued that the threat to pull the Hard Surface planes out of Saudi Arabia had "played an important role" in getting Faysal to back down.[205] The Pentagon agreed to extend the USAF mission.

But even as the White House managed to cobble together a minor victory on disengagement, it took a beating on aid. At virtually every level, Kennedy aides had warned their Egyptian counterparts that Nasser's behavior was creating trouble on Capitol Hill. They were not exaggerating. In Congress, Nasser was caught between the hammer and the anvil—between the Israel lobby on behalf of the Jewish state and Big Oil on behalf of the Arab conservatives. The two lobbies agreed on very little, but they agreed on Nasser: he was a menace for the region and a sinkhole for U.S. aid.[206] Nasser also did not endear himself to anyone in Washington by abruptly offering diplomatic recognition to North Korea on August 25 and North Vietnam on September 1.[207] And above all, the Senate strongly felt that "Nasser has played us for suckers in Yemen."[208]

On November 7, a stinging Senate debate led by Ernest Gruening of Alaska denounced both the administration's Nasser overture and Egypt's own transgressions. After visiting Cairo and meeting Nasser, Gruening had tried earlier to get Kennedy's goat by writing the president, "I fervently hope that no future historian will be able to write a book concerning this period of United States activity in the Middle East, entitled *While America Slept*"—a swipe at Kennedy's own famous senior thesis on appeasement, *While England Slept*.[209] Now, Gruening led the charge against Nasser on the Senate floor. "The United States is buying both butter and guns for aggressor nations," Gruening charged, "and we must stop it now."[210]

Even the laconic Talbot later privately described the debate as "an extraordinary anti-Nasser binge."[211]

After rejecting a watered-down alternative pushed by Senator Fulbright, the Senate voted 65 to 13 to amend the 1961 Foreign Assistance Act to bar foreign aid from going to any country that the White House felt was committing or planning aggression against either the United States or any country receiving U.S. aid.[212] For all the vagueness of that language, the Gruening amendment was aimed squarely at Nasser, and he knew it.[213] When the Egyptian leader received West Berlin's visiting mayor, Willy Brandt, Nasser "talked of little else,"[214] railing "bitterly and at length against the American tactics of using aid to put pressure on him."[215] He reportedly told Brandt that the Kennedy administration had initially made him retract his post-1956 assessment that the West could not be trusted; now, he felt that he was back to square one.[216]

The state-run Egyptian media shook with indignation. All three morning newspapers led with the story, and the common theme was not hard to discern: al-Ahram's headline read "Israel Hides Behind the American Senate," whereas al-Jumhuriyya opted for "Israel Creates a Crisis in Washington" and the editors of al-Akhbar al-Yom went with "America Tries to Protect Israel." Their stories blamed the Gruening amendment on Zionist perfidy; raged against statements from such villains as Gruening, Javits, Keating, and the American Jewish Congress; called the vote an attack on all Arabs; and vowed never to cave in to pressure. "Today the [Aswan] High Dam is being built, in spite of the will of imperialism and the imperialists," editorialized al-Jumhuriyya. "Let the U.S. understand such a reality, and that we pay no heed to its aid, if this aid impedes our aims or protects our enemies."[217]

Nor was all this merely for show. One Nasser adviser, Hassan Sabri al-Khouli, told Badeau that he was shocked that 65 senators had "voted against [the] UAR." If the Gruening vote accurately bespoke "Zionist strength in US," Khouli implied, trying to strengthen U.S.–Egyptian ties was futile.[218] Badeau found all this overly facile: Nasser had been warned ad nauseam that he would pay a price for Yemen and for his ongoing propaganda slurs, so what had the Egyptians expected? Still, the besieged ambassador wrote Talbot that Congress's handiwork had left him in a Waiting for Godot mood: "Offstage there is an impending but nebulous spectre that at any moment may appear radically to alter our position and destiny here."[219]

However annoyed they were with Nasser, Kennedy's men also resented Congress's meddling. If American aid was to be used to spank Nasser, it was the White House and not Congress whose hand would hold the paddle. "Other dispatches from Cairo make it clear that the Gruening Amendment has had a strong impact there, but unfortunately the effect is the opposite of what supporters of the Amendment must have intended," Bundy lectured Fulbright. "On the evidence so far, there seems no alternative to the conclusion that we make people more, and not less, nationalistic by actions which seem to them to be 'neo-colonial pressure.'"[220] Rusk concurred. And in his last press conference, the president was scathing about congressional attempts to impinge on the executive's supposedly traditional prerogatives over foreign policy.

"This is the worst attack on foreign aid that we have seen since the beginning of the Marshall Plan," Kennedy told the White House press corps. If America suffered a setback "in the Middle East, Africa, and Latin America, and South Vietnam, Laos," the blame would fall not on a senator but on the president.[21] Later, he was asked why he had not taken advantage of his ability to suspend aid to Egypt over its defiance of the United Nations' Yemen peace plan. Kennedy replied that 80 percent of aid to Egypt came from surplus PL-480 food but agreed that the rate of withdrawal from Yemen was too slow. The Senate's action, however, will not strengthen "our hands or our flexibility in dealing with the UAR. In fact, it will have the opposite result." In general, when dealing with aid to the Arab world, Washington had to resist the temptation to say, "Cut it off." "They are nationalist, they are proud, they are in many cases radical," Kennedy said. But threats from Capitol Hill would not help; after all, cutting off aid for the Aswan High Dam had proved foolish. "I think it is a very dangerous, untidy world," he added. "But we are going to have to live with it." That meant that Congress was going to have to let him do his job. "If we don't function, the voters will throw us out," Kennedy said. "But don't make it impossible for us to function by legislative restraints or inadequate appropriations."[222]

Many in the administration also had little doubt about the role the Israel lobby had played in Gruening's legislative craftsmanship. At lower levels, Israeli diplomats backpedaled, expressing hopes that Congress would give the president a waiver and fears that an Arab backlash could further destabilize the region and expose Israel to "thoughtless acts."[223] But higher up, few New Frontiersmen were buying. Averell Harriman was disturbed enough to cable Rusk from São Paulo, worrying that all the administration's good work with Egypt would be lost. "It seems to me that this shows the necessity for [a] prompt frank exchange of views on a high level with the more responsible and responsive Jewish leaders as to reasons for our Middle East policy and objectives," Harriman growled.[224]

Perhaps the frankest of those exchanges came from the frankest of New Frontiersmen, Bob Komer. On November 21, Komer had a contentious lunch with Mordechai Gazit, one of Israeli Ambassador Harman's top aides. A spat in the United Nations over the Palestinian refugees led both men to complain about the tenor of the U.S.–Israel relationship, and Komer fumed at what he considered Israeli narrow-mindedness. "Israel's whole effort since 1948 — in the UN, in the maneuvers for a public security guarantee, in demands for more arms, joint planning, etc. — seemed aimed at forcing us off of an ostensibly middle position which permitted us to maintain reasonable relations with the Arabs and thereby combat Soviet penetration of the Middle East," Komer wrote in his description of the meeting. "Israel might think that a net outcome in which the US backed Israel all-out, while the Arabs turned to Moscow, was in its overall security interest, but we most emphatically did not. We saw our ME [Middle East] policy as being in Israel's interest as much as ours. We had consistently tried to explain this to them, with little success."

Komer then blasted the Gruening amendment, which he said "had so limited our freedom of action with the Arabs" that the administration could help out Israel less on the refugees and other issues. Israel had had nothing to do with the amendment, Gazit protested, and could hardly be blamed for "the standard pro-Zionist reactions of [Rep. Leonard] Farbstein, Gruening, Keating, and Javits." Unimpressed, Komer told Gazit that Israel should have waved the pro-Israel senators off and preserved the administration's freedom of maneuver.

The argument raged on, but as the two men finally prepared to leave, Komer returned again to the administration's ill-appreciated search for middle ground in the Middle East. "Couldn't the Israeli Government acknowledge just once that the US had a defensible position in attempting to maintain good relations with the Arab states[?]" Komer asked. The strains in U.S.–Israel relations were "not always a question of the US failing to take Israel's security interests into account but of at least comparable failure on [Israel's] part to give any recognition to the possible validity of our policy." But Israel saw America's Middle East relations as a zero-sum game, and even Komer's energy could not convince Gazit that the now-dead Nasser overture had ever actually been in Israel's interest. "We were ships passing each other in the night," Komer sighed.[225]

COLD WAR FOLLIES

Kennedy's Nasser overture finished in failure. Some PL-480 aid continued to flow during the Johnson administration, but the idea of bringing Egypt into the Western orbit had to wait until the late 1970s. While Operation Hard Surface ended a few months after Kennedy's assassination, the ugly little war in Yemen smoldered on until the staggering humiliation of the 1967 Six Day War forced Nasser to rethink his regional posture.

By then, the Johnson administration had long since chosen Faysal over Nasser, offering the Saudis a series of programs to help beef up their armed forces, including a joint U.S.–U.K. air-defense program worth $400 million, a major Army Corps of Engineers initiative to build Saudi bases, and a $100 million program to buy trucks and other vehicles to make Saudi forces more mobile.[226] In turn, Nasser relied more and more on Soviet assistance in Yemen.[227] As the Soviets were getting in, the British were getting out, weary with imperial overstretch. In February 1966, Britain decided that "Aden was not vital after all" and said it would abandon its base there.[228] The old British protectorate and Yemen's southern governates soon fell to leftist rebels. Much as he had with the rump republican regime in what was now known as North Yemen, Faysal began trying to undermine the new radicals in South Yemen. By the time of the Six Day War, Nasser had about 60,000 troops in Yemen and had used chemical warfare repeatedly on the royalists. Sour, battered, and disgraced, he began to leave. In one cruel final twist, Nasser died in the bleak fall of 1970 while busily protecting his old royalist foe, King Husayn, from being overthrown by the young revolutionaries of the Palestine Liberation Organization, who were now providing some of the electricity in Arab politics that Nasserism had offered until 1967.

Early in the Johnson administration, the State Department's Intelligence and Research (INR) bureau filed a stinging dissent from Kennedy's Egypt policy, arguing that "where vital interests of Nasser and the UAR have been involved, we seem to have had little success." In reality, America's regional position had actually eroded as its engagement with Nasser deepened. "The UAR now has a considerable history of aggression," noted INR. Nasser's commitment to pan-Arabism was stubbornly unfeigned. No matter how much Washington hated seeming to side with the forces of reaction, Nasser's overall concept of "reform" entailed "driving the British out of the Arabian peninsula, the reduction of US influence in the area, the elimination of the Jordanian and Saudi regimes . . . and, eventually, a reckoning with Israel."[229]

Over the long term, then, there is reason to wonder how close unchastened Nasserite pan-Arabism could have come to America at the height of the Cold War. But there is also no way to know, because Nasser short-circuited the experiment. While other factors played their part in that, the truly fatal blunder was Egypt's "peanut war" in Yemen.[230] However much Nasser scorned Sallal and however much Kennedy wooed Nasser, Nasser in effect wound up choosing Sallal over Kennedy, Sanaa over Washington, Yemen over the United States.

Ultimately, Nasser would come bitterly to call Yemen "my Vietnam."[231] According to Anthony Nutting, Nasser told sympathetic Westerners that Yemen had been "a venture more futile and protracted than any other undertaken during his reign . . . an endless drain on Egyptian resources of men and money to win a war which could never be won."[232] In return, as the conflict wore on, the administration became increasingly tempted to let Yemen's belligerents stew in their own juices, and Nasser's frustration at the interminable futility of his Yemeni overstep came to echo the Vietnam mea culpas of the more repentant among Kennedy's best and brightest.

Nasser tied down much of his army and sacrificed much of his stature on behalf of a regime he disliked and a leader he distrusted. One sympathetic Nasser biographer described the strutting Sallal as a "complete simpleton," utterly bereft of "political knowledge or touch," and pathetically dependent on his patron—a reasonably accurate summary of the New Frontier's assessment of Ngo Dinh Diem.[233] In 1964, Nasser brought Sallal along on a Red Sea cruise with the visiting Khrushchev. "I just wanted you to see what I have to put up with," Nasser explained to the exasperated Soviet.[234] But of course, Nasser did not have to put up with Sallal, did not have to plunge into Yemen, did not have to refuse to admit that he had blundered into a dead end. He chose to.

It is also worth remembering, at least for the record, that Yemen almost became as much Faysal's Vietnam as it was Nasser's. After all, the unrepentant Faysal ran an almost infinitely wealthy country that poured its oil riches down a sinkhole on behalf of a deeply unpopular and ultimately doomed proxy. At least Nasser's Yemeni client survived. Still, even for the most ardent pan-Arabist, the costs and benefits of Yemen were wildly out of proportion. Nor, after Egypt and Saudi Arabia had indulged their ambitions and phobias, was there much of Yemen left for the revolutionaries to run.

The hubris of such New Frontiersmen as Robert McNamara, the brothers Bundy, and Maxwell Taylor has long since become the stuff of cautionary historical fable. But they also brought down with them many lesser-known colleagues, including Bob Komer, who went on from Nasser's Vietnam to America's Vietnam. The brio that he brought to his work on the Middle East would play much less well in Indochina. After shifting NSC portfolios, Komer became a devotee of the ill-fated and ill-named tactic of "pacification" and even made a play for the job of national security adviser when the tainted McGeorge Bundy quit in 1966. As it happened, the irrepressible Komer was well liked by the Saigon press corps, who found his optimism amusing. "Do you really believe all that stuff you put out and send back to Washington?" asked one reporter. "The difference between you and me is that I was sent out here to report on the *progress* in the war," Komer replied.[235] In his *New York Times* obituary, Vietnam, not Yemen, was featured as Komer's war.

Of course, the comparison between the quagmires is inexact; for one thing, while Kennedy sought to contain communism within North Vietnam, Nasser sought actively to expand pan-Arabism across all of Yemen, and quite conceivably as far as opportunity would permit. Moreover, Kennedy's idea of a political system worth exporting varied sharply from Nasser's. But the parallels remain intriguing. Above all, neither Cairo nor Washington in the early 1960s could free themselves from the shackles of crudely conceived notions of activism, toughness, and face. Fascinatingly, however, they could often see when the other fellow should.

It was an irony that Chekhov would have recognized: the folly that one could see in others was invisible when indulged in oneself. Yemen was primarily a political problem, Badeau lectured Nasser in March 1963, so Nasser's Yemen policy must put a premium on politics rather than armed might. The United States had "learned this in Korea and Vietnam," and in Nasser's "maturity and realism," Egypt should now follow suit.[236] That July, Nasser tried to explain away allegations that his forces had used chemical weapons in Yemen by saying they had merely employed a variant of Napalm—an unwitting Vietnam echo. Badeau urged Nasser to start pulling out of Yemen lest he might get dragged into a bruising and pointless guerrilla war. "What else can we do but keep on?" Nasser asked with a shrug—a sentiment that U.S. officials handling Vietnam would often utter.[237] One of them, Komer, proved as farsighted on Yemen as he was blinkered on Vietnam. "Basically, we and Nasser both miscalculated how long and how much it would take to subdue and pull together this non-country," Komer sighed in September 1963. "Nasser is trapped in Yemen," Komer added. "It's bleeding him," but Nasser felt he could not "afford the sharp loss of face in letting go."[238]

And there was one final grim commonality: neither president would live to see his nation recovered from their grand blunders. By the time Nasser died in 1970, almost half of the Egyptian army was still stuck in Yemen. What is perhaps most telling about the duration of Nasser's Vietnam is simply that Nasser could speak of Yemen of his own Vietnam—that the ordeal dragged on long enough that Vietnam had become "Vietnam," not merely a country but a metaphor. Kennedy reached out to Nasser because of his wider global strategy; Nasser fell into Yemen because of his pressing regional imperatives. Kennedy could see the futility of Nasser's Vietnam, and Nasser could see the futility of Kennedy's. Both men had their Vietnams because neither man thought wisely enough about his own cold war.

CHAPTER FIVE

Israel's Missile Gap

How America Began Arming the Jewish State

I N THE SPRING OF 1963, Shimon Peres did business for the first time with an American president. As he neared the age of 40, the future Israeli prime minister and Nobel Peace Prize winner already had many of his trademark features: thoughtful and somehow sad eyes; expressive, slow-moving hands with fat sausage fingers; a swept-back wave of hair that remained dark but had already receded above a high, shovel-flat forehead; a yen for aphorisms; and a position at the heart of the Israeli government. As deputy defense minister, the precocious Ben-Gurion protégé had helped build Israel's military infrastructure, which included tanks from Great Britain, airplanes (and, it was rumored, the bomb) from France, and now Hawk surface-to-air missiles from the United States. In Washington to finalize the terms of the Kennedy administration's watershed August 1962 decision to sell the first-ever package of sophisticated American weaponry to the Jewish state, Peres was escorted by Mike Feldman to the Oval Office, where Peres discovered that he was not the only strikingly young man charged with great responsibility. "Mr. President," Peres blurted out, "with so youthful an appearance, I doubt whether you would be elected mayor in my country."

JFK laughed. "You'll be surprised to hear that even in the United States I doubt whether I'd be elected mayor," he replied. "But president—that's something else." How, Kennedy continued, was Peres coming along with his requests?

He had come, Peres declaimed—unable, even then, to resist a witty inversion—to ask for a few Hawks on behalf of Israel's doves.

"In that case, you can have them," Kennedy said, playing along. "We've got plenty of hawks, and we can afford to supply a few even to our friends."[1]

For all the breezy banter, Kennedy and his men were in the midst of wrapping up a deadly serious policy shift toward the Jewish state—the very shift, indeed, that marks the origins of the U.S.–Israel alliance as we know it today. From Israel's founding until the summer of 1962, the United States had consistently refused to provide major armaments to Israel — fearing that even one big sale could set a precedent, pave the way for becoming Israel's arms supplier, and drive more Arab states toward the Soviet Union. Kennedy sought to change course gradually with the Hawk sale, not make an abrupt reversal. Still, the Hawk precedent remains perhaps the most underappreciated milestone in the U.S.–Israel special relationship. As Peres put it, the Hawks "were the first major weapons to breach the wall of America's arms embargo."[2] Israel became the first non-NATO country to receive such advanced technology — a state-of-the-art surface-to-air missile whose name was an acronym for Homing All the Way Killer.[3] No longer could Washington invoke its traditional refusal to introduce sophisticated weaponry to the Middle East in general or to Ben-Gurion's regional pariah in particular. What began with the Hawk in 1962 has become one of the most expensive and extensive military relationships of the postwar era, with a price tag in the billions of dollars and diplomatic consequences to match.

This shift should be understood as a part of an overall Kennedy policy toward the Arab-Israeli conflict that sought to expand the frontiers of American friendship and maneuver in the Middle East. As we have seen, the attempt to befriend Nasser failed, largely because Egypt valued inter-Arab political jousting more than American goodwill. The State Department's Arabists had long argued that the Arab-Israeli conflict harmed U.S. Cold War interests because America's closeness with Israel hampered its ability to court the Arabs. But now it turned out that the leading Arab nationalist was unwilling to take yes for an answer. Perhaps warmer ties to Israel would not harm America's standing in the Arab world as much as the grandees of U.S. diplomacy from George Marshall onward had feared. Nasser's friendship was falling out of reach, and the Arab kings who feared that Nasser wanted their thrones were in no position to shun the United States — even if America drew closer to Israel. Moreover, if Nasser's worldview did not place much stock in American friendship, Ben-Gurion's underlying strategy dictated acquiring as much U.S. support as he could get. The failed Nasser experiment, then, would stand in stark contrast to Kennedy's Israel policies, above all in the crucial area of arms sales.

The 1962 Hawk sale was even more striking because the Eisenhower administration had just two years earlier refused such an Israeli request on the grounds that such a sale would spur a perilous regional arms race and undermine America's Cold War position in the Middle East. Why the change? Embittered State Department officials revived Marshall's complaint: that the Kennedy administration, with the 1962 congressional midterm elections looming, bowed ignobly to pressure from the Israel lobby. The

State Department's senior Middle East official, Phillips Talbot, still ascribes the Hawk sale as much to these domestic considerations as to diplomatic ones.[4] Having watched the debate from Cairo, the administration's foremost Arabist, Ambassador John Badeau, granted that the Pentagon thought Israel legitimately needed the missiles. "But I don't think this is why it was done," Badeau said years later. "It was done because the Congress was facing the first election to Congress after Kennedy had been elected and individuals, who were contributors to the campaign funds of various candidates, withheld their contributions in that summer along into August and said, 'You don't get this until we know what you are going to do for Israel.' And finally, the president said, 'Well, I've got military justifications, I'm going to sell Hawk missiles to Israel' and then he got the funds."[5] An angry Arab world concurred. But the documentary record tells a different story.

There is an old Washington saw: to change policy, change personnel. After Israel, Egypt, and France attacked Egypt during the 1956 Suez crisis, Eisenhower and his aides came to view Israel as potentially aggressive, like a skittish dog that generally enjoys company but might bite if cornered or startled. Most of the key New Frontiersmen lacked the institutional memory of the Suez trauma, and Kennedy's men were generally contemptuous of many of the old general's cautious policies. That made the new administration more predisposed to hear out the Israeli case for arms sales. The Kennedy administration's absence of direct baggage from Suez let it seriously consider Israel's argument that it sought—for the time being—purely defensive weaponry to fend off Nasser's Soviet-made air force. The Eisenhower administration, by contrast, had been more sympathetic to the Arab complaint that boosting Israeli deterrence increased Israeli arrogance and eased the way to Israeli aggression.

The Kennedy administration's decision-making structure also dramatically helped Israel's chances. In 1960, a determined president, aided by a State Department whose Middle Eastern desks were staffed by Dulles loyalists and Arabists suspicious of Israel, could blunt Ben-Gurion's advances. Two years later, under a president determined to act as his own secretary of state, the center of policy-making gravity had swung away from the State Department and toward an invigorated National Security Council (NSC), abetted decisively by a willing Pentagon. The unsympathetic bureaucrats at the State Department's Near East affairs division (NEA) found themselves losing out to the NSC and the Pentagon.

A sustained campaign of Israeli diplomacy helped. Ben-Gurion himself was often unhelpfully bombastic, but many of his advisers were strikingly shrewd. Peres in particular put in a virtuoso diplomatic performance in 1962, sometimes aiming at U.S. objections with such lethal accuracy

In 1939, a 22-year-old John F. Kennedy visited Egypt *(above)* and Mandate Palestine, where he talked in Jerusalem with an officer from the ruling British administration *(right)*. "I have never seen two groups more unwilling to try and work out a solution that has some hope of success," JFK wrote his father.

His younger brother Robert made his own youthful pilgrimage in 1948, where the future attorney general witnessed Israel's birth—although not before being arrested and blindfolded by the mainstream Zionist militia known as the Haganah while strolling Jerusalem's streets.

As a congressman, JFK visited Israel in 1951, where he dined at Prime Minister David Ben-Gurion's Jerusalem residence, along with another young congressman, Franklin Delano Roosevelt, Jr., *(center)*. Ben-Gurion would be prime minister again when Kennedy was elected president nine years later.

President Kennedy met Israeli Foreign Minister Golda Meir at his Palm Beach compound in December 1962. Kennedy's top Middle East diplomat, Phillips Talbot *(center)*, and Israel's ambassador to Washington, Avraham Harman *(left)*, looked on. Kennedy offered support in case of an Arab invasion but warned Israel not to try to acquire nuclear weapons.

The New Frontier's Israel team: Phillips Talbot (*top, left*) with Ben-Gurion; Kennedy's envoy to the American Jewish community, Myer Feldman (*center, left*), with Israeli Education and Culture Minister Abba Eban; and Kennedy's ambassador to Israel, Walworth Barbour (*bottom, left*), presenting his credentials to Meir in May 1961 as Israeli President Yitzhak Ben-Zvi looks on.

The search for common ground with Egyptian President Jamal Abd al-Nasser, the nemesis of both Israel and the Arab monarchs, was the most innovative prong of Kennedy's Middle East policy. Nasser—a nationalist firebrand whom Kennedy's aides sometimes called the "Mister Big" of the Arab world—made the cover of *Time* on March 29, 1963. One of the strongest proponents of the Nasser initiative was Egypt's ambassador to Washington, Mustafa Kamel.

The overture to Nasser outraged the most important conservative Arab state, Saudi Arabia. Both King Saud—seen above with Kennedy and Secretary of State Dean Rusk at a 1962 White House visit—and the real power behind the kingdom, Crown Prince Faysal *(right)*, feared that after Nasser sent troops to finish off the doddering monarchy in Yemen, he would try next to topple the House of Saud.

Kennedy also butted heads with his Air Force chief of staff, General Curtis Le-May, who hated the idea of Operation Hard Surface—the June 1963 deployment of an American F-100D fighter squadron to Jidda to deter Nasser from attacking Saudi Arabia.

Two young Ben-Gurion protégés—Deputy Defense Minister Shimon Peres *(left)* and IDF Deputy Chief of Staff Yitzhak Rabin, seen here in January 1963—helped strengthen the U.S.–Israel security relationship.

In August 1962, Kennedy agreed to sell Israel cutting-edge Hawk anti-aircraft missiles—the start of the U.S.–Israel military alliance we know today. In June 1964, Israeli Prime Minister Levi Eshkol and Peres inspected a Hawk battery at Fort Bliss, Texas.

In the 1950s, the Eisenhower administration helped Israel build a small nuclear reactor at Nahal Soreq, outside Tel Aviv, for peaceful research.

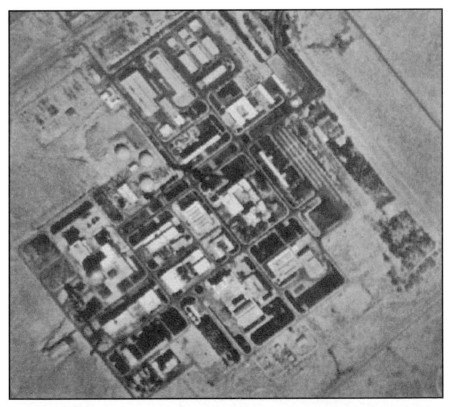

But Ben-Gurion was also determined to get the bomb. With French help, Israel secretly built a far larger reactor (seen here in a 1971 U.S. satellite photo) near the Negev desert town of Dimona to produce nuclear weapons, under the noses of U.S. inspectors.

In a press conference on November 14, 1963, Kennedy called the Senate's decision to cut aid to Nasser's Egypt "the worst attack on foreign aid that we have seen since the beginning of the Marshall Plan." Eight days later, Kennedy was assassinated in Dallas. On November 24, Eshkol signed the condolence book at the U.S. embassy in Tel Aviv.

On July 4, 1966, Eshkol, Barbour, and Supreme Court Chief Justice Earl Warren traveled through the Jerusalem hills to dedicate Yad Kennedy, a memorial to the slain president shaped like a tree felled before its time.

that one has to either suspect discreet assistance from within the White House, admire superlative Israeli intelligence work, or simply appreciate the instincts of a natural master. While Israel's arguments were couched exclusively in strategic terms, the looming midterm elections—however hushed—could hardly have been a disincentive.

Nor did the U.S. Treasury object to the sale. With the United States hobbled by a genuinely alarming balance-of-payments deficit, the administration (and for that matter Raytheon, the Hawk's manufacturer) was looking for opportunities to sell more arms, not less.[6]

The Hawk decision was also partially influenced by the Kennedy administration's attempt to reach out to Nasser. Israel argued that with Nasser receiving Soviet arms and American aid, some compensation was in order. Even the most ardent proponents of the Nasser initiative knew that it could only increase Israeli anxiety and fears of abandonment. The Hawk sale, Israel argued, would ease those jitters.

The historian Douglas Little has plausibly argued, too, that the Kennedy administration, preoccupied with nuclear proliferation, hoped that the Hawk sale would assuage Israel's security concerns—and that an Israel thus soothed with conventional arms would feel less need to get nuclear weapons.[7] Little's hypothesis is intriguing, but the available documents did not reveal any direct proof that Israel and the Kennedy administration were trading Hawks for Israeli concessions on nuclear issues.[8] The record does show, however, that once they realized that the Hawk sale was a foregone conclusion, NEA's officials sought to tie it to Israeli willingness to go along with the U.N.–sponsored Johnson plan to resettle or compensate Palestinian refugees.

For their part, Talbot, Badeau, and others ascribed the Hawk decision to Kennedy's disinclination to cross the Israel lobby. But the Israel lobby— a Washington powerhouse by the 1980s—was simply not that formidable in the early 1960s. American Jewry was less confident about its ability to throw its weight around, more intimidated by a Christian-dominated society exploring the limits of its tolerance, and less passionately identified with an Israel that had not yet gone through the galvanic experience of the Six Day War, which erupted five years after the Hawk sale. Moreover, the Israel lobby was young; when I. L. Kenen founded the American Israel Public Affairs Committee (AIPAC) in the 1950s, he was its sole employee. While his lobby made progress in grassroots mobilization, built up its paid membership, gained support in Congress, and had a sympathetic White House ear in the person of Mike Feldman, AIPAC had little true clout in the executive branch in the early 1960s.

To be sure, the Israel lobby could squeeze supportive resolutions out of Congress by 1961, but a few episodes give the flavor for AIPAC's attempts to get much out of Kennedy's White House. At a fruitless March 1961 meeting with NEA officials, for instance, pro-Israel lobbyists were reduced to praising the cogency and clarity of a presentation by Armin Meyer, one of the least pro-Israel diplomats in the entire State Department.[9] American Jewish pressure did not prevent the administration from cuffing Israel in the U.N. Security Council in April 1962 over Israeli reprisal raids against Syria (although it did seem to dissuade the administration from taking similar measures the next year). As telegrams poured into the White House from members of the American Jewish group B'nai Brith, a frustrated Mike Feldman wrote of one State Department draft response, "If it is the purpose of this correspondence to raise an anti-Kennedy issue in the Jewish community, then it is all right."[10] One Detroit rabbi cabled Kennedy to warn that the Jewish state was in more dire straits than ever: it was now facing "threats of war by the UAW"—confusing the United Arab Republic with the United Auto Workers.[11] It was all a far cry from the purring, powerful lobbying machine of the 1980s and 1990s.

Of course, Kennedy was a political animal, and he knew that the Hawk sale could only help him with pro-Israel voters and donors. But American Jews in the 1960s were mostly Democrats anyway. It is hard to imagine that political calculations did not cross Kennedy's mind, but it is hard to find proof that they drove his decision. For all the Arabists' worries, there is virtually no documentary evidence that the Hawk sale was driven by domestic considerations. "The Israelis made no effort to stimulate pressures from Jewish organizations and Congress," insisted AIPAC's Kenen.[12] This is surely overstated, but the Israel lobby's major proposal in 1962 was in fact related not to Hawk sales but to a comparatively trivial resolution urging the U.N. General Assembly to request direct Arab-Israeli negotiations. At the U.S. mission to the United Nations, Adlai Stevenson considered the measure meaningless and voted against it, to AIPAC's chagrin. Indeed, the only two countries in the Western Hemisphere to oppose the resolution were the odd couple of Kennedy's United States and Castro's Cuba—hardly a stirring testimonial to the young Israel lobby's brawn.[13]

But the final and probably decisive explanation for the Hawk sale is that that the balance of power in Washington was not the only one that had shifted. The ongoing Soviet arms sales to Nasser's Egypt had made Israel increasingly vulnerable. Ben-Gurion tended to paint the Egyptian threat in livid shades of scarlet and night-pitch black, but behind the nightmarish imagery of Nasser as Hitler's second coming was what more restrained Israeli representatives such as Peres and Ambassador Avraham Harman argued was a real vulnerability: Nasser's Soviet warplanes might well be able to deliver a knockout first punch by leveling Israel's handful of airfields and then using dominance of the air to prevent the Israel Defense Forces (IDF) from mobilizing to blunt an Arab invasion. The Pentagon agreed that Israel had a legitimate, defensive need for the missiles, leaving opponents of the sale elsewhere within the administration without a leg to stand on.

The irony, of course, is that five years after the Hawk sale, the Israelis would do to the Egyptians something not entirely dissimilar to what they had feared Nasser would do to them. During the preemptive airstrike that inaugurated the six days of sharp, one-sided combat in 1967, Israeli warplanes destroyed virtually the entire Egyptian air force on the ground. So did Egypt ever have a military edge, or was Israel casting itself as the underdog during the Kennedy years in order to secure the Hawk sale? In other words, was Israel too peddling a "missile gap"—a calculating Middle Eastern version of JFK's disingenuous 1960 campaign insistence that America had fallen dangerously behind the Soviet Union in intercontinental ballistic missiles?

The answer has to be both yes and no. Egypt was indeed getting state-of-the-art Soviet armaments, even as Israel was frequently relying on hand-me-downs from the West. On paper at least, Nasser's Soviet-made air force was formidable, and had it cratered even one Israeli airfield, it could have seriously snarled the IDF's all-important ability to mobilize its reserves. The question was how likely it was that Egypt could pull off such a tour de force. (After the Six Day War, one popular Middle Eastern joke had two mystified Egyptians trying to understand the enormity of their defeat. "It was the Russian weapons," gripes one. "No, they worked just fine," replies his comrade. "It was the Russian military strategy manual: first, draw the enemy onto your own territory. Second, wait for the winter.") Simply having planes has never been enough for any state; planes are only as good as their pilots. Pentagon analyses at the time pointed out that Israel probably retained important advantages in its armed forces' morale, training, command and control, and overall skill and grit. But neither prudent generals nor worried statesmen tend to be complacent about their adversaries' capabilities. The risks might have been smaller than Ben-Gurion, Meir, Peres, and Harman sometimes made out, but they were real.

Moreover, Israel's campaign for the Hawk was of a piece with the Jewish state's longstanding desire to forge an arms relationship with the West's mightiest great power—which was precisely why the State Department so doggedly resisted. Until Kennedy, Israel's leaders and generals had to content themselves with scraps: light arms, yesterday's technology, occasional training, arms manuals, and ammunition. With the sale of a major, state-of-the-art weapons system, America set the precedent that ultimately created the U.S.–Israel strategic relationship: a multimillion-dollar annual business in cutting-edge weaponry, supplemented by extensive military-to-military dialogues, security consultations, extensive joint training exercises, and cooperative research-and-development ventures. In 1962, of course, all that could have been no more than a glimmer in Ben-Gurion's eye; the full scope of the U.S.–Israel military alliance by the end of the twentieth century probably lay beyond the Israeli leader's fondest imaginings, if not beyond the State Department's direst fears. Even so, 1962 marked the year that Ben-Gurion finally got his foot in the door.

THE HAWK SALE THAT WASN'T

Israel's founding father was a man who kept his eyes on the prize. As the historian Zach Levey has noted, "obtaining arms from the United States remained the most important goal in Israel's foreign policy" between Suez and Kennedy's inauguration.[14] Economic and technical aid did not suffice; Ben-Gurion wanted American arms, he wanted them to be state-of-the-art, he wanted them to set a precedent, and he wanted them badly.

But until the United States would break its embargo, Israel made do with the other two Western great powers—its Suez comrades. France began selling arms to Israel in the summer of 1956 to press the hated Nasser to stop military aid to Algerian rebels. "In the six months preceding the Sinai campaign," a CIA report noted, "France poured 40,000 tons of military equipment into Israel," including the best planes in Israel's air force.[15] The French-Israeli marriage of convenience, in Nadav Safran's apt phrase, unexpectedly survived and intensified well past Suez. France used Israel to squeeze Nasser and to stoke its smoldering imperial ambitions, especially after the smart of being left out of the anticommunist regional alliance known as the Baghdad Pact and the humiliation of Suez.[16]

Britain proved more resistant to Israeli desires. But after cooperating (albeit haltingly) with Israel in 1958 in supporting King Husayn of Jordan against Nasserite upheaval, Britain decided to sell Israel the item that had topped its shopping list for about five years: the Centurion tank.[17] Centurions became the backbone of the IDF's armored corps until they were superseded by American M-60 Pattons in 1970.[18]

This all suited Eisenhower and Secretary of State John Foster Dulles fine. Helping arm Israel "would represent a major departure" in U.S.–Israel relations "which might adversely affect delicate relations with the rest of the area," wrote Dulles's State Department.[19] Even so, the eager Israelis tried as hard as they dared—either to buy arms outright from America or from British or French stockpiles of U.S.–manufactured weapons. In either case, they also hoped to receive American financial aid to defray the costs. The Israeli wish-list was substantial: tanks, helicopters, submarines, antitank rifles, transport planes, trucks, and antiaircraft missiles.

For years, Washington had wanted no part of this. But the fall of Hashimite Iraq in 1958 and the fear that communism was on the march in the Middle East changed things somewhat. Israel had let American planes overfly its airspace in 1958 en route to propping up the Jordanian monarchy. Moreover, Nasser's reputation for mischief making was growing. So the Eisenhower administration rewarded Israel with a one-time-only sale of the recoilless antitank rifles—easy to use, cheap, helpful for defending outlying Israeli towns from Arab attack, and largely defensive in nature. Israel asked for 350; Dulles signed off on 100 and turned down Israel's further request for heavy arms.[20] In October 1958, Dulles told Israel's doughty visiting foreign minister, Golda Meir, not to get carried away by the rifle sale. Washington's "basic policy had not changed; we still did not wish to become an important supplier of arms to Israel, preferring to concentrate on economic assistance, and did not wish to have the exceptions we had made become the rule." When Dulles succumbed on May 24, 1959, to an agonizing recurrence of the cancer diagnosed during the Suez crisis, he left behind a U.S. foreign policy bureaucracy set against arms sales to Israel.

Meir's boss did not do much better than she had done. In March 1960, Ben-Gurion traveled to Washington, bent above all on winning an American promise to sell Hawks. Before his arrival, the Arab diplomatic corps let their disapproval of the visit show; Lebanon's ambassador even hectored the new secretary of state, Christian Herter, about the forthcoming adaptation of Leon Uris's Zionist potboiler *Exodus* into a Hollywood movie, which the ambassador considered a shamefully transparent bid for American sympathy.[21]

The Lebanese diplomat need not have fretted. Ben-Gurion's trip was fated for frustration. On March 10, Eisenhower told Ben-Gurion that he "would not stand for the destruction of any nation in the Middle East," but Ben-Gurion "must realize that the United States does not want to establish itself as a partisan supporter of any nation in the Middle East," let alone its arms dealer.[22] State Department officials—including Undersecretary Douglas Dillon, the Republican Brahmin who would become Kennedy's treasury secretary—were equally unmoved by Ben-Gurion's arguments.[23]

But their boss, Herter, was not on the same page as the rest of the administration. To Ben-Gurion's surprise, the new secretary of state promised in a March 13 meeting to consider the Israeli request *"sympathetically and urgently."* It would probably be best to ship the missiles from some NATO country, Herter mused.

"Am I right in believing that I can consider your reply a positive one?" Ben-Gurion asked, seeing an opening.

"That is a fair assumption," Herter replied, hastening to add that there might be other factors of which he was unaware.

But Ben-Gurion seems to have heard that as an unambiguous yes. The excited prime minister told Herter that "Israel has deep faith in the spiritual world" and would try to repay the administration by "doing something worthwhile in the world."[24] Ben-Gurion left Washington thinking that he had finally cracked the iron wall of American refusal to sell the Jewish state a major, state-of-the-art weapons system.

He had not. Herter seems to have gone off the reservation. On April 11, Israeli Ambassador Avraham Harman was summoned to the State Department, where Dillon and the new assistant secretary for NEA, G. Lewis Jones, dashed cold water in Israel's face. The Pentagon now said that it could not offer any Hawks within Ben-Gurion's time frame. It could, however, offer a $10.2 million electronics package that included cutting-edge technology that many full-blown American allies lacked and was ten times larger than any previous arms deal with the Jewish state.[25]

A bitterly disappointed Ben-Gurion felt a promise had been broken. On June 9, he sent Herter a letter confessing that he could not "conceal my feeling of disappointment. . . . We face a possible attack of Soviet origin and manufacture," Ben-Gurion wrote. "I am sure that we will not be left to face it alone."[26]

The administration resented the guilt trip. When U.S. Ambassador to Israel Ogden Reid reported back to the State Department that Ben-Gurion wanted to hold Herter to his supposed commitment, someone in Herter's circle scrawled in the margin, "BG will not find people very anxious to talk with him if he uses the screws like this."[27]

Nor did turning the screws work. Meir was rebuffed again on another U.S. visit in late June. In early August, Herter—now back on message—wrote Ben-Gurion that the Hawks were a perfect illustration of why Washington had not sold "spectacular weaponry" to Israel. "While the Hawk system is purely defensive, it is easy to imagine that some other outside power [i.e. the Soviet Union], anxious to exacerbate tensions in the Near East, would yield to the importunities of Israel's apprehensive neighbors and equip them with missile weaponry," including surface-to-surface rockets that would sail past the Hawks and render them an expensive waste. The only one to benefit from having Egypt and Israel squander "their limited resources on unproductive and fabulously expensive weaponry" would be the Soviet Union.[28]

For his part, Nasser gave the administration scant credit for its messy refusal to sell the Hawks when he met Eisenhower during the annual kick-off of the U.N. General Assembly in New York on September 26. "Israel is the barrier to good U.S.–Arab relations," the Egyptian leader told Ike. While the West refused to sell weapons to the UAR, the Jewish state was raking in warplanes from France, tanks from Britain, and anti-tank rifles from America. Nasser seemed not much to care which Western great power sold the arms; for him, the blunt fact remained that the *"UAR cannot get arms from the West and Israel does get arms from the West."*

America had never sent offensive weapons to Israel, Ike protested, just "some radar equipment and defensive things."[29] At the time, the old general was quite right: America's arms policy was not France's. The Eisenhower administration had indeed refused to become a major arms supplier for Israel. But within two years, Ben-Gurion would get his Hawks after all.

STATE OF ISOLATION

Ben-Gurion had his work cut out for him in 1961. From the start of the Kennedy administration, the State Department's bureau of Near East affairs pushed to ensure that the New Frontiersmen did not change course on arms sales to Israel. The State Department stressed the wisdom of Eisenhower's policy to the influential new national security adviser, McGeorge Bundy. "The United States declined [to sell the Hawks] because of its reluctance to have a weapon of this sophistication introduced into the Middle East, inevitably producing a dangerous new element in the never-ending pursuit of better arms," noted a State Department memo. What Israeli Ambassador Harman might characterize to Bundy as a U.S. willingness to reconsider was the last verbal resort of "heavily pressed" officials, not a genuine openness to changing the U.S. position.

The State Department was also unimpressed with the threat posed to Israel by the MiG-19, the Soviets' first supersonic fighter, which Harman claimed the Soviet Union was now providing to Nasser. Harman insisted that the MiG-19 far outclassed Israel's best fighter, the French Super-Mystère. Without Hawks, Harman told Bundy in a none-too-subtle allusion to Kennedy's inaugural, Israel would face its "time of maximum danger."[30] But the State Department countered that the Super-Mystère was "virtually on a par with the MIG-19," which in turn was vastly inferior to the new Mirages that Paris had just agreed to provide to Jerusalem.[31]

Even if the State Department's opinion had not changed, however, the landscape had. The arrival of the New Frontiersmen put a different group of players on the field. One might have expected the new treasury secretary, Douglas Dillon, who as undersecretary of state under Herter had helped blunt Israel's push for the Hawk in 1960, to play a role in the sequel, but

Dillon seems not to have been involved in the Kennedy administration's deliberations. A more important shift came at the Pentagon, where the reliable, courtly former CIA official William P. Bundy—a Harvard-trained lawyer, lifelong Democrat, and son-in-law to Dean Acheson—now served as deputy assistant secretary for international security affairs.[32] (Bundy's courtesy became legendary. "Everyone at the State Department is trying to knife me in the back except for Bill Bundy," Henry Kissinger cracked early in the Nixon administration. "He is still enough of a gentleman to knife me in the chest.")[33] Under Kennedy, Bill Bundy sat at a fulcrum, both because his position as deputy to Assistant Secretary of Defense for International Security Affairs Paul H. Nitze put him close to U.S. decision making on overall global strategy and because his position as National Security Adviser McGeorge Bundy's lookalike brother put him close to the president's chief foreign policy adviser. Bill Bundy handled much of the Pentagon's staff work on the Hawks, but he was no freelancer. His overall view of the region was endorsed by his bosses as well. "Nitze and MacN. think mil. bal. has changed," Komer scrawled in a June 1962 note.[34] The sympathy of Bundy, Nitze, and Defense Secretary McNamara to Israel's military anxieties would help set an historic precedent.

In May 1961, an Eisenhower holdover aide at NEA named William Hamilton was unnerved to note how well disposed Bill Bundy was to the Israeli argument that the Hawk was a purely defensive system.[35] Letting Israel defend itself from aerial assault wouldn't necessarily change the regional balance of power, Bundy said. Nor was Bundy impressed with the old Eisenhower argument that the introduction of a system as spectacular as the Hawk would trigger a Middle East arms race. After all, the region was already awash in advanced weaponry from London, Paris, and Moscow; Bundy doubted that one defensive system would tip over the cart.

The Pentagon also kept one eye on the price tag of the Hawks. Throughout a U.S. administration bedeviled by a balance-of-payments deficit, Israel remained "one of our 'excess-currency' countries." McNamara and his aides were on the lookout for ways "to help reduce U.S. dollar outflow in this area."[36] The defense secretary was looking to say yes, not no: "Secretary McNamara feels very strongly that we must under no circumstances reject a valid credit request . . . and he and Secretary Dillon also feel strongly that we must stimulate this business from the standpoint of balance of payments—always, of course, subject to political judgment as to the merit of the request."[37] Where strategically feasible, McNamara's Pentagon was out to do more business with Israel, not less.

Overall, the Kennedy Pentagon's position on the Hawks reflected a subtle but important shift. Under Eisenhower, the Joint Chiefs of Staff had argued that Israel's qualitative superiority in personnel, training, and morale gave the Jewish state enough of an edge over the Arabs that there was no *military* reason for the United States to begin arming Israel. But the chiefs added that if there were compelling *political* reasons to offer arms or military aid, the focus should be on defensive systems.[38] In effect, the Eisenhower administration stressed the earlier part of that formulation; now, Bundy stressed the latter. This shifted the emphasis decisively. By hop-scotching the question of military necessity, Bundy could focus on the sort of weapon that should be considered if a political case were to be made for further helping Israel. With the former set of emphases, the Hawk sale made no sense; with Bundy's set, it was made to measure. By the time Ben-Gurion made his way to New York for his May 1961 meeting with Kennedy, NEA was fretting that it would be left alone to hold the line against the Hawk. Reinforcements from Bill Bundy's Pentagon would not be forthcoming.

THE OLD MAN AND THE YOUNG PRESIDENT

The change in personnel also mattered at the very top. When Kennedy met Ben-Gurion on May 30 at the Waldorf, the new president's tone was different from his predecessor's. Where Eisenhower had bluntly refused, Kennedy merely hesitated. The arguments about the Hawks were similar—indeed, sometimes identical—but the underlying firmness was gone.[39]

As he had with Ike, Ben-Gurion centered his security pitch around the Egyptian menace. Ben-Gurion described Nasser to Kennedy in the bleakest terms, as a cruel aggressor bent on Hitlerian genocide. The Israeli leader then moved directly on to the Hawks, echoing the arguments he had made during his March 1960 visit to Washington. A year ago, Ben-Gurion had asked the United States for arms, especially defensive ones, since "the UAR has 26 air fields and Israel has only four." When he asked whether he could end his visit by assuming that Israel would get the Hawks, Ben-Gurion told Kennedy, he had been told "that is a fair assumption." Ben-Gurion still saw no reason that Israel should be denied these weapons, particularly since it was in the U.S. interest for Israel to have defensive arms.

Tellingly, Ben-Gurion's Waldorf account of the Eisenhower administration's commitments on the Hawks revolved almost entirely around former secretary of state Herter's brief sympathetic comment. (NEA aides must have been driven to distraction by the amount of mileage that Ben-Gurion forced out of what many of them saw as one minor gaffe.) By actually quoting Herter's remark back to Kennedy, the Israeli leader implied that the "fair assumption" was a considered administration commitment rather than an unfortunate individual misstep. Once Ben-Gurion had the bit in his teeth, no amount of American repudiation would get it out. Sooner or later, the dogged prime minister seemed to be hoping, America's policy could be brought into line with Herter's "promise."

Kennedy's response borrowed from both Ike and Herter. The new president "had not found records which permit a firm conclusion about what had been committed by the previous Administration." (State groaned.) But while the Hawk was a defensive system, it was also a sophisticated missile whose introduction into the region could produce a dangerous spiral. (State sighed with relief.) Introducing state-of-the-art missiles into the region might drive the Arabs to seek ground-to-ground missiles against which the Hawks would be useless. (State began to relax.) On the other hand, Kennedy did not "want to see Israel at a disadvantage," and if the Arabs made a "critical break-through of weapons . . . we would have our views of what to do." (State tensed back up.) The administration would have to monitor the situation, but it hesitated "to be the ones to introduce missiles into the region."

Perhaps sensing that he had overplayed Herter's legacy, Ben-Gurion hastened to explain that he sought Hawks not "on the basis of a commitment made by the previous Administration but on the merits of the case." Fair enough, Kennedy replied, but he still did not want to be the president who brought the Middle East into the missile age.

The discussion then turned to the regional balance of forces. Nasser had 300 fighter planes, Ben-Gurion told Kennedy, as well as 200 more on hand from the other Arab leaders. To keep pace, Israel had ordered 60 new Mirages from France, but it would take a year before all of them arrived. Until then, Nasser's new Soviet MiG-19s were particularly worrisome. Washington could not "eliminate the hazard," Kennedy pointed out, but it would not want Israel in "such a position of inferiority that an attack on it would be encouraged." In that case, Ben-Gurion countered, sell us Hawks—the most elegant way to let Israel defend itself without threatening its neighbors.

Kennedy noted that only a handful of other countries had received Hawks and again warned of a missile race. "You don't feel that this is a satisfactory answer to your request," JFK said, "but you can be assured that we will continue to watch the situation." When the meeting wound down— after moving on to the Cold War, the Palestinian problem, and Ben-Gurion's admiration for the Peace Corps concept—Kennedy tried to summarize their discussion of the Hawk issue. "I expressed a desire to continually review the missile situation," he told Ben-Gurion. "We are reluctant to give Israel missiles and you understand that, but we would be disturbed if Israel should get into a situation that would invite attack. We will keep the matter under continuing review in our Administration, I can assure you."

Kennedy's summation was significantly more encouraging than anything Eisenhower had said on the subject. JFK sounded considerably less pro forma about promising to take the matter under advisement than Eisenhower and his aides had a year ago. By telling Ben-Gurion that the United States was "reluctant" to sell Hawks, Kennedy was hardly telling the Israeli prime minister anything he had not already heard before. Nevertheless, the ratios had changed: Kennedy offered two parts review, one part reluctance, and one part sympathy for Israel's security dilemma, whereas Eisenhower had offered one part review and three parts refusal. Ben-Gurion left the Waldorf more optimistic than he had been since Herter's semi-promise the previous year.

The State Department also began to adjust, over NEA's protests. In the fall, Secretary of State Rusk asked his assistant secretary for Near East affairs, Phillips Talbot, what Nasser's ongoing military buildup meant for Israel's security. Rusk may have been considering a shift in American policy, but Talbot and the State Department's Middle East specialists saw "no good reason for the United States to change its arms policy toward Israel." Citing a recent Pentagon study, Talbot argued that Israel's modernity, manpower, money, and morale still gave it a significant military edge, despite Nasser's latest Soviet acquisitions. That advantage would only widen with the pending arrival of the Mirage fighters. Arab fears of Israel's battlefield prowess necessitated "a wolf pack approach" in a fight—forcing the Jewish state to exhaust itself on multiple fronts—but any war coalition would be outclassed by Israel and riven by inter-Arab dissension. Scant surprise, then, that there had been no "major Arab military action" against Israel since 1948.[40] The Arabs were also deterred by the knowledge that the West would intervene if Israel seemed in real trouble. Nevertheless, Talbot sighed, the Israeli leadership "refuses to admit this, claiming to fear a surprise air assault"—despite its entirely adequate supply of weapons from non-American sources and its "own rapidly developing armaments industry."[41]

NEA had two major worries about Israeli security. On the one hand, an Israel that felt internationally isolated or immediately imperiled might lash out preemptively against Egypt or Syria; on the other, an Arab world that felt threatened by a Jewish state with ballistic missiles or atomic bombs might lash out desperately against Israel. Meanwhile, Jerusalem was pushing for both the Hawks and an American security guarantee—a presidential promise to come to Israel's aid if the Arabs invaded.[42] So the administration needed to soothe the Israelis by offering economic aid and political succor and soothe the Arabs by keeping an eye on Israel's nuclear program. Providing state-of-the-art missile technology to Israel, NEA fretted, would upset the precarious balance.

PERES SWIMS THE POTOMAC

When the visiting Shimon Peres first met Robert F. Kennedy in his Justice Department office, the attorney general began by reminiscing about his days as a cub reporter for the *Boston Post* in Israel in the spring of 1948. Peres told Kennedy that he had come to Washington to break America's "elegant arms embargo" against Israel by securing the Hawks.

"Well, what's stopping you?" RFK asked.

Peres replied that the Pentagon and the State Department were separated by the Potomac, whose bridges were blocked by heavy traffic.

"You look like a fit young man," the attorney general replied. "Why don't you swim across?"[43]

Bobby Kennedy had the dynamic right. As his brother's administration settled into office, the Pentagon's top policymakers were coming to view Israel's requests increasingly charitably, and NEA was finding itself increasingly isolated. When the State Department nixed an Israeli attempt to buy a defensive radar system from an American arms firm, the Pentagon's Bill Bundy sent Talbot a pointed note. "I realize that this is a straight political matter, but I am a little concerned whether we are getting into an unduly inflexible position on sales to Israel of sophisticated equipment," Bundy wrote. "The increasing Soviet deliveries to Egypt highlight the problem, which is largely one of preserving a military balance under which neither side would be tempted to attack the other."[44] A few days later, when the State Department circulated a draft of new formal policy guidelines for Israel that barred the "supply of major categories of arms to Israel," the Joint Chiefs simply signed off on them.[45] Bundy, however, tweaked the language to permit the sales of "equipment particularly suitable for defensive uses as evidence of our interest in Israel's welfare and to avoid charges of partiality arising from occasional United States sales to Arab Governments."[46] Talbot and his subordinates feared precipitating an arms race; Bundy feared prolonging an arms imbalance.

A few weeks later, in May 1962, Israel began to make a savvy new pitch for Hawks that hammered away at the Pentagon-NEA split. Israel sought to find sympathetic U.S. officials, which meant circumventing the State Department. With the Pentagon and much of the National Security Council feeling charitably toward Israel's request, the State Department found it had lost the ability to block Israel that it had enjoyed under Dulles.

Ben-Gurion's emissary was the 39-year-old Peres, who handled the day-to-day running of Israel's Ministry of Defense since Ben-Gurion was both defense and prime minister. His latter-day reputation for dovishness notwithstanding, Peres was then seen as a hard-liner; during his visit, the future architect of Oslo's New Middle East warned one disapproving NEA official that "the Arabs were emotional rather than logical people and thus could not be predicted."[47]

On his supposedly unofficial visit, Peres cut quite a swath across the District of Columbia, meeting with Defense Department aides, including Deputy Secretary Roswell Gilpatric and Assistant Secretary Nitze; enjoying a dinner thrown by Israeli Ambassador Harman; and visiting the White House to see McGeorge Bundy and Mike Feldman. "He will undoubtedly present a high pressure approach for us to sell Israel more sophisticated weapons," Bill Bundy alerted Gilpatric. "He has a reputation of being articulate, knowledgeable of world affairs, crafty and unscrupulous."[48] Feldman was more complimentary, calling Peres "one of the 5 leading politicians in Israel" and urging fellow Kennedy aides to meet him.[49]

The highest-ranking official whom Peres met was National Security Adviser McGeorge Bundy. On May 21, Peres told Bundy that Hawks for Israel were "now a necessary contribution to the stabilization of the Middle East." Bundy reported to the State Department that the Israeli emissary "appeared to believe that we should gradually get into a steady relation of military assistance to Israel, and I think it is predictable that he will have been making this point to Zionist leaders in this country."[50] While Peres also made pitches for a security guarantee and U.S.–Israel talks on the regional military balance, his main concern was the Hawk.

For its part, the State Department gave Peres a tepid welcome. Also on May 21, Undersecretary of State for Political Affairs George McGhee warned Peres that Israel's 1955 reprisal raid on the Egyptian-held Gaza Strip had spooked Nasser into seeking Soviet arms; Peres shot back that Nasser had only started showing restraint after his 1956 drubbing in the Sinai. McGhee then argued that new weapons for the IDF only drove Nasser to counter; Peres replied that Israel could not afford the casualties of an Arab invasion and therefore needed enough of an edge to deter an attack in the first place.[51]

In another meeting that day, Talbot and Peres squared off over the administration's Nasser overture. U.S.–UAR rapprochement had induced Egypt to mute its quarrel with Israel, the assistant secretary of state argued, and such diplomacy would make Israel more secure than new air defenses, which would "inevitably create new appetites" in the Arab world for Soviet missiles. Talbot and Peres disagreed over Israel's vulnerability to Nasser's airpower, which Talbot did not see as extraordinary; after all, as Talbot pointed out, even the United States would have only about 15 minutes of lead time in case of Soviet attack. Peres replied that the administration was undermining Israel's security by giving aid and comfort to Nasser. "Israel could not ask the United States to abandon its UAR policy," Peres admitted to Talbot. "It did feel, however, that as long as the United States

had increased Israel's risks, concessions should be made to Israel for purposes of balance."[52] Peres hit the same theme with the director of the office of Near East affairs, Robert Strong, over lunch on May 23 in Peres's
suite at the Mayflower Hotel. "Having worsened Israel's position by increasing aid to the UAR," the Israeli argued, "the US should make an
equivalent gesture to Israel."[53] The suggestion had a certain dash to it;
Israel's diplomats were using Kennedy's outreach to their nemesis as an
argument for why he should also reach out to them.

Over breakfast two days later with Bill Bundy, Peres lost no time work-
ing over the Defense Department official. Shrewdly, Peres sought to give
Bundy a counterargument to use against the State Department naysayers.
Washington should move to stabilize the region in the face of Syrian and
Egyptian disruptions "and above all to relieve Israel's sense of isolation" —
precisely the thing that the State Department worried could prompt rash
Israeli military moves.

Peres's return volley was not only aimed with pinpoint accuracy, it also
had a wicked spin. The State Department had sought to assuage Israel's
jitters via aid and diplomacy; but since that was clearly not doing the trick,
why not offer military help as well? In effect, Peres echoed NEA's diagno-
sis and offered a bolder prescription. The malady was Israel's fear of isolation; the remedy was a more elaborate demonstration of American friendship.

Ideally, Peres said, Israel would like to see the administration guarantee
Israel's frontiers, urge Britain and France to join in such a declaration, or
let Israel into some form of association with NATO. But if "such a major
initiative were not possible, the U.S. should *at least* be prepared to take a
more major role alongside France" as an arms supplier for Israel.[54] So
beyond the earlier, more modest items, such as small-arms sales, sonar
orders, and early-warning air-defense systems, Peres said, "the U.S. should
supply a Hawk missile unit." The Hawks would be a consolation prize to
make up for the lack of a security guarantee. And Peres pointedly asked
only for one unit. After all, if Israel got one now, it would be able to get
more later.

Peres then introduced a new argument: Israel could no longer rely on
Western Europe for arms as it had in the past. France was clearly poised to
seek to reassert its influence in the Arab world once it settled the Algerian
crisis; French Foreign Minister Maurice Couve de Murville had personally complained to Peres about the burden of arming Israel, adding that it
would be a relief if others would pitch in. Britain, too, was becoming
convinced that the less it dealt with Israel, the more sway it would command with the Arabs.

Peres also made a military pitch. Nasser's air force, he argued, was already stacked with IL-28 light bombers, and it was now about to be supple-

mented with brand-new MiG-21 fighters. Moreover, Israel had evidence that Egyptian technicians were being trained in the Soviet Union, a clear prelude to Egyptian acquisition of sophisticated missiles—probably the SA-2 surface-to-air system. (As it happened, Peres had it half-right; Nasser had indeed been promised SA-2s by the Kremlin, but his order would be diverted to Castro's Cuba.) All this made the Hawk a vital deterrent—and a "purely defensive" one, unlike such nonmissile systems as bombers. But the Hawk was crucial in both military and strategic terms. The "real key," Peres argued, was the administration's "willingness to supply something that would be a demonstrable indication of our concern for supporting Israel and maintaining a military balance."[55]

Peres urged Bundy to try to persuade the State Department. Israel had found a potential bureaucratic ally in the McNamara Pentagon. At the same time that Bundy asked for the State Department's input, he passed along to Talbot a new strategic assessment. The Defense Department still believed that Israel's air force would prevail over Nasser's—but only "if an effective defense of Israel's air facilities could be maintained." The Pentagon, in other words, now gave credence to Ben-Gurion's earlier assessment that Nasser had a real chance of knocking out Israel's airfields in a sharp first punch, which could snarl the mobilization of Israeli reserves and leave its cities vulnerable to bombardment. The Israelis were lagging behind the Egyptians in fighters, and providing *those* remained unthinkable. So while Bundy conceded that "one can read into their present insistence all kinds of collateral political motives," the Israelis had a "valid military basis" for asking for Hawks.[56]

For NEA to deny Israel the Hawks now, it would have to override a senior Pentagon aide's blunt finding that Israel had a genuine military need for the missiles. Peres's "informal conversations" around Foggy Bottom and the Pentagon, Rusk warned U.S. embassies in the Middle East, "laid [the] groundwork" for a new Israeli approach for American military concessions.[57] The Peres mission helped shift the burden of proof away from those who wanted to sell Israel Hawks and onto those who preferred the status quo. The Pentagon had become an Israeli proponent inside the Kennedy administration, endorsing Ben-Gurion and Peres's case in crisp military terms that the State Department found painfully awkward to refute.

FOGGY BOTTOM'S AMBER LIGHT

None of which stopped NEA from trying. On June 7, Talbot—a specialist in the Indian subcontinent who relied heavily on his subordinates' Middle East expertise—gave Rusk the second draft of a paper arguing against the

Hawk sales. Rusk had already sent back the first draft and told NEA to include arguments in favor of a security guarantee or Hawk sales. "They are few," Talbot and his aides wrote as they complied. NEA urged Rusk to defer the Hawk sale for a few years or until the Soviets introduced surface-to-air missiles of their own into the Middle East. But the anti-Hawk forces inside the administration were clearly on the defensive.

Peres's visit, NEA argued, had shown Israel's true objectives: Hawks, talks on the regional balance of power, and a security guarantee. "A principal argument used by both Peres and Harman was that the US, having worsened Israel's position by aiding the UAR, should now make a compensatory gesture to Israel," NEA wrote. With an election year coming up, Israel and its American supporters would make a serious push "to show that Israel faces a situation of unusual peril in the next two to three years."

Talbot's paper made clear NEA's determination to avoid selling the Hawk. The memo acknowledged that Hawks would "strengthen the weak link in Israel's defenses" and reduce Israel's temptation to solve its security worries on its own. Moreover, "American supporters of Israel would be pleased and would be less critical of US policy" as a result. But Israel's ability to deter Egyptian aggression was fine as it was, and while the Hawk was a defensive weapon, its sale "would pin on the US responsibility" for stepping up the Middle East arms spiral. Impartiality would then demand that Washington also consider selling Hawks to Israel's neighbors, who would not be able to handle so sophisticated an arms system. Meanwhile, Israel would ask for more "allegedly defensive" high-tech armaments. "We doubt that Israel would rest satisfied with having gotten the Hawk," NEA warned. Better to mollify Israel with aid, reassuring noises, and more modest sales of light arms. The State Department's Middle East specialists were determined "not to give in to Israeli and domestic pressures for a special relationship in national security matters," the memo noted. "To undertake, in effect, a military alliance with Israel would destroy the delicate balance we seek to maintain in our Near East relations."[58]

But not only had the Pentagon shifted its position on the Hawks, Rusk had too. The secretary of state agreed with much of the Talbot paper but found NEA's arguments on the Hawk so seriously unconvincing that he sent the paper back yet again—a clear sign that Talbot and his allies were climbing a steep hill. Surely plugging the gap in Israel's defenses should be seen in terms of deterring Egypt from attacking the Jewish state with modern Soviet warplanes, Rusk posited, not in terms of Israel's temptation to preempt. Similarly, the question was not whether the Hawk would balance out any surface-to-air missiles that the Kremlin might sell Nasser but whether Israel's air defenses were adequate against Egypt's air force.[59]

NEA's answers might have satisfied Dulles, but they had barely satisfied Herter, and they did not satisfy Rusk.

Rusk's Middle East aides tried one last time to circle the wagons. The Hawk sale was one of the items on the agenda of a conference of U.S. chiefs of mission to Middle Eastern states held in Athens. The assembled ambassadors included an unhappy Walworth Barbour, Kennedy's ambassador to Israel, who had been lobbied hard on the Hawks by Meir in Tel Aviv. As the ambassadors saw it, Talbot reported, the main problem was "not a defense 'gap' on either side" of the Arab-Israeli quarrel but the risk that one side might preempt if it came to feel that its vulnerability was intolerable.[60] Impartiality forbade a military relationship with Israel; word of the stronger bond would inevitably leak out and be promptly exploited by Moscow. A new security guarantee just for Israel was "both unnecessary and undesirable"; better simply to reaffirm the Tripartite Declaration's provisions condemning aggression in the region.

"From the standpoint of an abstract, solely military equation," the Athens conference concluded, one could make a case for selling the Hawks.[61] But the question was not merely military. Israel was basically secure, thanks not only to Arab fear of the IDF but also to Arab worries of Western intervention, inter-Arab rifts, and the threat that Nasser might lose Western and U.S. aid. Rather than accelerating the arms race by abandoning precedent and becoming Israel's military supplier, the administration should instead renew its push for regional arms control. Moreover, the Kremlin would surely use the Hawk sale to reingratiate itself with Nasser. The Hawk sale ran contrary to the underlying purpose of Kennedy's overall Nasser policy. Washington would be wiser to turn the arms spigot off, not on.

On the other hand, the gathered mission chiefs realized that they might well be fighting a losing battle by this point: a high-level administration review would probably end in a Hawk sale, Talbot said.[62] If the Soviets gave Nasser surface-to-air missiles of his own, the ambassadors reckoned that the administration would finally "be justified" in selling Hawks to Israel.[63] "In a strictly air defense sense, Israel does have considerable vulnerability to air attack," the NEA official James Grant conceded to Rusk back stateside.[64] But Israel's fighters were better, its army was better still, and the other deterrents to Arab adventurism—a possible Western intervention, the loss of Western aid, and the Arab cold war—were formidable. On June 25, Grant formally asked Bundy for a Defense Department assessment of the military impact of a Hawk sale. If NEA were to be backed into a corner by an unarguable Pentagon ruling, let it at least be a full investigation, not an individual judgment.

But the Pentagon had by now concluded that the Egypt-Israel balance had tilted enough that a Hawk sale was in order.[65] On June 24, Ben-Gurion wrote to Kennedy to follow up on the Peres visit and make a more general pitch for military aid, although he declined to mention the Hawks by name. He was less oblique, however, about his view of what was at stake for Israel in the talks over security. "What was done to six million of our brethren twenty years ago with the participation of Palestinian Arab leaders, among them the ex-Grand Mufti [of Jerusalem] and his henchmen, could be done to the two million Jews of Israel, if, God forbid, the Israel Defence Forces are defeated," Ben-Gurion wrote.[66]

The State Department's beleaguered Middle East experts were starting to bow to the seemingly inevitable. On July 9, Talbot reiterated to Rusk that "it is essential to avoid establishing a special military relationship with Israel. To create what would in effect be a military alliance with Israel would destroy the delicate balance we have so carefully maintained in our Near East relations and would bring insufficient compensatory advantages." As for a security guarantee, Kennedy's assurances of concern for the Jewish state's survival and success should have done the trick. But NEA was starting to qualify its insistence that the Hawk sale was folly. "Despite the justification found in a strictly military equation," Talbot wrote, Nasser was still deterred, a Middle East arms race was still dangerous, and a regional arms control push was still worth trying. If, however, Moscow could be shown to be providing Cairo with "comparable missiles," Washington should give in after consulting with the British and discussing the matter with the Egyptians.[67] Rusk finally scrawled his assent to this formula. At last, the State Department had a position, but it was an amber light, not a red one.

The Joint Chiefs had some sympathy with NEA, warning that the Hawk sale could hurt ties to Nasser and help the Soviets.[68] But the civilians in the Defense Department were flashing eager green. On July 16, as requested, Bill Bundy sent NEA the Pentagon's official assessment of the military utility of the Hawk. It was hardly the result for which the foot-draggers at NEA had hoped. "Israel is vulnerable to UAR air attack and is becoming increasingly so with the arrival of additional Soviet TU-16's," Bundy wrote. The Hawks "would fill an important gap" in Israel's air defenses but "would not alone act to shift the balance of military power between Israel and its neighbors."[69]

When Nasser tested two types of homegrown missiles on July 21, it dramatized Israel's fears.[70] At that, the State Department threw in the towel. In early August, Rusk sent the president a memo summarizing an "extensive and intensive" State Department review of Israel policy. Behind the scenes, he wrote, NEA had been haggling with the White House's point men on Israel, including Komer, Bundy, and Feldman. The result was "a meeting of the minds," as Talbot euphemistically put it—or, more baldly, a State Department climb-down on the Hawk.

So now, Rusk argued that America's "relatively high standing" in the Arab world gave it "a minor degree of maneuvering room in terms of adjustments in policy with respect to Israel." This extra flexibility had materialized at a time when, notwithstanding America's "unparalleled" economic assistance (amounting to $317 for each individual Israeli over the past decade, Rusk reckoned) and the ongoing Israeli-Syrian sparring over the Sea of Galilee, Israel was seeking "a close military relationship." Rusk reiterated his earlier formulation: a military alliance with Israel would pointlessly wreck America's delicate web of Middle Eastern ties. Instead of a new security guarantee, the administration should simply reiterate its commitment to the 1950 Tripartite Declaration—in which the United States, Britain, and France pledged not to arm Middle East aggressors and to uphold the armistices reached after the 1948–49 Arab-Israeli war—as a de facto guarantee to Arabs and Israelis alike against attack. Meanwhile, the administration would interpret Ben-Gurion's hedged suggestion of using other means than armed retaliation to handle terrorist incursions as an Israeli repudiation of disproportionate retaliatory raids; it would also urge the Arabs to restrain themselves from provoking Israel.

The time had now come, Rusk continued, for a presidential decision on the Hawk. "Greater confidence in its defenses would permit Israel the better to resist any temptation to engage in preemptive attack against the UAR air strike capability," Rusk noted, and this would help avoid any sequel to Suez. To be sure, he rehearsed NEA's old line: Israel's deterrent was sturdy; production and training would cost time and money; other American friends might object; and arms control would be wiser than arms sales. Nevertheless, Israel had a demonstrable need for the Hawks, which were purely defensive anyway. Rusk also added some critical new data: "United States intelligence clearly indicates that the UAR is in the process of obtaining comparable missiles from the USSR," so if the Hawk sale fed the sort of arms spiral that Eisenhower's aides had so feared, it would be the Soviets who had started it. Rusk recommended that Kennedy wait two months to make sure that an arms-control arrangement was out of reach, consult with the British, and alert the Egyptians. Thereafter, the United States should "offer the Hawk to Israel."[71] By outflanking the foes of the Hawk sale within the Kennedy administration, Israel had pushed America to the verge of broaching its arms embargo.

THE JOHNSON LINKAGE

Now that the State Department had caved on the Hawk sale itself, however, it wanted Israeli cooperation elsewhere. Above all, U.S. diplomats were concerned about getting Israel to go along with a new U.N. initiative on the Palestinian refugees. The State Department figured progress on the refugees would prove America's good faith to the Arabs, reduce the refugees' misery, and lance a political boil. In his May 1961 letters to the major Arab leaders, Kennedy had promised renewed efforts—under the auspices of the United Nations' long-inactive Palestine Conciliation Commission (PCC)—to do something about the Palestinian problem. Kennedy picked Joseph E. Johnson, the head of the Carnegie Endowment for International Peace, to handle the unenviable assignment for the PCC—a selection that left it unclear in many people's minds whether Johnson worked for the United Nations or the United States. Johnson's plan—a vague affair produced out of slogging rounds of regional consultations—called for compensating refugees who chose to remain in such host countries as Lebanon and for resettling others, including letting many of them return to Israel. Still, the State Department believed in Johnson's work and hoped to trade the Hawks for progress toward a Palestinian settlement. "Our resolve on the quid pro quo is firm and remains firm," Talbot wrote to Mike Feldman, the administration figure whose resolve here was most likely *not* to be firm.[72]

To seal the deal, the State Department wanted to send a special presidential envoy on a secret mission to Israel. "We judge Ben-Gurion to be increasingly confident that he will get the Hawk and perhaps even a security guarantee regardless of how he helps us at this time," Talbot worriedly wrote Feldman in August 1962. "Unless he is convinced we are not bluffing" about withholding Hawks and any security guarantee, the hard-nosed Ben-Gurion would not go along with the Johnson proposals.[73]

Kennedy had repeatedly mentioned a desire to do something about the refugee problem, which he saw as an ongoing threat to tranquility in the region. His approach to the Palestinians may sound either unduly modest or unwisely aimed today. After more than a year's quiet diplomacy and consultations with regional leaders and the State Department, Johnson came up with a plan to resettle some refugees and repatriate others that was flatly unacceptable to the Israelis and hardly palatable to the Arabs. His somewhat naïve proposals were largely humanitarian in emphasis and paid scant heed to the Palestinians' percolating sense of nationhood or fierce sense of dispossession. That should not be particularly surprising. The Johnson plan, after all, was designed for a pre-1967, pre–Palestine Liberation Organization era in which Palestinian nationalism had yet to find its voice and the Arab-Israeli conflict focused on clashes between Israel and the Arab states. Today it may strike readers as odd to imagine a settlement of the Palestinian refugee problem that makes no reference to statehood. But the Johnson plan was a well-intentioned attempt to offer the refugees something more lasting than the stop-gap relief aid offered by UNRWA, the U.N. refugee relief agency, not an attempt to foreshadow the 1990s Oslo peace process. References to Palestinian nationalism and its ideological keystone, the right of return, were absent and would have been anachronistic. On his many trips to the region, Johnson met with Arab heads of state, not with representatives of the displaced Arabs themselves—who were spoken of as refugees, not Palestinians. The plan spoke not of self-determination but of repatriation and resettlement, and managed to do even that in terms that none of the parties found appealing.

Feldman warned Kennedy that "the most violent opposition" to the Johnson plan would come from Ben-Gurion, who feared that an internationally mandated influx of refugees would create a fifth column within Israel. Ben-Gurion spoke grudgingly about taking in 100,000 Arabs at most. For their part, no one among the jousting Arab cold warriors wanted to be caught endorsing anything less than full repatriation.[74] Since a full settlement was "manifestly unattainable," Johnson envisioned "backing into the problem in small steps."[75] Assuming that Kennedy signed on and that no regional principal objected vehemently, the PCC would send out detailed questionnaires to refugees, asking for assessments of the value of lost property and such questions as "Do you prefer to return to what is now Israel whether or not you could return to your former home," "If you prefer not to return, indicate in order of preference the countries where you would like to live, in the Near East or elsewhere," and "If your preference is to return, would you agree to live at peace with your neighbors as a law-abiding resident of Israel?"[76] But the overall plan, as presented to the president by Rusk in an August 7 memo, remained vague on the balance between repatriation (as demanded by the Arabs) and resettlement and compensation (as preferred by the Israelis).

To some degree, the plan may have been left amorphous to let the administration sculpt a scheme that Johnson knew would fail without U.S. backing. Indeed, one of the few things Johnson had going for him was his ill-defined relationship with Kennedy's men; it was never entirely clear if he worked for U.N. Secretary General U Thant or for Kennedy. Now the latter was about to offer Israel a major sweetener. With the Hawk offer looming, perhaps a presidential emissary—working quietly out of the public eye—could discreetly cudgel the Israelis into assenting to the Johnson plan.

Johnson and Rusk wanted that envoy to be Feldman. A higher-level official would have been harder to sneak in and out of Israel. Moreover, having the friendly Feldman deliver a tough message would rob Ben-Gurion of the temptation to use domestic pressure to get the administration to back down; sending Feldman would send the message that the Kennedy administration was united on the Johnson plan.

But Feldman was not nearly as wedded to a Hawks-for-refugees swap as was Rusk, who was a good enough personal friend of Johnson's to be inextricably linked in Middle Eastern capitals to Johnson's mission. In a memo to Kennedy, Feldman noted that the president would have to decide whether "we should support the Johnson proposal which has only a slim possibility of acceptance by either Arabs or the Israelis." For this headache, Feldman wrote, the administration would have to shell out "about $30 million a year—if we are lucky." The only way the Israelis would possibly accept the plan was in return for Hawks and a security guarantee, but Feldman was skeptical. "We should not, in the meantime, defer for too long our offer to Ben-Gurion," he wrote, "for I should not like to be in the position of notifying him that we will provide Hawks at the time we request his acquiescence in the Johnson plan."[77]

Kennedy, too, was dubious about tethering the Hawk sale to a potentially doomed refugee plan.[78] On August 14, in a White House meeting on the plan with Johnson, Rusk, and Feldman, the president asked, "Why isn't the status quo more preferable for both the Israelis and the Arabs? We pay the bill [for UNRWA], and there is no compromise of principle." Johnson argued that both sides would be better off with the refugee problem solved, but Kennedy warned that the Israelis would balk. Feldman wanted to punt until after the midterm elections in November, but Johnson ruled that out.

That left hardball. "If we could tie in the Hawk, it might work," Feldman volunteered. But Kennedy nixed that idea. The Johnson plan "might be stillborne if we have word out of a big repatriation," the president said. "People would stir up because of elections. We should find out what Israel will do. I don't want to get into a costly fight without getting something." Kennedy was "still living with residue" from the December vote to censure Israel in the Security Council over its reprisals against Syria, and he did not "want to live with [the] residue of another fight for years and years." The president simply did not see the margin in forcing "a bloody battle" over a proposal that was probably DOA anyway. So the parameters of Feldman's mission shrunk dramatically. He was going to sound the Israelis out, not ram anything down their throats.

Kennedy also wanted to avoid a fight with Egypt. "We must talk to Nasser first on the Hawks," he insisted. If blindsided, Cairo might roll back some of the progress from the Nasser initiative. "All of this," Kennedy ordered, "must be carried out with the utmost secrecy."[79]

The administration thus began planning not one but two secret Middle East missions: Feldman to Israel and Robert Strong of NEA to Egypt. Strong was to float the idea of an arms-control initiative to Nasser, which could delay the Hawk sale. But Rusk warned that there was not "a chance in a thousand that Nasser would buy disarmament."[80] The next day, Kennedy sent a note to Ben-Gurion to let him know that Feldman was on his way; the combined pressures of the security guarantee, the Hawk sale, and the Johnson mission, the president explained, had created a situation too complicated for letters alone. While Kennedy avoided substance on the security questions, he did assure Ben-Gurion that his country would "not be endangered in the process of resolving the Arab refugee problem"—a hint that Washington was not likely to push hard on the Palestinian issue.[81] Johnson was concerned; if word got out that his plan had been cleared in advance with Israel, it would be doomed. In fact, it was doomed anyway.

SAY ANYTHING

With his wife along as camouflage, Feldman flew first to Paris, supposedly to discuss trade matters with the French.[82] He then caught an El Al flight on to Lydda airport on August 18. The purpose of his quick side trip, the State Department told its embassy in Tel Aviv, was to take up the Weizmann Institute of Science in Rehovot on its longstanding invitation to have Feldman see Israel for the first time. The deputy White House counsel would also pay a few "courtesy calls" on Israeli leaders; the U.S. embassy was to keep quiet, schedule no social appointments for Feldman, and ensure that he had a secure telegraphic line back to Washington.[83]

The day after Feldman's arrival, August 19, 1962, marks the start of the U.S.–Israel military relationship as we know it—and with it, the birth of the U.S.–Israel alliance. That afternoon, in the late-summer swelter of Tel Aviv, Feldman met for three and a half hours with Ben-Gurion, Golda Meir, and Teddy Kollek, a gifted young Ben-Gurion protégé deeply involved in the building of Israel's arms infrastructure who would become mayor of Jerusalem. Feldman began the meeting by telling this formidable trio that "the President had determined that the Hawk missile should be made available to Israel," albeit with a long lead time.[84] Payment terms would be worked out later, he added in response to a question from Ben-Gurion. The Israelis, Feldman recalled later, were "ecstatic."[85]

Feldman noted that Britain would also offer to sell its own surface-to-air missile, the Bloodhound, and claimed that the administration was not concerned about who got the sale. He also told Ben-Gurion that Nasser would receive advance warning about the missile sale. Ben-Gurion replied that he would gladly forswear the Hawks if Nasser would agree to arms control—which, of course, was not in the cards.

Neither was the Johnson plan. Ben-Gurion and Meir's initial reaction to the U.N. initiative was dour. No Arab player would accept anything less than repatriation, Ben-Gurion warned, and the forced absorption of large numbers of Palestinian refugees was a clear and present danger to Israel. After stressing that the plan gave Israel the authority to decide how many refugees to take back, Ben-Gurion offered to "acquiesce in the plan" if Nasser would resettle the refugees that Johnson directed him to and would not bully the refugees into choosing to return to Israel. It was not much of a glimmer of hope for Johnson; Nasser was unlikely to meekly let thousands of Palestinian refugees settle permanently in Egypt.

Indeed, Ben-Gurion took a firm line with Feldman, even amid his glee over the Hawks. He was even inflexible on the State Department's request that Israel stop the U.N. push for the so-called Brazzaville resolution, which called for direct negotiations between Israelis and Arabs—a bit of symbolic posturing that was causing Washington some minor U.N. headaches. Even when dealing with such a sideshow, Ben-Gurion offered only to consult with Washington while insisting that the United Nations should hear the resolution.

According to the Israeli account of the meeting, Feldman did not push hard on the Johnson plan.[86] If, after handling the first thousand refugees, it became clear that "more than [a] small proportion want to return, [the] U.S. will step in and say that the security of Israel is jeopardized. Let's drop the plan," the minutes report Feldman saying. "Give it a try," he told his Israeli hosts. "You have nothing to lose." He added, "We want you not to stand in the way." The administration knew that the plan's chance were slim, but Feldman urged Ben-Gurion, Meir, and Kollek to "look at it carefully." The White House would "keep you advised [about] our talks with Arabs but [we] don't want you to be [the] first to reject." Even that was not enough to lower Ben-Gurion's guard. "If there is a real settlement we will accept a certain number which will be decided only by ourselves," Ben-Gurion replied. "But, if the Arab attitude is that they must go back to Palestine, we will not accept a single one."

Despite the lack of movement, Rusk was surprisingly upbeat about Feldman's first round of meetings. The State Department cabled Feldman that the secretary was "reasonably satisfied" and considered the envoy "close to success" on the Johnson plan, notwithstanding Ben-Gurion's attempt to add prior commitments from Nasser before signing on. "I hardly need stress," Rusk stressed, "that it would be most unfortunate if Israelis were to end up with the Hawks and strengthened security assurances while being responsible for derailing the Johnson plan before it could even be given a good try."[87] NEA's Grant warned Feldman that Ben-Gurion's attempts to put conditions on his acceptance of the Johnson plan were "unacceptable to us."[88]

On August 21, Feldman held a final six-hour meeting with Meir, who had long suspected Johnson of pro-Arab sympathies. The stubborn Israeli foreign minister worked busily to avoid the Hawks-for-refugees linkage, offering a series of what were either stalling maneuvers or chances for the Arabs to demonstrate their good faith. Meir suggested a U.N. General Assembly vote on the Johnson plan, more time to discuss the matter with Israel's ruling Mapai Party's smaller coalition partners, further meetings between herself and Johnson, and at least a month's further delay. For good measure, she gave Feldman a six-page letter for Kennedy from Ben-Gurion, most of it devoted to "a discussion of the impracticability of the plan." Perhaps not wanting to seem ungrateful, Meir did offer to shelve the Brazzaville resolution. And she was as direct about the importance of missile technology as she was cagey about the Johnson plan. Israel had just received "concrete evidence," Meir told Feldman, that Egypt had bought guided missiles from West German sources for £250 million. At this, Feldman seems to have concluded that Israel should get the Hawks even if it later slipped the surly bonds of the Johnson plan. "Under the circumstances," Feldman cabled Kennedy and Rusk, "I recommend that we defer a final decision on the Johnson plan until I return Thursday night."[89]

Feldman then flew back to Washington, his cover largely intact. Washington's ambassador in Tel Aviv, Walworth Barbour, also sneaked back stateside to join the follow-up discussions. The next day, the Israeli tabloid *Ma'ariv* ran a lengthy, speculative, and vague article about Feldman's short visit; it quoted Feldman as privately telling reporters in Jerusalem, "I do not believe [the Israeli journalists] know why I am here."[90] He was right.

In Washington, Feldman and Barbour briefed McGeorge Bundy and Grant. The most straightforward concession Feldman had received was "a firm, secret commitment" from Meir not to push the direct-talks resolution during the forthcoming session of the General Assembly. On the Johnson plan, he secured only a commitment not to reveal the "true purpose of Mr. Feldman's visit" and not to "say anything" to obstruct the implementation of the plan unless Nasser began "propagandizing in favor [of] repatriation" or ultimately refused "to settle those refugees who opt for resettlement" within Egypt and other host countries. But on the Hawks, the Israelis had been blunt. Meir had told Feldman that Israel had no interest in the British-made Bloodhound antiaircraft missile, which Israel simply considered an inferior system. But even if the Hawks were not better missiles, Israel still "for other reasons, would purchase the United States system" over the British one.[91] Ben-Gurion wanted both the missiles and the marker.

THE MISSILES OF AUGUST

Meanwhile, another special administration envoy was in motion. Bob Strong, the director of the State Department's Office of Near East Affairs, had winged his way to Egypt to prime Nasser for the news of the Hawk offer. As Feldman's mission proceeded, Rusk cabled Strong that the "exploratory talks" in Israel had been "useful," but Washington was still not ready to commit itself to the Johnson plan while the Israelis hemmed and hawed. Tell Nasser about the Hawks, Rusk ordered, but make it clear that the offer came not out of U.S. enthusiasm but from its inability to "turn down repeated and insistent requests" for a defensive system as Nasser acquired new Soviet weapons.[92]

Strong and Badeau broke the news to Nasser during a sober August 24 meeting at the Egyptian leader's vacation cottage in Alexandria. Israel had been seeking the Hawks for years as Nasser built up his Soviet arsenal, the Americans noted. If Nasser had truly eschewed aggression against Israel, the Jewish state's ability to defend itself against an Egyptian attack that was never coming was irrelevant.

Nasser seemed "unperturbed by [the] military implications" of the Hawk offer, Badeau reported. Its politics, however, were something else. Jordan, Syria, and Saudi Arabia were already accusing Nasser of selling out Palestine in return for American aid. Now the entire Arab world would decry Kennedy for breaching precedent and getting into the Middle East arms business. It would be harder for Nasser to refute the charges that he had gotten too close to Washington. The Soviets would eagerly try to counter the sale of even defensive missiles, leaving the blame for the expansion of the Soviet arms role in the region squarely on America's door.[93]

Nasser could always agree to arms control before the Hawks arrived, the Americans replied. U.S. willingness to provide Hawks to Israel was "a statement in principle in the absence of arms limitation," not a firm undertaking to deliver missile shipments.[94] But Nasser was "gloomy and unenthusiastic" about arms embargoes, which had hampered the Arabs in 1948. After seeing the mockery that Britain and France made of the Tripartite Declaration during Suez, he "would not trust any arms agreement to be effective against Israel." Egypt's arsenal, Nasser insisted, was only as large as necessary to deter an expansionist Israel, especially after the "bitter experience" of Suez. Nasser was not about to be the first to step out of the arms spiral.

The Americans got somewhat further on the Johnson plan. Badeau called Nasser's response here "moderate and slightly encouraging." But Nasser did push for an untrammeled Palestinian right of return, without quotas, as what the U.S. minutes render unfelicitously as a "final solution" to the refugee issue—a way to replace the "basic Zionist concept" with a "bi-national state," even if it took 70 years.[95] Nasser was also open to Badeau's suggestion of an ongoing process of repatriation and resettlement within Israel and the Arab world, agreeing that repatriation later might make resettlement now more palatable. But he hardly leapt at the Johnson plan. His lukewarm response would ultimately encourage Kennedy to orphan it, thereby cutting an important string that the State Department was try-ing to attach to the Hawks.

Ben-Gurion, having given the Johnson plan due reflection, was even less enthusiastic. On August 20, he sent Kennedy a tough letter blaming the Arab states for creating the refugee problem in the first place by sup-posedly calling on the Palestinian Arabs to flee in 1948. "I must say that I can conceive of no practical plan which will bring about a settlement of the refugee problem in the near future as long as the Arab rulers are plan-ning the destruction of Israel," Ben-Gurion wrote. "There is only one way to resolve the refugee question, and that is for the Arab rulers, with Nasser in the lead – for until Nasser makes a move, no Arab ruler would dare to do so, even if in secret he was so disposed – to reconcile themselves both inwardly and publicly to the existence of the State of Israel."[96]

On August 27, at 5 P.M., Kennedy gathered his secret envoys together for an intensive, hour-long White House meeting. In attendance were Rusk, McGeorge Bundy, Feldman, Barbour, Strong, and Talbot. This session was not necessarily the most important of the meetings JFK held on the Arab-Israeli conflict, but it still offers the most comprehensive look at the administration's Middle East deliberations—for the simple reason that Kennedy secretly had a tape recorder running.[97] The resultant re-cording gives a superb sense of Kennedy's skepticism, desire to find a middle ground, and command of foreign policy.[98] It also shows that Kennedy him-self was probably the U.S. official who recognized that the Johnson plan was futile.

Strong began by reporting back on his and Badeau's Alexandria meet-ing with Nasser, speaking in a slow, deep drawl that made America's Cold War adversaries into the *Saahhviets*. Kennedy asked Strong whether Nasser was really being attacked by other Arabs for allegedly softening his hawk-ishness on Israel in order to curry favor with the United States (he was) and whether Nasser was trying to acquire surface-to-surface missiles from Moscow (he was). "Under the present circumstances," Rusk pointed out, "this is partly irrelevant because the Hawk missile is aimed at aircraft, and there's no question that the Egyptians already have the aircraft to which the Hawk missiles are a defense."

Kennedy remembered seeing figures showing that Israel had "a com-parable aircraft—in comparable quantity . . ."

"No," said Feldman, "no they don't."

"The Israelis do have the fighters," Barbour interjected, "but I think they do claim that they don't have the bombers."

"What have the UAR gotten in the way of bombers lately?" Kennedy asked.

They have low-flying TU-16s from Moscow, replied Talbot. But the point of looking at Nasser's surface-to-surface missiles was that, after the Hawk sale, Israel would probably be asking for such missiles next.

"One of the things we talked about," Kennedy said, "was making the proposition that we wouldn't give [the Israelis] the Hawk missiles if all missiles were removed"—that is, including Nasser's ground-to-ground rockets.

He had told Nasser that, Strong replied, but Nasser had riposted that he had little faith in Western arms control after Suez. Nasser had also complained that, "of course, [the Americans] would not sell missiles to the Arabs."

Would we? Kennedy asked.

Badeau had told Nasser that the administration would give "serious consideration" to an Egyptian request for Hawks, Strong replied. "The opening was given to [let Nasser ask for Hawks]. He did not pursue it."

Nasser had been warmer about the Johnson plan, Strong continued. While the Egyptian leader had dismissed Johnson's reported quota of returning 20,000 refugees to Israel as paltry, Nasser preferred to stay away from numbers entirely and hold out the long-term hope of return, in order to get the refugees themselves to back the plan. Badeau repeatedly told Nasser that the refugees must be free to choose whether to return to Israel or not, without outside propagandizing or pressure—Ben-Gurion's demand to Feldman. Nasser "did not react," Strong reported, but he clearly heard the point. "In no way did he link the discussion of the Hawk or the sale of the Hawk missile to the Johnson plan," he added.

Rusk asked Feldman if the Johnson plan could go ahead "without getting into numbers."

"Oh, yes, yes," Feldman replied. The Israelis thought that the refugees will "all take repatriation because of the pressure brought on them." Feldman had replied that, based on Johnson's regional soundings, "it's our best guess that not more than one in ten would take repatriation." The Israelis accepted that, he added.

"What did they figure?" Kennedy asked. "It's like a Negro wanting to go back to Mississippi, isn't it?"

The room filled with chuckles. "It's different," Feldman replied with a laugh, "because it's as if the dominant doctrine were Black Muslim doctrine in a sense . . ."

Israelis and Arabs had different views on Palestinian return, Kennedy noted, turning the problem over in his mind. "Nasser will think they all want to go back," the president said. "He doesn't think the Israelis will take them so he thinks it's going to collapse." The Israelis, on the other hand, hoped that most of the refugees could be fobbed off with compensation. "Isn't one group going to be horribly disappointed—either the Israelis by a lot more than one out of ten coming back, or the Arabs when only one out of ten wants to go back? Isn't it going to blow up, then, the plan when this fact becomes a pattern?"

"I would think that's a fair assumption," Strong admitted. The Johnson plan had just been gutted by Kennedy himself.

Could Nasser, Bundy asked, resist pressure from the other Arabs to push harder for more refugees to return to Israel?

Strong did not know. Nasser had said that he was taking heat from the other Arabs for his low-key policy on Israel.

"That's sort of a self-serving statement," snapped a dubious, irritated Kennedy. "Has he really been under attack?"

"Yes," Strong replied, "quite serious attack from the Saudis, from the Jordanians, and from the Syrians."

They had no other answer to Nasser's "Arab socialism" than to pillory him as soft on Israel, Feldman added.

Kennedy, still working the problem through, then asked if they needed to pull the trigger just yet on the Johnson plan. "Is this stage by stage, and can be dropped conveniently at different stages?" he asked.

"No," said Strong.

"Or once we launch this thing are we . . . have we really got hold of it there?" Kennedy continued.

Israel was worried that once the plan was started, "the onus will be on them" if too many refugees flooded back, Strong said.

"There's no way to sort of get this first stage going?" Kennedy asked. "Let's say you get 10,000, 9,000 [who] choose not to go back; 1,000 go back. Would that be acceptable to the Arabs? It would be acceptable to the Israelis. Would it be acceptable to the Arabs?"

"I don't know," Strong said. "This remains to be seen. This is an imponderable, Mr. President."

To Kennedy's mind, though, this was exactly the sort of thing one ought to ponder. He was being asked to put his prestige behind an irreversible initiative, and his own State Department could not assure him that the plan would be acceptable to either side. As his aides talked on, the president fell silent. He had heard what he needed to know: the Johnson plan was a nonstarter, and it could not be floated or started without a full American commitment to see it through. To link the plan to the Hawk sale would require a definitive presidential commitment, and Kennedy was not about to put his full weight behind an exercise in futility.

Feldman was unimpressed, too. "In my own mind, I don't see the need for doing it right now any more than I did before," he said. "It seems to me that it needs so much additional groundwork. You have only a tentative agreement from Nasser to consider it and I have more or less the same kind of agreement from Israel to consider it." Actually signing on was far away.

"One step at a time, gentlemen," said Bundy.

"As each step is taken," Strong said, "it becomes a little more difficult for them to be responsible for calling the whole show off."

If the Arabs started pressuring the refugees to return, Feldman pointed out, Israel would immediately nix the whole plan.

"Did you see any difficulty on going ahead and putting this to the PCC— the French and the Turks?" asked Rusk.

"Well, I wonder," replied Feldman. "So long as our prestige isn't committed at that point . . ."

At that, the president perked up. "Do you know if Joe Johnson will be regarded as an independent agent putting forward a . . . ?" he asked. "At what point do we become the sponsor of the Johnson plan?"

"I don't think we're kidding anybody about our sponsorship," Talbot said.

After 28 minutes, the tape recording ends, still on the question of whether Johnson worked directly for U Thant. Kennedy was clearly at least mildly curious to see whether the administration could take a flyer on the Johnson plan without being directly implicated if it flopped. But by late August, the president had also unmistakably given up any hopes of linking the Hawk sale to the Johnson plan.

The plan, then, was wilting. With Rusk still interested in pushing ahead in the PCC and with Feldman noncommittal, Kennedy seems to have felt that he did not have to decide just yet. But Israel's aversion would only harden over the coming months. "As I see it," Komer wrote, "Israel (having gotten its Hawks) is making an all-out effort to sink the Johnson plan."[99] When Feldman had dinner in September at the Hotel Pierre with Meir, who was in New York for the opening of the U.N. General Assembly, she began the conversation by declaring her "unalterable opposition to the plan."[100] After all, it set no ceiling on the number of refugees to be repatriated, gave a U.N. body a powerful say over whom to admit, and offered the refugees no incentives to stay put. Feldman concurred. "I am convinced that there is no hope for this plan," he wrote Kennedy.[101] Noting Feldman's advice with some asperity, the NSC urged turning the matter over to Rusk.[102] French officials complained that the Israelis had been coming at French

Foreign Minister Couve de Murville "like wild animals" over the Johnson plan.[103] The State Department, for its part, complained that Israel "has stirred up the American Jewish community against the refugee initiative despite a promise it would not do so."[104]

On December 5, Komer urged Kennedy to make "a basic decision as to whether the US ought to battle uphill any farther on this issue." The NSC aide urged the president to take the long historic view and try to ease a major underlying cause of Arab-Israeli strife. "Your Administration has done more to satisfy Israeli security preoccupations than any of its predecessors," Komer wrote. "We have promised the Israelis HAWKS, reassured them on the Jordan waters, given a higher level of economic aid (to permit extensive arms), and given various security assurances. In return, we have gotten nothing from our efforts. . . . The score is 4–0." To even out that ratio, however, Kennedy would have to press Israel hard enough to "entail a real domestic backlash," with no assurance that Nasser and other Arab leaders would concur—all for a plan that Komer gave "only a 50–50 chance of success" and could "easily get short-circuited by another Arab-Israeli flare-up."[105] Ultimately, Kennedy decided to put the Johnson plan out of its misery.[106] On December 27, the Johnson plan was mentioned during a meeting in Palm Beach between Kennedy and Meir. "That's gone," the president said.[107]

UNCLE SAM'S ARMFUL

It was just the sort of doodle guaranteed to spoil John Badeau's morning. On September 17, a disapproving Badeau cabled back to Washington that *al-Ahram*, the semiofficial Egyptian daily edited by the Nasser confidant Muhammad Hassanein Haykal, had run an editorial cartoon showing Uncle Sam presenting an armful of rifles to Ben-Gurion.[108] Ever since the Hawk decision, Badeau and his fellow ambassadors had been bracing for the inevitable howls of protest. Having spent years trying to convince Arab governments of American friendship, they would now have to explain away the first major U.S. arms sale to Israel—with, despite NEA's bureaucratic exertions, very few strings attached. But much of the venting from America's Arab friends was limited to splenetic denunciations in state-run media outlets, rather than serious diplomatic demarches. Moreover, Arab protests over the Hawk sale—from both conservatives and radicals—would be muted by the breaking crisis in Yemen.

During the Strong mission, Nasser had protested the Hawk sale but had not broken any furniture about it. Even so, Kennedy's Middle East team was taking nothing for granted about the potential ferocity of Nasser's reaction when the sale became public. Komer, who was more attached to the Nasser overture than the Johnson plan, began looking avidly for ways to "keep US/UAR rapprochement from going off [the] rails" over the Hawks.[109] At that time, Nasser's minister of economy, Kaissouni, was in Washington for an IMF meeting, and Komer and the State Department wanted the Egyptian aide to leave with either a previously promised $10 million in stabilization credit or as much new PL-480 aid as Congress would approve. Neither the Israelis nor their advocate, Feldman, were opposed this time, perhaps sensing that they had done rather well recently. The administration discretely placated Nasser over the Hawks with aid just as he was plunging into Yemen.[110]

The administration's hand was forced by a September 26 leak, which the State Department feared would include the wince-inducing tidbit that Nasser had been consulted in advance on the Hawk sale.[111] In Cairo, Badeau scrambled to find Nasser's confidant, Haykal; in Washington, Talbot summoned Egyptian Ambassador Kamel, whom he assured that the administration's willingness to sell Hawks to Israel was neither a precedent-setting departure nor an obstacle to long-range cooperation with Egypt. The usually excitable Kamel took the news calmly but lamented having been kept "in the dark."[112]

The Saudis were even more philosophical. Faysal, who was at the Waldorf in New York for the opening of the U.N. General Assembly, was briefed the same day in his suite by NEA's Persian Gulf officer, Talcott Seelye. "You know my feelings on the matter," the crown prince shrugged. America could do what it liked, Faysal continued, although the timing "would seriously jeopardize the Johnson initiative"—which, unbeknownst to Faysal, was already dead.[113] In Jidda, Ambassador Pete Hart reported that no Saudi officials had formally mentioned the Hawks to him in the days after the leak and that his private contacts seemed to accept the U.S. insistence that the Hawks were strictly defensive—a general lack of interest "due no doubt to preoccupation" with Yemen.[114]

On September 27, the BBC and the Associated Press both ran the Hawk story, and America's Middle Eastern diplomats swung with a communal sigh into damage-control mode. At 11 A.M., Badeau met a fuming Haykal, who was more upset about "this reverse" of "long standing American policy of disengagement from [an] arms race" than about the leak that revealed the administration's consultations with Egypt (although, for good measure, he did insist that the leaker was either an American or an Israeli spy within the State Department).[115]

The same day in Amman, King Husayn, whose large refugee population tied him uncomfortably closely to the Palestinian problem, summoned to the royal palace the visiting State Department official Samuel Lewis, then the special assistant to Chester Bowles. The king seemed almost as concerned about Nasser's Yemen meddling as he was about Israel's Hawk windfall, which both strengthened Israel and reminded the young king that he was "completely defenseless" against the Soviet jet bombers of his radical Arab foes.[116] The Jordanian media was less sanguine. "It is impossible for Arabs to accept any excuses justifying the U.S.'s gift of rockets to Israel on the eve of the Hebrew New Year," editorialized the Amman newspaper *Falastin*. It argued that Kennedy was both trying to help out Democratic congressional candidates (including the Massachusetts Senate candidate Edward M. Kennedy) and "requiting to world and American Jewry some of the debt he owes to those who . . . played a major role in the last Presidential elections."[117]

By September 28, the Nasserite media had weighed in sulfurously. While Yemen led the Cairo papers' news pages, most of their commentary was about the Hawks. From the massacres at Deir Yasin and Qafr Qasim to the Suez invasion, every weapon that America gives Israel "has been used to shed Arab blood," Haykal's *al-Ahram* boomed. Whoever arms a murderer, the editorial concluded, is himself a murderer. The editorial in *al-Akhbar* was even tougher, accusing Kennedy of having been brought to his knees by the Israel lobby and of selling Hawks to win a few votes. "Is it neutrality which makes the US refuse to supply the UAR with one single gun while supplying Israel with rockets?" *al-Akhbar* demanded. "Every bullet given to Israel is meant to kill an Arab, every rocket, thousand [*sic*] of Arabs."[118] "Arabs can expect to be stabbed in the back by the U.S.," fulminated a pro-Nasser paper in Beirut. "Arabs everywhere should beware of Kennedy."[119]

Arab reaction, however, was more muted outside Nasser's circles. Lebanese Prime Minister Rashid Karame complained "more in sorrow than in anger" to the U.S. ambassador, Armin Meyer.[120] To Meyer's relief, Karame refrained from grandstanding and expelling the visiting Sixth Fleet—although of the 650 Beirut dignitaries invited to a reception aboard the aircraft carrier U.S.S. *Forrestal*, fewer than 40 showed up.[121] The Iraqi media response, too, was mild; only 6 of Baghdad's 11 dailies ran Hawk stories, and Baghdad Radio limited itself to quoting a *Washington Post* editorial that called the sale a "major change" in U.S. policy.[122] The new regime in Damascus, seeking to curry favor with Washington, also had a "surprisingly moderate initial reaction."[123] And while the Kuwaiti press excoriated the administration, not one Kuwaiti official raised the Hawks with the American ambassador.[124]

The most genuine distress came from Egypt. In Washington, Kamel warned the administration not to be deceived by Nasser's aides' restraint; the problem was not Nasser's circle but the Egyptian army. Nasser's generals had "never been completely convinced" of the wisdom of a "policy of cooperation" with Washington, and the Hawk deal confirmed their "worst fears."[125] Through Haykal, Nasser expressed bewilderment to Badeau over American tactics, especially over the leak about Strong's consultations; either the administration was double-dealing with Nasser, or it was so riddled with Israeli spies that no policy could be made in secret. In Alexandria, many local dignitaries boycotted a farewell reception for the American consul, Rupert Prohme. One Stanford-educated engineering professor took Prohme aside bitterly to ask, "Why is it that the United States government always succumbs to the Jewish lobby?"[126] Badeau's Egyptian interlocutors concluded that the administration had been motivated solely by domestic politics, the ambassador reported. The only solace was that Nasser was foregoing the chance to pillory the administration over the Hawks or the failure of the Johnson plan, viewing Yemen as a vastly better arena in which to demonstrate his Arabist purity.[127] Still, Badeau cabled, "Having chosen the mess of potage we should not be surprised at [its] bitter taste."[128]

AN UNSTIFF UPPER LIP

Nasser was not the only one nonplussed by the Hawk sale. The British were startled by the American leap into the Middle Eastern arms-sales business. While they had no choice but to grudgingly give way, they did so in terms that would have been reckoned undiplomatic by any standards — let alone those of British decorum. Some of the tartness of Britain's complaint was due to an unflattering portrait of the Kennedy administration's deliberations sketched by Bob Strong and other grousing State Department officials to sympathetic British colleagues. But such gripes aside, Britain's competing surface-to-air missile, the Bloodhound, simply proved to be a dog that would not hunt.[129]

In 1959, Israel had first approached Britain about the Bloodhound; the following March, Ben-Gurion raised the matter personally with Prime Minister Harold Macmillan even as the Israeli leader was also pressing the Eisenhower administration for Hawks. In September 1960, the State Department told Whitehall that the administration had formally declined to sell Israel Hawks and added pointedly that selling the Bloodhound would be just as irresponsible.[130]

The British lineup on the Bloodhound looked rather like the American lineup on the Hawk, although London was more straightforward about its need for cold cash. The Foreign Office and Britain's ambassadors in the field were firmly opposed, arguing that the risk to British standing in the Arab world, staging rights in Libya, and overflight rights in the Sudan "outweigh the commercial benefits."[131] The Ministry of Aviation, however, favored the sale, agreeing with the Pentagon that Israel was vulnerable to an Egyptian bomber attack.[132] On February 14, 1962, Peres met British Secretary of State for War Jack Profumo, who warned the Israeli deputy defense minister that as "a matter of principle," London did not want to upset the regional balance of might by selling missiles. Peres told Profumo that Britain "was too nervous" about forthrightly supporting Israel.[133] After Peres left, Foreign Office and U.S. embassy officials agreed that the British refusal to sell surface-to-air missles (SAMs) to Israel "was exactly the American position," too.[134]

In early June, however, Strong of NEA tipped off the British embassy's first secretary, Denis Speares, that the administration's resolve was starting to waver.[135] Stung, Britain told its embassy in Washington that "we simply cannot risk reaching a position in which American firms secure a valuable order from Israel while we continue to block the entry of British firms into the field."[136] On June 24, Macmillan complained to the visiting Rusk about the rumored pending missile sale after dinner in Carlton Gardens. Taken aback, the secretary of state "replied that he did not think that this could be so."[137]

Of course, it was. On August 17, about a week before his mission to Egypt, an unhappy Strong privately told a British official in Washington about the Hawk decision, which Strong stressed had "been taken in the face of strong opposition from the State Department."[138] When the American embassy in London broke the news to Macmillan, the British stiff upper lip finally broke. The "prime minister has received your message," Macmillan informed the American chargé d'affaires. "He is amazed. He is sending a protest directly to the president."[139]

That got the administration's attention. A flabbergasted Rusk and Bundy summoned Viscount Samuel Hood, the minister of the British embassy, to reassure him. Rusk told the British diplomat that Washington had met its obligation to tell the British if the administration changed its mind about selling Hawks to Israel, which it now had. Feldman's mission was portrayed as centering on the Johnson plan.[140] The envoy "was in no sense attempting to close a Hawk deal," Rusk told Hood, and "there would be every opportunity for the British to attempt to sell Bloodhounds." Of course, the Americans knew that the Hawk was a better missile and that the United States was a better patron, but still, the British would have a chance to compete.[141]

After the meeting, a chastened Hood urged Macmillan to calm down lest he harm Anglo-American relations. "I hope you will agree that the Americans have acted like fools not knaves," he cabled London.[142] Partially mollified, Macmillan sent another message to Kennedy, promising to offer the Bloodhound to Ben-Gurion and expressing relief that "his concern was all based on a muddle."[143]

If Macmillan's concern had been alleviated, though, the Foreign Office's had not. The foreign secretary, Lord Home, understood that Ben-Gurion would surely buy the American missiles instead. "This is really a straight choice between the commercial gain and the political odium which we will undoubtedly incur with the Arab and Moslem world," Home wrote Macmillan, and London was likely to get "the odium without the order."[144]

By now, Macmillan was hearing protests from a British arms industry that was livid at having been "out-manoeuvred at every stage" by the Americans.[145] To save face, Whitehall told the British press that Israel really wanted the "vastly superior" Bloodhound and sniped that Kennedy had broken an "unwritten Anglo-American understanding on not supplying missiles to the Middle East."[146] Taking Lord Home's point that Israel would choose the Hawk over the Bloodhound, Macmillan's miffed cabinet decided to consider SAM sales to the Arab states instead.[147]

The shifting nature of America's special relationship with Israel, then, left behind some bruised feelings in America's special relationship with Britain. Clearly, Bundy admitted to Kennedy, the administration had not kept the British enough inside the loop, but "there was no justification for the violence of the Prime Minister's explosion . . . the way is now open for perfectly fair competition. The rub, of course," he added, "is that the British will not win. Nothing is harder for a merchant's feelings than to have to market a second-best product against alert competition."[148]

WHEN THE WIND IS SOUTHERLY

On October 1, the Israeli daily *Ma'ariv* ran a cartoon showing Kennedy, champing on a massive cigar, handing the cartoonist Dosh's famous stand-in figure for Israel a popsicle labeled "Hawk." On the side, Nasser stands, smoking a smaller cigar of his own, labeled "Offensive Rockets." The little sabra is looking at Nasser's stogie and saying, "I'd like one of those instead."[149]

If the Kennedy administration expected a swoon of Israeli gratitude for the Hawk sale, it was quickly disappointed. In early October, Israeli diplomats suggested procuring F-104 fighters and Genie air-to-air missiles—exactly what "we had feared" after the Hawk decision, Talbot groaned to Rusk.[150] An irritated Undersecretary of State for Political Affairs George McGhee seconded that emotion, directing Talbot "to make the HAWK our only exception to the policy on arms for Israel."[151]

That proved easier said than done. Israeli hopes for far-reaching security ties with the United States were now well and truly raised. When

Kennedy met Meir in Palm Beach in December 1962, he told her that America "has a special relationship with Israel in the Middle East really comparable only to that which it was with Britain over a wide range of world affairs." To Meir's delight, he added, "I think it is quite clear that in case of an invasion the United States would come to the support of Israel"—the most sweeping security guarantee of Israel yet from an American president.[152] Similarly, the Israeli press thrilled to Kennedy's more carefully hedged April 3 remarks at a press conference about maintaining the "military balance of power" in the Middle East.[153]

Word that Peres was returning to Washington in April 1963 did nothing to dampen Israeli optimism; the prompt leaks about Peres's supposedly secret meeting with Kennedy and about his success in securing credit terms for the Hawk did nothing to lift the State Department's pessimism. Peres had some reason to strut; financing the Hawks was no small matter. The total cost for one battalion of Hawks was about $27 million—a stupefying sum by 1962 standards.[154] The administration told Peres it would give Israel credit for the Hawk for 10 years, with 5 to 10 percent of the initial cost down, to be repaid at the 3.5 percent interest rate that was standard for development loans.[155] For a regional pariah that spent about 11 percent of its $2.5 billion GNP on arms, the Hawks—and the concomitant tighter ties to Washington—were a bargain. "When I look at our defense budget it makes me cry with one eye," Eshkol said later. "But I smile with the other eye because this purchases security."[156]

With the Hawks in train—Washington was slated to begin training the Israelis on the missiles in August 1963 at Fort Bliss, Texas, with an eye toward finishing the training in November 1964—Ben-Gurion kept up the pressure for more security help, especially after Nasser's spring 1963 bid to reconstitute the UAR with Iraq and Syria.[157] "I fully appreciate your decision to release the Hawk missiles to Israel, but I regret to say that this defensive weapon alone cannot serve as a deterrent to our neighbours," an agitated Ben-Gurion wrote Kennedy. "They are preparing weapons whose offensive potential cannot be reduced by the Hawk."[158]

Seeking to strike again while the iron was hot, Meir on September 30 formally told Rusk that Israel was now seeking U.S. tanks and ground-to-ground missiles, which would enable it to strike Egyptian targets and cities rather than just fend off Egyptian fighters. The secretary of state instead suggested that the sides trade evaluations of the Middle East security situation.[159] In Jerusalem, the new prime minister, Levi Eshkol, jumped at the idea and offered to send the IDF's deputy chief of staff—a taciturn, gruff veteran of some of 1948's worst fighting named Yitzhak Rabin—and Deputy Chief of Intelligence Aharon Yariv to Washington in November. Eshkol seemed to be seeking a "full-scale review" of the Israeli-Egyptian balance of forces as a preliminary to joint military planning, regular military consultations, and additional arms requests, but Rusk told him to cool it; the talks were simply to compare notes on Nasser's missile and nonconventional-weapons capabilities.[160] Yet they still heralded a new level of intimacy in U.S.–Israel security discussions.

Rabin spent much of November in the United States, visiting U.S. military bases in Texas and Oklahoma and meeting with Bill Bundy and other Pentagon officials.[161] On November 12 and 13, the future prime minister led an Israeli team that included Harman and Gazit in the unprecedented U.S.–Israel talks about the Middle Eastern balance of forces. The team sat opposite Talbot, Komer, and officials from the State Department and the Pentagon. The first three-hour session was given over mostly to Israel's assessment of Nasser's tanks, missiles, and order of battle; in the second session, the Americans argued that Israel was overstating the Egyptian threat.[162] On November 14, Rabin came to Komer's office, laid out a map of Israel, and began describing Nasser's most likely avenues of attack.

Why, complained Komer, didn't Washington's support over the years win it any trust? Because of 1948, Rabin replied.[163] Israel had been left alone, and the United States had embargoed arms shipments; the new-born state beat back the Arab armies with only Czech weaponry. A lot had happened since 1948, Komer retorted. Rabin replied that he "had a long memory"—perhaps a hint of his own harrowing combat experiences outside Jerusalem. However much he appreciated Washington's private assurances, Rabin continued, he could not rely on them without joint military planning.

Hearkening back to the previous days' talks, Komer told Rabin that the two sides' estimates of Nasser's capabilities differed widely. The general nodded assent. The underlying danger, Rabin argued, was that Nasser's overconfidence might one day lead him to underestimate Israel—quite a good description of Nasser's folly in May 1967. Komer, however, was not entirely sympathetic. Israel's assessments of threat, Komer said, struck him as the sort of exaggerations to which intelligence agencies were prone. America, too, had miscalculated "Soviet intentions in our original estimates of our 'missile gap.'"[164]

First Israel had argued that Nasser enjoyed a missile gap; now, with the Hawk sale in hand, it argued that Nasser enjoyed a tank gap and perhaps a naval gap. The month of Kennedy's assassination, Eshkol formally asked for "(1) surface-to-surface missiles to meet the growing UAR missile threat; (2) tanks to modernize Israeli armor; (3) some means of countering growing UAR naval strength." "Of course," Harman told Mac Bundy and Komer in January 1964, "Israel's immediate and primary need was for tanks."[165] Israel's British-made Centurions, French-made AMXs, and old Shermans were "completely outclassed" by Nasser's burgeoning stocks of Soviet T-54s, Stalin-3s, and older T-34s, warned Harman and Eshkol.[166] Although Israel could hardly argue that tanks were anything other than offensive weapons, the Pentagon again agreed that the IDF was lagging behind. The State Department's Middle East hands had feared that the Hawk sale would be a slippery slope; now the Israelis were pouring out the grease. After trying to steer the Israelis to West Germany instead and seeking to link the tank sale to inspections of the Israeli nuclear reactor at Dimona, President Lyndon B. Johnson closed a deal to sell 210 tanks to the Jewish state in February 1965. A year later, LBJ would agree to sell Israel 48 Skyhawk bombers.[167] America's old insistence that it was not in the Middle East arms business was dead. The Hawks, as it turned out, were harbingers.

For all of the State Department's attempts to minimize the significance of the Hawk sale, 1962 marked a watershed in Washington and Jerusalem's arms relationship. Kennedy shifted away from the parsimony of Eisenhower toward the liberality of Johnson, and, ultimately, laid important groundwork for today's full-blown military alliance. The sale of the Hawk remade the landscape of U.S.–Israel relations, to be sure, but the change came not from a sudden, unexpected earthquake but from the moment in an ongoing process of erosion when an accumulating pool of water finally overflowed, marking the start of a steady stream that would eventually carve asunder the rock of American reluctance to arm the Jewish state. The State Department might have tried to portray America's first major weapons sale to Israel as an attempt merely to provide an inoffensive tool to a friend, but Israel's founding father was after not just a projectile but a precedent. Ben-Gurion could tell a Hawk from a handsaw.

For his part, Kennedy considered the Hawk sale a reasonable middle ground. His Defense Department accepted Israel's argument that the Hawks were a strictly defensive system that would redress a legitimate military vulnerability to Nasser's Soviet fighters and bombers. The State Department argued that the Hawk sale would start a dangerous arms race; the Pentagon argued that it would stop a dangerous arms imbalance. Moreover, the administration felt pressure to compensate Israel for the tilt toward Nasser and to soothe Israel's security fears with conventional weapons. But Ben-Gurion felt that the Arabs were deadly serious about destroying Israel, and he wanted an ace in the hole. Israel's quest for nuclear weapons would lead it into its sharpest clash with the Kennedy administration—and help cement the origins of the U.S.–Israel alliance.

CHAPTER SIX

The Delicate Matter

Kennedy's Struggle to Deny Israel the Bomb

O N JANUARY 19, 1961, John F. Kennedy went to the White House as a guest for the last time. The day before he was sworn in as president, Kennedy met privately for 45 minutes with Eisenhower. The two men then walked over to the Cabinet Room—where the outgoing and incoming secretaries of state, defense, and treasury were sitting—to pass the foreign policy baton. Kennedy had asked Eisenhower and his aides to discuss hot spots (especially Berlin, Laos, and Formosa), the organization of the executive branch, and the personalities of America's closest allies, Britain's Harold Macmillan, France's Charles de Gaulle, and West Germany's Konrad Adenauer. The meeting with the Eisenhower team did not make Kennedy happy: the president-elect could not yet muster the old general's bland equanimity in the face of foreign policy crises that could lead to world war. Alone in the Oval Office, Eisenhower had showed Kennedy how to operate the "football," the ominous satchel carrying codes to the U.S. nuclear arsenal. Now, in the Cabinet Room, Kennedy wanted to know which countries might have both motive and opportunity to get the bomb.

"Israel and India," bluntly replied Christian Herter, John Foster Dulles's replacement as secretary of state. The Soviet Union was helping Nehru build a reactor. But the Israelis—furtively aided by the French—were ahead of the Indians, and might be able to produce weapons-grade plutonium before Kennedy came up for reelection in 1964. The new administration, advised Herter, should insist on inspections of the secret Israeli reactor at Dimona, in the heart of the Negev desert, lest the Middle East be dragged into a nuclear arms race. Kennedy left the meeting chilled by more than just the falling snow.[1]

Kennedy's presidency, more than any other Cold War administration, is associated with nuclear threat. The terror of the Cuban missile crisis left an indelible mark on the Kennedy administration, stimulating a new U.S. interest in nonproliferation. But the emphasis on stemming arms races also reflected an abiding concern of the president himself. Kennedy had no intention of trying to conduct a Cold War in a proliferated world where every theater was marked by its own precarious nuclear balance.

That put the Middle East high on the president's agenda. In addition to Israel, America's nuclear experts estimated that France, China, and Nasser's UAR had a high or near-high motivation to pursue the bomb.[2] (Trailing them were West Germany, Italy, Belgium, the Netherlands, Japan, Brazil, and Norway.) The part of the Third World, then, that posed the greatest threat of proliferation was far and away the Middle East.

This translated into a direct presidential interest in the Israeli nuclear program that dwarfed any other of Kennedy's Arab-Israeli concerns—including, for example, the Johnson plan. As Phillips Talbot put it later, JFK worried that what we today would call "rogue states" would upset the geopolitical apple cart by turning to nuclear weaponry.[3] In response to a burgeoning Israeli nuclear arms program, Nasser would probably seek more sophisticated armaments, including surface-to-surface missiles and a stepped-up nuclear research program, to try to narrow the gap.[4] Moscow might offer the Arabs a less direct sort of nuclear deterrent: overtly threatening Israel, guaranteeing the Arabs' security, and putting Israel in the cross hairs of Soviet missiles. Kennedy worried that the Jewish state's efforts would drive the Arab states toward the Soviet Union and trigger a regional arms race—all in all, an American nightmare.

Kennedy feared that Israel would let the nuclear genie out of the bottle. The satirist Tom Lehrer's question—"Who's Next?"—helps explain much of Kennedy's persistent, personal interest in Dimona.[5] Kennedy wanted the bottle corked and corked firmly. Israel in the early 1960s seemed fit to become the world's first undeclared nuclear-weapons state. Kennedy had no intention of letting that happen.

Moreover, if Kennedy was not going to let de Gaulle have the bomb, he was not going to let Ben-Gurion have it either. As Komer put it later, "We don't want Israel to have nuclears any more than France."[6] Over the bomb, America would wrangle with its formal ally; it could do no less with its *aspiring* ally.

The New Frontiersmen also resented the way Israel handled the nuclear issue. To steer the developing world's interest in nuclear technology away from bombs and toward power plants, the Eisenhower administration had started the Atoms for Peace program, which had provided numerous countries with nuclear know-how to use to advance their economic development; Israel had received a small U.S. research reactor in 1958. But Israel had gone secretly to France for a far larger reactor. That united the U.S.

bureaucracy in its alarm over what the Jewish state was up to. Using nuclear power for energy, technological gain, and water desalinization was fine; building nuclear weapons was not.

Small wonder, then, that the question of Dimona became the largest single bilateral obstacle to the warmer U.S.–Israeli ties that Ben-Gurion sought—at the same time as Ben-Gurion, ever mindful of the Holocaust, insisted that Israel needed the technological edge and deterrent power of the bomb. The ongoing U.S.–Israel wrangle over Dimona sometimes even carries odd echoes of America's more recent struggles to insert arms inspectors into Iraq.

Of course, Kennedy's willingness to clash with Israel should not be confused with eagerness. One tactful American diplomat in Tel Aviv took to referring to the nuclear issue as "the delicate matter."[7] Particularly in his first year in office, Kennedy's worries over Israel's nuclear program vied with his reluctance to force the issue. Kennedy never tried to link Israeli concessions on Dimona overtly to America's decision to sell Hawk missiles, but his administration had more general hopes that closer U.S.–Israel relations might make Ben-Gurion more tractable. On Dimona, that hope proved forlorn.

Domestic politics vanished as presidential engagement grew.[8] The stern tone of Kennedy's warnings to Ben-Gurion and his less combative heir, Levi Eshkol, would have done the administration no good at all in a 1964 reelection bid if word of them had ever gotten to the Israel lobby. Kennedy does not seem to have cared. Tellingly, Mike Feldman, who had sat in on meetings on such sensitive issues as the Hawk sale and the Johnson plan, was often out of the loop on Dimona.[9] On the nuclear issue, Kennedy was not much interested in what the American Jewish community thought. It is also hard to imagine that any amount of Israeli complaint, bluster, or threat would have driven him to permanently acquiesce to the Israelis' getting the bomb.

The stakes were simply too high. In addition to having deep Cold War concerns, Kennedy worried that a war might ensue if Egypt decided to stop Israel's nuclear program. The image of squadrons of Nasser's MiGs and TU-16 bombers roaring into Israeli airspace to try to reduce Dimona to rubble did little for the peace of mind of any of Kennedy's Middle East advisers.

Ben-Gurion's stated rationale for the Dimona program—the attempt to use nuclear technology to produce electricity for water desalinization—was not as transparent a pretext as it may appear to modern eyes. Throughout the 1960s, Israel's need for fresh water led it to jostle for control of the waters of the Jordan, Yarmuk, and Hasbani Rivers; the West Bank aquifers that supply much of Israel's water today were in Jordanian hands. The Jordan waters issue simmered away throughout the period, regularly causing bellicose Arab reactions. A secure and permanent water supply for Israel would remove a genuine worry. Nevertheless, Dimona was built to address a far larger one, and Kennedy either suspected or knew this.

In Ben-Gurion, however, Kennedy met a brick wall. The feisty Israeli prime minister was determined to defend Dimona and also to woo Washington. The administration grew irked with Ben-Gurion's evasions, stalls, and attempts to emasculate any Dimona inspections regime. But when the showdown came, Ben-Gurion went. At precisely the moment that Kennedy leveled his sharpest threats—icy warnings in the spring of 1963 that an Israeli refusal to permit real Dimona inspections would have the gravest consequences for the budding U.S.–Israel friendship—Israel's founding father abruptly resigned.

Ben-Gurion's resignation marked the climax of the fight over Dimona. Levi Eshkol, Ben-Gurion's finance minister and successor, proved a vastly more supple, adaptable chief executive who lacked both Ben-Gurion's combativeness and some of his fervor about the long-term indispensability of Dimona. Where Ben-Gurion fought, Eshkol fudged. Eshkol's mellower approach, his willingness to work with the New Frontiersmen rather than buck them, and his amenability to talking calmly about an ongoing inspections regime all helped soothe the inflammation caused by Israel's secret reactor. Unlike Ben-Gurion, Eshkol was willing to agree to ongoing U.S. inspections; like Ben-Gurion, Eshkol made sure that those inspections never found Israel's best-hidden secrets. That bought room to develop both the U.S.–Israel special relationship and the Dimona nuclear program. Under Eshkol, Israel behaved as if it had nothing to hide even as it was doing the hiding.

Of course, much of Kennedy's atomic diplomacy was conducted orally, leaving no documentary record. ("Never write it down," Bobby Kennedy once wrote CIA Director John McCone, passing along advice the attorney general originally got from his father.)[10] Many nuclear documents—both U.S. and Israeli—remain secret or censored. Until the full record is declassified, we cannot completely reconstruct the administration's decision making. But the upshot is plain enough: the Kennedy administration and Eshkol cleared away the single thorniest bilateral issue in U.S.–Israel relations during the early 1960s. Israel never really had to choose between Dimona and Washington. It is hard to know just how Ben-Gurion would have weighed those risks; what is clear is that, with Dimona, Israel's founder was deeply committed to a policy that carried the seeds of confrontation. Eshkol did not uproot those seeds, but he managed to tamp them far deeper down into the soil.

The fact that Dimona never became a lasting obstacle—indeed, *the* obstacle—to the warming trend in U.S.–Israel relations epitomized by the Hawk sale had much to do with Eshkol's skill but also something to do with the tragic change of U.S. leadership on November 22, 1963. Lyndon B. Johnson never quite shared Jack Kennedy's determination in the pursuit of arms control. Kennedy always saw himself primarily as a foreign policy president, whereas Johnson's dreams of his place in history came to center around his beloved Great Society. Moreover, with Nasser farther and farther away from the American orbit in the aftermath of his Yemen blunder, LBJ had less cause to bemoan the damage that America's friendship with Israel was causing with the Arabs. Kennedy and Ben-Gurion were on a collision course over Dimona; Johnson and Eshkol were both inclined to steer clear. In a sense, the way the Kennedy administration handled the problem of Dimona and regional arms proliferation ultimately helped create the U.S.–Israel alliance by helping remove—or find a route around—perhaps the largest single obstacle blocking the road.

SCOOP

On December 16, 1960, the London *Daily Express* got the sort of scoop of which journalists dream. For weeks, rumors had been swirling about a big nuclear story. On December 13, *Time* had reported that a small, nonaligned power was developing a nuclear weapons program. Now the *Daily Express* could name names: the small power was Israel, and it was well on its way to developing "an experimental nuclear bomb."[11]

Dwight Eisenhower might have been surprised, but he was not shocked. His administration had been wondering for months what Israel was up to at a remote, isolated compound outside Dimona—a small town inhabited primarily by recent immigrants from Morocco, located some 25 miles southwest of Beersheva in the parched heart of the Negev desert. In fact, the groundwork for the secret reactor had been laid years ago.

The story began when French workers broke ground on a secret reactor in the Rhône Valley town of Marcoule in 1952. After the Suez crisis, a humiliated France had plunged ahead with its nuclear program in the hope that an independent *force de frappe* would ensure that France could not be bullied in the future. In October 1957, France agreed to sell Israel—its Suez ally—both a big reactor that could produce large amounts of plutonium and a reprocessing plant to separate plutonium from the irradiated reactor fuel. Such separation facilities remain a hallmark of a nuclear-arms program. The reactor and ancillary facilities—including labs, a waste-disposal plant, offices, a facility for cooling rods, and a medical unit—

would cost about $34 million.[12] Norway, Europe's only producer of the heavy water used as a moderator and coolant in nuclear fission, agreed quietly to handle Dimona's needs. By 1961, France had provided Israel with 85 tons of natural uranium.[13] In Paris, Prime Minister Maurice Bourges-Maunoury pushed the deal over the objections of Foreign Minister Christian Pineau, who feared that it would get Israel not cheap energy but the bomb. As a result of this cabinet squabble, the French Foreign Ministry forced Israel to sign a pact vowing that it would use the French package strictly for peaceful, energy-related research—thereby, as the atomic historian Avner Cohen has noted, leaving Israel "with no choice but to make a commitment it could not keep."[14] Ben-Gurion and his protégé Shimon Peres, who was the godfather of the French-Israeli entente, overrode the hesitations of Golda Meir, who distrusted the French and disliked Peres's ability to drive Israeli foreign policy from the Defense Ministry.

When Charles de Gaulle returned to power in May 1958, he worried that Bourges-Maunoury's brand of closeness with Israel could hamper Paris's post-Suez attempts at rapprochement with the Arab world and complicate its dilemma in Algeria, the North African colony where France was fighting a losing battle against nationalist rebels.[15] As if to symbolize the extent of Israel's nuclear indebtedness to France, some 150 French families were living in Beersheva while working on the reactor.[16] In February 1960, France tested its first homegrown bomb, announcing to the world—and a mute United States—that France was not merely a faltering imperial metropole but also a new nuclear power. In May 1960, Pineau's pro-Arab successor as foreign minister, Maurice Couve de Murville, told Israel that it must lift the veil of secrecy, declare that Dimona was peaceful, and let the International Atomic Energy Agency (IAEA) into the compound. Until these conditions were met, France would not supply Dimona with uranium. In August, the sides struck a compromise: the French government would cut its ties to Dimona, but French companies would continue carrying out preexistent contracts so that Israel could finish the plant on its own. Meanwhile, Israel would publicly reveal the existence of Dimona and pledge that it was peaceful, in return for which France would drop its demand for outside inspections.

Even as Israel secretly built Dimona, it was asking formally for nuclear research aid from the United States. In 1955, under the terms of Ike's Atoms for Peace initiative—designed to share the peaceful fruits of nuclear technology with such developing nations as Greece, Iran, Pakistan, and Lebanon—the United States "undertook to assist Israel with its atomic energy development program."[17] On May 2, 1958, Israel signed an Atoms for Peace contract with American Machines and Foundry Atomics to build a small, one-megawatt research reactor at Nahal Soreq, outside Rehovot.[18]

In 1958, an American U-2 flight saw the Dimona construction site, but the administration was slow to grasp what it had found.[19] The U-2 photographs were inconclusive, perhaps because Dimona's plutonium processing facilities are now thought to have been located underground. Still, CIA analysts—noting the suspiciously long security fence, the depth and scope of the digging, its road network, its power lines, and its attendant secrecy—called Dimona a probable nuclear site. After rumors began swirling in June 1960 about French-Israeli nuclear collaboration, the American embassy in Tel Aviv formally asked Israel for the first time about Dimona.[20] Initially, perhaps in deference to one of Dimona's major industries, Israel called the facility a "textile plant"; in September, Israel changed its mind and told the United States that the compound was actually a "metallurgical research installation."[21]

As the Eisenhower presidency wound down, the administration's suspicions of Israel wound up. In late November 1960, U.S. Ambassador Ogden Reid reported that when Israel broke ground on its new university at Beersheva, Ben-Gurion would announce that a "new 10 to 20 megawatt natural uranium and heavy water nuclear reactor [was expected] to go critical in about a year and a half."[22] An unnamed source—identified by Avner Cohen as Henry Gomberg, a University of Michigan nuclear scientist who had visited Israel—told the State Department that Dimona "was actually a Marcoule-type reactor being constructed with French technical assistance."[23] In December 1960, London told Washington that Norway had given Israel 20 tons of heavy water, and the U.S. Joint Atomic Energy Interagency Committee formally concluded that the facility near Beersheva was a large atomic plant.[24] That was enough for the CIA; on December 8, Director of Central Intelligence Allen Dulles told an NSC meeting that Israel was building a secret nuclear reactor.

The next day, Secretary of State Herter summoned Israeli Ambassador Avraham Harman to Foggy Bottom. An angry Herter presented Harman with U.S. intelligence about Dimona—including photographs snapped from the ground that clearly showed a water tower to cool the reactor[25]—and berated Harman for the inconsistencies in Israel's earlier explanations.[26] Harman "disclaimed any detailed knowledge" of the reactor and asked for time to consult with Jerusalem.[27]

There matters lay, until the *Daily Express* landed its scoop. The Israeli embassy in London promptly denied that Israel had "either the means or the intention" of developing a bomb.[28] Ernest Bergmann, the chair of Israel's Atomic Energy Commission, called the story "flattering but false."[29] On December 18, the chair of the U.S. Atomic Energy Commission— John McCone, soon to become Kennedy's director of central intelligence—was grilled on NBC's *Meet the Press* about Dimona. "Would it not be a very perfect opportunity for the government of Israel," asked Arthur Krock of the *New York Times,* "considering that it has been the beneficiary of great help from the United States government . . . to agree to be the model for an inspection system whereby the benevolence of intent could be proved, not only to us but to the world?" McCone concurred. Dimona, he admitted, had come as a surprise.[30] In a White House meeting on Dimona the next day, Defense Secretary Thomas Gates said bluntly that Dimona was "not for peaceful purposes."[31] In Beirut, one American diplomat warned of the need to "allay hysterical Arab suspicions"; throughout the Arab world, calls erupted for an Arab bomb.[32] In Cairo, a startled Nasser vowed to destroy the Israeli nuclear program.[33]

Now that the cat was out of the bag, Ben-Gurion tried to soothe the world. Hoping to avoid a showdown with Eisenhower, the prime minister told the Knesset on December 21 that Dimona, which would not be ready for three or four more years, was "designed exclusively for peaceful purposes." France concurred, likening Dimona to the much-larger but still peaceful reactor that Canada had helped India build.[34] French officials promised to keep an eye on the plant, provide all the uranium for its use, and receive all the plutonium it produced.[35] The only reason for the secrecy, Ben-Gurion insisted, was the fear that the Arab economic boycott would have forced the foreign companies helping Israel build the reactor to sever their ties.[36] Since Israel had no uranium to fuel the reactor, Ben-Gurion promised the Americans that Israel would return any plutonium Dimona produced to the uranium-supplying country.[37]

In Washington, Harman passed along a similar message to Herter, who had been stewing over having been made to wait.[38] Harman portrayed Dimona as part of Israel's wider program to make its deserts bloom. But Israel continued to behave as if Dimona was anything but innocuous. One Israeli official, for instance, complained in December 1960 to Israel's *Yediot Ahronot* newspaper that an American naval aide's photographing of a military installation amounted to American espionage inside Israel; the American embassy retorted that the officer who took the snapshots had been told by Israel that all he was looking at was a metallurgical research plant.[39] Moreover, Ben-Gurion dissembled on how powerful Dimona was; while he said in the Knesset that it was a 24-megawatt facility, CIA operatives put its true power level at 40 megawatts, and it may well have had more juice than that.[40] The more powerful the reactor, of course, the more military use it could have. Ben-Gurion also did not mention Israel's French connection. Nor was a claim by Teddy Kollek, the director-general of the prime minister's office, that Israel's Atomic Energy Commission had been placed under the auspices of the Defense Ministry purely out of "administrative convenience" particularly plausible.[41]

Some members of Congress expressed irritation over Israel's duplicity. When Herter testified before the Senate Foreign Relations Committee in early January 1961, the magnificently named Senator Bourke B. Hickenlooper, a conservative Iowa Republican, growled that the Israelis "have just lied to us like horse thieves on this thing."[42] A few days later, Senator Albert Gore of Tennessee—the chair of the Near East subcommittee of the Senate Foreign Relations Committee and the father of Bill Clinton's vice president—quietly summoned Assistant Secretary of State for Near East Affairs G. Lewis Jones and a few senators for an informal meeting at a low-key Senate staff office to find out why Israel was lying to the United States. "Peacefully applied atomic energy is like electricity," Hickenlooper told the gathering. "Whether we like it or not countries are going to get it." But what was Israel up to? Gore was annoyed that Israel had not merely tried to conceal the project but had "deliberately misled" American officials. Israel kept saying it had nothing to hide, noted Senate Foreign Relations Chair J. William Fulbright, so why was it hiding Dimona? Worse, Gore fretted, if Dimona began producing weapons-grade plutonium, it might push the Arabs into the Soviets' arms. Nasser had already asked the Kremlin for help in building a 30- to 40-megawatt reactor "comparable to Dimona."[43] The senators resented the bind in which Israel had put them: letting Israel get the bomb could drive the Arabs toward the Soviet Union, but the more of a fuss the United States made, the more of a fuss the Arabs would make, too.

Angry as Congress was, Eisenhower seems to have hoped to be able to look the other way. And Ben-Gurion, for all his bombast, was ultimately willing "to say almost anything" that Washington wanted to hear, as the historian Avner Cohen has argued.[44] Still, the president also asked for safeguards on the plutonium that Dimona produced and an inspection of the plant by either an American or an IAEA representative.[45] Israel formally promised the administration to let "visitors" from America or "another friendly country" into Dimona when the "present intense public interest in the question has subsided." Herter's aides, holding down the fort until the New Frontier finished staffing up, accepted that, figuring that an extended public flap would do vastly less good than "persistent but quiet" diplomacy.[46] Dimona simply came too late in Eisenhower's presidency for him to do much about it. Eisenhower extracted an Israeli promise of inspections but failed to implement it. Israel's nuclear program was about to become John F. Kennedy's problem.

INHERITING DIMONA

For Ben-Gurion and his closest aides, the question was not whether the White House would be angry about Dimona. It would be. The question was how angry. If Israel had asked America for help building Dimona in the first place, Peres and Moshe Dayan had reportedly argued before the Israeli cabinet, it would surely have been refused. By going to France instead, Israel had sought to create a fait accompli. Ben-Gurion and his men were gambling that the United States would decide that its vital interests were not materially affected by the Dimona revelation and settle for mere expressions of pique. The Israeli cabinet was said to have been persuaded by Peres and Dayan that America "would do no more than display [an] angry attitude."[47] As the initial shock was absorbed, the fledgling Kennedy administration had to calibrate its anger—to decide, as it were, whether Dimona was a core issue.

Dimona was on President Kennedy's mind from the start. On January 30, 1961, Secretary of State Rusk sent the president a briefing memo on Israel's nuclear program, one of the secretary of state's first presidential communications on the Middle East, offering a full chronology of Israel's atomic history.[48] While Israel and France's assurances did much to assure Rusk that Israel was not trying to acquire nuclear weapons, he still worried about the regional consequences of an Israeli bomb—"not the least of which might be the probable stationing of Soviet nuclear weapons on the soil of Israel's embittered Arab neighbors." On February 6, Kennedy sat in on one of Rusk's staff meetings and fretted that Dimona might drive Nasser to seek Soviet help in getting the bomb. That might force the administration to state publicly that the reactor was peaceful—something Washington did not really know.[49]

The outgoing ambassador to Israel, Ogden Reid, was less troubled by the conundrum. On January 4, he had been told again by Ben-Gurion that the reactor was peaceful; the Israeli leader had also agreed to a "free and open," quiet visit to Dimona by an American scientist or representatives from friendly powers.[50] In an Oval Office exit interview, Reid told Kennedy that the administration could "accept at face value" Ben-Gurion's assurances.[51] Reid later guessed that most of Ben-Gurion's aides, including even Foreign Minister Golda Meir, had not known that the prime minister was building such an ambitious nuclear program until Dimona hit the newspapers.

No great help was forthcoming from the American intelligence services.[52] An early CIA Information Report was longer on prejudice than analysis. "With reference to the recent revelation of the existence of a nuclear reactor in Beersheba [sic]," the CIA appraisal began, "the fact that Israel is working in this field should have come as no surprise inasmuch as almost every nuclear scientist who has contributed to the development of nuclear weapons in the U.S. has been a Jew and a great number of prominent nuclear scientists have come to Israel."[53]

Absent good intelligence, Kennedy had no way of knowing whether to trust Reid's optimism or Rusk's skepticism. If Israel genuinely was only trying to harvest the scientific fruits of peaceful nuclear research, Kennedy wondered, why all the secrecy? If Dimona was nonmilitary, why did Ben-Gurion so dislike the idea of regular, rigorous inspections of the Negev facility by American scientists? If Israel had nothing to hide, why was it acting as if it did?

This uncertainty may have driven his policy to center on nuclear inspections. Letting the United States see for itself what Israel was up to at Dimona let Kennedy bypass any assessment of Israeli veracity. If Israel was telling the truth about the peaceful nature of its atomic program, it had no reason to fear inspections. If Israel was not telling the truth—well, the New Frontiersmen did not like to dwell on that. On-site visits, usually conducted by the IAEA, were a standard part of U.S. contracts for Atoms for Peace reactors, including Israel's reactor at Nahal Soreq, so extending similar visits to Dimona was no conceptual leap for America's atomic experts.[54]

The push for inspections was embarrassing for Israel to resist publicly since it amounted to little more than verification of Ben-Gurion's public and private assurances—assuming they were sincere. Kennedy just had to make sure that Ben-Gurion kept his word to Eisenhower. If the inspections gave Dimona a clean bill of health, the administration could use that independent assessment to soothe the Arab world—a boon to both JFK's overarching nonproliferation policy and his attempts to ease Arab-Israeli tensions. Ultimately, the administration's problem was twofold: it had to keep Israel from making weapons, and it had to convince the Arabs that Israel was not making weapons. Inspections blunted both prongs.

The inspections policy was in train even before the administration was fully staffed. On January 31, Reid had told Kennedy that Israel had agreed to have an American scientist visit "within the next month," so the president had no reason not to push early.[55] In early February, before a meeting on Arab refugees, the lame-duck NEA chief Jones pulled Harman aside for a private chat. Washington took Ben-Gurion at his word about Dimona, Jones said, but it still wanted a quiet American on-site visit. An unhappy Harman replied that the timing was wrong, with Ben-Gurion's Mapai Party being torn apart by the calamitous domestic scandal known as the Lavon affair. But there was no great mystery at Dimona, Harman insisted: the reactor would take two years to complete, which meant that there was no fissile material and plenty of time to inspect the site. What was America's rush? Proliferation was "anathema" to the United States, Jones replied. Now that a cloud of suspicion had fallen across an American friend, the sooner it could be lifted, the better. Clearly not enjoying being put on the spot, Harman agreed that "getting the visit over with" would be a relief.[56]

It was not the last time Harman would think such things; throughout Ben-Gurion's showdowns over Dimona, Israel's Washington embassy repeatedly found itself wishing for a less confrontational Israeli policy that did less to imperil the wider U.S.–Israel relationship. Meanwhile, the State Department began prodding the Israelis almost weekly about an inspection.

To his chagrin, Harman soon found that the administration's concerns went all the way to the top. In mid-February, National Security Adviser McGeorge Bundy warned the Israeli ambassador that Dimona could have a dreadful impact on Arab opinion.[57] News of the plant had "spilled out" inelegantly, Harman wearily conceded, but it was peaceful and three years or more away from "going critical"—that is, starting a sustained chain reaction. Indeed, Dimona was small enough that Israel would not mind seeing Nasser develop a similar, peacefully oriented reactor. The point of the program, Harman insisted, was the development of a cadre of nuclear-trained scientists who might be able to reap the scientific benefits of peaceful atomic research, not anything more sinister. Moreover, Ben-Gurion objected to *international* inspections, both because other suspected proliferators—notably India—had not been forced to accept them and because the Israeli leader feared Soviet interference.[58]

A few weeks later, Teddy Kollek told Jones that there was no reason that a visit could not occur during March.[59] On March 27, Kennedy called the State Department to ask again where matters stood. Jones promptly summoned Harman to Foggy Bottom and told him that the president himself wanted Israel to hurry up. Kollek's month was almost up, Jones noted, and the impression that Israel was "stalling" would do the country no good.[60] Harman said again that Israel's political crisis was monopolizing Ben-Gurion's attention and offered one of the feeblest stalls yet, pointing out that little government business would get done during the week of Passover in early April. At a minimum, the flap over the discovery of Dimona would have to subside before the administration could take a better look. On inspections, the administration felt, the question was not whether but when.[61] In fact, the better question would have been how—whether Israel would permit inspections that would mean anything.

AMERICANS IN DIMONA

In April of 1961, Abe Harman was let off the hook. At the end of Passover, Jerusalem finally ordered its long-suffering ambassador to invite an American inspector to visit Dimona secretly during the week of May 15. The administration suggested sending a pair of scientists, under cover of a quiet consultation lest word of the inspection leak out. While the visit itself would remain under wraps, the administration told Israel that it would ask its permission to pass along the results—presumably, the White House told the Israelis, confirming Ben-Gurion's earlier insistence that Dimona was harmless. On April 28, the U.S. embassy in Tel Aviv formally accepted the Israeli invitation. Ulysses Staebler, the senior assistant director of the U.S. Atomic Energy Commission's (AEC) division of reactor development, and Jesse Croach, a Dupont scientist and a heavy-water expert at the AEC's Savannah River lab, were chosen as the American inspectors, and the sides agreed that they would visit on May 18.[62]

In early May, Rusk passed on the good news to the president.[63] Kennedy suggested adding a scientist from a neutral country to the team, but both Rusk and Bundy replied that it had been agonizing enough to get the Israelis to agree to a purely American inspection and advised the president to leave well enough alone.[64] During a brief meeting with Walworth Barbour, the administration's ambassador-designate to Tel Aviv, Kennedy underscored the need for secrecy during the visit but complained again of the absence of a neutral inspector, which would have given the inspection additional credibility.[65]

With the visit finally set, Harman formally asked Rusk on April 13 for a face-to-face meeting between Ben-Gurion and Kennedy—to, among other things, discuss Dimona, which was clearly the most contentious issue in U.S.–Israel relations thus far.[66] Perhaps partially as a reward for his allowing the inspections, Kennedy decided to see Ben-Gurion at the end of May—after the Dimona visit. To ease Arab concerns over such an early meeting with the Israeli prime minister, the president sent out his opening round of letters to Arab leaders. So by May, the Dimona issue was heating up, with American inspectors on their way to Israel and Ben-Gurion on his way to New York.

Israel's strategy, it now seems, was to permit a visit—but ensure that the inspectors did not find anything. The two AEC scientists landed in Tel Aviv on the evening of May 17. Their official host was Ephraim Katzir-Katchalsky, the head of the Department of Biophysics at the Weizmann Institute of Science in Rehovot, near Tel Aviv. During their four-day stay in Israel, Staebler and Crouch were shown the Atoms for Peace reactor at Nahal Soreq, the nearby Weizmann Institute, the Technion (Israel's MIT) in Haifa, and some Galilee scenery. But the heart of the visit took place on Saturday, May 18, when most of Israel was relaxing for the Jewish sabbath. Staebler and Crouch spent the day being shown around the Dimona complex—some 750 square meters, surrounded by a large security area with barbed-wire fencing.[67] The ground rules were simple: the Dimona scientists would answer all of the Americans' questions; no written material was handed out lest it leak; and no pictures were permitted.

The two American atom scientists were greeted cordially by the reactor's director and visited several installations engaged in nuclear activity, including the reactor itself. In 1957, they were told in a background briefing, an Israeli committee had first considered moving its nuclear program beyond the lab, but the committee ultimately decided that the cost of the original proposal — building two large reactors to produce industrial power — was prohibitive. Instead, the committee had opted to build a smaller research reactor to pave the way for a larger nuclear power program. Israel had broken ground at Dimona in 1959, and Israeli nuclear officials told their visitors that the plant would not go on-line until 1964. The Americans found "strong evidence of close French scientific collaboration and support," and they were told that Dimona's design was based on French EL-3 reactors. Staebler and Crouch guessed that the completed reactor would cost $15 million, plus another $20 million for the ancillary labs, fuel dumps, storehouses, and so on.

When the two scientists reported back to the State Department on May 25, they gave Dimona something close to a clean bill of health. Like other such reactors, Dimona would eventually produce "small quantities of plutonium suitable for weapons," they noted, but "there is no present evidence that the Israelis have weapon production in mind." Israel seemed bent on secrecy not because it was seeking the bomb but because it feared sabotage, a boycott from foreign manufacturers, and unnecessary Arab knowledge of Israeli technological capacities. A second verification of Dimona's nonmilitary usage, the scientists suggested, could safely wait for another year — at least from the scientific standpoint. The reactor was "entirely as advertised."[68]

The Israelis must have heaved a sigh of relief. From the outset, Meir had opposed the visit, seemingly "concerned about the implications of misleading the American scientists."[69] But as it happened, the scientists had not shown up bristling with suspicion — either because they were letting scientific curiosity rather than strategic anxiety be their lodestar, because they were enjoying the novelty of a secret government mission to an exotic country far from Savannah River, or because they simply had not been ordered by the administration to interrogate every Israeli protestation of innocence. The administration had focused so closely on just *holding* an inspection that it had let Israel limit that inspection's scope to a few closely supervised hours on a shabbat afternoon, with American representatives who were not inclined to grill their Israeli hosts.

As Kennedy prepared for his summit at the Waldorf with Ben-Gurion, Mike Feldman sent him a briefing memo on Dimona that accepted the thrust of the two scientists' report: their findings, Feldman wrote, "confirm the peaceful purposes of the reactor."[70] But even Feldman urged

Kennedy to seek similar return visits at regular intervals just to make sure. The mere appearance of a secret Israeli drive to get the bomb—let alone an *actual* secret Israeli drive to get the bomb—could well make the Arabs do something rash. As Bundy warned the president, "while the reactor is clean as a whistle today, it could be turned in a dirty direction at any time."[71]

THE APPEARANCE OF VIRTUE

On his way to New York, after a state visit to Canada, even the hard-bitten Ben-Gurion was tense.[72] Even with the first inspection behind him, he knew that two of his most cherished policies—nuclear power and American friendship—might collide at the Waldorf. Kennedy's aides were suspicious, and Ben-Gurion, never terribly discreet, had reportedly told Canadian Prime Minister John Diefenbaker that "if the Arab threat continued to grow and Israel's defensive capability became heavily outweighed, Israel might as a matter of self-defense be required to develop nuclear weapons capability."[73] On May 30 at 4:45 P.M., a nervous Ben-Gurion entered suite 28A of the Waldorf Astoria to meet Kennedy, along with Feldman, the newly confirmed Talbot, and Harman.

The prime minister's apprehensions were not entirely misplaced. The two men had barely finished exchanging pleasantries and posing for photographs before they "plunged into a discussion" of Dimona.[74] It is some measure of Ben-Gurion's preoccupation with Dimona that the Israeli minutes of the meeting are divided into two sections: a report on the reactor, and another section on everything else.

That discussion of Dimona, however, might well have been much tougher on Israel if not for the somewhat lackadaisical inspection a few weeks earlier. Kennedy told the Israeli leader that he was glad to have had "a good report" of the American visit. Even so, "on the theory that a woman should not only be virtuous but also have the appearance of virtue," Kennedy said, he wanted to find ways to reassure others about Israel's nuclear intentions. "We must take away any excuse for the argument that what you are doing is connected with the proliferation of nuclear arms."[75]

Kennedy's tone could have been far more skeptical. The main purpose of Dimona, a relieved Ben-Gurion reiterated, was to help Israel use atomic energy for the affordable desalinization of salt water—a way to solve the country's chronic fresh-water shortage that was even more effective than tapping the Jordan. "For the time being the only purposes are for peace," he added—leaving the door open a crack.[76] Less reassuringly, he added, "we do not know what will happen in the future; in three or four years we might have need for a plant to process plutonium." For now, the Kremlin did not seem to want to give Nasser nuclear help, but he would probably develop such technology on his own in 10 to 15 years.

Perhaps so, Kennedy replied, but why goad him? If Israel seemed to be on the road to the bomb, Nasser would surely follow. To reassure the Arabs on this score, could the administration publish the scientists' report? "You are absolutely free to do what you wish with the report," Ben-Gurion said.[77]

Of course, Kennedy continued, "because we are close friends," some might not take America's word that Dimona was pacific. Perhaps neutral scientists might also have a look.

"What do you mean by neutral?" Ben-Gurion asked.[78]

"Do you think, like Khrushchev, that no man can be neutral?" Kennedy shot back. "Take Nehru."

"Yes, Nehru is neutral," Ben-Gurion said, "though after his experience with China he is not so neutral."

"Yes," Kennedy said. "Or Switzerland or Sweden or Denmark. Would you object to our sending such a neutral scientist?"

"Yes, if you wish," Ben-Gurion replied, and the meeting moved on to a discussion of Israel's conventional security needs and Nasser's ambitions.[79] But while Dimona started off the meeting, it did not sour it. Instead of a showdown, JFK contented himself with Israeli commitments to let him publicize the inspectors' report as he saw fit and to permit a future Dimona visit by a neutral scientist. As Kennedy walked Ben-Gurion to the hotel elevator, the prime minister was relieved: the Waldorf meeting could have gone much worse for him.[80]

That impression is borne out by the administration's reports after the meeting. When Senator Fulbright asked the State Department where matters stood with the Dimona inspections, Foggy Bottom replied that Kennedy had raised the issue with Ben-Gurion at the Waldorf and been told that the reactor was intended for desalinization—something that neutral scientists could verify.[81] When Talbot met with the Arab ambassadorial corps to brief them on the meeting, he made it clear that the nuclear issue had topped the president's agenda and that Kennedy had warned that "the United States would have to use its weight against" nuclear proliferation.[82]

The administration was sufficiently concerned about Dimona to push for an inspection but not so concerned that it picked a fight at the Waldorf. Even Ben-Gurion's hint that Israel might one day need a plutonium-separation plant—a key prerequisite for a nuclear-arms program—set off no particular alarm. The half-hearted Dimona visit and Kennedy's temperate attitude at the Waldorf offered Ben-Gurion a way to fob off American apprehensions without ever being forced to choose between pursuing the bomb and wooing Washington. But over time, that balancing act would become more difficult. While the Kennedy administration was not looking for a confrontation, it was not prepared to let the matter drop, either. On June 22, Talbot suggested to Harman that the administration hold "another quiet visit by US scientists to [the] Dimona reactor."[83] The previous month's visits had helped ease regional tensions over Israel's nuclear program, Talbot argued; a sequel "could serve to prolong" this new "relaxed attitude." Harman promised to check. The inspections tango was about to begin anew.

GUTS AND BRAINS

In sharp contrast to its interagency brawling over the Hawks, the Kennedy administration was basically united on Dimona. The rivalries and disagreements between the State Department, the Pentagon, and the NSC that Israel so skillfully exploited over conventional arms sales did not extend to Israel's nuclear program. Moreover, the tone over Dimona was set by Kennedy himself, which discouraged the bureaucracy from wandering off in disparate directions. Kennedy sometimes sighed that his diplomats had no guts and his generals had no brains.[84] On Dimona, however, both guts and brains were in rough agreement.

In the summer of 1961, the Joint Chiefs of Staff (JCS) prepared a strategic analysis of the Dimona reactor.[85] The new facility gave Israel the ability to produce plutonium, the JCS reported, and France's fingerprints were all over it—including "plans, materials, equipment, and technical assistance."

If Israel got the bomb, the chiefs reckoned, its fear of the superpowers' wrath would probably prevent it from actually starting a Middle East war. But a nuclear Israel would possess "a powerful psychological weapon" that would make it more obdurate and assertive toward the Arabs. For their part, the Arabs would blame the United States and France for letting Israel get the bomb; led by Nasser, a rattled and more unified Arab world would lash back at France in particular and the West in general, perhaps by cutting off oil supplies or the Suez Canal. The Soviet Union "would almost certainly not provide nuclear weapons to the UAR" in return, but it would offer the UAR other compensatory military assistance and political support.

In fact, the chiefs argued, the Soviet Union's desire to make hay out of a nuclear Israel would probably be outweighed by its concern with nonproliferation. True, Moscow could use the issue to press Washington and London for a test ban or arms cuts, to rally Third World neutralists, and to agitate for a nuclear-free Middle East. But such opportunism aside, the Kremlin knew that if Israel got the bomb, China and Egypt would be baying for Soviet help to develop their own nuclear capabilities.

As for the West in general, the closer Israel came to developing nuclear weapons, the more pressure there would be from the smaller NATO nations and neutral powers to slow the spread of nuclear arms. If Israel went ahead anyway, such technologically advanced countries as Sweden, Switzerland, and perhaps even Japan would feel less inhibited about pursuing bombs of their own. Another headache would surely be the projection of U.S.–French tensions, which were already bedeviling NATO, into the Middle East.

The Joint Chiefs thus recommended using "all feasible means, official, quasi-official and private, to convince Israel and France" that a nuclear-armed Israel was in the interest of neither the West, the Middle East, nor Israel. An Egyptian nuclear-arms program would be no more salubrious. Washington should push the Israelis toward peaceful nuclear research and away from the bomb.

The State Department agreed. The May inspections "satisfied us that, for the present, the Government of Israel is not actively engaged in programs aimed at nuclear weapons production," Rusk wrote Deputy Secretary of Defense Roswell Gilpatric in response to the JCS study.[86] Nor should it be. "As a matter of well-considered policy, we remain opposed to acquisition by Israel of a nuclear weapons capability," insisted NEA's Meyer shortly before being sent to Beirut.[87] Dimona would remain right at the top of Foggy Bottom's Arab-Israeli agenda.

THE OSIRAQ FACTOR

Not the least of the reasons for the Kennedy administration's consensus in favor of further inspections was what might in retrospect be called the Osiraq factor, after the Iraqi nuclear reactor destroyed by Israel in 1981. In effect, the Kennedy administration was concerned that Nasser might do to Dimona what Menachem Begin did to Osiraq. Unless Arab radicals—especially Egypt and, to a lesser degree, Syria—were reassured that Israel was not on the verge of getting the bomb, they might be tempted to launch a surprise air raid to take out Dimona.[88] Worse, they might even "launch in desperation a combined arms attack on Israel."[89]

Dire as this scenario was, the administration did not seem eager to face its full implications in 1962. Dimona was moved to the back burner after the first inspection and the Waldorf non-showdown. With the nuclear issue at least temporarily defused, the administration's Middle East team focused its energies on the Nasser initiative, the Hawk question, the Johnson plan, and such perennial lower-level worries as Israeli-Syrian raids and reprisals, the ongoing dispute over the Jordan River's precious waters, and the U.N. forums handling Arab-Israeli issues.

Over the long term, the most important U.S.–Israeli development in 1962 was the Hawk sale. Did it have anything to do with Dimona? The historian Douglas Little has compellingly argued that the Hawks represented an American attempt to soothe Israel's security jitters and lull it out of its nuclear program.[90] The argument runs that both Nasser's adventurism and Israel's atomic bid drove Kennedy to abandon his more evenhanded approach to Arab-Israeli relations—epitomized by the Nasser initiative and the Johnson plan—in favor of a frank recognition that a strong Israel was a Cold War asset and a weak Israel a Cold War obstacle. An Israel that could not resolve its security worries with conventional weapons would go nuclear, thereby driving the Arabs toward Moscow. So Kennedy is said to have offered Hawks to Ben-Gurion to dissuade him from plunging ahead with Dimona.

The nuclear historian Avner Cohen also hints at a linkage between the Hawks and Dimona. While on the surface, it seems that security and nuclear issues were two separate questions, both Feldman and the late Bob Komer gave interviews to Cohen in which linkage between the two issues was "presented as a fact, if unstated and tacit." As Komer put it, "There was [sic] never really two tracks, security and atom, there was always really only one track."[91] According to the investigative reporter Seymour Hersh, "The most important factor, clearly, in Ben-Gurion's decision to permit the [Dimona] inspections was the Kennedy administration's decision in mid-1962 to authorize the sale of Hawk surface-to-air missiles to Israel."[92]

A linkage between nuclear weaponry and closer U.S.–Israel security ties may well have been in the air, but it is not in the documents. There is abundant documentary evidence of other tradeoffs in Kennedy's Middle East policy—say, security guarantees and the 1963 McCloy mission on Israeli-Egyptian disarmament discussed later in this chapter—but there is no paper trail to show that the nuclear issue had anything to do with the Hawk sale. We do know that the administration tried to link the Hawks to the Johnson plan, and it is unlikely that the administration would simultaneously try to trade the Hawks for Israeli concessions on the Johnson plan *and* on its nuclear program. There is only so much mileage one could get out of one arms sale, however historic.[93] On the wider question of the U.S. military relationship with Israel, by the time the Dimona question heated back up again in 1963, the precedent of major American arms sales to Israel had already been set.

Even if Dimona and the Hawks were not linked in Kennedy's mind, they may well have been linked in Ben-Gurion's. What if the real military reason Ben-Gurion so badly wanted the Hawks was not for a national air defense against Nasser's MiGs but for a perimeter defense to protect Dimona from the Egyptian air force? It would be an eminently sensible tactical use of antiaircraft missiles. As a weapon system, the Hawks were better suited to defending Dimona than defending Tel Aviv.[94]

Such supposition remains speculative. The relevant documentation—if it even existed, which is by no means clear in light of Ben-Gurion's closed circle on atomic decision making—would be off limits in the Israeli defense archives in Tel Aviv. Moreover, Nasser, who had the most to lose from the use of Hawks to defend Dimona, never mentioned such fears to American officials. Even so, it is an intriguing thought. If the Hawks were indeed intended to defend Dimona from a Nasserite version of Osiraq, then the two seemingly contradictory elements of Ben-Gurion's policy—courting Kennedy for Hawks and aggravating him over Dimona—would come together. Washington was almost certainly pursuing two different policies with its stances toward Dimona and the Hawks. But if the Hawks were an insurance policy against the Osiraq factor, then for Israel, the two policies may have been different sides of the same coin. And on June 5, 1967, the Israeli air force inadvertently gave strong evidence that Israel had hoped to use the Hawks to defend Dimona. On the first day of the Six Day War, Israeli jets destroyed Nasser's painstakingly built air force in a preemptive strike that shocked the Egyptians. Israel lost just eight jets in the first wave of attack—including one wounded plane, limping home in radio silence, that wandered into Dimona's air space and was shot down by a Hawk.[95]

A LONG TWILIGHT STRUGGLE

In mid-August 1962, Robert Strong of NEA told British diplomats that the "Israelis were clearly dragging their feet" on whether to permit a second visit to Dimona—perhaps hoping that in the interval, the United States would conclude that further inspections were unnecessary.[96] In early August, Ben-Gurion told the Knesset that both Nahal Soreq and Dimona were "intended for peaceful aims and would be open to foreign students just as the reactor which Canada set up in India [was]."[97] Why, then, had he still not responded to Washington's June 22 request for a second visit to Dimona? To the New Frontiersmen, the attempt to watch Israel's nuclear program was threatening to become a long twilight struggle—particularly since twilight was about as much illumination as Israel wanted cast on its nuclear secrets.

On August 24, the State Department again asked Harman for a follow-up visit. After three more weeks passed, the administration suggested taking advantage of a forthcoming routine, semiannual trip to Israel by two American AEC scientists to inspect the smaller U.S.–funded reactor at Nahal Soreq. Despite the State Department's warnings that "this was a matter of primary importance," Harman replied that Israel could not respond until Ben-Gurion returned from a trip to Scandinavia in late September.[98]

This time, however, Ben-Gurion decided to seize the opportunity to get the visit out of the way. As the State Department grumbled about Israel's stalling, Israel quietly prepared for an impromptu look at Dimona that would catch the Americans unprepared. On September 26, the AEC scientists were abruptly taken on a 40-minute tour around Dimona.[99] The scientists noted being barred from entering one large building, but they still had found no smoking gun.

Again, the administration did not seem eager to pick a fight. "There is no evidence of preparation for nuclear weapons production," Rusk cabled U.S. embassies after the visit.[100] In a meeting with the British ambassador to Washington, Sir David Ormsby Gore, NEA's Strong said that the admittedly brief visit had been enough "to conclude that the situation at Dimona had not changed: i.e., the installation appeared to be intended for peaceful purposes only, and there was no evidence of preparations for the military use of plutonium."[101] Dimona, then, still formally had a clean bill of health from the United States—an assessment passed along to Jordan, Iraq, Lebanon, Syria, Saudi Arabia, and Norway (which was suspected of aiding the Israeli program). Badeau also confidentially shared the update with Nasser.

But the visit—it hardly merits the name "inspection"—was scarcely enough to offer certainty. The administration passed along the second visit's results to Western Europe and the Arabs with a confidence that it did not really feel. In a briefing paper for Kennedy, the State Department complained that the two inspectors "were allowed only 40 minutes at the site, which was inadequate, and were not given opportunity to see all sides of the operation."[102] As with the first Dimona visit, the lightning September 1962 tour may have been intended to clear the air before a presidential meeting with an Israeli leader, in this case Foreign Minister Golda Meir, who was slated to meet Kennedy in late December.

However annoyed the White House may have been, any follow-up was temporarily halted during the harrowing Cuban missile crisis. On December 27, with the cataclysm past, a tired but triumphant Kennedy took time out of a working vacation in Palm Beach to spend 70 minutes with Meir.[103] The president's briefing papers focused not on nuclear issues but on payback after the Hawk sales; the State Department was annoyed that its pro-Israel moves had not been reciprocated, especially over the Johnson plan for Arab refugees and the general need to keep up good ties with the Arabs. Komer, too, complained that "our policy to date toward Israel has been one of all give and no get."[104]

Kennedy's aides were also not enthusiastic about their interlocutor. "Mrs. Meir is as tough and driving" as Ben-Gurion but "more repetitious and less intellectually flexible," read the character sketch that the State Department prepared for Kennedy. "It requires a determined persistence in discussion to persuade her to hear out or accept an opinion contrary to her own."[105] Even Barbour—the U.S. ambassador in Tel Aviv, who became a close friend of Meir's—tended to agree. "I would not say that she was the world's most flexible individual," he later said.[106]

The president sat in a rocking chair on the porch of the Kennedys' Florida house, without a tie, shirt sleeves rolled up. Kennedy struck Meir as "so handsome and still so boyish" that she later said that she found it hard to remember that he was president—although she supposed that she did not fit his mental image of a foreign minister, either.[107] Kennedy found Meir concerned about Israel's security vulnerabilities, just as his briefers had predicted. The Pentagon tended not to view Egypt's nuclear program as a serious threat, but Meir offered a fresh (and probably false) allegation: Nasser was secretly spending about $250 million per year on an atomic warfare program, she warned.[108] More pressingly, Meir asked Kennedy, if Nasser's TU-16s could fly from Egypt, bomb royalist targets in Yemen, and then return, what could they do to Israel? (The Hawk sale seemed not to have allayed such concerns.) The president listened sympathetically enough, but toward the end of the meeting, he specifically cautioned the Israeli foreign minister about Dimona. Kennedy spoke with unprecedented warmth about the U.S.–Israel bond, but he warned that the special relationship was "a two-way street." In the long run, Israel's security depended both on how it dealt with the Arabs and on how it dealt with the United States. So the president hoped that Israel would "give consideration to our problems" about Dimona. "We are opposed to nuclear proliferation," he said bluntly. "Our interest here is not in prying into Israel's affairs but we have to be concerned because of the over-all situation in the Middle East." Meir, who had long feared that Ben-Gurion's attempts to deceive the United States about Israel's nuclear program would cause a U.S.–Israel rift, assured Kennedy that "there would not be any difficulty between us" over Dimona. That was wishful thinking.

ATOMIC DIPLOMACY

The superpower showdown in Cuba produced a new American seriousness about proliferation. In early 1963, the administration's wheels began turning in earnest about the Israeli-Egyptian balance of forces, real in-spections of Dimona, and the question of a Middle East arms race. "Per-sonally," said Kennedy in March 1963, "I am haunted by the feeling that by 1970, unless we are successful, there may be ten nuclear powers instead of four, and by 1975, fifteen or twenty."[109]

Part of this renewed focus resulted from warnings by France, especially via Foreign Minister Couve de Murville, a former ambassador to Cairo and the leading pro-Arab figure in French politics. Under his direction, the French Foreign Ministry began warning the Kennedy administration that Israel's nuclear program was close to bearing fruit.[110] France began scaling back from its earlier deals with Peres, seeking belatedly to ensure that Israel's nuclear program was strictly peaceful.[111]

The dire consequences of an Israeli bomb were increasingly underscored by the U.S. intelligence community. With CIA Director Allen Dulles's repu-tation tarnished by the Bay of Pigs, Kennedy had replaced him in Septem-ber 1961 with John McCone, a rock-ribbed Republican, California plutocrat, and committed anticommunist. McCone had been head of the Atomic Energy Commission in 1960 when Dimona was discovered, and his con-cerns about nonproliferation made him an administration player on Middle East arms control. His agency's findings in 1963 were far from hysterical, but they did point to looming strategic worries for Washington.

"No Arab state will be able to develop a nuclear weapon capability for many years to come," the CIA declared in January 1963.[112] Meir's claims notwithstanding, Nasser had no nuclear program to speak of, except a small, Soviet-provided research reactor at Inschass, outside Cairo. He also lacked the capacity for biological warfare, although he did "have a small stock of toxic chemical munitions" from the Soviet bloc.

The American intelligence community was also not terribly alarmed about Nasser's rocketry. True, Egypt's homegrown surface-to-surface mis-siles (SSMs) had some psychological and propaganda value. But neither of his two homemade missiles—al-Kahir (the Conqueror), which wasn't much more powerful than one of Germany's World War II-vintage V-2 rock-ets, and the somewhat smaller al-Zafir, or the Victor—seemed ready for firing from mobile launchers or for carrying nonconventional warheads.[113] On the other hand, Israel was close to finalizing a deal with France on a more effective SSM of its own, the Jericho. But McCone's spies knew that Israel was not nearly as sanguine. Jerusalem had been rattled by Nasser's July 1962 missile demonstrations. An Israel-Egypt missile race might not yet have been underway, but the runners were certainly taking their marks.

Worse, with no real way to know what was going on at Dimona, the prospect of a nuclear-armed Israel was very real. McCone's CIA worried that an Israeli bomb would do "substantial damage to the US and Western position in the Arab world."[114] Moreover, the CIA argued that a nuclear-armed Israel "would become more rather than less tough." It would probably try to cow the Arabs, sow dissension within the Arab world by mocking the impotence of the key Arab states, and launch more painful retaliatory raids. As the Arabs then rushed into the Soviet embrace, Israel would tell America that it was both the only friend in the region that could be had and the only one worth having. In effect, if Israel got the bomb, America got Israel.

The Arab reaction to Israel's getting the bomb would be disorganized, unsophisticated, and outraged, the CIA warned. The more clinical realization that Israel would still be wildly unlikely ever to *use* its nuclear arms would do little to stem the tide of opprobrium, recriminations, and frustration. Since the Arabs saw the United States as the lone power able to stop Israel's nuclear program, Washington would become a key target of Arab resentment. Inevitably, "charges of US complicity in the Israeli achievement would be widely made and widely believed in the Arab world."

Nor was there much the Arabs themselves could do but seethe. Nasser might toy with an air strike on Dimona, but he would probably be deterred by the fear of Israel's new A-bombs. Nasser was more likely to bloviate, jostle with other radical Arabs to goad the world into futile attempts to place the Israeli nuclear program under international controls, and perhaps pursue chemical and biological weapons programs to compensate.

"The obvious recourse of the Arabs would be to turn to" Moscow, McCone's analysts wrote. But even if Nasser and the other Arab radicals were forced to trade their tarnished neutralism for a pro-Soviet alignment, the Kremlin was unlikely to give the Arabs the atomic technology it had denied its own Eastern European satellites. The CIA considered riskier schemes—stationing a few Soviet nuclear warheads on Arab soil, or setting up missile bases in the Arab world—similarly unlikely. But the Soviets would make political hay out of an Israeli bomb: they would make "resounding declarations of sympathy and support" for the Arabs and "dire threats against Israel" or its friends. It would be a Cold War windfall: without any major new commitments, the Soviet Union would dramatically boost its influence in a crucial region.

On balance, the White House decided, the combination of a missile race and a nuclear-armed Israel was a migraine well worth avoiding. With the Johnson mission hors de combat in early 1963, Komer began urging Kennedy to move instead on arms control.[115] Komer suggested a secret mission, along the lines of the Anderson shuttle of 1956 (a model of discretion if not of efficacy), to sound out Cairo and Jerusalem about a "tacit agreement to refrain from acquiring" cutting-edge weaponry.

In late March, Komer reported to Kennedy that the administration was "pushing ahead on plans for [the] next inspection" of Dimona. Meanwhile, via Mike Feldman, the Israelis continued warning that Nasser was developing his own missile and nuclear capacities, with the help of former Nazi scientists. Komer told the president that "this effort looks far less menacing than the Israelis suggest" and that atomic warheads probably lay beyond Egypt's technological grasp. Even so, Komer wrote, Israel's nerves meant trouble. "We ought to try hard to forestall a new UAR/Israel missile and nuclear arms race," and he offered to test the waters on his own upcoming April visit to Egypt.[116]

Three days later, Kennedy himself met with McCone and asked him about Israel's nuclear program. On March 26, on the president's behalf, Bundy sent a full-blown National Security Action Memorandum to the CIA, the Atomic Energy Commission, and the State Department ordering them "as a matter of urgency" to find out what the Israelis were up to—a sign of renewed interest at the highest levels. Kennedy wanted "the next informal inspection of the Israeli reactor complex to be undertaken promptly and to be as thorough as possible." He ordered the State Department to find ways of forestalling Israeli and Egyptian nuclear programs, including making it clear to Nasser and Ben-Gurion "how seriously such a development would be regarded in this country."[117] Unlike in other aspects of his Arab-Israeli policy, Kennedy was now driving the nuclear issue himself.

The reengaged White House also decided to put some steel behind its old policy on inspections. Rusk ordered Barbour to tell Ben-Gurion that Washington now wanted "semi-annual visits to Dimona, perhaps [in] May and November, with full access to all parts and instruments in the facility, by qualified US scientists."[118] No longer would it be fobbed off with lightning tours under strict Israeli control. Ben-Gurion did not demur in Barbour's presence, but thereafter, the prime minister did his best again to stall.[119] It gives some sense of how constricted Ben-Gurion's nuclear decision-making circle was that Meir, who attended the meeting, seemed genuinely surprised to hear that the last U.S. visit to Dimona had been so short. She had thought that had been Washington's idea, she told Barbour.[120] It is not hard to imagine the earful that Ben-Gurion got when the American ambassador left the room.

Shimon Peres, who *was* in the loop on Dimona, got a stern talking-to of his own. With the American bureaucracy goosed by Kennedy's personal interest, the Israeli deputy defense minister found himself peppered with questions about the bomb during his return visit to Washington in April 1963 to follow up on the Hawk sale. When Peres met with Deputy Undersecretary of State for Political Affairs U. Alexis Johnson, the American official answered Peres's summation of Nasserite perfidy by downplaying the military significance of Nasser's budding missile programs, which were causing a furor in Congress because of their reliance on German scientists with possible Nazi links. Johnson also warned that the United States "deeply opposed" introducing nuclear weapons to the Middle East.[121]

Peres got a similar message at the highest level. When Peres "bumped into" the president while walking through the White House corridors with Feldman on April 5, Kennedy asked the Israeli official to drop by later.[122] At the resultant meeting, Peres explained that the only Arab country that Israel "really fears" is Egypt and began describing Nasser's missile program. According to Feldman, who came along as a chaperone, JFK warned Peres that "the United States is very concerned about proliferation of nuclear weapons" and that Kennedy "would strongly hope that Israel would not develop or obtain this kind of weaponry." Peres gave JFK "an unequivocal assurance that Israel would not do anything in this field unless it finds that other countries in the area are involved in it."[123]

The Israeli account of the meeting was even blunter. "You know that we follow very closely the discovery of any nuclear development in the region," Kennedy is said to have told Peres from his rocking chair. "This could create a very dangerous situation. For this reason we kept in touch with your nuclear effort. What could you tell me about this?"

In response, Peres claims to have ad-libbed what has become Israel's nuclear mantra.[124] "I can tell you most clearly that we will not introduce nuclear weapons to the region, and certainly we will not be the first," Peres told Kennedy, thinking fast. "Our interest is in reducing armament, even in complete disarmament."[125] That formula, improvised or not, would become Israel's standard rhetorical touchstone on the bomb. It has worked on most presidents since 1963, but it did not do much for JFK.

KENNEDY GOES NUCLEAR

With the administration increasingly engaged on the issue of arms control, Ben-Gurion would finally face a showdown with Kennedy. The U.S.–Israel tensions over Dimona had simmered for years; in the spring of 1963, they would boil over. The result was the nastiest exchange in U.S.–Israel relations since Suez, with fateful consequences for the countries' special relationship—and for the career of Israel's founding father.

Ben-Gurion was shaken on April 17, when Egypt, Iraq, and Syria issued a three-way union declaration, reconstituting an expanded UAR and vowing to liberate Palestine. In response, Ben-Gurion sent out a barrage of letters to world leaders, protesting that never before had a state's founding charter called for the annihilation of another sovereign state.[126] His Foreign Ministry groaned; Gideon Rafael, the ministry's deputy director general, called the prime minister's tone "hysterical," and both Harman and Gazit were baffled by Ben-Gurion's seeming panic.[127] Kennedy also told Ben-Gurion to calm down; in a May 4 letter to the anxious Israeli prime minister, Kennedy wrote that for now, "Israel is more than able to defend itself."[128] It was the long-term threat of a high-tech arms race that worried the administration, not the short-term specter of a futile Arab invasion. Forestalling such a spiral required solid American relations with the Arabs, Kennedy added—a clear hint to the Israelis not to gripe too much about the flagging Nasser overture. When Barbour delivered the president's message to Ben-Gurion, he added that Kennedy still had a "deep interest" in semiannual American inspections of Dimona, beginning that month. Ben-Gurion hedged, grumbling that regular visits looked like a "satellite relationship."[129]

The next day, Harman tried to find a more sympathetic ear by inviting Mike Feldman to lunch. With midterm elections on the horizon, the White House was having the State Department clear all cables and actions that could have a "domestic political impact" past Feldman, much to the department's chagrin.[130] But Feldman's say on nuclear issues was waning. The Israeli ambassador argued that Ben-Gurion had promised to let *neutral* inspectors examine the reactor, and while the Israelis were also willing "to permit American inspection," a regular schedule of such visits was "offensive to their sovereignty." Ben-Gurion also was not willing to decide on the inspections without Meir, who had been briefly hospitalized. Moreover, Harman added, why wasn't the administration trying to inspect Arab nuclear plants? Feldman offered no rebuttal. At the NSC, Komer read Feldman's account of the lunch with irritation.[131] In the memo's margin, he scrawled a series of rebuttals for Bundy, noting—correctly—that the only Arab state with a nuclear program was Egypt, whose lone reactor was far too puny to produce an atomic bomb. "Why in hell do we always let ourselves be put on [the] defensive," he groaned. "Mac—we just can't negotiate with Israelis if Mike is our interlocutor. You've really got to take this over."[132]

In Israel, Barbour was ordered to start prodding Ben-Gurion regularly, reflecting the "intensity of Presidential concern" for a prompt Israeli assent to "semi-annual Dimona visits" starting immediately. Kennedy saw the nuclear issue as a matter of "global responsibility," not a mere bilateral bargaining chip, Barbour told Ben-Gurion. Rusk warned his ambassador to push hard.[133]

Back home, the pace of meetings intensified. On May 8, in the middle of the civil rights crisis over Birmingham—where Martin Luther King,

Jr., was leading protests for desegregation of department store facilities—Kennedy took time at a press conference to mention his support for "the security of both Israel and her neighbors" and his strong opposition to "the use of force or the threat of force in the Near East." To thwart aggression, he added, the United States would back U.N. action or "adopt other courses of action on our own"—a far-reaching statement clearly tailored to meet at least some of Israel's desire for a security guarantee, as well as a warning to Israel not to try to take advantage of the April coup scare in Jordan.[134]

The same day, Kennedy spent a half-hour with Rusk, Komer, Feldman, Bundy, and Strong and ordered them to start preparing an Israel-Egypt arms-control initiative. A small working group was formed, under the supervision of the State Department, to follow up. Meanwhile, McCone held lengthy meetings on Dimona with Rusk and Kennedy, although the details remain classified.[135]

Ben-Gurion began to feel the heat. On May 12, he sent Kennedy another agitated letter, asking for a formal U.S. pledge to come to Israel's defense if it were attacked and arguing that "to ensure that another Holocaust would not be inflicted on the Jewish people, Israel must be able to threaten a potential perpetrator with annihilation." Foreign Ministry staffers winced at the tone and urged that it be muted or not sent, but Ben-Gurion was adamant.[136] In the Knesset, he lambasted JFK's arms policy as dangerously one-sided (notwithstanding the Hawk sale) and lamented that "not all our friends" grasped the need to boost the IDF's deterrent.[137]

He was right: the Kennedy administration did not see things his way. Instead, on May 14, the administration's working group on arms control proposed "a highly secret probe of UAR and Israeli willingness to cooperate with us to increase their security" by decreasing their arsenals.[138] Such a mission was hardly guaranteed to succeed, Talbot admitted, but the timing was propitious: Israel was pushing hard for a security guarantee, Nasser was embarrassed by the furor over word of his German scientists, Israel was on the verge of developing serious SSMs, and a regional arms spiral was looming.[139]

As the mercury rose in Washington, so did the administration's annoyance. Talbot dunned Harman again on May 16 about Dimona. "There is enormous concern here," Talbot told the ambassador. "There never was a hint of conditions laid down for our visits. There was complete expectation that this was going smoothly. This matter should be worked out very promptly."[140]

By the spring of 1963, U.S.–Israel relations were in, as the Israeli diplomat Gazit put it, a "hullabaloo." Israeli diplomats had begun asking the White House for formalized reassurances of American support in times of crisis—a so-called security guarantee. A suspicious Komer called Gazit to his office, where the NSC aide asked whether the recent statements from Ben-Gurion and Dayan about strengthening Israel's defenses and the threat of Nasser's "Nazi scientists" were actually "part of a campaign to justify Israeli development of nuclear weapons, or to threaten this as an alternative if we didn't come through with a security pact." Gazit grinned.[141] The administration was less amused. An unhappy State Department, resentful of Israeli pressure, suggested to Kennedy that any talks about a presidential letter guaranteeing Israel's security be conditioned on Israeli cooperation on Dimona. Komer also wanted to go slowly on security assurances. "Given the Hawk/refugee episode of last year," he told Kennedy, "we want to avoid giving if possible before we've taped down the quid pro quos."[142]

In Tel Aviv, Barbour was finding the going rough. On May 14, 1963—15 years to the day after Ben-Gurion had declared the independence of the state of Israel—the usually affable Barbour held a long, testy exchange with Israel's founding father over Dimona in which the American diplomat again stressed Kennedy's personal, "keen interest" in regular inspections. The United States should inspect Nasser's reactor twice a year, Ben-Gurion retorted. After all, Nasser had already used gas in the Yemen war. When Barbour argued that, to the best of his knowledge, Egypt had "only some kind of medical reactor," Meir claimed to have "interesting information" on the Egyptian plant, and Foreign Ministry adviser Gideon Rafael added that Egypt was planning a second reactor. "We know they are building something bigger," Ben-Gurion bristled.

Barbour tried to drag the conversation back to inspections, but Ben-Gurion kept hammering away at the threat Nasser posed to Israel. "We know he is making unconventional weapons," the prime minister said. "He has some foreign experts, he is sending some people abroad, there is a chemist. We are afraid when he has missiles with nuclear warheads he will do it. What will you do to him?"

America would take "all necessary measures" to help Israel if it was attacked, Barbour replied. Ben-Gurion waved that off, insisting that Washington did not understand the mortal threat that Israel faced. Sharply, Barbour cut in and asked again what Ben-Gurion's answer was on Dimona inspections. "Twice a year?" the prime minister asked. For that, he would have to ask his cabinet, unless he could tell them that Egypt was getting the same treatment. The two situations were not remotely comparable, interrupted the exasperated Barbour, as they went around in circles. Egypt's program was far less advanced. "We need to see Dimona," the ambassador insisted. Peres's White House assurances to Kennedy would not suffice.

What right, Ben-Gurion asked, did Nasser have to ask for such inspections? Telling Nasser the results of the previous inspections might be too soothing; perhaps it was better for Cairo to "be a little afraid." Barbour replied that he simply could not grasp why Israel would want to risk a nuclear arms race and a war; surely inspections were a safer course. "No, no, no!" Ben-Gurion exclaimed.

Perhaps, Barbour ventured, Ben-Gurion thought that keeping Nasser guessing would deter him—which, indeed, was the logic behind Israel's policy of nuclear opacity. In fact, Barbour warned, such anxiety would just force Nasser to redouble his nuclear efforts. Ben-Gurion insisted that Nasser had already done so. Why reassure him now? Barbour, fed up, simply asked again for an "urgent reply" on inspections. The Israeli leader promised to check with his cabinet.

Israel now seemed to be backing off its promise to permit inspections. "Our growing suspicion that [the] procrastination of [the Israelis'] response to our request betokened [a] change in their attitude [is] now confirmed," a weary Barbour reported back to Washington. Indeed, one Ben-Gurion aide had reminded Barbour of Kennedy's comment at the Waldorf that a woman should not only be virtuous but also have the appearance of virtue. But there are times, the Israeli noted, when a "virtuous woman might not want to appear virtuous."[143]

Back home, the ferocity of Barbour's sparring match with Ben-Gurion was met with surprise and bewilderment. Talbot warned Harman that Israel had never before hinted of conditions being placed on visits to Dimona; awkwardly, Harman insisted that there had never been any previous discussion of regular visits.[144] All along, Harman had winced at Ben-Gurion's confrontational instincts, fearing they might lead to a crisis in U.S.–Israel relations. His worst fears were about to be justified.

On May 18, Kennedy finally resorted to the diplomatic equivalent of unconventional weaponry: a blunt, written presidential threat. Kennedy's starkest threats—and they were stark indeed—were leveled only after the Cuban missile crisis, after the 1962 midterm elections were safely over, after the decision to sell Hawks had already been made, after Ben-Gurion had repeatedly tried to buck an American inspections regime, and after Kennedy concluded that the problem of Dimona could not be swept under the rug. Kennedy went nuclear (figuratively) to prevent Ben-Gurion from going nuclear (literally).

The sudden flash of steel seems to have been caused by word of the rancorous Barbour meeting with Ben-Gurion, which made it clear to the administration that its old tactics were not conveying its full seriousness about Dimona. Israel's obduracy only made the White House more suspicious. So Kennedy's May 18 letter to Ben-Gurion noted that he had seen Barbour's report of his nuclear wrangle with Ben-Gurion and then offered—lest the Israeli leader doubt the depth of Kennedy's engagement—

"to add some personal comments on that subject."[145] He needed not re-state the dangers of nuclear proliferation, Kennedy wrote. "When we spoke together in May 1961 you said that we might make whatever use we wished of the information resulting from the first visit of American scientists to Dimona and that you would agree to further visits by neutrals as well. I had assumed from Mrs. Meir's comments that there would be no problem between us on this."

He had been wrong, it seemed. "I cannot imagine that the Arabs would refrain from turning to the Soviet Union for assistance if Israel were to develop a nuclear weapons capability – with all the consequences this would hold," Kennedy wrote. "But the problem is much larger than its impact on the Middle East. Development of a nuclear weapons capabil-ity by Israel would almost certainly lead other larger countries, that have so far refrained from such development, to feel that they must follow suit."

Then came the bombshell.[146] As Kennedy had noted in his May 8 press conference, "we have a deep commitment to the security of Israel." The United States supported Israel in many ways. "This commitment and this support," Kennedy wrote, sticking in the shiv, "would be *seriously jeopar-dized* in the public opinion in this country and in the West as a whole if it should be thought that this Government was unable to obtain reliable information on a subject as vital to peace as the question of the character of Israel's effort in the nuclear field." One could almost hear the Israeli Foreign Ministry gasp.

He understood Ben-Gurion's concerns about Egypt's weapons program, Kennedy continued. "But I see no present or imminent nuclear threat to Israel from there," he wrote. Nasser had nothing comparable to Dimona. "But, of course, if you have any information that would support a contrary conclusion, I should like to receive it from you through Ambassador Barbour," Kennedy wrote. "We have the capacity to check it." There were no niceties to soften the blow. "I trust this message will convey the sense of urgency and the perspective in which I view your Government's early assent to the proposal first put to you by Ambassador Barbour on April 2," Kennedy concluded. The rest was silence.

THE RETREAT TO SDEH BOQER

In Jerusalem, Kennedy's letter was greeted with shock. Israeli diplomats saw the president's tone as "harsh" and even "brutal," hinting as it did that the entire underlying special relationship could be sacrificed over Di-mona.[147] The tensions between Ben-Gurion's attempts to court Washing-ton and build Dimona had been hurled into precisely the sharp relief that Jerusalem had hoped to avoid.

To raise tensions even higher, the French diplomat Charles Lucet met on May 25 with McCone and shared some of Paris's rising anxieties. There might be parts of Dimona that even France did not know about, Lucet now warned, and Israel had recently been foiled while trying to buy uranium from suppliers other than France, including Gabon and other French colonies.[148]

If Kennedy had hoped that Israel would simply concede after his May 18 salvo, he was disappointed. Ben-Gurion met privately with selected aides and ministers, presented the matter to the full cabinet on May 26, and personally drafted Israel's response.[149] On May 27, a somber Ben-Gurion handed Barbour his reply. It did little to take Jerusalem off its collision course with Washington. The letter began by assuring Kennedy that Israel's policy on nuclear research had not changed since the 1961 Waldorf meeting. But while Ben-Gurion sympathized with Kennedy's global concerns over nonproliferation, keeping the genie in the bottle was not Israel's problem. "I fear that in the absence of an agreement between the great powers on general disarmament," Ben-Gurion wrote, "there is little doubt that these weapons will, sooner or later, find their way into the arsenals of China and then of various European states and India."

As for Israel's part in the proliferation question, Ben-Gurion continued, France's nuclear assistance had been strictly dependent on devoting Dimona "exclusively to peaceful purposes. I regard this condition as absolutely binding, both on general grounds of good faith" and because of France's unique military aid to Israel from 1948 onward. Similarly, Ben-Gurion had told JFK at the Waldorf that Dimona was the crux of Israel's drive to get atomic energy. "I went on to add that we should have to follow developments in the Middle East," the prime minister continued. "This is still our position today."

Israel and France had much the same arrangement over Dimona as Israel and the United States had over Nahal Soreq, Ben-Gurion wrote. "While we do not envisage a system of formal United States control at the Dimona reactor which the United States has not helped to establish or construct, as in the case of the reactor at Nachal Sureiq, we do agree to further *annual visits* to Dimona by your representatives, *such as have already taken place.*" The "most suitable" time for the next visit would be late 1963 or early 1964, when Dimona reached its "start-up" time and Israel's French contractors handed over control of the reactor; all the Americans would see today was construction. A visit from a neutral scientist would be acceptable, too.

He appreciated Kennedy's commitment to Israeli security, Ben-Gurion concluded. But while he understood Kennedy's concerns about proliferation, "we in Israel cannot be blind to the more actual danger now confronting us . . . destructive 'conventional' weapons in the hands of neighboring governments which openly proclaim their intention to attempt the annihilation of Israel."[150]

It was a feisty response. Ben-Gurion said that Dimona was strictly for nonmilitary use—but in the next breath noted that Israel reserved the right to shift the reactor's purposes if regional circumstances so demanded. It was hardly the sort of categorical assurance that would have eased Kennedy's apprehensions. On a wider plane, taking issue with Kennedy's basic view of nuclear danger was hardly a diplomatic move; implying that the inevitability of proliferation was the superpowers' fault was even less so. While Ben-Gurion bent somewhat on opening Dimona, he studiedly avoided the word "inspection," speaking instead of "visits." Instead of the two assessments per year that Kennedy was demanding, Ben-Gurion proposed one, like those that had already occurred—in other words, a short, guided tour under strict Israeli control, rather than a serious inspection. Even that visit would not be viewed by Israel as a regime of American supervision of Dimona, and Ben-Gurion seemed to contemplate either American visits or neutral visits, not both. Finally, having browbeaten Barbour about American hypocrisy in not monitoring a looming nuclear danger from Nasser, Ben-Gurion now explicitly and unapologetically stated that the threat Israel faced from its neighbors had to do with conventional weapons, not weapons of mass destruction. Kennedy had called Ben-Gurion's bluff in demanding to see evidence of an Egyptian nuclear menace, which proved to be a phantom, and Ben-Gurion had folded—without any acknowledgment that he had been fear-mongering.

Washington was underwhelmed. Talbot and the rest of NEA saw Ben-Gurion's letter "as a step backward."[151] Komer, too, warned that Kennedy might have to try again.[152] But the administration's bottom line seems to have been set in June, when the CIA, the Atomic Energy Commission (AEC), and the Arms Control and Disarmament Agency (ACDA) all agreed that Ben-Gurion's proposal fell short of the standards required to have any confidence in the inspections' verdict.[153] The International Atomic Energy Agency (IAEA) minimum inspections system would have required two inspections per year of a facility of Dimona's size. The reason was simple: if a Dimona-sized reactor was being used for peaceful purposes, it would take about two years to go through a single load of fuel; if Dimona was producing weapons-grade plutonium, it would burn through such a load every six months. Annual visits might not be able to spot the telltale fingerprint of the reactor's fuel-use rate.[154] The U.S. intelligence and scientific agencies therefore agreed that there must be a Dimona visit in the summer of 1963; another in June 1964, as the reactor grew nearer to completion; and then regular, thorough, untrammeled inspections every six months thereafter. That bent a little toward Ben-Gurion's once-a-year schedule, but not much. America's spooks and scientists were clear: doing half a job on Dimona inspections was the equivalent of doing no job at all. Kennedy would have to hang tough.

Presidents often lament that their specialists fail to see the big picture, but this time, an angry Kennedy did not demur. On June 15, Kennedy sent Ben-Gurion another scorching letter, insisting on the terms set by the CIA, AEC, and ACDA's ruling.[155] Given Ben-Gurion's commitment to eschew nuclear weapons, Kennedy wrote that he was sure that the Israeli leader would agree that the inspections should "more nearly be in accord with international standards, thereby resolving all doubts as to the peaceful nature of the Dimona project." Then he brought down the hammer again. "As I wrote you on 18 May, *this Government's commitment to and support of Israel could be seriously jeopardized* if it should be thought that we were unable to obtain reliable information on a subject as vital to peace as the question of the character of Israel's effort in the nuclear field." It was an even tougher threat than the first one.

To dispel uncertainty, JFK wrote, Israel should follow the inspection schedule demanded by his nuclear experts. "I am sure that such a schedule should not cause you any more difficulty than that which you have proposed," Kennedy wrote, just a tad sardonically. "It would be essential, and I take it that your letter is in accord with this, that our scientists have access to all areas of the Dimona site and to any related part of the complex, such as fuel fabrication facilities or plutonium separation plant, and that sufficient time be allotted for a thorough examination." Of course, such unimpeded inspections were a far cry from the guided tours mentioned in Ben-Gurion's last letter. Playing hardball, Kennedy's men would force Ben-Gurion to either accept real inspections or argue forthrightly against them—not an easy case to make. Kennedy's peroration was a trace more polite than last time, although the tone was faintly ironic. "Knowing that you fully appreciate the truly vital significance of this matter to the future well-being of Israel, to the United States, and internationally," Kennedy concluded, "I am sure our carefully considered request will *again* have your most sympathetic attention."

The letter was even rawer than the previous demarche—the starkest threat yet to hold the entire special relationship hostage to Dimona. Kennedy's letters were the flash of anger designed to make the Israelis put their nuclear sword back in its scabbard. Barbour was supposed to add a verbal message underscoring the scientific basis for the inspections, but the American ambassador never got the chance. Kennedy's bombshell was dated June 15. On June 16, before Barbour could deliver the letter, Ben-Gurion dropped a bombshell of his own. Israel's founding father resigned.

As Avner Cohen has noted, the reasons for the Old Man's resignation remain murky. Ben-Gurion always ascribed it to personal reasons, and in cabinet, he denied that policy had anything to do with it. By the spring of 1963, there were numerous signs that Ben-Gurion's powers and patience were waning. A lengthy April 19 profile in *Ha'aretz* had called his rule "almost monomaniacal" and described Israel's founding father as a "semi-retired chief national prophet whose only real interest is defense policy and who has escaped to Buddhism, the Bible and abstract calls to duty instead of providing necessary leadership to country and party."[156]

Nevertheless, Yuval Ne'eman, the head of the Nahal Soreq reactor, who was deeply involved in crafting Israel's replies to JFK, attributed Ben-Gurion's demise to Kennedy's pressure on Dimona. Several ministers, including Commerce Minister Pinhas Sapir and Yisrael Galili of Ahdut Ha'avodah, also said as much.[157]

Some authors even suspect that Kennedy was trying to topple Ben-Gurion. "I have a feeling that the agenda of the Kennedy administration was to get rid of Ben-Gurion," notes the Israeli scholar Zaki Shalom. "He's stubborn, there's no way to deal with him, so we have to get rid of him."[158] Seymour Hersh, noting Kennedy's irritation at Israeli mendacity, has written, "One solution was to help get Ben-Gurion, then embattled in the most serious crisis of his political career, out of office."[159] On balance, though, Dimona was almost certainly not the dominant factor in Ben-Gurion's decision. Exasperated as Kennedy was, there is no documentary evidence that the president or his aides ever entertained the idea of driving Ben-Gurion from power over Dimona.

Indeed, if Dimona had been uppermost in Ben-Gurion's mind, he might well not have bowed out. All along, Ben-Gurion sought to safeguard Israel's nuclear program from American pressure; it is hard to imagine that he thought his likely successor, the more tractable Levi Eshkol, would do that job any better.

At the time, Ben-Gurion's abrupt decision to quit his three posts — as prime minister, defense minister, and Mapai Party leader — seemed more a blast of frustration than a planned strategy; a startled Barbour cabled that "Ben-Gurion's triple resignation apparently took [Israel's] cabinet and certainly everyone else by complete surprise."[160] Barbour reported that Ben-Gurion probably figured that his lonely retreat to Sdeh Boqer — his spartan Negev kibbutz — would be only temporary, as it had been when he briefly made way for Moshe Sharett in 1953, only to return two years later. The resignation could well be a "mere hiatus in B-G era," cabled Barbour. "I cannot quite see Eshkol as more than [a] transitional" prime minister. But if Ben-Gurion's underlying motivation had been Dimona, why would he even temporarily take himself out of the battle? And why would he leave just as the fight reached its fiercest pitch? "If it'd been Dimona," argues Ben-Gurion's leading biographer, Shabtai Teveth, "he'd have ducked."[161]

The impetus for Ben-Gurion's resignation was almost certainly domestic politics, not Dimona. The reactor was, of course, the major foreign policy issue on Ben-Gurion's desk when he quit, but Dimona was a complication, not a cause. The Old Man's problem was not his fight with Kennedy; it was that he did not have a government with which to wage that fight. "He didn't jump," argues Shalom. "He was pushed." The nuclear option was never truly popular within Mapai, let alone its leftist coalition partners, but Ben-Gurion's downfall was caused by something much less titillating: by internal bickering, dreary party rivalries, and the metastasizing Lavon affair.

That protracted, internecine scandal—Israel's Watergate—began in 1955, when Defense Minister Pinhas Lavon quit in disgrace after being linked to a string of clumsy covert operations the previous year; Israeli agents had hoped to turn the United States and Britain against Nasser's new regime by bombing U.S. targets in Cairo and then blaming the Free Officers. Lavon insisted that he had not known about the failed plan. A 1960 commission of inquiry cleared Lavon, and while the rest of the cabinet accepted his protestations of innocence, Ben-Gurion bitterly refused. Lavon's campaign to rehabilitate himself, which included blaming his downfall on Dayan and Peres, wound up ripping Mapai apart.[162]

Moreover, by 1963, the party's old guard—including Eshkol, Meir, and Sapir—were convinced that Ben-Gurion was out to overleap the entire older generation and install Peres and Dayan as Israel's new leaders. In April, Peres sacked Yisrael Harel, the director of military intelligence—a display of muscle-flexing not lost on the Mapai elders. The old-timers rebelled en masse. Ben-Gurion was still willing to fight Kennedy over Dimona, but he had wound up virtually a minority of one. "You can lift 50 kilos when there's solid ground beneath you," Teveth notes, "but if you're on shaky ground and everything is falling around you, sometimes you find it very difficult to lift a 10-kilo bag." Abandoned, isolated, and exasperated, Israel's founding father quit in a huff.

Whatever combination of factors sent Ben-Gurion stalking off to Sdeh Boqer, Dimona suddenly became Levi Eshkol's problem. The mild, shrewd former finance minister and long-time Mapainik remains Israel's most underrated prime minister, receiving scant credit for his dexterity in general or the Six Day War in particular. The good-humored Eshkol was keenly aware of America's strategic importance; there is an old Israeli story about a group of farmers marching into the prime minister's office to complain about a terrible drought. "Where?" Eshkol asks, alarmed. "In the Negev, of course," the farmers reply. "Thank goodness," a relieved Eshkol sighs. "I was afraid it was in America."

But if Eshkol realized how important America was to Israel, he had not fully understood how irritated America was with Israel. Eshkol got the message on the fourth of July. Barbour had urged Washington to hold off on any demarche until Eshkol assembled his cabinet, but the president was in no mood to wait.[163] To greet the new Israeli leader, Kennedy sent Eshkol what must be one of history's most hostile letters of congratulation. After a few thin lines of cordial pablum, JFK immediately raised probably the most sensitive issue on Eshkol's desk: Dimona. The language did not merely echo Kennedy's last letter to Ben-Gurion; it repeated it almost verbatim—an act that bordered on rudeness.

"As I wrote Mr. Ben Gurion, *this Government's commitment to and support of Israel could be seriously jeopardized* if it should be thought that we were unable to obtain reliable information on a subject as vital to peace as the question of Israel's effort in the nuclear field," Kennedy warned. "If Israel's purposes are to be clear beyond reasonable doubt, I believe that the schedule which would best serve our common purpose would be a visit early this summer, another visit in June 1964, and thereafter at intervals of six months. I am sure that such a schedule should not cause you any more difficulty than that which Mr. Ben Gurion proposed in his May 27 letter. It would be essential, and I understand that Mr. Ben Gurion's letter was in accord with this, that our scientists have access to *all areas* of the Dimona site and to any related part of the complex, such as fuel fabrication facilities, or the plutonium separation plant, and that sufficient time be allotted for a thorough examination."[164]

Instead of giving Eshkol a welcoming handshake, Kennedy lunged for his jugular. It was an extraordinarily effective way of getting a new prime minister's undivided attention. Eshkol opted to punt. On July 17, he wrote Kennedy that he would carefully study the Dimona issue and soon offer a fuller response. Kennedy's threat had caused him real "surprise," Eshkol told Barbour, searching about for the mot juste. Beyond the administration's wider concern about a nuclear-armed world, Barbour replied, in the "explosive atmosphere" of the Middle East, the introduction of nuclear weapons "would be especially grave." Eshkol nodded, and Barbour thought that the Israeli prime minister seemed to be agreeing.[165] "I don't feel any special pressure," Eshkol told a group of foreign correspondents a few days later when questioned about Dimona.[166] Not for the first time in the history of Israel's nuclear program, a prime minister was lying.

RAISING CANE

In the summer of 1963, the Kennedy administration's concerns over the Middle East's arsenals extended beyond Dimona. The New Frontiersmen also worried that Egypt was increasingly interested in long-range missiles and might even accelerate its nuclear program. Since tackling Israel's nuclear program head-on was proving painful, a broader approach to arms control was well worth trying, not least because it would alleviate Israel's fears of being singled out. Kennedy decided to send a presidential emissary on a secret mission to get the two adversaries to set limits on their arsenals. Kennedy hoped that more general progress on arms control would make the Arab-Israeli conflict less dangerous, the Middle East less susceptible to Soviet penetration, and both Israel and Egypt more tractable. The key was Nasser; without his cooperation, Israel would fear that arms control amounted to tying one arm behind its back. With this new shuttle, the administration's Nasser initiative would meet its emphasis on nonproliferation—with uninspiring results.

For several reasons, the administration thought the timing ripe. Israel was pushing for a security guarantee; the CIA feared that Israel would be able to detonate a homegrown atomic bomb by late 1965 or 1966; and Israel was poised to overtake Egypt in missile technology.[167] The mission had its genesis with a small working group—chaired by NEA's Jim Grant and including Henry Byroade, Bob Strong, several NEA aides, and James Spain of the CIA—formed to follow up on Kennedy's orders to produce a "practical course of action which might achieve an informal voluntary suspension of the Arab-Israel arms race."[168] The highly secret cable traffic on the subject was slugged with the codename CANE.[169]

The officials staffing CANE had their work cut out for them. As ordered by Kennedy, the CIA's McCone presented in early May his agency's latest assessment of the Israeli and Egyptian arms competition.[170] Both were trying to produce surface-to-surface missiles (SSMs) with a range of over 200 nautical miles. Nasser, whose program began in 1960, had gotten a head start, but Israel was clearly poised to take the lead. The last time Nasser had shown off his missiles, Badeau had been unimpressed to see their rickets sticking out;[171] General Ezer Weizman, the head of Israel's air force and its future president, also tended to view Nasser's missiles mostly as a political challenge, not a military one.[172] After all, with sweeping French support, Israel could have SSMs capable of carrying a 4,000-pound payload as early as 1965. By contrast, even with the help of its German scientists—some of dubious ethical pedigree—Egypt could probably deploy over the short term only a few SSMs with 500-pound payloads.[173] Komer told Kennedy that Egypt's missile program "looks far less menacing than the Israelis suggest."[174]

The CIA was also far from panicked about the adversaries' doomsday arsenals. "Neither country can produce radiological warfare weapons," the CIA concluded, although clearly Israel was closer than Egypt. Nasser's lone reactor—an IAEA-monitored, two-megawatt research facility near Cairo built by Soviet technicians—was too small to pose any real worry.[175]

In its attempts to forestall an Israel-Egypt arms race, CANE focused less on the weapons that the sides had than on the weapons they might get. "As it were, it is easier to give up a 'bird in the bush' than one in the hand," wrote NEA's William Polk in a top-secret planning paper. In its initial approach, the arms-control initiative would need to demonstrate the depth of American commitment, sound out Israel and Egypt, lay the groundwork for more talks, and think of ways to induce both Egypt and Israel to sign onto a secret arms-limitation understanding.[176]

The CANE mission should have been the apogee of the administration's ongoing Nasser initiative—the chance for the Kennedy Middle East team to prove that its patient efforts to conciliate Cairo had made the Egyptian leadership more tractable. To get things going, Kennedy needed to have yet another frank word with Nasser. "The arms race holds the seeds of disaster, too, for all of us," Kennedy wrote the Egyptian leader in late May, sidling up to the Arab states' fears of a nuclear Israel. Pleased as he was to see Israel and Egypt putting the atom to peaceful use, the president wrote, without proper safeguards, "power reactors can be diverted to military objectives. Thus, Israel could have the capability to develop nuclear weapons in the next few years if it were to divert its efforts in that direction." Keeping Arab "views and interests very much in mind," Kennedy primed Nasser to expect an administration initiative to "help avoid serious trouble in the area."[177]

That meant that the president would need a representative who showed that CANE was serious. The administration bruited about such names as Walt Rostow, John McCone, General Lauris Norstad (who had recently stepped down as supreme allied commander in Europe), and Ellsworth Bunker. Its top choice, however, was John McCloy, the virtual embodiment of the American establishment—the man who was to American WASPs what Jacob Blaustein was to American Jews. Entirely immune to fuzzy feelings about the Jews or their state, McCloy was more a friend of Big Oil than of Israel, let alone Nasser. A protégé of Henry Stimson, a former assistant secretary of war, and the virtually omnipotent high commissioner of Allied-occupied Germany, McCloy was by 1963 a senior partner at the New York law firm of Milbank, Tweed, Hadley & McCloy. He struck the Kennedy administration as an appealing choice for several reasons: he was well versed in the Middle East from working as general counsel to the Seven Sisters, as the major American oil companies were known; he had met Nasser in 1956, when McCloy worked on the postwar agreements to clear and reopen the Suez Canal; and Kennedy often tapped him for advice. After the disastrous 1961 Vienna summit, a shaken president had invited McCloy to the White House to discuss Soviet strategy in the Middle East.[178] During the Cuban missile crisis, the Kennedys had toyed with sending McCloy to New York to stiffen the spine of U.N. Ambassador Adlai Stevenson. McCloy was also a particularly obvious choice because he was already charged with helping plot administration strategy on arms control and disarmament, making the Middle East probe a natural extension of his preexistent role.

On June 4, the crusty McCloy spent four hours with Talbot and other State Department officials discussing his potential new assignment.[179] He was intrigued but wondered whether he could take the job without disclosing it to his oil-industry clients—the concern that had made him pass up the chance to negotiate JFK's test-ban treaty. In the end, McCloy signed on, squeezing the mission in between a trip to Italy and a long-planned Aegean vacation with his daughter. He would be assisted by Hermann Eilts, a former NEA officer now tasked to the U.S. embassy in London.[180]

McCloy would first go to Cairo in late June and then, if things went well, fly to Israel in mid-July. His marching orders were to cut separate deals with Israel and Egypt eschewing nuclear weapons and long-range missiles, since it was unthinkable for Nasser to sign an arms-control pact with Israel. So McCloy's bargains would have to be secret, tacit, and limited. Even if he succeeded, Israel and Egypt would hold onto whatever they now had in their holsters. But the United States would then "maintain unobtrusive, reasonably simple surveillance" of the Israeli and Egyptian arsenals just to be safe.[181]

It would be a tough sell. Nevertheless, Nasser might sign on simply because Israel already had such a large lead in nuclear technology and was on the verge of overtaking him on missiles, too. He might well not want to run a race he was destined to lose.[182] For its part, Israel might assent if given some sort of presidential security guarantee—probably building on the Tripartite Declaration's promises to oppose aggression from either Arabs or Israelis.[183] On balance, though, Komer gave McCloy "a 50/50 chance at best."

At 10 A.M. on June 15, a working White House Saturday morning, Kennedy convened a meeting of his top Middle East advisers—including Bundy, McCone, Komer, Talbot, Grant, and McCloy—to discuss the upcoming mission.[184] Tellingly, Mike Feldman was absent. The president said that the McCloy exercise was rooted in his worries about both the bomb and Jordan, which was still woozy after the April coup scare. If King Husayn were toppled, JFK noted, Nasser might actually be glad that the Israelis had asked for a security guarantee; the renewed American commitment to the region's frontiers and the Jewish state's deepened reliance on American patronage would prevent Israel from snatching a West Bank buffer—a move that would otherwise oblige Nasser to start an Arab-Israeli war in which "he'd get licked." But the Israelis were after more than just a guarantee, Talbot and Komer warned. They wanted "a full-fledged defensive alliance with close joint planning" for American help during an Arab invasion, as well as "substantial military assistance."

In particular, Kennedy seemed perturbed by the prospect of trouble in Jordan. If the administration sat back while Israel took the West Bank, the Arabs would fume; if the administration were to "pull a Suez" and force Israel out of the West Bank, the Israelis would howl. "We are in the soup either way," JFK noted.

At this point, McCloy stepped in and tried to limit his mission's scope — not to mention its chances for failure. He preferred to deal just with arms control, rather than adding Jordan and the security guarantee to the mix. Kennedy agreed, adding that if Nasser asked about Jordan, McCloy should reaffirm America's opposition to aggression by either side. For now, McCloy should target both nuclear weapons and missiles. True, McCone and the CIA did not think much of Nasser's nuclear program for now. But after all, Bundy noted, if France or the Soviet Union began giving atomic warheads to their respective clients, the means to deliver them would abruptly become painfully relevant, no matter how feeble Egypt's present program might be.

The first stop for McCloy would be Cairo. If Egypt was not interested in cooperating, the administration would have no way of inducing Israel to play along. "To go to Israel without being able to deliver Nasser puts us at Israel's mercy," Komer told Kennedy.[185] That would throw the White House back to its old policy of handling Israeli proliferation through inspections, admonitions, and ongoing vigilance—not a prospect the administration relished. If McCloy succeeded in Cairo, he would fly on to Jerusalem in mid-July.

Nasser's initial response to the idea of a shuttle was lukewarm. If America was so concerned about arms control, he wrote Kennedy in early June, why had it sold Hawks to Israel? Since Israel was the aggressor, Nasser wrote, did the Arabs not have the right to "be ready to face the worst?"[186] Most of the rest of the letter was taken up with complaints about Jordanian and Saudi perfidy in Yemen. Still, Nasser did agree to see Kennedy's envoy. Beyond that, the mission's fate was anyone's guess.

THE CHAIRMAN IN CAIRO

On June 26, McCloy boarded a KLM flight from Rome and flew to Cairo, accompanied by his daughter Ellen and one of her friends from Smith

College.[187] The young women, who were in the midst of a long-planned postgraduation tour of the Mediterranean, provided useful cover for CANE. McCloy's party would stay at the U.S. ambassadorial residence in Cairo for a few days, during which time McCloy would rekindle his old acquaintance with Nasser.[188] The press often kept an eye on McCloy, but this itinerary was anodyne enough not to pique much journalistic curiosity.

At 7 P.M. the next evening, Badeau escorted the presidential envoy to Nasser's office and, after a round of affable greetings, left the two principals to talk privately. Underscoring Kennedy's personal interest, McCloy began by making a general pitch for regional arms control. A nuclear arms race in the Middle East would be a disaster, he argued. Nasser's missile program — made worse by its association with the German scientists — was goading Israel toward getting the bomb. The statesmanlike and sensible course was renouncing nuclear arms and long-range missiles.

Nasser replied that he would have to consult with his army chief of staff, Marshal Amr, who was then in Yemen. But Nasser's initial reaction was skeptical, reciting again his familiar litany of complaints about Israeli attacks and Western fecklessness. Why was the UAR being "singled out from all the non-nuclear powers" to make such a commitment to self-denial? It was not, McCloy replied; Israel was also being asked to do likewise. Even so, Nasser said, he firmly opposed "any form of inspection" as imperialist meddling, and he was deeply worried that agreeing to arms control with the United States would be tantamount to an Israeli-UAR pact. His strategy was "purely defensive," and his missile and nuclear programs were benign, Nasser insisted. After two hours, the meeting broke up, with a follow-up session set for two days later.[189]

Ironically, even as McCloy was meeting Nasser, Washington was shying away from another complaint about Egypt's nonconventional arsenal. U.S. intelligence had come to believe that Nasser had, during his war with the Yemenite royalists, used both tear gas and some form of Vasicant-group poison — mustard gas. Children playing near the spot where Egyptian bombs landed reportedly developed blisters hours later; several Yemenis died painful deaths after protracted vomiting. Such results, and the way the toxin lingered, were hallmarks of mustard gas.[190] Such complaints eventually wound up winning Cairo a series of scoldings from Washington. But in the very midst of the McCloy mission, Badeau told the State Department that the timing was "injudicious" for him to protest Egypt's use of poison gas in Yemen.[191] The bomb that Nasser did not have bothered the administration more than the gas he did. Not until July 12, with the McCloy shuttle safely over, did Talbot summon Ambassador Kamel, whereupon the usually affable American diplomat "reamed him on gas."[192]

Back in Cairo, however, the focus remained on missiles and the bomb. McCloy met Nasser again on Saturday night for just over an hour, this time accompanied by Badeau and the State Department's Eilts.[193] Kennedy's envoy began by trying to keep Nasser from feeling singled out, noting that India and several South American countries were also being asked for similar assurances.

Having consulted with his aides after the first meeting, Nasser was now prepared to be more definitive, if not more encouraging. While he appreciated and shared Kennedy's desire for regional stability, he said, he "could not enter into an agreement with the US to renounce the weapons." If it curtailed its sovereignty in any way, Egypt would look like an American "protectorate" or "satellite." For Nasser, agreeing to an American arms-control proposal would violate anticolonialist principle. He might be open to some form of arms renunciation in a collective forum such as the United Nations, but a bilateral pact with the United States was out of the question. Nor, for similar reasons, could Nasser "accept any inspection or observation arrangement." Egypt's traditional refusal to permit inspections stood. "Besides," Nasser added, "so far as nuclear matters were concerned, there was nothing to inspect." Nor was his missile program anything to fear. He was simply trying to maintain a balance of power, even while Israel was receiving American Hawks and French Mirages. On the central thrust of the CANE proposal, Nasser's answer was a resounding no.

McCloy suggested an alternative to a formal U.S.–Egypt pact: instead, Kennedy could write Nasser to ask him about his nuclear intentions, Nasser could reply that he had no intentions of developing the bomb, and the administration could publish the exchange. That, Nasser replied after a moment's thought, was possible; he had recently said something similar in Addis Ababa about the need to keep nuclear weapons out of Africa. But Nasser evinced no particular enthusiasm for the idea. Nor did he seem to be seeking any reaffirmation of the Tripartite Declaration, which he had concluded was feeble after the Suez crisis of 1956.

Regional arms control was a priority for Kennedy, McCloy reiterated. Did Nasser have any suggestions of his own? He was sensing, McCloy added, a "little suspicion" that Nasser saw the United States as overly favorable to Israel. Nasser smiled; he had "a little more than a little" suspicion.

McCloy then reminded Nasser of Dimona, which the Egyptian leader agreed should continue to be inspected. What would happen, Badeau asked, if Nasser learned that Ben-Gurion was using Dimona to produce military material? "Protective war," replied Nasser unhesitatingly. "We would have no other choice."

It was an unhappy ending to an ill-fated mission. On June 30, a discouraged McCloy left Cairo for Athens and his Aegean cruise, suggesting in his parting cable stateside that he consult further when he returned to Washington in late July.

Badeau, as usual, tried to see the glass as half full. The usual "Arab play of refusal is to avoid [the] negative and spin out discussion until it dies [a] natural death," he wrote. That Nasser had not strung the administration along but rather forthrightly told McCloy of his opposition was a sign of both Nasser's intractability on Israel and his regard for America. But Badeau also recognized that Nasser's Arab rivals were ready to jeer at him at the slightest provocation, which made anything that smacked of submission to superpower diktat intolerable.[194]

Back in Washington, Komer also refused to lose heart. Nasser's amenability to renouncing the bomb in a letter to Kennedy or at the United Nations was a step forward, and McCloy had not played one of his strongest cards: Israel's commanding lead in the nuclear race. There was no point going to the Israelis just yet, Komer argued; better to have Badeau keep talking to Nasser and thereby underscore Egypt's interest in tamping Dimona down. Even if Nasser's no was final, sounding him out had still been useful; it would let the administration explain to Nasser just why it had been compelled to offer Israel any future security guarantee.[195]

Kennedy concurred. On July 11, Badeau met again with Nasser to follow up on the McCloy mission.[196] The ambassador assured Nasser that the arms-control push was in Egypt's interest, not merely an "Israeli stalking horse." While Dimona was still peaceful, the plant would soon be capable of producing the fuel for nuclear warheads, Badeau warned. By stiffing the administration on arms control, Nasser would hand Israel a pretext to pursue the bomb. Washington was willing to avoid any "elaborate overt inspection apparatus" and rely on "some sort of tacit, perhaps even private, understanding" that would not cost Nasser ground in the Arab cold war.[197] But Nasser proved no more tractable this time than the last, responding again that any inspections or repudiations would smack of renewed Western control of Egypt's destiny. With the Yemen crisis worsening, Nasser could not afford to be called an American stooge by his Arab rivals. Such obduracy, Badeau warned, meant that Nasser's only way to control Israel's nuclear arms program would be "preventative military action," which would be disastrous. Nasser shrugged that only within some context of "collective security" would true verification of any arms control understandings be possible. That was "exceedingly vague," Badeau protested, but Nasser would go no further. He was off to Washington for the summer, Badeau added as he left, but Kennedy would still be interested in CANE upon the ambassador's return in the fall.[198]

"Badeau's pitch to Nasser clarifying our arms limitation ideas drew rather a blank," Komer later sighed to Kennedy.[199] When McCloy reported back to Rusk on July 18, there was scant enthusiasm for pressing on with a visit to Tel Aviv.[200] Even the patient Talbot groaned about "Nasser's political schizophrenia."[201]

At 4:30 P.M. on July 23, Kennedy gathered his Middle East arms-control team — McCloy, George Ball, Talbot, the recently returned Badeau, McCone, Bundy, Komer, the Pentagon's Nitze, and NEA's Eilts — to take stock.[202] Again, Feldman was absent. Kennedy told his aides that he had gone about as far as he wanted to on a security guarantee for Israel; anything further risked "inviting the Soviets into the Middle East." The president did not think the time had arrived to do anything more drastic with Israel; in Tel Aviv, Barbour could keep meeting with Eshkol to see if anything could be finessed.

For Middle East arms control to work, Kennedy continued, "some inspection is needed in both Israel and the UAR." That was easier said than done. Nasser, with his lone puny Soviet research reactor, had still bucked at the idea of visits by either the United States, the United Nations, or the IAEA. And Dimona inspections would have to restart soon in order to ensure that Israel had not acquired nuclear weapons.

The president asked when Israel might actually produce a bomb. "[A]bout one year after Dimona goes critical," McCone replied, "Israel will be able to make a nuclear device."[203] The reactor would go on-line in either late 1963 or early 1964, the CIA guessed. "Thereafter, they can build up to two or three per year," McCone added.

This new assessment only added to Kennedy's alarm over Nasser's warning of a "protective" war if Dimona were found to be producing A-bombs. America's earlier assurances to the Arabs that Dimona was peaceful — backed up by inspections — had hitherto helped prevent such pronouncements, Badeau said. The Pentagon, Nitze added, doubted that Nasser could launch a "successful attack against Israel." Instead, Badeau said, "Nasser would simply mount an air raid to wipe out Dimona" and wait for U.N. intervention to calm matters down.

That was not an appetizing prospect. Although he deferred a McCloy visit to Israel, Kennedy ordered his men to keep working on inspections for both Israel and Egypt's nuclear programs. The superpowers were about to ratify the limited test-ban treaty concluded in the wake of the Cuban missile crisis. The administration could then start pushing for across-the-board international inspections of suspected proliferators.[204] The test ban offered a good "opportunity to test Israeli intentions," Ball noted. Seeing Israel at the vanguard of those adhering to the test-ban pact would augur well; if Israel hung back, the administration should worry. Just signing up would not suffice, JFK replied. "We must also have inspection," the president insisted. That meant that Levi Eshkol's life was not about to get any easier.

SPEAK SOFTLY AND HOLD ONTO A BIG STICK

Thanks to Kennedy's harsh July 4 letter, Dimona was the opening act of Eshkol's premiership. In Jerusalem, rumors were flying about serious U.S. pressure over the reactor.[205] As the administration waited for Eshkol's counteroffer, Komer braced Kennedy for the likelihood that Israel would try to trade concessions on Dimona for a security guarantee. The State Department hated this idea, fearing that additional protestations of American friendship for Israel would be overkill that "will only spook the Arabs, to Israel's disadvantage and our own."[206] The Pentagon also had scant interest in going any farther than Kennedy's May 8 press conference statement on upholding the regional balance of power. The Joint Chiefs argued that one of the key items on Israel's wish list—joint military planning between the Pentagon and the IDF—was unnecessary, since the most help the IDF was likely to need was airstrikes.[207] "Our evaluation is that the true desire of the Israelis is for more public and open alignment and support from the U.S.," wrote one senior Defense Department official, "rather than a great interest in advanced weaponry or purely military planning."[208]

But if Kennedy did not offer Israel a security guarantee, what incentive did Eshkol have to abandon or curtail the Dimona program? "In any case," Komer wrote Kennedy, "*Israel will not give us nuclear promises unless we either: (1) literally force them to back down; or (2) pay a price.*" Perhaps that price could be more arms sales, along the lines of the Hawk precedent, or a reassuring public letter to Eshkol. "*Our dilemma is that the more we talk about inspection, nuclear self-denial, and Jordan the more the Israelis will see leverage to get [a security] guarantee, arms, and joint planning from us.*" Still, Israel's calculus seemed clear enough to Komer. "Israel wants a full-fledged alliance," he wrote, "with all the trimmings."[209]

In his heart of hearts, Eshkol would not have disagreed. First, however, he had to get U.S.–Israel relations off their collision course. The domestic pressure was intense. To Eshkol's right, the Herut Party—the forerunners of the Likud—urged the prime minister to simply get the bomb and be done with it; to his left, the socialists of Mapam, who had a soft spot for Moscow, argued that Israel should lead a drive to make the Middle East a nuclear-free zone. Eshkol's own Mapai was torn. One puckish communist Knesset member suggested that Eshkol, a former finance minister, simply sell Dimona to the Americans, thereby both stopping proliferation and balancing the budget.[210]

Even Eshkol's closest advisers were split over how to respond, according to Teddy Kollek. On the one hand, Peres wanted to turn the Americans down cold and refuse to tolerate such an infringement on Israeli sovereignty; on the other, Harman urged protecting the U.S.–Israel relationship above all else.[211] Ben-Gurion had tried to avoid choosing between Israel's nuclear deterrent and its budding patron. Unlike Ben-Gurion, however, Eshkol realized that Israel could not simultaneously defy America and make ever-larger claims on its affections. Unlike his combative predecessor, Eshkol wanted an accommodation, not a showdown. In early August, a senior Foreign Ministry official told Barbour that he need "have no sleepless nights" waiting for Eshkol's response.[212]

On August 19, Eshkol wrote again to Kennedy.[213] Under new management, Israel finally chose to bend with the wind. "Fully conscious as I am of the special intimacy of the relationship between the United States and Israel," Eshkol wrote, "we are ready to agree to visits by United States representatives." The next visit could take place in late 1963, before the reactor went critical but after the French contractors had handed over the keys to Israel. As for Kennedy's demand for inspections every six months, "I believe that we shall be able to reach agreement on the future schedule of visits." Israel would continue to return to France all irradiated uranium fuel, which would contain plutonium produced during the nuclear reaction. But if Kennedy was skeptical, "your representatives will be enabled to observe the procedure of uranium control during their visits." For a final grace note, Eshkol congratulated Kennedy on the test-ban treaty, which "would not have been possible without your *personal* initiative and tenacity at many stages." He only hoped that the superpower thaw would make its way to the Middle East.

As he handed the letter to Barbour, Eshkol noted that he was offering three concessions: a visit before Dimona went critical, an assurance that visits after June 1964 would "give no trouble," and American scrutiny of Israel's uranium-control procedures.[214] But the results were not to be passed along to Nasser—a reversal of Ben-Gurion's position. Eshkol's mind was not firmly made up about this, but for now, he preferred to let Nasser sweat a little. "When you don't have certain weapons," Eshkol later told Barbour, it "may be just as well not [to] tell everybody."[215]

Israel's new stance, Barbour observed, was a response to Kennedy's direct, personal interest. The new prime minister's response was "not entirely what we wanted," Ball wrote Kennedy, but it was probably "the most we can hope to get at this time."[216] Both Komer and the State Department agreed that the administration should act as if Eshkol had simply given in.[217]

He had not. Pace Theodore Roosevelt, by August 1963, Eshkol decided that only by speaking softly could he hold onto the big stick that was Dimona. So where Ben-Gurion had bucked, Eshkol bent. The administration had sought Dimona inspections in the summers of 1963 and 1964, to bracket the period when the reactor would go critical; Eshkol offered a visit in late 1963. The administration had sought visits every six months thereafter; Eshkol studiously avoided any firm commitment but murmured soothingly about reaching agreement. The administration had sought unhindered access to the entire Dimona complex; Eshkol was vague on the inspections' scope, although he hinted that they would be limited to the reactor alone. The administration had sought Israeli assent to passing along its findings to Egypt, if only to dissuade Nasser from launching a raid on Dimona; Eshkol told Barbour that he did not want the Arabs to know what the Americans found. It was vintage Eshkol: flexible where Ben-Gurion had been firm, subtle where Ben-Gurion had been severe, conciliatory where Ben-Gurion had been combative.

In the end, Kennedy opted to declare victory. On August 26, he sent Eshkol a vastly friendlier letter, noting that Eshkol's suggestions had been "most welcome here. I appreciate that this was a difficult decision, yet I am convinced that in generously agreeing to invite our scientists to visit the Dimona complex on the regular basis that was proposed you have acted from a deep wisdom regarding Israel's security in the longer term and the awesome realities which the atomic age imposes on the community of man." Eshkol, Kennedy concluded, clearly partook of the historic spirit of the test ban.[218]

For all the rhetorical flourishes, Kennedy's letter was tightly parsed. He held Eshkol to his promise of regular inspections and put the Israeli leader on notice that the next year's inspections, during Dimona's startup phase, would have to occur "at a time when the reactor's core is being loaded and before internal radiation hazards have developed"—in other words, when America could find out what the Israelis were up to. Barbour was also dispatched to add that the administration emphatically wanted to leave open the question of passing the inspectors' findings along to Nasser, which might prevent the Egyptian leader from pursuing a nuclear program of his own—to say nothing of a preemptive airstrike.[219]

On August 28, Barbour gave Kennedy's letter to Eshkol, adding a pitch for passing the results on to Nasser. "Do I have to read it twice—anything between the lines?" Eshkol asked, chuckling. "Not that I know," Barbour replied.[220] The Israeli leader expressed his satisfaction over the end of the crisis. To some degree, Eshkol had been able to ease the tensions over Dimona because his leadership style was less abrasive than Ben-Gurion's, but the two men had differed on doctrine, not merely temperament. Eshkol never saw Dimona as being quite as central to Israel's long-term security as did Ben-Gurion. Rather than being hell-bent on acquiring a nuclear deterrent, Eshkol sought to balance Israel's interest in continuing a nuclear program against its interest in cultivating an alliance with Washington. Ben-Gurion was more prickly about state sovereignty and more worried that American monitoring would ultimately foreclose Israel's nuclear options. But Eshkol was not about to surrender, either. He surely recognized that unrestricted American inspections could tear the veil off Dimona and bring the full weight of Kennedy's displeasure to bear. So along with the new openness to American scrutiny necessarily came a new degree of duplicity: Israel would simply have to hide the evidence from prying American eyes and carry on with its nuclear-arms program nonetheless. If that kept Nasser guessing, so much the better. Eshkol sought to defuse Dimona as an issue, not as a reactor.

WHAT KIND OF RELATIONSHIP IS THIS?

Eshkol's compromise was enough to get the Kennedy administration to back off—for now. JFK's personal suspicions about Dimona might well have led him into another showdown with Israel had he lived. But in the event, his administration's immediate worries about an atomic Middle East faded as the fall of 1963 approached. Almost a year after the Cuban missile crisis, the world seemed a safer place. In Moscow on July 25, Soviet Foreign Minister Andrei Gromyko and Averell Harriman, the wily old crocodile of the State Department, had initialed an historic treaty banning atomic tests in space, the atmosphere, and the oceans. Khrushchev was ebullient. Two days later, Nasser—who had no bombs to test in the first place—announced that he would adhere to the treaty. On July 31, Israel announced that it, too, would join the limited test ban. Despite grousing from Menachem Begin's rightist Herut that Israel had caved in to American pressure, and despite a rumor that one Mapai minister— perhaps Moshe Dayan—had been opposed, the rest of the cabinet decided Israel had nothing to lose by signing on.[221]

Amid its gratification, however, the administration was still troubled by the failure of the CANE mission. In retrospect, both Nasser and Eshkol had been sunk far too deep into their respective security dilemmas to have made military self-abnegation viable. Worse, Nasser's pan-Arab ambitions made him reliably nettlesome, and the fact that the reconstituted union between Egypt, Iraq, and Syria was now falling apart did little for his mood. On August 11, Nasser gave a blistering speech at Port Said.[222] "Disarmament must be preceded by the liquidation of imperialism and the liquidation of all traces of imperialism," he thundered. "For us here in the United Arab Republic, disarmament cannot be achieved while the rights of the Palestine people are lost and usurped." While he applauded the test-ban treaty, he warned that Israel would use disarmament as "a ruse in order to enable the criminal to get away with the booty, and, at the same time, to deprive justice of all ability to give chase."

A frustrated Rusk suggested picking up on the hint from McCloy's Cairo mission and trying to get a written assurance from Nasser that Egypt would neither attack Israel nor pursue the bomb.[223] Kennedy agreed. On September 12, Badeau was given a draft letter from Kennedy to Nasser, written under the pretext of thanking the Egyptian leader for endorsing the test-ban treaty.[224] In that signature, Kennedy wrote, he saw a welcome acknowledgment that Cairo already "regards itself as committed, in a broader sense, not to seek or acquire nuclear weapons through any means." Nasser's confirmation of that commitment would be welcome, the president continued. He also encouraged Nasser to expound on his past statements and formally pledge not to attack his neighbors. McCloy had failed to cut a deal, but perhaps Kennedy could still elicit a response. On October 5, Nasser read Kennedy's letter and told Badeau that some sort of reply "might be possible."[225] But the crack-up of the reconstituted UAR, which had meant scalding propaganda from his rivals in the Ba'ath Party, was limiting his options.

Beset by Arab conservatives and radicals alike, Nasser then indulged his final major display of churlishness on Kennedy's watch. In September, Egyptian scientists had visited U.S. nuclear reactors, with an eye toward eventually building a 150-megawatt power reactor near Alexandria. The Egyptians had been told that any U.S. reactor would come with at least one string attached: international safeguards similar to those on the Indian reactor at Tarapur. In October, the IAEA General Conference in Vienna voted 57 to 4 to create a system of safeguards for such large reactors, with support from both NATO and Warsaw Pact nations. The UAR was one of the four naysayers, protesting that such oversight was a discriminatory infringement of the sovereignty of small states, designed to hamstring their technological progress.[226] After the failure of the Egyptian-Iraqi-Syrian union talks and Yemen, Nasser hated to be seen to buckle under American pressure.

Meanwhile, Israel was determinedly getting as much as it could out of the White House. During the opening of the U.N. General Assembly in New York, the visiting Meir again painted a dire picture of Nasser at a meeting with Rusk.[227] Nasser was getting his troops into fighting trim in Yemen, using mustard gas on the Yemeni royalists, relying on Nazi scientists, upgrading his missile program, and possibly pushing ahead on a nuclear program to boot. Perhaps to avoid having to refute Israel's charges, Rusk suggested that America and Israel compare notes on Nasser's military capabilities instead.[228] Meir jumped at the suggestion.

Rusk may have been acting on impulse, but his suggestion of these balance-of-forces talks may also have been part of a wider administration ploy. The timing is suggestive: just as Eshkol was getting the good news on the security consultations, he got the definitive bad news on the security guarantee. On October 2, Kennedy formally turned down Ben-Gurion's May 12 request for a pledge to come to Israel's aid in the same way America would assist a NATO ally.[229] For all of America's sympathy with the Zionist enterprise, Kennedy wrote, the existing series of informal arrangements were quite enough. For one thing, the IDF could fend for itself; for another, American help was never far away; for a third, nobody in the region could have misread Kennedy's May 8 press conference. But Kennedy insisted that both U.S. and Israeli interests were best served by retaining the ability to talk frankly to the Arab states. "A bilateral security relationship such as Mr. Ben-Gurion suggested would, I fear, have a distinct contrary effect," Kennedy wrote. "There is no doubt in Arab minds as to how we would respond to unprovoked aggression by them," he added. Being more explicit would only hurt Israel's security by encouraging the Soviets to sell more arms to the Jewish state's foes. "Nonetheless," Kennedy concluded, "I know you need no reassurance as to the constant and special United States concern for the security and independence of Israel." And should the Arab military menace loom larger in the future, the administration would be willing to consider evening the odds, as it had with the Hawk sale. It was Jack Kennedy's last letter to an Israeli prime minister.

Jerusalem swallowed its disappointment the best way it knew how: by trying to take maximum advantage of the new offer of U.S.–Israel consultations. The security guarantee was off the table, but the security talks were now squarely on it. As a sign of its seriousness, as we have seen, Israel chose two key officials as its delegates: IDF Deputy Chief of Staff Yitzhak Rabin and IDF Deputy Director of Intelligence Aharon Yariv. Indeed, the Israelis were so keen for a sweeping security consultation that an irritated Rusk eventually told Barbour to warn them not to try to broaden the scope of the upcoming talks.[230] On November 4, Eshkol wrote Kennedy that without American promises to come to Israel's rescue, his government would have to find other ways to defend itself from Nasser's arsenal.[231] Citing a Russian proverb, Eshkol told Barbour that it was the patient and not the doctor who truly knows how ill he is.[232]

Even though the administration worked hard to limit the security talks' purview, they nevertheless set an important precedent—detailed U.S.–Israel talks on regional security—that is still operative today. On November 12 and 13, Talbot chaired two three-hour sessions that attempted to assess how much of a threat Nasser posed to Israel. Around a table in Room 1205 of the State Department, Talbot, Komer, a few NEA advisers, a CIA official, and several Pentagon aides faced off with Rabin, Yariv, Harman, Gazit, and four other Israeli officials.[233] While the two sides disagreed on the scope of the Egyptian threat to Israel and while no actual policy decisions were made, the talks still had an unmistakably business-like tone that bespoke a growing intimacy—albeit not yet a full-blown alliance.

That point was vividly made on the penultimate day of John F. Kennedy's life, when Bob Komer got into an argument. Over a November 21, 1963, luncheon with Gazit, Harman's deputy at the Israeli embassy, the two men vented their frustrations over the state of U.S.–Israel relations.[34] Komer accused the Israelis of always trying to force the administration into taking pro-Israel positions that would hamper its ability to keep lines of communication open to the Arabs; Gazit accused the Americans of unwarrantedly holding Israel at arms length.

During the recent security talks headed by Rabin, Gazit said, the Israelis had "laid out all of their intelligence" on Egypt's arsenal while the Americans had kept "mum." Komer retorted that the American side had given more information on Nasser's weaponry than ever before and that they certainly did not offer such data to the Arabs. "Moreover," he continued, "if one were going to talk about lack of candor, it was strange to me that Israel was so consistently coy about describing its own defense plans and programs to its guarantor, banker, and strongest friend in the world." The Americans "were expected to subsidize Israel, both privately and publicly, to support her to the hilt on every issue, to meet all of her security requirements, and to defend her if attacked. In return, we did not even know what she intended to do in such critical fields as missiles and nuclear weapons." Israel's evasiveness on Dimona, he noted, had created "real suspicion on our part" that Israel was bent on getting the bomb. "What kind of a relationship was this?" Komer asked.

What indeed? For all the warming trend exemplified by the Hawk sales, Kennedy pressured Ben-Gurion and Eshkol well beyond the bounds of politesse on Dimona. The president did not care. Nuclear proliferation was for Kennedy an issue that transcended more localized considerations. If Israel had to be pressed hard so that the United States could keep a watchful eye on a suspiciously constructed, dangerously located, and evasively concealed nuclear reactor, then Israel had to be pressed hard. To be sure, Kennedy failed to stop the weapons program at Dimona. But the intensity with which he pushed in 1963 suggests that he would probably have assertively revisited the issue if the U.S. deal with Eshkol proved too weak—an attitude quite unlike his successors'.

Early on, Kennedy seems to have hoped that Dimona would just go away as an issue, so he let himself be temporarily mollified by brief American visits to the reactor that the administration had to have known offered no real guarantee of its peaceful nature. But with rumors about an Israeli bomb being nervously traded in Cairo, Baghdad, Riyadh, Washington, and Paris, the administration realized that simple Israeli assurances of Dimona's harmlessness would scarcely suffice. Kennedy tried first to see if he could receive credible Israeli assurances of pacific intent, then realized later in his term that only a more muscular approach could soothe Arab anxieties, avert a serious escalation of regional tension, and deprive the Kremlin of a particularly potent appeal to Arab fidelity. As the president grew more comfortable in office, he increasingly treated Dimona not as an issue to be deferred but as a problem to be solved. By 1963, riding high on his post–Cuban missile crisis popularity and deep into negotiations with the Soviet Union for a partial nuclear test ban, Kennedy was willing to finally force a showdown with Israel over Dimona.

Ironically enough, the U.S.–Israel tussling over Dimona had the long-term result of strengthening the special relationship, not weakening it. Kennedy presided over the worst of the U.S.–Israel struggle over the Jewish state's nuclear program, and that searing experience ultimately led both Washington and Jerusalem to shy away from further confrontations over Dimona. Eshkol decided to permit regular American visits to the reactor and then set about making sure that Israel's guests never found anything. For his part, Lyndon Johnson proved more willing to be convinced by the sham inspections because he had less stomach than Kennedy for an all-out slugfest over Dimona. After the summer of 1963, neither side was eager for a sequel.

And, of course, all of Kennedy's suspicions about Dimona's capacities — if not his fears about its consequences — were correct. Today, Peres's mantra notwithstanding, Dimona has produced the only nuclear arsenal in the region. Even with a veil of opacity, Ben-Gurion and his protégés indeed introduced nuclear weapons into the Middle East by about the time of the Six Day War.

A Time to Cut Bait

I met Murder on the way,
He had a mask like Castlereagh
Very smooth he looked yet grim
Seven bloodhounds followed him

     —John F. Kennedy
     journal entry quoting Shelley,
     Jerusalem, 1951

NOVEMBER 1963 HAD BEEN a relatively quiet month in the Middle East. The only event of any real note had been a brief flap over a few ill-advised remarks by Ben-Gurion in the *New York Times*. On November 16, C. L. Sulzberger of the *Times* had interviewed the former prime minister at his Negev kibbutz of Sdeh Boqer, and Ben-Gurion had railed against Egypt's missile program. "As a result," Sulzberger had written, "he hints grimly that in its nearby Dimona reactor Israel itself may be experimenting with military atomics." Two days later, the Old Man cabled a denial to the editors of the *Times*. In Israel, the press buzzed that Ben-Gurion had sought to deliberately embarrass Eshkol. Meanwhile, the government tried to squelch the story.[1] "After all, what constitutes a 'hint'?" asked one Israeli Foreign Ministry official of an American diplomat in Tel Aviv. "Is it [a] twitch of eyebrow, facial expression or what?"[2] The episode did little to alleviate the State Department's irritation over Dimona. "If the Israelis go ahead with military development in this area," said Averell Harriman, "we shall have to come down on them like a ton of bricks."[3]

But beyond this short-lived flare over Dimona, November 1963 was reasonably routine: on November 5, a Syrian infiltrator was killed by the Israelis near the Galilee town of Kfar Ha'nassi; on November 11, two Israelis were shot and wounded by Syrians near Kibbutz Dan, close to the Syrian-held Golan Heights; also on November 11, the American Jewish leader Jacob Blaustein, with his perpetual worries about "dual loyalty," arrived in Israel for a short visit; on November 14, the United Nations named a Brazilian lieutenant general the new commander of the U.N. peacekeeping force in Sinai; on November 16, it also named a new commissioner general of

UNRWA, the Palestinian refugee relief agency; and on November 21, Egyptian planes again bombed Saudi territory, and the USS *Tallahatchie* arrived in Haifa for a four-day visit to Israel.[4]

The next day, the world changed. As he had written in his last diary entry in Jerusalem, a decade before becoming president, John F. Kennedy indeed "met Murder on the way." It was a horror that riveted the Middle East. Television was still a relatively new technology in the United States; in the Middle East, the radio still ruled. If the American experience of Kennedy's assassination—the country's first fully televised, real-time mass-media trauma—consisted of sitting around suburban living rooms watching Walter Cronkite, the Middle Eastern version consisted of huddling around the radio, hearing the tidings over state-run newscasts. Throughout the region, the reaction was galvanic—perhaps the first truly global instant of tragedy, briefly uniting even Middle Eastern adversaries in startled grief. To be sure, some of the response came from sheer shock, but some of it paid tribute to the innovations that Kennedy brought to his Middle East diplomacy and to the widespread regional perception of JFK as a progressive with no grudge against Arab nationalism. By contrast, imagine how the Middle East might react today to the assassination of an American president.

November 22 was a slow day in Cairo. At the American embassy, one of Nasser's advisers, Hassan Sabri al-Khouli, popped by to tell an American diplomat that his government did not object to Washington's ongoing attempts to broker détente between Yemen and Saudi Arabia.[5] That evening, Nasser turned in early in order to read. At 9:30 P.M. local time, Nasser's confidant Muhammad Haykal heard a news flash from Dallas and called Nasser to tell him that Kennedy had been shot. Haykal sat for hours, stunned, in front of the Associated Press wire ticker in his office at *al-Ahram* watching each bulletin come in.[6] A horrified Nasser called Haykal repeatedly throughout the evening for more information, until the final bleak news arrived. At a loss for what to do with himself, Nasser felt somehow compelled to go in to the office. "My God, why have I dressed, why have I come here?" he asked when he arrived. "There is nothing any of us can do about it."[7]

The next day, Ambassador Badeau cabled, "Cairo was overcome by a sense of universal tragedy." His embassy left out a book of condolences for three days, during which time almost a thousand people came by to sign— including Vice President Anwar al-Sadat, who would also ultimately be assassinated. The army chief of staff, General Amr, signed, as did the foreign ministers of Yemen and Algeria, both of whom happened to be in town. Almost the entire staff of many embassies stopped by, including the Italian embassy's grieving code clerk. But the American diplomats were even more moved by the long, snaking line of ordinary Egyptians out front, waiting patiently to write impassioned messages. "After the way he handled the Cuba crisis," one Egyptian said, "I was never afraid for the security of the world." "You can understand it when someone kills a leader in a society where no one can express their political opinions," said another, standing near the book containing Sadat's words of sympathy. "Then perhaps assassination is the only means of political self-expression. But in America, where anyone could say what he wanted against the president, how is it possible that someone should want to shoot him?"

Nasser's state-run press set the tone. For a week, "there was quite literally no other news" on the front pages of Cairo's four Arabic dailies, reported the U.S. embassy.[8] Nasser al-Din Nashashibi, a reliably and sometimes rabidly anti-American columnist for *al-Jumhuriyya*, was abruptly transformed and insisted on delivering a televised, ten-minute eulogy. Newspaper eulogies were effusive. The columnist George Aziz wrote that JFK's whole life had been made up of acts of courage, from PT-109 to civil rights to Cuba to (rather less grandly) "his defense of foreign aid." Haykal's own *al-Ahram* editorialized that Kennedy had made the United States "the cherished rich brother of the human family rather than the repugnant rich brother." Cairo television showed the film of Kennedy's funeral in its mournful entirety, four times.[9]

The sorrow lingered among Nasser's aides. Khouli asked one American diplomat, Donald C. Bergus, when the most appropriate time to issue a memorial postage stamp would be; Bergus gently explained that America, which did not share the Muslim 40-day *arba'in* interval, would end its official mourning period on December 22.[10] When the U.S. embassy in Cairo canceled an upcoming concert by Duke Ellington, the minister of culture wrote back, "Compared to the loss of the late President Kennedy everything else counts for very little."

The public reactions were, if anything, even more heartfelt. One man wrote the embassy that he had named his new son Kennedy, enclosing a copy of the birth certificate for proof; another apologized for sending a belated note of condolences, explaining that he had been delayed by the death of his only son. Throughout the country, pupils stood for a moment of silence on Saturday morning. A requiem mass at downtown Cairo's St. Joseph's Cathedral, which seats about 600, somehow managed to cram in some 4,000 people, with 1,500 more clustered outside. The embassy staff watched in sorrow and gratitude. Kennedy, Badeau told one staff meeting, "represented what Egyptians want most to believe about Americans."[11]

Indeed, in death, Kennedy came to represent such hopes for people across the Middle East. In Tehran, Navab Street, which ran from the city's downtown core to Mehrabad Airport, was renamed for the late president; in 1964, on a bitterly cold January morning, Sargent Shriver attended the dedication ceremonies as both director of the Peace Corps, symbol of America's development strategy, and bereft brother-in-law.[12] In Basra, the southern Iraqi city that would become the base for Saddam Husayn's 1990 occupation of Kuwait, hundreds of ordinary Iraqis crowded the streets in silence during memorial services for Kennedy.[13] In Lebanon, peasants in the Bekaa Valley tumbled disbelievingly out of their fields to listen to the radio news. The headmistress of Beirut's College Protestant des Jeunes Filles gathered her students the Saturday after the assassination and wrote on her blackboard, "Ask not what your country can do for you; ask what you can do for your country." In Beirut, flags flew at half-mast, and the long-planned anniversary celebrations for the November 23 founding of the Phalange—the Maronite Christian party whose troops would run amuck in Sabra and Shatila in 1982—were canceled, except for a session of eulogies.[14] One of the first people to call the American embassy in Amman was King Husayn, who had looked on in horror in 1951 as his grandfather, Abdallah, was assassinated by a Palestinian gunman; since the young king called only minutes after the first radio reports from Dallas, he had to pass his shock and grief on to the embassy's counselor for economic affairs.[15] And in Yemen, the republican government that Kennedy had recognized shut all its offices on November 24 and 25 in his honor.[16]

In Algeria, the shock was particularly intense. The country had felt a special bond with JFK since his 1957 Senate speech backing Algerian independence; when France grudgingly recognized Algerian statehood in July 1962, Kennedy had responded warmly and hosted President Ahmed Ben Bella at the White House. Upon hearing the news that Kennedy had been shot, a flabbergasted Ben Bella now rushed to call the American ambassador, who was in the middle of hosting a reception. A few minutes later, Ben Bella called again, having been told by the local UPI reporter that the president had died. The ambassador gathered his guests, told them of the murder, and ended the reception. Algeria sent its foreign minister and the president of the National Assembly to Washington for the funeral and flew its flags at half-staff for a week; Ben Bella himself renamed the main square of al-Biar, an Algiers suburb, "Place John Kennedy" as the entire cabinet looked on. Televised coverage of the funeral was beamed straight to Algiers, local radio switched entirely over to mournful classical music, and eulogies repeatedly invoked the 1957 Senate speech. Kennedy, eulogized the semiofficial daily Le Peuple, "constitutes a small part of our own heritage."[17]

Saudi Arabia was also rattled by the loss of the president who had sent USAF planes to defend its borders. An anonymous Saudi called the U.S. embassy in Jidda around 10:30 P.M. the night of the murder and tipped off the Marine Guard. Amid the familiar mobbing to sign the embassy condolence book, one man stood out: he had come from Medina especially for this. On his own visit to the U.S. embassy, the country's ailing finance minister, Shaykh Abdallah Sulayman, practically had to be carried by other Saudi royals. Egypt's November 21 bombings of Saudi soil were crowded off the front pages with news from Dallas and Washington. Ambassador Pete Hart was overrun with diplomats expressing their regret, including one who also conceded some surprise at the outpouring, adding, "I did not know we liked you Americans so much." But even in its grief, the kingdom kept its own counsel. Only a handful of women stretched the limits of the House of Saud's puritanical Wahhabi mores by calling on Hart's wife; when the Jidda embassy held an outdoors memorial ceremony on November 25, which featured both a visiting Catholic chaplain and several readings from the Bible, the limits of decorum forbade inviting any Saudi citizens.[18]

The Arab world found the loss as baffling as did many Americans. Long before the Warren Commission or the rantings of Oliver Stone, conspiracy theories began to crisscross the Middle East. The Soviet-oriented Algerian daily newspaper, *Alger Républican*, called Dallas a hotbed of reactionary hatred, sneered at the incompetence of the authorities, and blamed the murder on rightists out to create a new era of "hysterical McCarthyism."[19] Ben Bella blamed "les partisans de la ségrégation raciale."[20] In Basra, it was the death of Lee Harvey Oswald that did it; with many people convinced that such a lapse could only be the work of a conspiracy, Basrawi opinion divided over whether the plotters were communists or Zionists.[21] In Beirut, American diplomats were overwhelmed with questions about a nefarious plot against the American way of life, probably of communist origin.[22] (The now-famous AP photo "showing police looking [the] other way while Oswald [was] being shot point-blank does nothing to reassure foreigners of [the] competence of American police authorities," cabled Ambassador Armin Meyer.)

The ugliest speculations of all, however, burbled out from the twin wellsprings of Palestinian resentment and Saudi insularity. In Jordan, with its huge population of Palestinian refugees, early speculation about revenge from a rightist or racist fanatic quickly came to center instead on a "Zionist conspiracy," which had supposedly killed Oswald to cover its tracks. The major Jordanian newspapers thrummed with rumors, noting that Jack Ruby had been born "Rubinstein," reporting (falsely) that Oswald was also Jewish, and hyperventilating over the lax security precautions of the Dallas police. "It is quite possible," editorialized the newspaper *al-Manar*, "that the wrath of Zionism has led some Zionist agent to kill in order to terrify Kennedy's successor and America's policy in general."[23] Other pundits argued that the Zionists had planned Dallas because of Kennedy's opposition to Israel's nuclear program. In Jidda, Pete Hart had the unenviable task of soothing Saudi elites leery of Lyndon B. Johnson, which left the ambassador endlessly refuting theories that the new president had had his predecessor murdered on Zionist orders.[24] In Amman and Jidda, the logic flowed ineluctably: since Zionism was automatically the root of "any evil in the world," as a dispirited U.S. diplomat in Amman put it, Zionism's finger must have been on the Book Depository trigger.[25] Such squalid surmise—four decades before Gallup polls would reveal that millions of Arabs blamed the Mossad for the September 11, 2001, terrorist attacks on the World Trade Center and the Pentagon—remains a sobering reflection on the depths and distortions of anti-Israel animus in the Arab world.

In Israel, Kennedy died on shabbat. While tradition-minded Israelis were finishing off Sabbath evening meals over candles, wine, and challah, Wally Barbour was dining in Tel Aviv at the Italian ambassador's table—a particular pleasure for the portly Barbour, a man fond of his food and wine. But the American ambassador's enjoyment was dashed when word of Dallas came over the radio, which reported that Kennedy was shot but still alive. As Barbour was absorbing the news, the phone rang; it was Israel's president, Zalman Shazar, calling to formally offer his condolences.

Barbour rushed back to the embassy through the streets of a Tel Aviv now quieted down for its lone day off. The U.S. embassy, too, was shutting down for shabbat, but Barbour opened it back up. As he and his staff tried to follow the news and to think through the implications of the president's death, Barbour realized that he had a singularly Israeli problem on his hands: the embassy would need to buy a book of condolences, but Tel Aviv's stores had all closed for shabbat. On Saturday, an embassy official discreetly tracked down a stationery store willing "to open the back door." The next day, Eshkol and his cabinet filed gravely by the embassy to sign the contraband condolence books.[26]

Shortly after 9 P.M. on November 22, Ben-Gurion turned on his radio at his home in Sdeh Boqer to tune into the evening news on Kol Yisrael (Voice of Israel) radio. He tuned in a bit late for the headlines but was still in time to hear that Kennedy had been shot and that Catholic priests had been summoned. "Where were his security forces?" Ben-Gurion scribbled in his diary.[27] Shortly after 11, the Old Man turned on the radio again and heard that the president was dead. "Was it because of Kennedy's relations with the blacks?" Ben-Gurion wrote. "He was a brave man, sensible and so young, where were the guards?" The next day, Ben-Gurion's bewilderment persisted. "Still in shock over the murder of Kennedy," he wrote in his diary.[28] In a personal letter of condolences to Barbour, Ben-Gurion ended by scrawling, "I am asking why? Why?"[29]

Yitzhak Rabin—who would himself fall to an assassin's bullets in Tel Aviv in another grim November 32 years later—seems to have been astonishingly close to Dallas on the day of Kennedy's murder.[30] Having wrapped up his mid-November talks with U.S. officials in Washington over Nasser's military capabilities, the red-headed young IDF deputy chief of staff embarked upon a round of meetings with various U.S. military officials. It was his wife Leah's first trip to America.[31] A Pentagon schedule has Rabin visiting the U.S. Army Field Artillery and Missile School at Fort Sill, Oklahoma, on November 21, 1963.[32] Fort Sill lies about 210 miles northwest of Dallas, just across the Texas-Oklahoma state line—about a four-hour drive from the Texas School Book Depository.

Back home, an Israeli press shocked by the assassination now "largely dismissed" the recent strains in U.S.–Israel relations as fleeting and tactical, Barbour reported. Israel's response was sorrow, he recalled, not anxiety that LBJ might be harder to handle.[33] For the first time in its 31-year history, *The Jerusalem Post* broke the Sabbath to put out a Saturday edition. The Knesset held a special short mourning session, and on November 24, the regular Sunday cabinet meeting was turned over entirely to eulogizing Kennedy. Eshkol and his ministers then saw off President Shazar and Foreign Minister Golda Meir, who were to represent Israel at the funeral in Washington.[34]

At the memorial service in the National Cathedral, Meir recalled, among the handful of people not kneeling were herself, Shazar, and Charles de Gaulle—the two Israelis because Judaism forbids kneeling to any authority other than God, the Frenchman because of Gallic pride.[35] After the funeral, Meir lined up to shake hands with Jacqueline Kennedy and murmur a few words of condolence. "I can't forget how she stood there, pale and with tears in her eyes, but still finding something special to say to each one of us," the sorrowful foreign minister wrote later. At the somber state dinner thrown by the new president that evening, Meir waited again in a receiving line to meet President Johnson, whom she remembered from his vocal opposition to Eisenhower's threat of anti-Israel sanctions during the Suez crisis, when LBJ was Senate majority leader. When Meir approached the new president, he put his arm around her. "I know that you have lost a friend," Kennedy's heir said, "but I hope you understand that I, too, am a friend."[36]

THE VIEW FROM YAD KENNEDY

Southwest of Jerusalem, past the plain, blue-collar neighborhoods of Kiryat Ha'yovel and Katamonim, past the mixed Arab-Jewish town of Ein Kerem, past the winding hillsides around the small village of Ora, stands a bulky, concrete block shaped faintly like a tree trunk. Yad Kennedy, as the official

Israeli memorial to JFK is known, commands a dramatic view of the surrounding countryside, looking out toward Ramallah over misty hills with terraced slopes, new Jewish neighborhoods built for recent immigrants, and Arab villages studded with minarets. The memorial itself is a large slab of crenellated concrete, adorned with the seals of all 50 states of the union, that borrows its shape—a tree felled before its time—from a traditional Jewish cemetery design for children's tombstones. Inside the gray stump sits a round, black version of Arlington's eternal flame.

The memorial was dedicated on July 4, 1966, by Supreme Court Chief Justice Earl Warren. Looking on, beneath the dazzling sun of an Israeli summer and amid the rushing wind around the hilltop, were Levi Eshkol and Walworth Barbour. A plaque called the site "an eternal expression of American-Israel friendship." Yad Kennedy's design stamps it indelibly as a relic of the 1960s; with its modernist lines and blocky architecture, it could scarcely have been built in any other decade.

Near the memorial, three saplings are struggling out of the dry earth, planted in August 1999 in memory of John F. Kennedy, Jr., Carolyn Bessette Kennedy, and Lauren Bessette. Another, larger, grove was planted by visiting members of the Kennedy family, including Edward Kennedy, Jacqueline Kennedy Onassis, Jean Kennedy Smith, and Sargent Shriver. From the younger generation, trees have been planted by Joseph Kennedy, Kerry Kennedy Cuomo, and Kathleen Kennedy Townsend, who planted her sapling in honor of her late father, Robert, assassinated by the deranged Palestinian Sirhan Sirhan in 1968.

Nor were Irish Catholics from Boston the only ones planting trees in the dry earth outside Jerusalem. The landscape around Yad Kennedy looks far different than it did in 1966. The hills around the memorial have been overrun with trees planted by the Jewish National Fund (JNF), softening the harsh terrain with an overlay of foliage.

That seems fitting. It is not only the JNF that transformed the landscape; JFK did, too. The thousand days of the Kennedy presidency were enough time for a series of important shifts on Middle Eastern affairs. The Kennedy administration removed several roadblocks to a full-blown U.S.–Israel alliance. It broke the taboo on arms sales to Israel; it fudged a compromise that smoothed over the nuclear issue; it set the precedent of professionalized security talks; and it began the process of minimizing the costs of friendship with Israel by discovering the limits of friendship with the Arab states. These laid the foundations upon which presidents from Lyndon Johnson to George W. Bush could build. Harry Truman was the father of the U.S.–Israel special relationship; John Kennedy was the father of the U.S.–Israel alliance.

Kennedy's Arab-Israeli policy was designed to take full advantage of whatever regional openings he could find or create. His administration, however frequently mired in internecine bickering, managed in the aggregate to produce an overall strategy that sought to give the president more Cold War options in the Middle East. That meant constant attention to maintaining a regional balance of power in which Nasser did not menace Israel, in which Israeli actions did not create openings for greater Soviet influence in the region, and in which the Arab cold war was kept under control. Kennedy was willing to consider wider attempts to resolve the underlying tensions of the Arab-Israeli conflict—most notably the Johnson refugee mission—but his pragmatism tended to drive him in less messianic directions. He was out not to solve the Arab-Israeli conflict but to circumscribe it.

Nor did the administration make it a priority to revamp American policy in the Middle East. "The jokes around the place used to be that every day we're not on page one is another great triumph," Talbot recalled. "[I]n the balance of all of these things, we never got the Israelis really angry at us, and you never got Faisal to the point where he'd just blow through the ceiling. We were working with Nasser in a way which quieted him at least for some time and that was quite important. . . . And we were trying very hard to convey the impression that a third round conflict would make no sense at all. . . . We didn't solve any of the fundamental problems. We didn't solve the refugee problem. We didn't solve the Jordan waters problem. We didn't solve the problem of frontiers between Israel and its neighbors. But maybe the combination of everything we were doing helped to keep it tamped down. I hope so."[37]

Talbot's assessment is not far off. Tamping down regional tensions entailed reaching out to Cairo, but by 1963, Washington had failed twice to solidify relations with the largest and most important Arab power. In the 1950s, Eisenhower and Dulles had haltingly reached out to Egypt, but they remained predisposed to see Third World nationalism as an automatic threat. In contrast, Kennedy was willing to see neutralist leaders such as Tito, Sukarno, Nehru, and Nasser as something other than communist pawns and began an important attempt to start afresh with Egypt.

As U.S.–Egypt ties warmed and pan-Arabism recovered from the shock of the collapse of the Egypt-Syria union in 1961, Ben-Gurion began to fear that Israel would be left out in the cold. But when the overture to Nasser ground to a halt over the Yemen war—hors de combat of inter-Arab bickering—Kennedy found that his Cold War strategy was frustrated by the Arabs' own cold war.

It was also hindered by the Arab-Israeli conflict itself, but Kennedy seems to have been immune to any sweeping temptations here. He had no intention of trying to wrap up the entire Arab-Israeli conflict. Kennedy's resoundingly pragmatic conception of Middle East peacemaking was more

Henry Kissinger than Jimmy Carter: modest steps to address manageable problems, rather than bold leaps toward a comprehensive solution. As such, Kennedy's one major attempt to grapple with an underlying source of Arab-Jewish tension—the Johnson mission on Palestinian refugees—was never much of an administration priority. When Kennedy did focus on the Johnson plan, he deemed it unworkable, one of the direst insults in the New Frontier lexicon.

Even without a major peacemaking push, Kennedy's meliorism shifted the underlying basis of the U.S.–Israel relationship. Komer's November 1963 description of America as Israel's "guarantor, banker, and strongest friend in the world" may have sounded mildly overblown (as was Komer's wont) at the end of the Kennedy administration, but it would have been unutterable at the end of the Eisenhower administration.

The context for the origins of the U.S.–Israel alliance is, in a very real sense, Suez. The shadow of Israel's aggressive protection of its security interests still fell heavily upon the Eisenhower administration. It was only the newer Kennedy appointees, less encumbered by the memory of 1956, who were willing to move closer to a post-Suez Israel. Arguing that the Hawks were simply defensive weapons worked only if one assumed that Israel was not an aggressor state. Kennedy made that assumption, even if Eisenhower did not.

With that view, Kennedy made considerable changes. He sold major arms to Israel for the first time, paving the way for America to become, as it were, the arsenal of Jewish democracy; he began security consultations, paving the way for full-blown military-to-military joint planning; he gave Israel its warmest security assurances to date, paving the way for even more formal American commitments to repel Arab aggression; and he even re-placed Marshall's old refusal to even think about domestic political con-straints when handling Israel policy, paving the way for the misty-eyed invocations of eternal U.S.–Israel friendship that are staples of any mod-ern presidential aspirant's standard foreign policy speech.

It is instructive to consider the markedly different style of Lyndon Johnson, who took a romanticized view of the Middle East legacy of Harry Truman. In June 1967, shortly after the Six Day War, the president held an impromptu summit meeting with Soviet Premier Alexei Kosygin in Glassboro, New Jersey. At the meeting, Kosygin asked why Johnson had chosen to squander the friendship of the numerous Arab states and in-stead chosen to support Israel. "Because it's right," Johnson reportedly replied.[38] It is not easy to imagine the supremely unsentimental Kennedy uttering—let alone believing—such a sentiment. But it would be far too neat to assume that the increasingly warm U.S.–Israel relationship of the late 1960s was an accidental byproduct of Kennedy's assassination or a mere extrapolation of Johnson's blunter preconceptions. Rather, the Johnson administration built upon the foundations laid by its predecessor. It was Kennedy's policy shifts, not simply the change in personalities in the Oval Office, that guided the special relationship in the direction of outright alliance.

Until the spring of 1967, the Middle East was not a top priority for LBJ. But when the time came to find his footing, he did so on a landscape reshaped by Kennedy. Nasser drifted away from the United States even as Israel drifted closer. To borrow JFK's variation on Ecclesiastes, the Kennedy administration had been a time to fish; the Johnson administration was a time to cut bait.

One could hear the lines being snipped in virtually every area. The visit to the White House by Nasser that the State Department had sought so avidly never materialized; instead, on June 1, 1964, Eshkol became the first Israeli prime minister to be welcomed formally to a summit at the executive mansion. It was an apt summation of what had happened with Washington's relationships with both countries. Shimon Peres remembers an Oval Office meeting in which the hulking Johnson told Eshkol, Ambassador Harman, and Peres that America stood "foursquare behind Israel." With a wink, Eshkol whispered to Peres, "You hear, young man, four squares. Not three squares, but four." That evening, at a formal reception, LBJ swept up Eshkol's wife Miriam and whirled away into a waltz. A nervous Harman nudged Eshkol toward Lady Bird Johnson, but the imperturbable Eshkol staffed out his dance-floor duties with the first lady. "*Ich tanz nisht*," he said in Yiddish, and pointed at Peres. "Young man, you dance."[39]

As LBJ circled the dance floor with Miriam Eshkol, U.S.–Egypt relations were circling the drain. Nasser's Vietnam was draining his resources, his patience, and his pan-Arabist ambitions. As he plunged deeper into Yemen, Nasser was increasingly embittered and embattled. For Washington, befriending both Nasserite Egypt and the conservative monarchs was proving a bit like trying to stay on cordial terms with the Capulets and the Montagues. Aid to Egypt continued to come under congressional attack. In Bobby Kennedy's 1964 Senate race against Kenneth Keating, the distinguished, white-haired New York Republican beloved of the Israel lobby, the frustrated incumbent used the Kennedy administration's Middle East record to jab at his carpetbagging foe. "Keating," the GOP signs read, "Nasser's Number One Enemy, Israel's Number One Friend."[40]

A suspicious Johnson increasingly started to fear that Nasser had gone over to the Soviet camp and to fret that Western influence was under assault throughout the Middle East. Meanwhile, Nasser's fellow neutralists had not been faring well, which lowered Johnson's interest in trying to make headway with Third World nationalists; Algeria's Ben Bella was toppled in June 1965, followed by Indonesia's Sukarno in October and Ghana's Nkrumah the following February. More and more, Nasser feared that an American noose was tightening around his neck. Meanwhile, Johnson began to liken the Palestinian nationalists of the newly founded al-Fatah to the Vietcong, and the now solidly pro-Soviet regime in Damascus to its counterpart in Hanoi. An exasperated Nasser let U.S.–Egypt relations tank: in Cairo, Nasserite students burned a U.S.–run library to the ground, and in Congress, LBJ signed off on a bill to slash the PL-480 wheat sales so crucial to Kennedy's overture to Cairo. "Those who do not accept our behavior," bellowed Nasser, "can go and drink from the sea."[41] When the devastating defeat of 1967 arrived, after a series of aggressive missteps by Cairo, the humiliated Nasser blamed the Arabs' thrashing in the Six Day War on an imaginary conspiracy between Israel and the United States. On the phone with a similarly embarrassed King Husayn of Jordan, Nasser asked, "Should we say the United States and Britain, or only the United States?"[42] It was a dismal ending to Kennedy's attempted rapprochement. Relations with Egypt would get worse before they got better, in the aftermath of the Yom Kippur War.

Meanwhile, the U.S.–Israel arms relationship became increasingly expansive. As the Kennedy administration gave way to the Johnson administration, the opponents of arms sales to Israel found that they were now on the defensive. The old precedent of U.S. standoffishness had been overridden. The Hawk sale had eased the way to future arms sales, rather than making them foregone conclusions. But the shift was an important one nevertheless.

With the Hawk precedent behind him, Eshkol pushed Johnson hard for tanks—which could hardly be described as strictly defensive weapons, unlike the Hawks. "Mike Feldman, who loses no time, says he's already talked to LBJ about tanks for our friends," a disgusted Komer wrote McGeorge Bundy three weeks after Kennedy's murder. "Latter seems sympathetic."[43] So, too, did the Pentagon, which ruled that Israel was lagging in armor. In 1965, after heading off several administration attempts to steer them elsewhere, the Israelis sealed a deal to buy 210 American M-48 tanks.

In 1966, Johnson agreed to let Israel buy 48 Skyhawk bombers—the first sale of U.S. warplanes. After the Six Day War, Israel found itself cut off from its traditional airplane suppliers, the French, who were furious that Eshkol had disobeyed de Gaulle's insistence that Israel not strike first. The loss of the French alternative only increased the intensity of Israeli pressure on Washington. In December 1968, as the Soviet Union's Middle East friends struggled to hide their humiliation, the Johnson administration agreed to another major sale, this time letting Israel buy 50 F-4 Phantom bombers.[44]

The U.S.–Israel arms relationship was, by the late 1960s, almost unrecognizable from the trickle it had been at the start of the Kennedy administration. This is not to say that the tap was simply cranked open. Johnson administration officials remember considerable bureaucratic opposition to Eshkol's post–Six Day War request for Phantoms.[45] But the question had shifted: the administration was asking *which* arms it should be selling to Israel, rather than asking *whether* it should be selling arms to Israel in the first place.

That still left the thorniest issue remaining from the Kennedy administration: the bomb. But the intensity had faded considerably here. The dyad of Johnson and Eshkol was considerably less quarrelsome than that of Kennedy and Ben-Gurion. Had Kennedy lived, the internal contradictions of his fuzzy 1963 arrangement with Eshkol would inevitably have been cast into sharper relief; it is hard to imagine that Kennedy's ongoing suspicions that Israel was building a nuclear weapons program in the Negev would have led to anything other than more U.S.–Israel clashes. But Johnson was much less interested in nonproliferation and much less skeptical of Eshkol's protestations of good faith, and that let Eshkol's 1963 gambit work. But it is hard not to wonder how events might have gone in Dimona if Kennedy had lived.

Johnson did not have Kennedy's fire in the belly about nonproliferation, but he was still willing to revisit the issue. In 1964, after Israel asked for five hundred new U.S. tanks to balance Nasser's Soviet-made T-54s, Badeau and Talbot decided the time was ripe to try another arms control probe—a sequel to McCloy's failed 1963 CANE mission.[46] This time, there was no need to send a special outside emissary to Cairo since Talbot would be in the region anyway in early March. Johnson approved, although Talbot did not get any farther with Nasser than had John McCloy. Still, with Johnson at the helm rather than Kennedy, the White House was more philosophical than frustrated about the futile sequel to CANE. "Current Arab-Israeli tensions are such that I see almost no chance of a successful tacit arms arrangement emerging," noted an uncharacteristically sanguine Komer.[47] As Rusk pointed out, Israel was being asked to give up something it had—its very real nuclear program—in return for something Nasser did not have—his nonexistent nuclear program.[48]

If Eshkol was less combative than Ben-Gurion, he was also suspicious of arms control. After all, in the face of sustained Nasserite hostility, why should Israel give up a major deterrent? "The potential threat of Israeli nuclear development has already served as a useful psychological weapon against the Arabs," noted one State Department study, "and the Israeli military will not wish to lose it."[49] So the more the administration pushed on arms control, the more Eshkol demanded—on a security guarantee, arms sales and aid, joint military planning, and assurances that the West Bank would remain demilitarized—to offset Israel's potential losses.

Moreover, Eshkol moved quietly ahead on Israel's nuclear program—albeit without Ben-Gurion's doggedness or penchant for confrontation. American visitors continued to keep an eye on Dimona, but they went on supervised visits rather than the inspections for which Kennedy had fought. Instead of inspections every six months, in practice Johnson settled for a quick visit once a year or so—in January 1964, January 1965, April 1966, April 1967, and June 1968.[50] The ongoing Dimona visits made their way into the daylight every now and then; on June 28, 1966, John Finney of the Washington bureau of the *New York Times*, almost certainly acting from an administration leak, reported that a quiet inspection of Dimona had "affirmed" the administration's "tentative conclusion that the plant was not being used for making atomic weapons."[51] But for all the administration's attempts to put a brave face on it, the hasty visits offered no real certainty that Washington was getting the real story about what Israel was up to at Dimona. By the time of the Six Day War, writes the nuclear historian Avner Cohen, Israel "already had a rudimentary, but operational, nuclear weapons capability."[52]

Eventually, even the Johnson administration's modest level of nuclear oversight fell away. The last Dimona visit by Americans came on July 12, 1969. By the time Richard Nixon was sworn in, the Israelis had shifted over to a de facto schedule of one brief visit per year to Dimona, pleading "domestic difficulties if the visits were to take place more frequently."[53] Instead of Kennedy's insistence on muscular, independent inspections in rough accordance with IAEA norms of oversight, the Johnson administration had wound up settling for one day-long visit per year, under the watchful eyes of the American visitors' Israeli hosts.

Israel, too, underwent a change of leadership: Eshkol died in 1969 and was replaced by Golda Meir. Kennedy and Ben-Gurion had clashed over Dimona; Johnson and Eshkol had skirted the issue; now Nixon and Meir, despite some half-hearted attempts at activism from the State Department, basically let the matter drop.[54] For all of the suspicion of the CIA and the irritation of the State Department, Johnson had not been looking for a fight over Dimona; he was willing to settle for a mutually tolerable level of duplicity. The Israelis may well have sensed this. By the end stages of the inspections dance, Israel was hardly doing all it could to hide its ongoing nuclear efforts. "Don't you be the first power to introduce nuclear weapons into the Middle East," Rusk warned the new Israeli foreign minister, Abba Eban. "No," grinned Eban, "but we won't be the second."[55]

Even in the nuclear field, then, the Johnson administration moved steadily closer to Israel's preferred position. The showdowns of 1963 were things of the past. With a deepening and widening arms relationship, up-graded diplomatic ties, a see-no-evil Dimona policy, and a new, post-1967 willingness to write off the battered Arab radicals, Washington was chart-ing a dramatically different course on Israel than it had under Eisenhower and Dulles. Moreover, on Egypt, the strains between Washington and Cairo from Suez in 1956 and the Eisenhower Doctrine interventions in 1958 had only been deepened by Yemen in 1963. Continuity ultimately tri-umphed over change in Kennedy's Egypt policy; change triumphed over continuity in Kennedy's Israel policy.

By the end of the Johnson administration, Arabs and Israelis had cho-sen their sides in the Cold War, or had had their choices made for them. Kennedy's presidency was a fluid moment in the Middle East —America's last Cold War time to fish. But from Sdeh Boqer, Ben-Gurion may well have wondered, with a smile of satisfaction, just who had hooked whom. In late 1958, Ben-Gurion had told a meeting of the Mapai Central Com-mittee that it was "the future of relations with the United States which will have the greatest bearing of all."[56] All along, Israel's founding prime minister had had his eyes on the prize. With both Israel and Egypt listen-ing, Jack Kennedy had pronounced himself ready to support any friend. The Egypt of Nasser, unlike the Egypt of Sadat, had proven too hemmed in by the Arab cold war to take the new president at his word. The Israel of Ben-Gurion and Eshkol had struggled to make use of the opening. Kennedy's willingness to support any friend was, in their eyes, a fine place to begin.

Chronology

The United States and the Arab-Israeli Conflict, 1917–1963

I: From Wilson to Kennedy

1917   Balfour Declaration; British capture Palestine from Ottomans; JFK born

1918   World War I ends

1920   Britain granted League of Nations Mandate for Palestine

1924   Ibn Saud ousts Hashimites, founds Saudi Arabia

1929   Anti-Jewish riots in Hebron and Jerusalem

1933   Hitler becomes chancellor of Germany

1936   Arab Revolt begins in Palestine; Faruq becomes king of Egypt

1937   Peel Commission proposes partitioning Palestine

1939   World War II begins; British White Paper halts Jewish immigration to Palestine; JFK visits Palestine and Egypt

1945   World War II ends; Nazis have slain six million Jews; FDR meets Ibn Saud; FDR dies, replaced by Truman

1946   Anglo-American Committee of Inquiry reports; Irgun bombs King David Hotel; JFK elected to House of Representatives

1947   U.N. General Assembly votes for partition

1948   Israel declared; War of Independence begins; Truman recognizes Israel; about 700,000 Palestinian refugees created; RFK visits Israel

1949   Arab-Israeli armistice agreements signed on Greek island of Rhodes

1951   King Abdallah of Transjordan assassinated; JFK visits Middle East

1952   Nasser's Free Officers overthrow King Faruq of Egypt; Eisenhower elected president; JFK elected to Senate

1953   Ben-Gurion resigns as Israeli prime minister, replaced by Moshe Sharett

1954   Lavon affair begins with bungled Israeli covert operation in Egypt

1955   Baghdad Pact; major Israeli raid on Gaza; Czech-Egyptian arms deal; Ben-Gurion returns to power

1956   Suez crisis

1957   Eisenhower Doctrine announced; France agrees to sell Israel a large nuclear reactor and reprocessing plant; JFK gives Algeria speech

1958   Syria and Egypt create United Arab Republic; crises in Lebanon and Jordan; coup in Iraq topples King Faysal; Israel signs Atoms for Peace reactor deal

1960   Israel's secret Dimona reactor revealed; JFK elected president

II: The Kennedy Administration

1961

Jan. 19	Eisenhower and aides warn JFK Israel is seeking nuclear arms
Jan. 20	JFK inaugurated as 35th president of the United States
Feb. 7	UAR Ambassador Kamel meets Secretary of State Rusk
Feb. 20	First Nasser letter to JFK, on the Congo crisis
March 1	First JFK letter to Nasser
April 17	Bay of Pigs landing in Cuba
May 11	JFK letters to six Arab heads of state
May 18	Two U.S. scientists visit Dimona
May 30	JFK and Ben-Gurion meet at the Waldorf-Astoria Hotel, New York
June 3	JFK-Khrushchev summit in Vienna
June 27	National Intelligence Estimate on "Nasser and the Future of Arab Nationalism"
Sept. 28	Coup in Syria; new regime leaves UAR
Nov. 3	Assistant Secretary of State Talbot visits new regime in Damascus

1962

Feb. 13	King Saud meets JFK in Washington
Mid-Feb.	State's Bowles makes three-day visit to Egypt
March	U.S. envoy Mason's economic assessment visit to Egypt
April	Egyptian Minister of Economy Kaissouni in Washington for aid talks
May	U.N. envoy Joseph Johnson in Cairo to consult on 1948 refugees
May 21–25	Israeli Deputy Defense Minister Peres in Washington to urge Hawk sale
June 21	Warmest Nasser letter to JFK
July 21	Egypt tests homegrown missiles
Aug. 7	Rusk endorses Hawk sale
Aug. 16	Warmest JFK letter to Nasser
Aug. 18–21	Feldman in Tel Aviv to announce Hawk sale and discuss refugees
Aug. 18	British Prime Minister Macmillan protests Hawk sale
Aug. 24	NEA's Strong in Alexandria to tell Nasser about Hawk decision
Aug. 27	JFK tapes White House meeting on Feldman and Strong missions
Sept. 19	Yemeni leader Imam Ahmad dies
Sept. 26	Coup in Yemen topples the monarchy; second U.S. visit to Dimona
October	Cuban missile crisis; Nasser sends 20,000 Egyptian troops to Yemen
Oct. 5	Saudi Crown Prince Faysal meets JFK in Washington
Oct. 27	Soviet SA-2 missile originally intended for Egypt downs U.S. Major Rudolf Anderson's U-2 spy plane over Cuba during missile crisis
Dec. 19	United States recognizes new regime in Yemen
Dec. 27	JFK meets Israeli Foreign Minister Meir in Palm Beach, Florida

1963

Feb. 8	Coup in Iraq ousts Qasim
March	Coup in Syria; rising influence of Ba'ath Party in Iraq and Syria
April	U.S. Air Force plan for Saudi tripwire mission excludes Jewish troops
April 3	Nasser agrees to U.S. envoy Bunker's Yemen disengagement plan

April 5   JFK meets Peres in Oval Office
April 6   Saudi Arabia's Faysal signs onto Yemen disengagement plan
April 17   Declaration by Egypt, Iraq, and Syria reconstitutes the UAR
April 21–29 Nasserite rioting creates coup scare in Jordan
May 18   JFK letter to Ben-Gurion: U.S. support for Israel "seriously jeopardized"
             by Dimona
June 10   Rep. Celler tells *New York Times* of Jewish troops in Saudi mission
June 15   JFK reiterates threat to U.S.–Israel ties in letter to Ben-Gurion
June 16   Ben-Gurion resigns; Eshkol becomes Israeli prime minister
June 27–30   U.S. envoy John McCloy meets Nasser in Cairo for arms control talks
July 2   JFK approves Operation Hard Surface, sending U.S. Air Force squadron
             to Saudi Arabia
July 4   JFK repeats Dimona warnings in first letter to Eshkol
July 11   Ambassador Badeau rebukes Nasser for using poison gas in Yemen
August   U.S. military begins training IDF on Hawks
Aug. 19   Eshkol agrees to U.S. visits to Dimona
September   Kaissouni in Washington again; Egypt offers United States the Temple of
             Dendur
Sept. 1   Nasser recognizes North Vietnam
Sept. 24   JFK signs U.S.–Soviet Nuclear Test Ban Treaty
Oct. 2   Last JFK letter to Eshkol
Oct. 19   Last JFK letter to Nasser
Nov. 7   Senate approves Gruening amendment cutting aid to UAR, with vote of
             65 to 13
Nov. 12–13   U.S.–Israel security talks, including IDF Deputy Chief of Staff Rabin
Nov. 22   JFK assassinated in Dallas, Texas

Dramatis Personae

The Kennedy Administration

In the White House:

John F. Kennedy, president
Lyndon B. Johnson, vice president
McGeorge Bundy, national security adviser
Walt W. Rostow, deputy national security adviser
Carl Kaysen, deputy national security adviser after Rostow
Robert W. Komer, NSC aide for Middle East
Theodore C. Sorensen, counsel to the president and chief speechwriter
Myer Feldman, deputy to Sorensen and in-house envoy to American Jewry

In the State Department:

Dean Rusk, secretary of state
Adlai E. Stevenson, ambassador to the United Nations
U. Alexis Johnson, undersecretary of state for political affairs
George Ball, undersecretary of state for economic affairs
Chester Bowles, president's special representative for the Third World
Phillips Talbot, assistant secretary of state for Near East affairs (NEA)
John S. Badeau, ambassador to Egypt
Walworth Barbour, ambassador to Israel
William B. Macomber, ambassador to Jordan
Parker T. Hart, ambassador to Saudi Arabia
Armin Meyer, ambassador to Lebanon
Robert Strong, NEA official
James Grant, NEA official
Talcott Seelye, NEA officer for the Arabian Peninsula
George McGhee, member of Policy Planning staff and later undersecretary of state
Roger Hilsman, director of the Intelligence and Research bureau
Ellsworth Bunker, presidential envoy on Yemen

In the Pentagon:

Robert S. McNamara, secretary of defense
Roswell Gilpatric, deputy secretary of defense
Paul H. Nitze, assistant secretary of defense for international security affairs
William P. Bundy, deputy assistant secretary for international security affairs
Maxwell Taylor, chairman, Joint Chiefs of Staff
Curtis LeMay, Air Force chief of staff

And elsewhere:

Robert F. Kennedy, attorney general
Douglas Dillon, secretary of the treasury
John McCone, director of central intelligence
John McCloy, president's adviser on arms control
Edward R. Murrow, head of the U.S. Information Agency
George McGovern, director, Food for Peace
Sargent Shriver, director, Peace Corps

Israel

David Ben-Gurion, prime minister and defense minister
Levi Eshkol, finance minister under Ben-Gurion and later prime minister
Golda Meir, foreign minister
Shimon Peres, deputy defense minister
Teddy Kollek, director general of the prime minister's office
Moshe Dayan, aide to the prime minister
Avraham Harman, ambassador to the United States
Mordechai Gazit, counselor in Washington and Harman's deputy
Yitzhak Rabin, deputy chief of staff, Israel Defense Forces
Aharon Yariv, deputy chief of intelligence, Israel Defense Forces
Ernest Bergmann, chairman, Atomic Energy Commission
Pinhas Sapir, commerce minister
Pinhas Lavon, disgraced former defense minister
Menachem Begin, Herut Party leader
Zalman Shazar, president

Egypt (United Arab Republic)

Jamal Abd al-Nasser, president
Anwar al-Sadat, vice president
Muhammad Hassanein Haykal, editor of *al-Ahram* and confidant to Nasser
Abd al-Hakim Amr, army chief of staff
Mahmud Fawzi, foreign minister
Zulfikar Sabri, deputy foreign minister
Mustafa Kamel, ambassador to Washington
Abd al-Moneim Kaissouni, minister of economy
Sami Sharaf, Nasser's aide-de-camp
King Faruq, deposed by the Free Officers' coup in 1952

Saudi Arabia

King Saud bin Abd al-Aziz bin Abd al-Rahman al-Saud
Crown Prince Faysal bin Abd al-Aziz bin Abd al-Rahman al-Saud

Yemen

Abdallah Sallal, rebel leader and prime minister
Ahmad ibn Yahya Nasir al-Din Allah, imam until his death in 1962
Muhammad al-Badr, crown prince and then imam; deposed by Sallal
Prince Hassan, royalist leader after Badr

Jordan

King Husayn ibn Talal
Wasfi Tell, prime minister

Syria

Ma'mun Kuzbari, prime minister after 1961 coup

Iraq

Abd al-Karim Qasim, prime minister after 1958
Abd al-Salam Arif, prime minister after 1963
King Faysal, deposed by 1958 coup

Lebanon

Fuad Chehab, president
Rashid Karame, prime minister

Soviet Union

Nikita Khrushchev, secretary general of the Communist Party
Andrei Gromyko, foreign minister

Great Britain

Harold Macmillan, prime minister
Lord Home, foreign secretary
Jack Profumo, secretary of state for war

France

Charles de Gaulle, president
Maurice Couve de Murville, foreign minister

The United Nations

U Thant, secretary general
Ralph Bunche, special envoy on Yemen
Joseph E. Johnson, special envoy on Palestinian refugees

The Eisenhower Administration

Dwight D. Eisenhower, president
Richard M. Nixon, vice president
John Foster Dulles, secretary of state
Chester Herter, secretary of state after Dulles
Douglas Dillon, undersecretary of state
Henry Byroade, assistant secretary of state for Near East affairs
G. Lewis Jones, assistant secretary of state for Near East affairs after Byroade
Ogden Reid, ambassador to Israel

The Truman Administration

Harry S. Truman, president
George C. Marshall, secretary of state
Dean Acheson, undersecretary of state and later secretary of state (after Marshall)
Robert Lovett, undersecretary of state to Acheson
Loy Henderson, head of State's Near East affairs division
George F. Kennan, director of policy planning at State
Dean Rusk, head of State's U.N. office
James Forrestal, secretary of defense
Clark Clifford, counsel to the president
David Niles, adviser to the president
Eddie Jacobson, friend of the president and haberdasher

The Roosevelt Administration

Franklin D. Roosevelt, president
Harry S. Truman, vice president
Henry Morgenthau, Jr., secretary of the treasury
Breckinridge Long, State Department official responsible for immigration

The Wilson Administration

Woodrow Wilson, president
Robert Lansing, secretary of state
Edward House, adviser to the president
Louis D. Brandeis, associate justice of the Supreme Court
Henry Morgenthau, ambassador to the Ottoman Empire

Notes

INTRODUCTION: A Time to Fish

1. Author conversation with Shabtai Teveth, July 30, 2001, Tel Aviv.

2. Michael Bar-Zohar, *Ben-Gurion: A Biography* (New York: Adama Books, 1986), p. 273.

3. In transliterating Arabic and Hebrew names and terms, I have usually followed academic conventions. The one major exception has been cases when I feared that pedantry might interfere with many readers' ease of comprehension. To match the documents of the day, I have therefore used "Nasser" rather than the more academic but less familiar "Nasir" or "Abd al-Nasir." (Names in documents are quoted verbatim.) To avoid confusing general readers, I have also left out diacritical marks and usually dropped the Arabic prefix "al-" after first reference.

4. A word on scope: this book focuses on American diplomacy in the Arab-Israeli theater. Such major questions as Kennedy's Iran and Iraq policies lie largely beyond its reach.

5. Author interview, Shabtai Teveth, July 30, 2001, Tel Aviv.

6. February 14, 1963, press conference, *The Kennedy Presidential Press Conferences* (New York: Earl M. Coleman Enterprises, 1978), pp. 444–45.

7. Diplomatic historians often differentiate between an outright alliance and a "special relationship"—a term that originated with U.S. relations with Great Britain but has since become commonplace in discussions of U.S.–Israel relations. This book relies on Stephen M. Walt's sensible definition of an alliance: "a formal or informal arrangement for security cooperation between two or more sovereign states." Like Walt, I think insisting on a formal treaty relationship—as in, say, NATO—is overly constraining. A special relationship, by contrast, is considerably looser. Perhaps the most useful way to think of a special relationship is as an interaction between two states, characterized by modest geopolitical assistance and warm rhetorical expressions of friendship; a special relationship falls short of a full-blown patron-client dynamic but extends beyond the level of interaction that most obviously serves both parties' narrowly defined self-interests. "Many, even all, relationships are special, George Orwell might have said, had Animal Farm been a foreign ministry," David Schoenbaum has written. "But some relationships are more special than others." This study is about one of those—about a special relationship that went deeper than boilerplate. Pace Potter Stewart, we know a special relationship when we see it, be it America's ties to Great Britain, Germany, Canada, Mexico, or Israel. Scholars

remain split on whether special relationships rest on hard or soft factors, on sharply defined realities of power or amorphously expressed aspirations of value. For our purposes, it is enough to note that whatever sort of relationship the regional pariah and the superpower had, it was special from 1948 on. Cf. Stephen M. Walt, *The Origins of Alliances* (Ithaca: Cornell University Press, 1987), p. 12; and David Schoenbaum, "More Special Than Others," *Diplomatic History*, Spring 1998, Vol. 22, No. 2, p. 274. For an important discussion that hints at the difficulties in defining such terms, cf. Yaacov Bar-Siman-Tov, "The United States and Israel since 1948: A 'Special Relationship'?" *Diplomatic History*, Spring 1998, Vol. 22, No. 2, pp. 231–62.

8. Needless to say, the source must remain anonymous.

9. David Schoenbaum, *The United States and the State of Israel* (New York: Oxford University Press, 1993), p. 79.

10. Translator's Summary, No. 33935, April 3, 1962, WHCSF, Box 60, CO 126 10-1-61/9-10-62, JFKL.

11. "The Round Freedom," talk at Rutgers University in Newark by Special Assistant to the President Harris Wofford, Jr., March 19, 1962, MH 3377/9, ISA.

12. Quoted in Alan Brinkley, *Liberalism and Its Discontents* (Cambridge: Harvard University Press, 1998), p. 214.

13. Timothy Naftali, Ernest R. May, and Philip D. Zelikow, eds., *The Presidential Recordings: John F. Kennedy—The Great Crises, Vol. II* (New York: W. W. Norton, 2001), p. 588.

14. Bar-Zohar, p. 274.

15. Barbour OH, May 22, 1981, p. 21, JFKL.

16. Comay to Harman, Nov. 5, 1963, MH 3377/6, ISA.

17. Theodore C. Sorensen, *Kennedy* (New York: Bantam, 1966), p. 20.

18. JFK letter to Nasser, May 27, 1963, State Department telegram to U.S. ambassador to Egypt John Badeau, NSF, Box 446, Robert W. Komer Papers, UAR 1/63–11/63, JFKL, italics mine.

19. "Framework and Tactics for Negotiation," undated 1963, DOSF, NEA Files, NEA/IAI, Near East Arms Initiative 1963–64, Box 1, CANE – Resumption of Near East Arms Limitation 1964, NA.

20. Sorensen, p. 329.

CHAPTER ONE: Kennedy's Inheritance

1. David Schoenbaum, *The United States and the State of Israel* (New York: Oxford University Press, 1993), p. 35.

2. Peter Grose, *Israel in the Mind of America* (New York: Knopf, 1984), p. 66.

3. Cf. Thomas J. Knock, *To End All Wars: Woodrow Wilson and the Quest for a New World Order* (Princeton: Princeton University Press, 1995).

4. Grose, p. 67.

5. Ibid., p. 70.

6. N. Gordon Levin, Jr., *Woodrow Wilson and World Politics: America's Response to War and Revolution* (New York: Oxford University Press, 1968), p. 247.

7. Ibid., p. 248.

8. Steven L. Spiegel, *The Other Arab-Israeli Conflict: Making America's Middle East Policy, from Truman to Reagan* (Chicago: University of Chicago Press, 1985), p. 11.

9. Levin, p. 248.

10. Spiegel, p. 68.

11. Ibid., p. 69.

12. Grose, p. 67.

13. Sir Isaiah Berlin, *Personal Impressions* (London: Pimlico, 1998), p. 27.

14. Warren F. Kimball, *The Juggler: Franklin Roosevelt as Wartime Statesman* (Princeton: Princeton University Press, 1991), p. 8.

15. Grose, p. 113.

16. Ibid., p. 146.

17. Ibid., p. 115.

18. Zvi Ganin, *Truman, American Jewry, and Israel, 1945–1948* (New York: Holmes & Meier, 1979), p. xiii.

19. Grose, p. 139.

20. Spiegel, p. 12.

21. Cf. Manfred Jonas, *Isolationism in America 1935–1941* (Ithaca: Cornell University Press, 1972).

22. Philip Mattar, *The Mufti of Jerusalem: Al-Hajj Amin al-Husayni and the Palestinian National Movement* (New York: Columbia University Press, 1988), p. 148.

23. David M. Kennedy, *Freedom from Fear: The American People in Depression and War, 1929–1945* (New York: Oxford University Press, 1999), p. 414.

24. Ibid., p. 415.

25. Grose, p. 127.

26. On this episode, cf. Kennedy, p. 795.

27. Kenneth Ray Bain, *The March to Zion: United States Policy and the Founding of Israel* (College Station: Texas A&M University Press, 1979), p. 15.

28. Spiegel, p. 13.

29. Grose, p. 149.

30. Spiegel, p. 13.

31. Bain, p. 26.

32. Paul F. Boller, Jr., *Presidential Anecdotes* (New York: Oxford University Press, 1981), pp. 281–82.

33. Alonzo L. Hamby, *Man of the People: A Life of Harry S. Truman* (New York: Oxford University Press, 1995), p. 405.

34. Ibid., p. 412.

35. Walter Isaacson and Evan Thomas, *The Wise Men: Six Friends and the World They Made* (New York: Touchstone, 1988), p. 452.

36. Michael J. Cohen, *Truman and Israel* (Berkeley: University of California Press, 1990), p. 279.

37. Spiegel, p. 20.

38. Cohen, *Truman and Israel*, p. 276.

39. Spiegel, p. 20.

40. David McCullough, *Truman* (New York: Touchstone, 1992), p. 599.

41. Ganin, p. xvi.

42. Spiegel, p. 20.

43. Cohen, *Truman and Israel*, p. 134.

44. Cited in Harry S. Truman, *Memoirs, Volume Two: Years of Trial and Hope* (Garden City, NY: Doubleday, 1956), p. 137.

45. Ibid., p. 278.

46. Bain, p. xv.

47. Dean Acheson, *Present at the Creation: My Years in the State Department* (New York: W.W. Norton, 1969), p. 181. A more likely explanation was what Paul Kennedy has called imperial overstretch. With his nation battered and broke after World War II, Attlee told Parliament just six days later that Britain was also withdrawing from India; cf. Howard M. Sachar, *A History of Israel: From the Rise of Zionism to Our Time* (New York: Knopf, 1989), p. 276.

48. Walter Laqueur and Barry Rubin, eds., *The Israel-Arab Reader: A Documentary History of the Middle East Conflict* (New York: Penguin, 1987), p. 108.

49. Spiegel, p. 26.

50. Ibid., p. 56.

51. Benny Morris, *The Birth of the Palestinian Refugee Problem, 1947–1949* (Cambridge: Cambridge University Press, 1989), p. 7.

52. Hamby, p. 412.

53. Ibid.

54. Truman, p. 164.

55. Robert Donovan, *Crisis and Conflict: The Presidency of Harry S. Truman, 1945–1948* (New York: W.W. Norton, 1977), p. 377–79.

56. Morris, p. 7.

57. Spiegel, p. 35.

58. Clifford, *Counsel to the President: A Memoir* (New York: Random House, 1991), p. 7. The following description of the May 12 showdown, in all its irresistible detail, draws heavily on Clifford's version, but his dialogue is largely corroborated by Marshall's own version of the meeting for State's files—a noteworthy exception to the old Foggy Bottom rule that one should never come off second best in one's own memcon.

59. Isaacson and Thomas, p. 390.

60. Clifford, p. 12.

61. Ibid.

62. Ibid.

63. Isaacson and Thomas, p. 452. Marshall's own version of the meeting rendered his intervention thus: "I remarked to the President that, speaking objectively, I could not help but think that suggestions made by Mr. Clifford were wrong. I thought that to adopt these suggestions would have precisely the opposite effect from that intended by Mr. Clifford. The transparent dodge to win a few votes would not in fact achieve this purpose. The great dignity of the office of the President would be seriously diminished. The counsel offered by Mr. Clifford was based on domestic political considerations, while the problem which confronted us was international. I said bluntly that if the President were to follow Mr. Clifford's advice and if in the elections I were to vote, I would vote against the President." Cited in Clifford, pp. 13–14.

64. McCullough, p. 617.

65. Clifford, p. 15.

66. Melvyn P. Leffler, *A Preponderance of Power: National Security, the Truman Administration, and the Cold War* (Stanford: Stanford University Press, 1992), p. 30.

67. James M. Goldgeier, *Not Whether But When: The U.S. Decision to Enlarge NATO* (Washington: Brookings Institution Press, 1999), p. 9.

68. Clifford, p. 19.

69. Michael J. Cohen, *Palestine and the Great Powers, 1945–1948* (Princeton: Princeton University Press, 1982), p. 385.

70. Cohen, *Palestine and the Great Powers*, p. 387.

71. McCullough, p. 618.

72. Ibid., p. 620.

73. Forrest C. Pogue, *George C. Marshall: Statesman, 1945–1959* (New York: Penguin, 1989), p. 373.

74. Ehud Barak made roughly the same offer at the abortive Camp David summit in 2000.

75. Spiegel, p. 46.

76. Grose, p. 300.

77. Zachary Karabell, *The Last Campaign: How Harry Truman Won the 1948 Election* (New York: Knopf, 2000), p. 5.

78. Cohen, *Palestine and the Great Powers*, p. 355.

79. Dan Kurzman, *Ben-Gurion: Prophet of Fire* (New York: Simon and Schuster, 1983), p. 416.

80. Selwyn Ilan Troen and Moshe Shemesh, *The Suez-Sinai Crisis, 1956: Retrospective and Reappraisal* (New York: Columbia University Press, 1990), p. 193.

81. Spiegel, p. 50.

82. Robert H. Ferrell, ed., *The Eisenhower Diaries* (New York: Norton, 1981), p. 318.

83. David Reynolds, *One World Divisible: A Global History Since 1945* (New York: Norton, 2000), p. 168.

84. John Lewis Gaddis, *Strategies of Containment: A Critical Appraisal of Postwar American National Security Policy* (New York: Oxford University Press, 1982), p. 129.

85. Fred I. Greenstein, *The Hidden-Hand Presidency: Eisenhower as Leader* (New York: Basic Books, 1982), p. 57.

86. On the New Look, see Gaddis, pp. 127–97.

87. If Dulles's hyperbole suggested that the hallmark of the New Look was *futuwwa*—the traditional set of Arabic virtues associated with young men, including brashness, courage, and impetuosity—then Ike's stewardship showed that the New Look was actually based on *muruwwa*—the virtues of older men, including sagacity, prudence, restraint, and the knowledge of when to refrain from the use of force.

88. Gaddis, p. 152.

89. The phrase is Melvyn Leffler's.

90. Gaddis, p. 153.

91. Spiegel, p. 51.

92. Donald Neff, *Warriors at Suez: Eisenhower Takes America into the Middle East* (New York: Simon & Schuster, 1981), p. 386.

93. Baker's unprintable quote elicited the memorable headline "Same to You, Buddy" from the pro-Israel *The New Republic*.

94. Spiegel, p. 57.

95. Neff, p. 44.

96. Ibid., p. 45.

97. Ibid., p. 44.

98. Ibid., p. 43.

99. Spiegel, p. 55.

100. In one of the more original and provocative recent additions to the literature, Steven Z. Freiberger has argued that the United States actively sought to replace Britain as the main imperial power in the Middle East, even at the expense of considerable damage to the Anglo-American partnership. But as scholars, including Peter L. Hahn, one of the period's most judicious students, have noted, responsibility for the region was a cup that Washington would just as soon have let pass. The deepening involvement of the late Eisenhower years, especially 1958, would not have been necessary had Britain not suffered the self-inflicted wound of Suez. Britain's Middle East presence, in a word, was a useful Cold War asset, and there is no particular reason to think Eisenhower wanted to fritter it away. See Steven Z. Freiberger, *Dawn Over Suez: The Rise of American Power in the Middle East, 1953–1957* (Chicago: Ivan R. Dee, 1992).

101. Mohamed H. Heikal, *Cutting the Lion's Tail: Suez Through Egyptian Eyes* (London: Andre Deutsch, 1986), p. 53.

102. Ibid., p. 66.

103. Ibid.

104. Spiegel, p. 67.

105. Working Paper No. 2, Airlie House Discussions, June 12–14, 1964, DOSF, NEA Files, NEA/IAI, Near East Arms Initiative, Box 1, Project Alpha, NA.

106. Schoenbaum, p. 101.

107. For Eisenhower's thoughts on the Anderson shuttle, cf. Ferrell, p. 308.

108. Ray Takeyh, *The Origins of the Eisenhower Doctrine: The US, Britain and Nasser's Egypt, 1953–57* (New York: St. Martin's Press, 2000), p. 156.

109. Cf. Aleksandr Fursenko and Timothy Naftali, "Frankly, We Don't Want You to Give a Dam: Khrushchev and Nasser's Aswan High Dam Project," Russian Academy of Sciences, June 8, 2000. I'm particularly grateful to Tim Naftali for his insights about Nasser and the Kremlin, which are drawn from an impressive excavation of heretofore classified Soviet documents.

110. Peter L. Hahn, *The United States, Great Britain, and Egypt, 1945–1956: Strategy and Diplomacy in the Early Cold War* (Chapel Hill: University of North Carolina Press, 1991), p. 245.

111. Heikal, p. 115.

112. Townsend Hoopes, *The Devil and John Foster Dulles* (Boston: Atlantic Monthly Press, 1973), p. 347.

113. Keith Kyle, *Suez* (New York: St. Martin's Press, 1991), p. 257.

114. Maurice Vaïsse, "France and the Suez Crisis," in Wm. Roger Louis and Roger Owen, eds., *Suez 1956: The Crisis and its Consequences* (Oxford: Clarendon Press, 1991), p. 134.

115. Vaïsse, p. 143.

116. Robert A. Divine, *Eisenhower and the Cold War* (New York: Oxford University Press, 1981), p. 83.

117. Henry A. Kissinger, *Diplomacy* (New York: Simon & Schuster, 1994), p. 531.

118. Mordechai Bar-On, "David Ben-Gurion and the Sèvres Collusion," in Louis and Owen, p. 153.

119. Kyle, p. 256.

120. Peter L. Hahn, "Suez," *Reviews in American History*, Vol. 20, No. 4, Dec. 1992, p. 570.

121. Spiegel, p. 74.

122. Herbert S. Parmet, *Eisenhower and the American Crusades* (New York: Macmillan, 1972), p. 473.

123. Isaacson and Thomas, p. 572.

124. Spiegel, p. 75.

125. Diane B. Kunz, "The Importance of Having Money: The Economic Diplomacy of the Suez Crisis," in Louis and Owen, p. 215.

126. Ibid., p. 85.

127. Divine, p. 85.

128. Anthony Nutting, *No End of a Lesson: The Story of Suez* (New York: Clarkson N. Potter, Inc., 1967), p. 94.

129. Divine, p. 88.

130. Schoenbaum, p. 115.

131. Parmet, p. 475.

132. Ibid., p. 485.

133. Neff, p. 433.

134. Schoenbaum, p. 122.

135. Bernard Reich, ed., *An Historical Encyclopedia of the Arab-Israeli Conflict* (Westport: Greenwood Press, 1996), p. 145.

136. Spiegel, p. 87.

137. Kenneth M. Pollack, *The Threatening Storm: The Case for Invading Iraq* (New York: Random House, 2002), p. 8.

138. Itamar Rabinovich, *The War for Lebanon, 1970–1985* (Ithaca: Cornell University Press, 1989), p. 28.

139. Spiegel, p. 89.

140. Isaac Alteras, *Eisenhower and Israel: U.S.–Israeli Relations, 1953–1960* (Gainesville: University Press of Florida, 1993), p. 311.

141. Ben-Gurion to Dulles, Aug. 5, 1958, MH 3377/9, ISA.

142. Cf. Thomas L. Friedman, "Iraq Without Saddam," *New York Times*, September 1, 2002.

143. Peter L. Hahn, "Special Relationships," *Diplomatic History*, Vol. 22, No. 2 (Spring 1998), p. 268.

144. For a fascinating alternative perspective, cf. Abraham Ben-Zvi, *Decade of Transition: Eisenhower, Kennedy, and the Origins of the American-Israeli Alliance* (New York: Columbia University Press, 1998).

145. Barbour OH, May 22, 1981, p. 30, JFKL.

146. Ben-Zvi, p. 73.

C H A P T E R   T W O : The Making of the President

1. John Lukacs, *The Duel: The Eighty-Day Struggle Between Churchill and Hitler* (New Haven: Yale University Press, 1990), p. 74.

2. *John F. Kennedy on Israel, Zionism and Jewish Issues* (New York: Herzl Press for the Zionist Organization of America, 1965), p. 12.

3. JFK letter to Joseph Kennedy, undated 1939, POF, Box 135, JFKL.

4. On the young Bobby's trip to Palestine, cf. RFK Papers, Pre-Administration Personal Files, Trips, Box 24, Palestine 1948, JFKL; and Arthur M. Schlesinger, Jr., *Robert Kennedy and His Times* (New York: Ballantine, 1978), pp. 74–77.

5. Sirhan was born in March 1944 in Jerusalem. His family had a momentous time of the first two Arab-Israeli wars: in 1948, they fled the fighting, and in 1956, when Sirhan was 12, his family were among some two thousand Palestinian Arabs granted special visas by the Eisenhower administration. Sirhan's apologists have tried to portray RFK's murder as a politically motivated act. But the assassin's diary entries, which feature rantings and repetitions aplenty but no mention of Kennedy's support for Israel, offer clear evidence of serious mental imbalance rather than serious political zealotry. For the dreary details, with the predictable whiff of conspiracy theory, cf. Godfrey Jansen, *Why Robert Kennedy Was Killed: The Story of Two Victims* (New York: The Third Press, 1970) and William Klaber and Philip H. Melanson, *Shadow Play: The Murder of Robert F. Kennedy, the Trial of Sirhan Sirhan, and the Failure of American Justice* (New York: St. Martin's Press, 1997).

6. Schlesinger, p. 76.

7. JFK Personal Papers, 1951 Travel Journal, Box 1, Book 2, Oct.–Nov. 1951, JFKL.

8. Ibid., p. 15.

9. Ibid., p. 17.

10. Ibid., p. 19.

11. Ibid., p. 21.

12. Ibid., p. 23.

13. Ibid., p. 30.

14. Ibid., p. 31. Ben-Gurion's diary makes no mention of the dinner; a photograph of the evening is found at Ben-Gurion House in Tel Aviv.

15. Ibid., pp. 33–34.

16. Radio Report on Trip to Middle and Far East, Nov. 14, 1951, POF, Box 135, JFKL.

17. *John F. Kennedy on Israel, Zionism and Jewish Issues,* p. 11.

18. Theodore C. Sorensen, remarks, April 5, 2001, American Jewish Historical Society, New York.

19. John F. Kennedy, *Profiles in Courage* (New York: Perennial Classics, 2000), pp. 193–205.

20. Yossi Melman and Dan Raviv, *Friends in Deed: Inside the U.S.–Israel Alliance* (New York: Hyperion, 1994), p. 108.

21. *John F. Kennedy on Israel, Zionism and Jewish Issues,* p. 15.

22. Douglas Little, "From Even-Handed to Empty-Handed: Seeking Order in the Middle East," in Thomas G. Paterson, ed., *Kennedy's Quest for Victory: American Foreign Policy, 1961–1963* (New York: Oxford University Press, 1989), p. 158.

23. Author conversation with Harris Wofford, Council on Foreign Relations, Dec. 13, 2000.

24. Abba Eban, *Personal Witness: Israel Through My Eyes* (New York: G. P. Putnam's Sons, 1992), p. 323.

25. Theodore C. Sorensen, *Kennedy* (New York: Bantam, 1966), p. 72.

26. Ibid., p. 161.

27. JFK letter to Goldstein, Aug. 10, 1960, DOSF, NEA Files, Lot File 62D435, Box 3, Democratic and Republican Platforms, NA.

28. Stephen D. Isaacs, *Jews and American Politics* (Garden City, NY: Doubleday, 1974), p. 144.

29. Theodore H. White, *The Making of the President 1960* (New York: Atheneum Publishers, 1961), p. 330.

30. Howard M. Sachar, *A History of the Jews in America* (New York: Vintage Books, 1992), p. 730.

31. At that point in the campaign, the speechwriter would almost certainly have been Sorensen, with substantial help from Richard Goodwin and input from the Washington office, whose staff included Feldman. Sorensen does not remember who wrote the phrase, but it certainly sounds like him; author conversation with Sorensen, May 18, 2001.

32. JFK speech to ZOA, Senate office press release, Aug. 26, 1960, DOSF, NEA Files, Lot File 62D435, Box 3, Democratic and Republican Platforms, NA.

33. Sorensen remarks, April 5, 2001, American Jewish Historical Society, New York.

34. Sorensen, *Kennedy,* p. 283.

35. On the trial, cf. Hannah Arendt, *Eichmann in Jerusalem: A Report on the Banality of Evil* (New York: Penguin Books, 1977).

36. Feldman OH, July 29, 1967, p. 514, JFKL. The State Department found it even harder to empathize; in declining Israel's invitation to have U.S. embassy officials attend any sessions of the trial, NEA's Armin Meyer sneered that "we should not participate in a spectacle of this type" and told the interim chargé d'affaires in Tel Aviv to claim, falsely, that the embassy did not have the staff to spare; cf. Meyer to Jones, Feb. 13, 1961, DOSF, NEA Files, Lot File 62D435, Box 5, Eichmann Trial, NA.

37. Richard Reeves, *President Kennedy: Profile of Power* (New York: Touchstone, 1993), p. 144. Reeves's source is Charlie Bartlett, a Washington journalist and old JFK friend who repeatedly discussed such matters with the president. The remark does not appear in the Waldorf meeting memcon. Talbot, who attended the Waldorf parley, does not remember Kennedy's making any such comment but was told by the Kennedy Library oral history team that the episode occurred during a 15-minute interlude when the leaders were alone.

38. Sachar, p. 730.

39. Michael Bar-Zohar, *Ben-Gurion: A Biography* (New York: Adama Books, 1986), p. 274.

40. Reeves, p. 144.

41. Bar-Zohar, p. 274.

42. Phillips Talbot OH, Dec. 5, 1964, p. 24, JFKL.

43. Robert D. Kaplan, *The Arabists: The Romance of an American Elite* (New York: The Free Press, 1995), p. 7.

44. Harry S. Truman, *Memoirs, Volume Two: Years of Trial and Hope* (Garden City, NY: Doubleday, 1956), p. 164. Loy Henderson was a particular target of suspicion.

45. Meyer letter to Bundy, July 2, 1962, DOSF, NEA Files, Lot File 62D435, Box 6, Memoranda to White House, NA. He meant AIPAC's I. L. Kenen.

46. Seymour M. Hersh, *The Samson Option: Israel's Nuclear Arsenal and American Foreign Policy* (New York: Random House, 1991), p. 96.

47. Memcon: Eisenhower meeting with members of the Conference of Major National Jewish Organizations, Sept. 20, 1960, *FRUS*, 1958–60, Vol. 13, pp. 369–72.

48. Memcon: Eisenhower meeting with Nasser, Sept. 26, 1960, *FRUS*, 1958–60, Vol. 13, pp. 600–607.

49. Sorensen, *Kennedy*, p. 199. As David Greenberg points out, the Nixopedia was a sequel to the "Ikelopedia," which made for a better pun.

50. Isaacs, p. 3.

51. Komer OH, December 22, 1969, pp. 81–82.

52. Talbot OH, Dec. 5, 1964, p. 26, JFKL.

53. Hersh, p. 100. Hersh cites an oral history interview with RFK at the Kennedy Library as his source.

54. Minutes, JFK meeting with Ben-Gurion, May 30, 1961, MH 3294/28, ISA.

55. Notes of meeting, Aug. 14, 1962, *FRUS*, 1961–63, Vol. 18, pp. 59–60.

56. Badeau OH, Feb. 25, 1969, p. 3, JFKL.

57. Sachar, p. 729.

58. On the evolution of U.S. aid to the Middle East, cf. Scott B. Lasensky, "Paying for Peace," Council on Foreign Relations, forthcoming 2003.

59. Blaustein letter to JFK, May 23, 1961, WHCSF, Box 60, CO 126 Israel 1-1-61/8-31-61, JFKL, italics mine.

60. David Halberstam, *The Best and the Brightest* (New York: Ballantine, 1992), p. 31.

61. Spiegel, p. 101.

62. Phillips Talbot OH, Dec. 5, 1964, JFKL, p. 3.

63. Chester Bowles OH, Feb. 2, 1965, p. 84, JFKL.

64. William B. Macomber OH, Feb. 14, 1969, p. 1, JFKL.

65. Ibid., p. 18.

66. Mordechai Gazit, *President Kennedy's Policy Toward the Arab States and Israel: Analysis and Documents* (Tel Aviv: Shiloah Center for Middle Eastern and African Studies, 1983), p. 16.

67. John S. Badeau, *The Middle East Remembered* (Washington: Middle East Institute, 1983), p. 174.

68. Heikal, *The Cairo Documents: The Inside Story of Nasser and His Relationship with World Leaders, Rebels, and Statesmen* (Garden City, NY: Doubleday, 1973), p. 201.

69. Halberstam, p. 61.

70. George Lenczowski, *American Presidents and the Middle East* (Durham: Duke University Press, 1990), p. 73.

71. Heikal, p. 192.

72. Even Sorensen could not resist noting this one; cf. *Kennedy*, p. 24.

73. William B. Macomber OH, Feb. 14, 1969, p. 20, JFKL.

74. David Halberstam, *The Unfinished Odyssey of Robert Kennedy* (New York: Random House, 1968), p. 23.

CHAPTER THREE: Uncle Sam and Mister Big

1. Josh Gerstein, "Float and Move: Clinton Does the Rounds in New York City," ABCNews.com, September 8, 2000.

2. The Temple was formally offered to the United States by Egyptian Ambassador Mustafa Kamel in a September 18, 1963, meeting in Washington with Assistant Secretary of State for Near East Affairs Phillips Talbot; cf. Rusk memo to Badeau, Sept. 19, 1963, NSF, Box 169, UAR General, JFKL.

3. Tarek Atia, "Exhibition Overdrive," *Al-Ahram Weekly*, September 16–22, 1999.

4. Thomas J. Noer, "New Frontiers and Old Priorities in Africa," in Thomas G. Paterson, ed., *Kennedy's Quest for Victory: American Foreign Policy, 1961–1963* (New York: Oxford University Press, 1989), p. 255.

5. The idea of an "Arab cold war" is Malcolm Kerr's.

6. Kennedy Statements on Israel, DOSF, NEA Files, Lot File 62D435, Box 3, Democratic and Republic Platforms, NA. The translation is by the U.S. government's Foreign Broadcast Information Service (FBIS).

7. Mohamed Hassanein Heikal, *The Cairo Documents: The Inside Story of Nasser and His Relationship with World Leaders, Rebels, and Statesmen* (Garden City, NY: Doubleday, 1973), p. 189.

8. Ibid., p. 190.

9. "Highlights of 1960 Democratic Platform," *Washington Post*, July 13, 1960, p. A5.

10. "News of the United Arab Republic," August 1960, DOSF, NEA Files, Lot File 62D435, Box 3, Democratic and Republic Platforms, NA.

11. Jones memo to Herter, July 6, 1960, DOSF, Records of the UAR Affairs Desk, Box 2, UAR-Kennedy, NA.

12. Thacher memo to Jones, Aug. 26, 1960, DOSF, NEA Files, Lot File 62D435, Box 3, Democratic and Republican Platforms, NA.

13. Meyer letter to "Nick" [Thacher], Aug. 28, 1960, DOSF, NEA Files, Lot 62D435, Box 3, Democratic and Republican Platforms, NA.

14. Komer memo to Bromley Smith, Dec. 27, 1961, NSF, Box 445, Komer Papers, UAR 1961–1962, White House Memoranda, JFKL.

15. On the Congo crisis, cf. Noer, pp. 261–69.

16. Reinhardt telegram to Rusk, Feb. 21, 1961, NSF, Box 169, UAR, Nasser Correspondence, JFKL.

17. Bowles memo to JFK, Feb. 27, 1961, NSF, Box 169, UAR, Nasser Correspondence, JFKL.

18. Rusk telegram to Reinhardt, March 1, 1961, NSF, Box 169, UAR, Nasser Correspondence, JFKL.

19. G. McMurtrie Godley to Governor Williams, Dec. 15, 1963, DOSF, NEA Files, Lot 62D435, Box 6, Correspondence, Assistant Secretary of State for Near East Affairs, NA.

20. Jernegan to Talbot, Dec. 17, 1963, DOSF, NEA Files, Lot 62D435, Box 6, Correspondence, Assistant Secretary of State for Near East Affairs, NA.

21. Nasser telegram to JFK, March 2, 1961, NSF, Box 169, UAR, Nasser Correspondence, JFKL.

22. JFK letter to Nasser, April 17, 1961, NSF, Box 169, UAR, Nasser Correspondence, JFKL.

23. Bowles memo to JFK, April 27, 1961, NSF, Box 169, UAR, Nasser Correspondence, JFKL.

24. JFK letter to Nasser, May 3, 1961, NSF, Box 169, UAR, Nasser Correspondence, JFKL.

25. Nasser letter to JFK, May 18, 1961, NSF, Box 445, Komer Papers, UAR 1961–62, Folder 4, JFKL. Walt Rostow remembers this exchange as being much warmer; he called Nasser's response "a quite remarkable letter . . . expressing respect for the way the President handled" the Bay of Pigs (Walt W. Rostow OH, April 11, 1964, p. 59, JFKL).

26. Conor Cruise O'Brien, *The Siege: The Saga of Israel and Zionism* (New York: Simon & Schuster, 1986), p. 16.

27. Robert W. Komer OH, July 16, 1964, p. 2, JFKL.

28. "Fight in Congress Foreseen on 'Nullified' Clause against Arab Blockade," JTA report, July 25, 1961, FM 3293/35, ISA.

29. Rusk telegram to Reinhardt, Feb. 8, 1961, *FRUS*, 1961–63, Vol. 17, pp. 18–20.

30. For JFK's preparations for the meeting, see Rusk memo to JFK, May 5, 1960, DOSF, NEA Files, Lot File 62 D435, Box 4, 1961-Chron White House Correspondence, NA.

31. Komer OH, July 16, 1964, p. 4, JFKL.

32. Bowles telegram to Badeau, May 11, 1961, NSF, Box 445, Robert W. Komer Files, UAR 1961–1962 (Folder 4), JFKL.

33. Komer OH, July 16, 1964, p. 5, JFKL.

34. Nasser telegram to JFK, May 6, 1961, NSF, Box 169, UAR, Nasser Correspondence, JFKL.

35. Battle memo to Dungan, May 11, 1961, NSF, Box 169, UAR, Nasser Correspondence, JFKL.

36. Feldman memo to JFK, May 26, 1961, *FRUS*, 1961–63, Vol. 17, p. 131.

37. Memcon: JFK meeting with Ben-Gurion, May 30, 1961, NSF, Box 118, Israel, General, JFKL.

38. JFK memo to Bundy, July 10, 1961, *FRUS*, 1961–63, Vol. 17, p. 183.

39. Rusk memo to JFK, July 13, 1961, *FRUS*, 1961–63, Vol. 17, pp. 187–93.

40. NIE 36-61, June 27, 1961, *FRUS*, 1961–63, Vol. 17, pp. 164–66.

41. Komer memo to Rostow, June 30, 1961, NSF, Box 445, Komer Papers, UAR 1961–1962, White House Memoranda, JFKL.

42. On Nasser, Qasim, and Khrushchev, cf. Fawaz A. Gerges, *The Superpowers and the Middle East: Regional and International Politics, 1955–1967* (Boulder: Westview Press, 1994), pp. 125–28.

43. "The Camel Driver," *Time*, March 29, 1963, p. 24.

44. Komer OH, July 16, 1964, p. 5, JFKL.

45. Unsigned White House memo to Senator Fulbright, "Extract from Kennedy-Khrushchev talks in Vienna," undated, NSF, Box 169, UAR, Nasser Correspondence, JFKL.

46. Humphrey memo to JFK, Oct. 23, 1961, NSF, Box 445, Komer files, UAR 1961–1962 (Folder 4), JFKL. The voluble senator, one of JFK's rivals in the 1960 primaries, sent the administration about 50 pages of reflections on his trip.

47. Nasser's reply is summarized and quoted in Rusk circular, Sept. 7, 1961, NSF, Box 169, UAR, Nasser Correspondence, JFKL.

48. Battle memo to Bundy, Aug. 30, 1961, NSF, Box 169, United Arab Republic, Nasser Correspondence, JFKL.

49. Nasser letter to JFK (State Department translation), Aug. 22, 1961, President's Office File (POF), Box 127, UAR Security 1961, JFKL.

50. 1961 was no match for 1967, of course.

51. George Lenczowski, *American Presidents and the Middle East* (Durham: Duke University Press, 1990), p. 77.

52. Memorandum for the record, Sept. 28, 1961, *FRUS*, 1961–63, Vol. 17, pp. 259–61.

53. Komer memo to Bundy, Sept. 28, 1961, *FRUS*, 1961–63, Vol. 17, pp. 261–62.

54. Ibid.

55. Bowles telegram to Macomber, Sept. 28, 1961, *FRUS*, 1961–63, Vol. 17, pp. 262–64.

56. Ibid., p. 263.

57. Bowles telegram to Macomber, Sept. 29, 1961, *FRUS*, 1961–63, Vol. 17, p. 267.

58. Battle memo to Bundy, Sept. 30, 1961, *FRUS*, 1961–63, Vol. 17, pp. 268–71.

59. Komer memo to Bundy and Rostow, Sept. 30, 1961, *FRUS*, 1961–63, Vol. 17, pp. 272–73.

60. Heikal, pp. 204–5.

61. Rusk circular telegram, Oct. 2, 1961, *FRUS*, 1961–63, Vol. 17, pp. 277–79.

62. Macomber telegram to State, Oct. 1, 1961, *FRUS*, 1961–63, Vol. 17, pp. 273–76.

63. Rusk circular telegram, Oct. 3, 1961, *FRUS*, 1961–63, Vol. 17, pp. 279–80.

64. Rusk telegram to Badeau, Oct. 3, 1961, *FRUS*, 1961–63, Vol. 17, p. 281.

65. *FRUS*, 1961–63, Vol. 17, p. 290.

66. Rusk memo to JFK, Oct. 7, 1961, *FRUS*, 1961–63, Vol. 17, pp. 289–90.

67. *FRUS*, 1961–63, Vol. 17, p. 290.

68. Talbot memo to Strong, Nov. 3, 1961, DOSF, NEA Files, Lot File 63D33, Damascus, NA.

69. Komer OH, July 16, 1964, p. 5, JFKL.

70. Hilsman memo to Rusk, Oct. 27, 1961, NSF, Box 445, Komer Papers, UAR 1961–62 (Folder 4), JFKL.

71. INR Research Memorandum, Oct. 30, 1961, RNA-8, "The Outlook for Nasser," DOSF, NEA Files, Lot 62D435, Box 4, NA.

72. National Security Action Memorandum No. 105, Oct. 16, 1961, DOSF, NEA Files, Lot File 62D435, Box 4, Cairo 1961, NA.

73. *FRUS*, 1961–63, Vol. 17, p. 303.

74. John S. Badeau, *The Middle East Remembered* (Washington: Middle East Institute, 1983), p. 184.

75. Badeau, p. 197. One wonders whether the senator might have been Alaska's Ernest Gruening, who actually visited Cairo before the 1963 aid debate.

76. Badeau airgram to State, "United States Objectives in the United Arab Republic," May 18, 1963, NSF, Box 446, Komer Papers, UAR 1/63–11/63, JFKL.

77. Heikal, pp. 191–92.

78. William S. Gaud memo to Hollis B. Chenery, April 25, 1963, NSF, Box 446, Komer Papers, UAR 1/63–11/63, JFKL.

79. Quoted in George Liska, *The New Statecraft: Foreign Aid in American Foreign Policy* (Chicago: University of Chicago Press, 1960), p. ix.

80. David Schoenbaum, *The United States and the State of Israel* (New York: Oxford University Press, 1993), p. 135.

81. Gaud memo to Chenery, April 25, 1963, NSF, Box 446, Komer Papers, UAR 1/63–11/63, JFKL.

82. Talbot memo to McGhee, May 30, 1961, *FRUS*, 1961–63, Vol. 17, pp. 142–45.

83. Komer memo to Rostow, June 2, 1961, NSF, Box 445, Komer Papers, UAR 1961–1962, White House Memoranda, JFKL.

84. Rostow to McGhee, June 6, 1961, NSF, Box 445, Komer Papers, UAR 1961–1962 (Folder 4), JFKL. India had a three-year PL-480 deal, which Talbot called normal; cf. Talbot OH, Aug. 13, 1970, p. 40, JFKL.

85. *FRUS*, 1961–63, Vol. 17, p. 156. Throughout the fall of 1961, the administration also toyed with the idea of sending an expert American consultant to advise the Egyptians on their overall economic strategy. At the same time, it began working on a financial stabilization program, with International Monetary Fund (IMF) assistance. If that went well, Washington would consider setting up an international consortium to help develop the UAR—a pet idea of Rostow's.

86. Memcon: Talbot meeting with Kamel, Dec. 1, 1961, DOSF, NEA Files, Lot File 62 D435, Box 4, 1961 - Chron memorandum of conversation, NA.

87. Komer memo to JFK, Dec. 8, 1961, NSF, Box 445, Komer Papers, UAR 1961–1962, White House Memoranda, JFKL.

88. Douglas Little, "The New Frontier on the Nile," *Journal of American History*, Vol. 25, No. 2 (Sept. 1988), p. 509.

89. Komer memo to JFK, Jan. 15, 1962, NSF, Box 445, Komer Papers, UAR 1961–1962, White House Memoranda, JFKL.

90. Rusk memo to JFK, Jan. 20, 1962, DOSF, NEA Files, Lot File 62 D435, Box 6, Memoranda to the White House, NA.

91. Ball memo to JFK, Jan. 31, 1962, NSF, Box 169, UAR, Proposed Nasser Visit, JFKL.

92. Memcon: JFK–King Saud meeting, Feb. 13, 1962, *FRUS*, 1961–63, Vol. 17, p. 471. With more wishful thinking than evidence, Saud added that Nasser's days "appeared to be numbered."

93. Heikal, p. 206.

94. Feldman memo to Komer, Jan. 17, 1962, NSF, Box 445, Komer Papers, UAR 1961–62 (Folder 3), JFKL.

95. The observation was relayed in Komer memo to JFK, Feb. 15, 1962, NSF, Box 445, Komer Papers, UAR 1961–1962, White House Memoranda, JFKL.

96. Bowles telegram to State, Feb. 19, 1962, *FRUS*, 1961–63, Vol. 17, pp. 478–79.

97. Bowles telegram to State, Feb. 21, 1962, POF, Box 127, UAR Security 1962, JFKL.

98. Badeau telegram to Rusk, Feb. 25, 1962, NSF, Box 169, United Arab Republic, Proposed Nasser Visit, JFKL.

99. March 28, 1962, SNIE 36.1-62, *FRUS*, 1961–63, Vol. 17, pp. 549–50.

100. Komer memo to Bundy, Feb. 20, 1962, NSF, Box 445, Komer Papers, UAR 1961–62 (Folder 2), JFKL.

101. Murrow memo to JFK, Feb. 27, 1962, DOSF, NEA Files, Lot File 62 D435, Box 6, Cairo, NA.

102. Komer memo to JFK, Feb. 28, 1962, POF, Box 127, UAR Security 1962 file, JFKL.

103. Badeau letter to Talbot, March 21, 1962, DOSF, NEA Files, Lot File 62 D435, Box 6, Cairo, NA.

104. For one example of McGovern's interest in the UAR, see McGovern memo to Bundy, Jan. 25, 1962, NSF, Box 445, Komer Papers, UAR 1961–62, Folder 3, JFKL.

105. Report on Mission to the United Arab Republic (by Mason), undated, 1962, POF, Box 127, UAR Security 1962 file, JFKL.

106. Memcon: follow-up meeting between Rusk and Kaissouni, April 26, 1962, NSF, Box 445, Komer Papers, UAR 1961–1962 (Folder 2), JFKL. Egypt drew the line at contemplating aid from France, however.

107. State paper, "WHITHER UNITED STATES–UNITED ARAB REPUBLIC RELATIONS," May 24, 1962, NSF, Box 445, Komer Papers, UAR 1961–1962 (Folder 2), JFKL.

108. Brubeck memo to Bundy, June 4, 1962, *FRUS*, 1961–63, Vol. 17, pp. 706–07.

109. Harold Saunders (NSC aide) memo to Bundy, June 27, 1962, *FRUS*, 1961–63, Vol. 17, p. 759.

110. Thacher (now chargé d'affaires in Jidda) to State, Sept. 26, 1962, NSF, Box 169, UAR, Nasser Correspondence, JFKL.

111. *FRUS*, 1961–63, Vol. 17, pp. 691–92.

112. Cairo embassy telegram to State, May 3, 1962, *FRUS*, 1961–63, Vol. 17, pp. 656–57.

113. Steven L. Spiegel, *The Other Arab-Israeli Conflict: Making America's Middle East Policy, from Truman to Reagan* (Chicago: University of Chicago Press, 1985), p. 111.

114. Ball memo to JFK, Jan. 31, 1962, NSF, Box 169, UAR, Proposed Nasser Visit, JFKL.

115. Kaysen memorandum for the record, June 16, 1962, *FRUS*, 1961–63, Vol. 17, pp. 733–34.

116. Brubeck memo to Bundy, Aug. 3, 1962, Department of State, NEA Files, Lot File 62 D435, Box 6, Memoranda to the White House, NA.

117. Komer memo to Feldman, May 31, 1962, *FRUS*, 1961–63, Vol. 17, pp. 691–92.

118. "Courting Nasser," *The New Republic*, June 25, 1962, pp. 7–8.

119. Brubeck memo to Bundy, June 21, 1962, NSF, Box 445, Komer Papers, UAR 1961–1962 (Folder 2), JFKL.

120. The article wrongly accused the White House of not consulting the State Department about the JFK-Nasser letters and attributed the birth of the Nasser initiative almost entirely to William Polk, a Middle East specialist on the State Department's Policy Planning staff. It also accused the White House of not staffing out Kennedy's correspondence with Nasser properly, boosting Nasser's desire for regional dominance, and actually seeking Nasser's approval before recognizing the breakaway government in Syria.

121. Komer OH, July 16, 1964, p. 6, JFKL.

122. Heikal, p. 189.

123. *FRUS*, 1961–63, Vol. 17, p. 157.

124. Badeau letter to Talbot, March 21, 1962, DOSF, NEA Files, Lot 62 D435, Box 6, Cairo, NA. Badeau also offered a blast of Marshall-style rectitude: "If, as I suspect, it is really domestic considerations that have postponed the visit, this ought frankly to be stated in the policy directive."

125. Komer memo for the record, "Mike Feldman's views on Nasser visit," Dec. 20, 1961, NSF, Box 445, Komer Papers, UAR 1961–1962, White House Memoranda, JFKL.

126. Rusk memo to JFK, "Modified Presidential Guest Visit of Gamal Abd al-Nasser," Dec. 17, 1962, NSF, Box 445, Komer Papers, UAR 1961–62 (Folder 1), JFKL.

127. Komer makes JFK's hesitancy clear in Komer OH, July 16, 1964, p. 7, JFKL.

128. Bundy memo to JFK, Feb. 1, 1962, NSF, Box 169, United Arab Republic, Proposed Nasser Visit, JFKL.

129. *FRUS*, 1961–63, Vol. 17, pp. 451–53. The *FRUS* account confuses some of the memos' authorship.

130. Bowles letter to Bundy, May 3, 1962, *FRUS*, 1961–63, Vol. 17, p. 658.

131. Komer memo to Bundy, May 11, 1962, NSF, Box 445, Komer Papers, UAR 1961–1962, White House Memoranda, JFKL.

132. Bundy memo to Bowles, May 12, 1962, NSF, Box 445, Komer Papers, UAR 1961–1962 (Folder 2), JFKL. Bundy's language clearly echoed that of Komer, who may well have drafted the memo.

133. Nasser letter to JFK, June 21, 1962, NSF, Box 169, UAR, Nasser Correspondence, JFKL.

134. Brubeck memo to Bundy, June 25, 1962, NSF, Box 169, UAR, Nasser Correspondence, JFKL.

135. Brubeck memo to Bundy, July 10, 1962, NSF, Box 169, UAR, Nasser Correspondence, JFKL.

136. Komer memo to Bundy, July 12, 1962, NSF, Komer Papers, UAR 1961–1962, White House Memoranda, JFKL.

137. JFK letter to Nasser, Aug. 16, 1962, NSF, Box 445, Komer Papers, UAR 1961–62 (Folder 1), JFKL.

CHAPTER FOUR: Nasser's Vietnam

1. Richard Reeves, *President Kennedy: Profile of Power* (New York: Touchstone, 1993), p. 442.

2. The Kremlin's man in Cairo was imagined to have protested this, whereupon he had supposedly been given the "silly answer" that the U.S. ambassador was "a well-known Orientalist with whom Nasser likes to discuss Oriental affairs."

3. Badeau telegram to Rusk, May 3, 1963, NSF, Box 446, Komer Papers, UAR 1/63–11/63, JFKL.

4. Komer memo to JFK, May 4, 1963, NSF, Box 446, Komer Papers, UAR 1/63–11/63, JFKL.

5. JFK letter to Nasser, Aug. 29, 1962, WHCSF, Box 72, CO 304, UAR, JFKL.

6. Harold Macmillan, *At the End of the Day, 1961–1963* (New York: Harper & Row, 1973), p. 271.

7. The paraphrase is State Department Executive Secretary William H. Brubeck's; cf. Brubeck memo to Bundy, undated 1963, NSF, Box 169, UAR General 1963, JFKL.

8. For instance, cf. John S. Badeau OH, Feb. 25, 1969, p. 16, JFKL.

9. Reeves, p. 448.

10. John S. Badeau, *The American Approach to the Arab World* (New York: Council on Foreign Relations, 1968), p. 132.

11. The description is not from one of his admirers; cf. Mohamed Hassanein Heikal, *The Cairo Documents: The Inside Story of Nasser and His Relationship with World Leaders, Rebels, and Statesmen* (Garden City, N.Y.: Doubleday, 1973), p. 212.

12. Anthony Nutting, *Nasser* (New York: E.P. Dutton, 1972), p. 321.

13. Heikal, p. 213. The story, however irresistible, should probably be taken with a grain of salt, if not of *qat*.

14. Nutting, p. 322.

15. Malcolm H. Kerr, *The Arab Cold War: Gamal 'Abd al-Nasser and His Rivals, 1958–1970* (London: Oxford University Press, 1981), p. 25.

16. Memcon: Rusk and Talbot meeting with Faysal, Sept. 27, 1962, *FRUS, 1961–63*, Vol. 18, pp. 136–40.

17. Ball telegram to Rusk, Sept. 27, 1962, POF, Box 127, UAR Security 1962 file, JFKL.

18. Badeau telegram to State, Oct. 1, 1962, *FRUS, 1961–63*, Vol. 18, pp. 150–51.

19. Memcon: Talcott Seelye of NEA with Yemeni chargé d'affaires, Oct. 3, 1962, *FRUS, 1961–63*, Vol. 18, p. 155.

20. Komer OH, December 22, 1969, p. 85, JFKL.

21. Komer memo to JFK, Oct. 4, 1962, *FRUS, 1961–63*, Vol. 18, pp. 158–59.

22. Memcon: JFK-Faysal meeting, Oct. 5, 1962, *FRUS, 1961–63*, Vol. 18, pp. 162–67.

23. Heikal, p. 215.

24. Ball telegram to Cairo embassy, Oct. 5, 1962, *FRUS, 1961–63*, Vol. 18, pp. 167–68.

25. Hart OH, April 15, 1969, p. 13, JFKL.

26. Phillips Talbot OH, Aug. 13, 1970, p. 33, JFKL.

27. For a vivid journalistic account, cf. Dana Adams Schmidt, *Yemen: The Unknown War* (New York: Holt, Rinehart and Winston, 1968).

28. Talbot memo to Rusk, Oct. 9, 1962, *FRUS, 1961–63*, Vol. 18, pp. 172–73.

29. Memorandum for the record, Oct. 18, 1962, NSF, Box 445, Komer Papers, UAR 1961–62, White House Memoranda, JFKL.

30. Komer memo to JFK, Oct. 5, 1962, NSF, Box 445, Komer Papers, UAR 1961–1962, White House Memoranda, JFKL.

31. Badeau telegram to State, Oct. 10, 1962, *FRUS*, 1961–63, Vol. 18, pp. 174–75.

32. Macomber telegram to Rusk, Oct. 15, 1962, NSF, Box 125, Jordan, General, JFKL.

33. Komer memo to Talbot, Oct. 12, 1962, *FRUS*, 1961–63, Vol. 18, pp. 177–78.

34. State telegram to Badeau, Oct. 13, 1962, *FRUS*, 1961–63, Vol. 18, pp. 179–82.

35. Badeau telegram to State, Oct. 18, 1962, *FRUS*, 1961–63, Vol. 18, pp. 184–86.

36. *FRUS*, 1961–63, Vol. 18, p. 170.

37. Paper by Seelye on recognizing new Yemeni government, Oct. 17, 1962, *FRUS*, 1961–63, Vol. 18, pp. 182–83.

38. Hart OH, April 15, 1969, p. 18, JFKL.

39. JFK letter to Faysal, in Rusk telegram to Hart, Nov. 2, 1962, *FRUS*, 1961–63, Vol. 18, pp. 198–99.

40. *FRUS*, 1961–63, Vol. 18, pp. 199–200.

41. Rusk telegram to Riyadh embassy, Nov. 7, 1962, NSF, Box 125A, Jordan, General, JFKL.

42. Komer memo to JFK, Nov. 9, 1962, POF, Box 120, Jordan Security 1961–63, JFKL.

43. King Husayn letter to JFK, Nov. 19, 1962, POF, Box 120, Jordan Security 1961–63, JFKL.

44. Paul Dresch, *A History of Modern Yemen* (Cambridge: Cambridge University Press, 2000), p. 91.

45. On the rise and fall of British hegemony in the region, cf. Elizabeth Monroe, *Britain's Moment in the Middle East 1914–1971* (London: Chatto & Windus, 1981).

46. JFK letter to King Husayn, Nasser, Faysal, and Sallal, Nov. 16, 1962, *FRUS*, 1961–63, Vol. 18, pp. 228–29.

47. Hart telegram to State, Nov. 19, 1962, *FRUS*, 1961–63, Vol. 18, pp. 229–36.

48. Hart OH, April 15, 1969, p. 60, JFKL.

49. Komer memo to JFK, Nov. 21, 1962, *FRUS*, 1961–63, Vol. 18, pp. 237–38.

50. Badeau, p. 145.

51. Komer memo to JFK, Nov. 28, 1962, *FRUS*, 1961–63, Vol. 18, pp. 238–39.

52. Ball telegram to Badeau, Dec. 14, 1962, *FRUS*, 1961–63, Vol. 18, pp. 266–67.

53. Rusk telegram to Macomber, Dec. 7, 1962, NSF, Box 125, Jordan, General, JFKL. Kennedy's message, which was enclosed, was to be conveyed "[a]fter rpt after" Macomber got word of U.S. recognition of the YAR.

54. Ernest R. May and Philip D. Zelikow, eds., *The Kennedy Tapes: Inside the White House During the Cuban Missile Crisis* (Cambridge: Belknap Press of Harvard University Press, 1997), p. 670.

55. May and Zelikow, p. 316.

56. Badeau telegram to Rusk, Nov. 1, 1962, NSF, Box 445, Komer Papers, UAR 1961–62 (Folder 1), JFKL.

57. Brubeck memo to Bundy, Nov. 13, 1962, NSF, Box 169, UAR, Nasser Correspondence, JFKL.

58. Talbot memo to Rusk, Nov. 9, 1962, NSF, Box 445, Komer Papers, UAR 1961–62 (Folder 1), JFKL.

59. Brubeck memo to Bundy, Nov. 13, 1962, NSF, Box 169, UAR, Nasser Correspondence, JFKL. Even so, Nasser was considerably less blunt in his own postcrisis cable to Khrushchev. The State Department suggested that the White House view Nasser's message as *de rigeur* neutralist compensation for his earlier congratulatory note to Kennedy. "There is very little in the Khrushchev message which we could criticize," the State Department added, except its "slightly warmer tone than the message to President Kennedy." In fact, in a November 5 message broadcast over Moscow radio, Nasser told

the Soviet leader that the Egyptian people had appreciated his "wise method in meeting the crisis which arose in the Caribbean Sea because of Cuba"—a novel reading of the showdown's cause that neglects to mention the Soviet decision to slip ICBMs into Cuba. "Your decision to change the direction of some of the ships sailing to Cuba to prevent a clash between them and the American blockade forces was a wise decision dictated by a sincere desire for peace," Nasser purred to the Soviet leader. So, too, was Khrushchev's decision to "to remove the weapons bases upon which the American side had based its attitude toward Cuba, an attitude which might have had consequences whose effect on mankind God alone knows." Khrushchev's "courage in meeting this crisis recorded [a] high standard of a sense of duty toward humanity," Nasser added. Tommy Thompson seems to have been right about the limits of Nasser's friendship with Washington and the necessity of his friendship with Moscow. Nasser message to Khrushchev, Nov. 6, 1962, FBIS 80, NSF, Box 169, UAR, Nasser Correspondence, JFKL. Moscow radio broadcast the message on November 5; the translation is by FBIS.

Indeed, Egypt's behavior during the Cuban missile crisis underscored the country's core reliance on the Soviet Union for, at a minimum, the arms that made possible the campaign in Yemen and the confrontation with Israel. In the early 1960s, the communist bloc gave Nasser about $600 million per year in military assistance. On the other hand, the more aid that *Washington* gave Cairo, the more vulnerable the Kennedy administration was to charges that U.S. taxpayers were subsidizing Nasserite mischief making. In fact, Nasser paid the Soviets for his arms with Egyptian goods, primarily cotton, or bought them on credit—none of which was affected by U.S. surplus food aid. Even so, such pro-Israel senators as New York's Kenneth Keating began calling American aid fungible. American assistance was "meeting needs which resources used to pay for arms – i.e., cotton and Soviet Bloc credits – could not be effectively mobilized to meet," the State Department wrote. Brubeck memo to Bundy, May 8, 1963, NSF, Box 446, Komer Papers, UAR 1/63–11/63, JFKL (note that Nasser received $415 million in cash and credit and $185 million in outright grants); Badeau letter to Talbot, July 2, 1962, NSF, Box 445, Komer Papers, UAR 1961–62 (Folder 1), JFKL; Brubeck memo to Bundy, July 7, 1962, NSF, Box 445, Komer Papers, UAR 1961–62 (Folder 1), JFKL.

60. On Lantphibex, cf. Aleksandr Fursenko and Timothy Naftali, *"One Hell of a Gamble": Khrushchev, Castro, and Kennedy 1958–1964* (New York: W.W. Norton, 1997), p. 166.

61. Ibid., p. 167.

62. Ibid., p. 170.

63. Rusk telegram to Badeau, Dec. 24, 1962, NSF, Box 445, Komer Papers, UAR 1961–1962 (Folder 1), JFKL. Hearkening back to his famous 1957 Senate speech, JFK dryly told Nasser that, "As you know I have long taken a special interest in Algeria" and urged him to cooperate to keep the breakaway former French colony from making trouble in North Africa.

64. Badeau telegram to State, Dec. 30, 1962, *FRUS*, 1961–63, Vol. 18, pp. 285–88.

65. Macomber telegram to Rusk, Dec. 5, 1962, NSF, Box 125, Jordan, General, JFKL.

66. Macomber telegram to Rusk, Jan. 4, 1963, NSF, Box 125, Jordan, General, JFKL.

67. Badr cable to JFK, Dec. 8, 1962, WHCSF, Box 72, CO 304, UAR, JFKL.

68. Rusk telegram to Badeau, Dec. 31, 1962, *FRUS*, 1961–63, Vol. 18, pp. 288–89.

69. Talbot telegram to embassies in Amman, Beirut, Damascus, Jidda, and Cairo, Jan. 4, 1963, NSF, Box 446, Komer Papers, UAR 1/63–11/63, JFKL.

70. Ball telegram to Badeau, Jan. 4, 1963, *FRUS*, 1961–63, Vol. 18, p. 299.

71. Komer memo to Bundy, Jan. 2, 1963, NSF, Box 169, United Arab Republic, Proposed Nasser Visit, JFKL.

72. Badeau telegram to State, Jan. 9, 1963, *FRUS*, 1961–63, Vol. 18, pp. 301–03.

73. State telegram to Badeau, Jan. 19, 1963, NSF, Box 169, United Arab Republic, Nasser Correspondence, JFKL.

74. Badeau telegram to Rusk, Jan. 24, 1963, NSF, Box 169, United Arab Republic, Nasser Correspondence, JFKL.

75. Hart OH, April 15, 1969, p. 18, JFKL. Hart assumes that there were originally 110 bundles and that 2 had already been picked up.

76. Nadav Safran, *Saudi Arabia: The Ceaseless Quest for Security* (Ithaca: Cornell University Press, 1988), p. 99.

77. Komer memo to Bundy, Feb. 7, 1963, *FRUS*, 1961–63, Vol. 18, pp. 338–39.

78. Talbot OH, Aug. 13, 1970, p. 57, JFKL.

79. Hart OH, April 15, 1969, p. 50, JFKL.

80. Komer memo for the record, Jan. 28, 1963, NSF, Box 446, Komer files, UAR 1/63–11/63, White House Memoranda, JFKL.

81. Joseph Alsop, "Matter of Fact: The Yemen Crisis," *The New York Herald Tribune*, Feb. 25, 1963. A copy is found in NSF, Box 447, Yemen 1961–4/1963, White House Memoranda, JFKL.

82. Memo for the record: JFK meeting on Yemen with Talbot, McGhee, Nitze, Komer, and various Pentagon generals, Feb. 25, 1963, *FRUS*, 1961–63, Vol. 18, pp. 363–66.

83. Rusk telegram to Badeau, March 2, 1963, NSF, Box 169, United Arab Republic, Nasser Correspondence, JFKL.

84. Nasser letter to JFK, March 3, 1963, POF, Box 127, UAR Security 1963, JFKL.

85. March 10, 1963, Rusk telegram to Badeau, NSF, Box 169, UAR, Nasser Correspondence, JFKL.

86. Badeau telegram to Rusk, March 5, 1963, NSF, Box 169, UAR, Nasser Correspondence, JFKL.

87. Komer memo to JFK, March 5, 1963, NSF, Box 169, United Arab Republic, Nasser Correspondence, JFKL.

88. Komer memo to Bundy, March 9, 1963, NSF, Box 446, Komer Files, UAR 1/63–11/63, White House Memoranda, JFKL.

89. Komer memo to Bundy, March 6, 1963, *FRUS*, 1961–63, Vol. 18, p. 397.

90. Memcon: JFK meeting on Yemen, March 11, 1963, NSF, Box 447, Komer Files, Yemen, 1961–4/63, White House Memoranda, JFKL.

91. *FRUS*, 1961–63, Vol. 18, p. 431.

92. Komer memo to JFK, March 13, 1963, *FRUS*, 1961–63, Vol. 18, p. 423.

93. Ball telegram to Bunker, Badeau, and Hart, March 16, 1963, POF, Box 127, UAR Security 1963, JFKL.

94. Bunker telegram to State, from Cairo embassy, April 3, 1963, *FRUS*, 1961–63, Vol. 18, pp. 447–48.

95. Rusk telegram to Badeau, April 13, 1963, *FRUS*, 1961–63, Vol. 18, pp. 464–65.

96. Komer OH, July 16, 1964, p. 17, JFKL.

97. Nadav Safran, *Saudi Arabia: The Ceaseless Quest for Security* (Ithaca: Cornell University Press, 1988), p. 99.

98. JFK letter to Nasser [in State telegram to Badeau], April 18, 1963, POF, Box 127, UAR Security 1963 file, JFKL; italics mine.

99. Anwar el-Sadat, *In Search of Identity: An Autobiography* (New York: Harper & Row, 1979), p. 147.

100. Ball telegram to Tel Aviv embassy, April 4, 1963, *FRUS*, 1961–63, Vol. 18, pp. 449–50.

101. Memcon: phone call between Talbot and Feldman, April 5, 1963, *FRUS*, 1961–63, Vol. 18, pp. 450–51.

102. Komer OH, December 22, 1969, p. 88, JFKL.

103. *FRUS*, 1961–63, Vol. 18, pp. 342–43.

104. Patrick Seale, *Asad of Syria: The Struggle for the Middle East* (Berkeley: University of California Press, 1988), p. 75.

105. Rusk telegram to embassies in Baghdad, Damascus, Cairo, and London, April 19, 1963, NSF, Box 169, United Arab Republic, Nasser Correspondence, JFKL.

106. Kerr, p. 76.

107. Fouad Ajami, *The Arab Predicament: Arab Political Thought and Practice Since 1967* (Cambridge: Cambridge University Press, 1981), p. 44.

108. Ben-Gurion's letter is summarized in Brubeck memo to Bundy, April 27, 1963, *FRUS*, 1961–63, Vol. 18, pp. 481–82. On the Hawk sale, cf. chapter V.

109. Supplementary Briefing Memorandum – Jordan, undated, NSF, Box 125, Jordan, General, JFKL.

110. Zaki Shalom, *The Superpowers, Israel and the Future of Jordan 1960–1963: The Perils of the Pro-Nasser Policy* (Portland: Sussex Academic Press, 1999), p. 47. Shalom's work, based on somewhat different primary source material than my treatment, offers a useful account.

111. Ibid., p. 26.

112. Macomber memo to Rusk, April 21, 1963, NSF, Box 125, Jordan, General, JFKL.

113. FBIS broadcast monitoring contained in Rusk telegram to embassies in Cairo, Amman, and Tel Aviv, April 21, 1963, NSF, Box 125, Jordan, General, JFKL.

114. Stevenson telegram to Rusk, April 25, 1963, NSF, Box 125, Jordan, General, JFKL.

115. Barbour telegram to Rusk, April 27, 1963, NSF, Box 125, Jordan, General, JFKL.

116. Memcon: Ball phone call to McNamara, April 27, 1963, *FRUS*, 1961–63, Vol. 18, p. 483.

117. Ball telegram to Tel Aviv, April 27, 1963, NSF, Box 125, Jordan, General, JFKL. The embassies in Beirut, Cairo, Baghdad, Damascus, Jidda, London, and Amman all were notified before Tel Aviv.

118. Memorandum for the Record, April 27, 1963, NSF, Box 125A, Jordan, General, JFKL.

119. Joint Chiefs of Staff telegram to Rusk, April 27, 1963, NSF, Box 125A, Jordan, General, JFKL.

120. Barbour telegram to Rusk, April 27, 1963, NSF, Box 125, Jordan, General, JFKL.

121. On how Israel actually took the West Bank in 1967, cf. Nadav Safran, *Israel: The Embattled Ally* (Cambridge: Belknap Press of Harvard University Press, 1981), p. 247. On the IDF's order of battle in the West Bank in 1967, cf. Chaim Herzog, *The Arab-Israeli Wars: War and Peace in the Middle East from the War of Independence through Lebanon* (New York: Vintage Books, 1984), pp. 167–83.

122. Ball telegram to Badeau, April 27, 1963, NSF, Box 125A, Jordan, General, JFKL.

123. Badeau telegram to Rusk, April 27, 1963, POF, Box 127, UAR Security, JFKL.

124. Macomber telegram to Rusk, April 29, 1963, NSF, Box 125A, Jordan, General, JFKL.

125. Macomber telegram to State, April 28, 1963, NSF, Box 125A, Jordan, General, JFKL.

126. Memcon: Ball meeting with Israeli Ambassador Avraham Harman, Israeli Minister Mordechai Gazit, and Grant of NEA, April 28, 1963, *FRUS*, 1961–63, Vol. 18, pp. 494–96.

127. Memcon: Bundy phone call to Ball, April 29, 1963, *FRUS*, 1961–63, Vol. 18, pp. 496–98.

128. Badeau telegram to Rusk, April 29, 1963, POF, Box 127, UAR Security 1963, JFKL.

129. Ball telegram to Baghdad and Damascus, May 1, 1963, NSF, Box 125, Jordan, General, JFKL.

130. Komer memo to Bundy, April 30, 1963, NSF, Box 125A, Jordan, General, JFKL. Komer even indulged one of his trademark flights of fancy, which echoed Dulles and Eisenhower: perhaps Ben-Gurion was protesting too much about Jordan? "Israel's patent attempt to embrace Hussein" was clearly "so much a kiss of death to the brave young king" that Komer wondered whether that wasn't the idea. Perhaps Ben-Gurion was getting ready to let the king fall and snatch the West Bank while Nasser's army was still tied down in Yemen.

131. Memorandum for the record: Daily White House staff mtg., May 1, 1963, *FRUS*, 1961–63, Vol. 18, pp. 505–6.

132. Badeau telegram to Rusk, April 30, 1963, NSF, Box 125, Jordan, General, JFKL.

133. Brubeck memo to Bundy, May 8, 1963, NSF, Box 446, Komer Files, UAR 1/63–11/63, JFKL.

134. Deputy Assistant Secretary for NEA Grant memo to Rusk, May 11, 1963, *FRUS*, 1961–63, Vol. 18, pp. 526–27.

135. Macomber OH, Feb. 14, 1969, p. 28, JFKL.

136. Komer OH, December 22, 1969, p. 79, JFKL.

137. Komer OH, June 18, 1964, p. 6, JFKL.

138. Hart OH, April 15, 1969, p. 32, JFKL.

139. Safran, p. 96. In 1961, King Saud gave the administration the requisite year's notice that he wanted the Dhahran airfield to return to full Saudi control. The USAF used Dhahran for refueling propeller aircraft on long routes. The base, which dated back to the Truman administration, was of largely symbolic importance, and the Saudi regime had grown tired of pan-Arabist catcalling about it; cf. Hart OH, April 15, 1969, pp. 4–5, JFKL.

140. Komer memo to Bundy, Jan. 8, 1963, NSF, Box 447, Komer Papers, Yemen 1961-4/1963, White House Memoranda, JFKL. The italicized text here is actually underlined in the original, but the emphasis is Komer's, who, for all his emphatic nature, rarely used such highlights.

141. After the Jordan crisis, the United States also made a few minor shows of military interest there. In May, a brigadier-general led a joint U.S.–U.K. survey mission, which the NSC let Nasser think might have been there to discuss joint military planning. In addition, 13 U.S. paratroopers were teaching at a Jordanian paratroop school, and the Pentagon sent a dozen or so more troops and two planes along in May for the school's graduation exercises. "All these will give Nasser and Iraqis pause," wrote Komer. Komer memo to JFK, May 2, 1963, NSF, Box 125, Jordan, General, JFKL.

142. The British got there first, sending a variety of materiel and advisers to help bail out the Saudis.

143. Badeau, p. 212.

144. Komer memo to JFK, May 24, 1963, *FRUS*, 1961–63, Vol. 18, p. 555.

145. JFK letter to Nasser, in State telegram to Badeau, May 27, 1963, NSF, Box 446, Komer Papers, UAR 1/63–11/63, JFKL.

146. Douglas Little, "The New Frontier on the Nile: JFK, Nasser, and Arab Nationalism," *Journal of American History*, Vol. 75, No. 2 (Sept. 1988), p. 524.

147. Badeau, p. 175. Badeau does not say which letter was under the knife.

148. *FRUS*, 1961–63, Vol. 18, pp. 574–75.

149. Komer OH, July 16, 1964, p. 19, JFKL.

150. Komer memo to JFK, June 13, 1963, *FRUS*, 1961–63, Vol. 18, pp. 580–81.

151. Safran, p. 97.

152. Deputy Assistant Secretary of Defense for International Security Affairs Frank K. Sloan letter to Talbot, March 4, 1963, DOSF, NEA Files, Lot File 62D435, Box 7, Operation Hard Surface, NA.

153. Edward Weintal and Charles Bartlett, *Facing the Brink: An Intimate Study of Crisis Diplomacy* (New York: Charles Scribner's Sons, 1967), p. 45. The book recycled the term "Komer's war," and Komer mentions his dim view of the overall scholarship on Yemen in his Kennedy Library OH interviews. Hart quite liked the book.

154. Talbot OH, Aug. 13, 1970, p. 53.

155. Sloan letter to Talbot, March 4, 1963, DOSF, NEA Files, Lot File 62D435, Box 7, Operation Hard Surface, NA.

156. Komer OH, December 22, 1969, p. 93, JFKL.

157. Sloan letter to Talbot, March 4, 1963, DOSF, NEA Files, Lot File 62D435, Box 7, Operation Hard Surface, NA.

158. Rusk telegram to Hart in Riyadh, June 14, 1963, *FRUS*, 1961–63, Vol. 18, pp. 587–88. The more risk-averse Pentagon proposed on March 4 that the USAF fighters simply destroy any "hostile intruder" into Saudi airspace.

159. Sloan letter to Talbot, March 4, 1963, DOSF, NEA Files, Lot File 62D435, Box 7, Operation Hard Surface, NA.

160. Cf. Grant letter to Sloan, April 29, 1963, DOSF, NEA Files, Records of the Director 1958–63, Box 7, Operation Hard Surface, NA.

161. Ibid.

162. Rodger P. Davies memo to Strong, April 23, 1963, DOSF, NEA Files, Records of the Director 1958–63, Box 7, Operation Hard Surface, NA.

163. Celler OH, April 11, 1972, p. 2, JFKL. One dodge often helped ease the perennial problem of Jewish servicemen in Saudi Arabia: most U.S. military personnel simply entered the kingdom on American-issued I.D. cards, not Saudi visas. But the "the general practice of our own people was simply to just not send out people there who were going to get into difficulties," as Kennedy's ambassador to Saudi Arabia, Pete Hart, delicately put it. Hart OH, April 15, 1969, p. 6, JFKL.

164. Komer memo to JFK, June 13, 1963, *FRUS*, 1961–63, Vol. 18, pp. 580–81.

165. Hart OH, April 15, 1969, p. 11, JFKL.

166. Taylor Branch, *Parting the Waters: America in the King Years 1954–63* (New York: Touchstone, 1989), p. 819. On the hasty drafting of the June 11 speech, cf. the account by its author, Theodore C. Sorensen, *Kennedy* (New York: Bantam, 1966), pp. 556–57.

167. *FRUS*, 1961–63, Vol. 18, pp. 581–83.

168. Strong memo to Grant, May 20, 1963, DOSF, NEA Files, Records of the Director 1958–63, Box 7, Operation Hard Surface, NA.

169. Badeau telegram to Rusk, July 1, 1963, DOSF, Central Foreign Policy File 1963, Box 3727, DEF ISR, NA.

170. Branch, p. 824.

171. The analogy was suggested to me by Ted Sorensen. Still, a basic question remains. Were there actually any Jewish soldiers in Operation Hard Surface? Even a full roster of the mission's troops would not truly answer the question. But surely if Celler had had it wrong when he went to the *Times*, the White House could have avoided some real Saudi hysteria by simply offering a flat denial, even privately. That the Kennedy administration did not do so suggests powerfully that there were indeed Jews among the Hard Surface personnel; that the mission went ahead suggests powerfully that the Saudis let the matter slide.

172. Komer OH, July 16, 1964, p. 13, JFKL.

173. Interview with Kenneth M. Pollack, then director for Near East and South Asian affairs, National Security Council, Feb. 16, 2001.

174. Kaysen OH, July 11, 1966, p. 51, JFKL.

175. Kaysen memo to JFK, June 28, 1963, *FRUS*, 1961–63, Vol. 18, pp. 614–15.

176. Komer memo to JFK, July 2, 1963, *FRUS*, 1961–63, Vol. 18, pp. 621–22.

177. Hart OH, April 15, 1969, p. 56, JFKL.

178. Memorandum on State-JCS Meeting, Aug. 16, 1963, *FRUS*, 1961–63, Vol. 18, pp. 676–77.

179. Komer paper (for JFK's weekend reading), Sept. 20, 1963, *FRUS*, 1961–63, Vol. 18, pp. 711–13.

180. John Lewis Gaddis, *Strategies of Containment: A Critical Appraisal of Postwar American National Security Policy* (New York: Oxford University Press, 1982), p. 215.

181. Komer memo to Bundy, Jan. 8, 1963, NSF, Box 447, Komer Papers, Yemen 1961-4/1963, White House Memoranda, JFKL.

182. Badeau telegram to State, July 11, 1963, *FRUS*, 1961–63, Vol. 18, pp. 639–41.

183. July 15, 1963, Komer memo to Bundy, NSF, Box 169, United Arab Republic, General, 6/63–8/63, JFKL.

184. Rusk telegram to Badeau, July 23, 1963, DOSF, NEA Files, Lot File 67 D497, Box 3.

185. Komer memo to Bundy, Aug. 5, 1963, NSF, Box 446, Komer Papers, UAR 1/63–11/63, White House Memoranda, JFKL. One can only speculate as to why the identity of the CIA's interlocutor still needed to remain secret when the document was declassified in 1999 with most of one line of text blacked out. It is hard to imagine why, some 40 years later, such documents cannot be released to the public.

186. Senators' letter to JFK (Hugh Scott, Jacob Javits, Thomas Dodd, Winston Prouty, Kenneth Keating, and Thomas Kuchel), April 5, 1963, WHCSF, Box 72, CO 304, UAR, JFKL.

187. Badeau telegram to Rusk, Oct. 2, 1963, NSF, Box 169, UAR General, JFKL.

188. Komer OH, Dec. 22, 1969, p. 75.

189. Badeau telegram to Rusk, July 12, 1963, NSF, Box 169, UAR General 1963, JFKL.

190. Komer memo to JFK, July 31, 1963, NSF, Box 169, United Arab Republic, General, 6/63–8/63, JFKL.

191. Kerr, p. 88; INR Research Memorandum RNA-34, "Tripartite Arab Unity a Casualty of the New-Elite Power Struggle," Aug. 7, 1963, NSF, Box 446, Komer Papers, UAR 1/63–11/63, JFKL.

192. Komer memo to JFK, Aug. 16, 1963, *FRUS*, 1961–63, Vol. 18, p. 680.

193. Memorandum for the record, Oct. 8, 1963, *FRUS*, 1961–63, Vol. 18, pp. 726–27.

194. National Security Action Memorandum No. 262, Oct. 10, 1963, *FRUS*, 1961–63, Vol. 18, pp. 729–30.

195. State memo to Bundy, Sept. 6, 1963, NSF, Box 169, United Arab Republic, General, 9/63–11/63, JFKL.

196. Rusk memo to Badeau, Sept. 20, 1963, *FRUS*, 1961–63, Vol. 18, pp. 708–9.

197. Memcon: Rusk meeting with Kaissouni, Oct. 8, 1963, NSF, Box 446, Komer Papers, UAR 1/63–11/63, JFKL.

198. Rusk letter to British Ambassador David Ormsby Gore, Oct. 19, 1963, *FRUS*, 1961–63, Vol. 18, p. 746.

199. Komer memo to Bundy, Nov. 12, 1963, NSF, Box 446, Komer Papers, UAR 1/63–11/63, White House Memoranda, JFKL.

200. Rusk telegram to Badeau, Oct. 19, 1963, NSF, Box 169, United Arab Republic, General, 9/63–11/63, JFKL.

201. Badeau telegram to State, Oct. 21, 1963, *FRUS*, 1961–63, Vol. 18, pp. 753–57.

202. Badeau telegram to State, Oct. 27, 1963, NSF, Box 169, United Arab Republic, General, 9/63–11/63, JFKL.

203. Hart telegram to State, Oct. 24, 1963, *FRUS*, 1961–63, Vol. 18, pp. 757–58.

204. Talbot telegram to Hart in Jidda, Oct. 28, 1963, *FRUS*, 1961–63, Vol. 18, pp. 759–60.

205. Talbot letter to William Bundy, Nov. 6, 1963, *FRUS*, 1961–63, Vol. 18, pp. 769–70.

206. Moreover, Kennedy's ongoing aid and balance-of-payments problems made each dollar that much more precious. For some flavor of the administration's budgetary constraints, cf. for instance Komer memo to JFK, Aug. 28, 1963, POF, Box 120, Jordan Security 1961–63, JFKL. Such strictures are a major theme of Robert Dallek's forthcoming major Kennedy biography.

207. *Current Foreign Relations*, Issue No. 37, Sept. 9, 1963, NSF, Box 446, Komer Papers, UAR 1/63–11/63, JFKL. On a related point, when King Husayn established diplomatic ties with the Soviet Union in late August, Macomber argued that he was trying to prove that he was not "a puppet of the West." This ever-present worry had been exacerbated by "growing anxiety that our policy towards Nasser is working against his regime," so the king had sought a counterweight. Macomber telegram to Rusk, August 23, 1963, NSF, Box 125, Jordan, General, JFKL.

208. Talbot letter to Badeau (personal and confidential), Dec. 3, 1963, DOSF, NEA Files, Lot File 67D497, Box 3, Aid, General Policy, UAR 1963, NA.

209. Ernest Gruening, *Many Battles: The Autobiography of Ernest Gruening* (New York: Liveright, 1973), p. 457.

210. Ibid.

211. Talbot letter to Badeau, Dec. 3, 1963, DOSF, NEA Files, Lot File 67D497, Box 3, Aid, General Policy, UAR 1963, NA.

212. Rusk circular telegram 884, Nov. 8, 1963, POF, Box 127, UAR Security 1963, JFKL.

213. Gruening did also take the odd pot-shot at Indonesia's Sukarno, who was then menacing Malaysia.

214. Badeau telegram to Rusk, Nov. 9, 1963, NSF, Box 169, UAR General, JFKL.

215. Bundy memo to Senator J. William Fulbright, Nov. 11, 1963, NSF, Box 169, United Arab Republic, General, 9/63–11/63, JFKL.

216. Badeau telegram to State, Nov. 9, 1963, POF, Box 127, UAR Security 1963 file, JFKL.

217. Badeau telegram to State, Nov. 9, 1963, NSF, Box 169, UAR General, JFKL.

218. Badeau telegram to Rusk, Nov. 9, 1963, NSF, Box 169, UAR General, JFKL.

219. Badeau letter to Talbot, Nov. 16, 1963, NSF, Box 446, Komer Papers, UAR 1/63–11/63, JFKL.

220. Bundy letter to Fulbright, Nov. 11, 1963, POF, Box 127, UAR Security 1963 file, JFKL.

221. *The Kennedy Presidential Press Conferences* (New York: Earl M. Coleman Enterprises, 1978), p. 585.

222. Ibid., pp. 588–89.

223. Memcon: Israeli Counselor Shaul Bar-Haim with NEA Staff Assistant Lee F. Dinsmore, Nov. 14, 1963, NSF, Box 169, UAR General, JFKL.

224. Harriman telegram to Rusk, Nov. 11, 1963, NSF, Box 169, UAR General, JFKL.

225. Memorandum for the record: Komer lunch with Gazit, Nov. 21, 1963, *FRUS*, 1961–63, Vol. 18, pp. 797–801.

226. Safran, p. 119.

227. Galia Golan, *Soviet Policies in the Middle East from World War Two to Gorbachev* (Cambridge: Cambridge University Press, 1990), p. 56.

228. Dresch, p. 102.

229. Robert B. Elwood of INR memo to Talbot, Jan. 7, 1963, DOSF, NEA Files, Lot File 62D435, Box 7, Cairo, NA.

230. The derisive phrase is Komer's.

231. Nutting, p. 323.

232. Ibid.

233. Ibid., p. 339.

234. Kerr, p. 112.

235. Halberstam, p. 632.

236. Badeau telegram to Rusk, March 5, 1963, NSF, Box 169, UAR, Nasser Correspondence, JFKL.

237. Badeau telegram to State, July 11, 1963, *FRUS*, 1961–63, Vol. 18, pp. 639–41.

238. Komer paper (for JFK's weekend reading), Sept. 20, 1963, *FRUS*, 1961–63, Vol. 18, pp. 711–13.

CHAPTER FIVE : Israel's Missile Gap

1. Shimon Peres, *David's Sling* (New York: Random House, 1970), p. 96. The "doves seeking Hawks" line from the aphorism-loving Israeli may rank as the earliest recorded Peres-ism.

2. Ibid., p. 100.

3. "U.S. Will Supply Israel Missiles in Policy Change," *New York Times*, Sept. 27, 1962, p. A1.

4. Author interview, May 21, 2001.

5. Badeau OH, Feb. 25, 1969, p. 23, JFKL.

6. On the balance-of-payments crisis, cf. the forthcoming JFK biography by Robert Dallek; cf. also Raytheon President Charles F. Adams letter to Bill Bundy, Oct. 16, 1962, DODF, OASD-ISA, Box 89, Israel 1962, NA.

7. Douglas Little, "The Making of a Special Relationship: The United States and Israel, 1957–68," *International Journal of Middle East Studies*, No. 25 (1993), pp. 563–85.

8. On May 21, 2001, Phillips Talbot said he did not remember any linkage between the Hawks and Israel's nuclear program.

9. Memcon: Jones, Thacher, and Hamilton meeting with AIPAC delegation, March 20, 1961, DOSF, NEA Files, Lot File 62D435, Box 4, 1961 – Chron Memorandum of Conversation, NA.

10. Feldman memo to Ted Reardon, May 21, 1962, WHCSF, Box 73, CO 304, JFKL. "Shocked at United States taking lead to censure Israel through Security Council at United Nations," cabled the president of Louisiana's B'nai Brith; Brooklyn's Jewish district attorney, Edward Silver, pronounced himself "completely bewildered" (WHCSF, Box 73, CO 304, JFKL).

11. Dungan memo to Brubeck, May 3, 1963, WHCSF, Box 73, CO 304, JFKL.

12. I. L. Kenen, *Israel's Defense Line: Her Friends and Foes in Washington* (Buffalo: Prometheus Books, 1981), p. 166.

13. Ibid., p. 158.

14. Zach Levey, *Israel and the Western Powers*, 1952–60 (Chapel Hill: University of North Carolina Press, 1997), p. 80.

15. "The French-Israeli Relationship," CIA Report, POF, Box 119A, Israel, Security, David Ben-Gurion 1/1961–5/1961, JFKL.

16. Nadav Safran, *Israel: The Embattled Ally* (Cambridge: Belknap Press of Harvard University Press, 1981), p. 370.

17. In 1962, for instance, the British Foreign Office (FO) argued that selling 45 more Centurions to Israel would prevent the Arab states from gaining a destabilizing edge; cf. FO 371/164345, PRO, Kew, London.

18. On the Centurion sale, cf. in particular Levey, pp. 101, 112–14.

19. Rountree memo to Dulles, Aug. 22, 1958, *FRUS*, 1958–60, Vol. 13, pp. 88–91.

20. Ibid.

21. Memcon: Herter and Jones meeting with Arab ambassadors, March 7, 1960, *FRUS*, 1958–60, Vol. 13, p. 280.

22. Memcon: Eisenhower meeting with Ben-Gurion, March 10, 1960, *FRUS*, 1958–60, Vol. 13, pp. 280–88.

23. Memcon: Undersecretary of State Douglas Dillon and aides with Ben-Gurion, March 10, 1960, *FRUS*, 1958–60, Vol. 13, pp. 289–90.

24. Memcon: Herter and Ben-Gurion, March 13, 1960, *FRUS*, 1958–60, Vol. 13, pp. 296–300. All italics are in the original.

25. Jones memo to Dillon, May 26, 1960, *FRUS*, 1958–60, Vol. 13, pp. 327–29.

26. Ben-Gurion letter to Herter, June 9, 1960, *FRUS*, 1958–60, Vol. 13, pp. 333–34.

27. Reid telegram to Herter, July 18, 1960, *FRUS*, 1958–60, Vol. 13, pp. 350–53.

28. Herter letter to Ben-Gurion, Aug. 4, 1960, *Documents on Foreign Relations of the State of Israel, 1960* (Jerusalem: Israel State Archives, 1998), pp. 289–91; cf. also *FRUS*, 1958–60, Vol. 13, pp. 358–61.

29. Memcon: Eisenhower meeting with Nasser, Sept. 26, 1960, *FRUS*, 1958–60, Vol. 13, pp. 600–607.

30. Memcon: Bundy meeting with Harman, Feb. 16, 1961, DOSF, Central Decimal File 1960–63, Box 2059, File 784A.5612, NA.

31. State Department Executive Secretary Walter Stoessel, Jr., memo to Bundy, Feb. 24, 1961, NSF, Box 118, Israel, General, JFKL.

32. Kai Bird, *The Color of Truth: McGeorge and William Bundy, Brothers in Arms: A Biography* (New York: Simon & Schuster, 1998), p. 183. William Bundy went on to serve as editor of *Foreign Affairs*. While I was an associate editor for the magazine, between 1998 and 2000, Bundy and I spoke once briefly.

33. Walter Isaacson, *Kissinger: A Biography* (New York: Simon & Schuster, 1992), pp. 193–94.

34. Komer handwritten note, June 18, 1962, NSF, Box 428, Komer Papers, Israel, Security (Missile), Development Sale of Hawks, JFKL.

35. Memcon: "Hawks" for Israel, May 8, 1961, *FRUS*, 1961–63, Vol. 17, pp. 102–03.

36. Director of DOD Office of Foreign Economic Affairs Joseph W. Darling memo, "Proposal for Use of U.S.–Owned Israeli Pounds to Help Reduce the U.S. Balance of Payments Deficit," Aug. 6, 1962, DODF, OASD-ISA, Box 89, Israel 1962, NA.

37. Most of McNamara's papers remain unavailable for researchers. The criteria are found in Talbot memo to Chenery, April 7, 1962, DODF, OASD-ISA, Box 89, Israel 1962, NA.

38. The Joint Chiefs basically bought Israel's assessment about "the magnitude of the gap in armaments," but they did not think that weapons capabilities told the whole story. True, the combined Arab states still had a qualitative advantage over Israel in military materiel. "Arab weapons, particularly those of the United Arab Republic, are also generally more modern and effective than those currently held by the Israelis," the Pentagon concluded. But the IDF enjoyed "overwhelming military superiority in the non-matériel areas" such as "mobilization capability, leadership, training, organization, morale, and determination," and that would let it "defeat the military forces of any combination of Israel's Arab neighbors." To be sure, the Arab arsenals were growing steadily better, and this inevitably threatened Israel's military position, but the erosion was not dramatic. And Israel still had its traditional suppliers, France and Britain. So there was "no valid military reason to accede at this time to Israel's request for military assistance from the United States or for economic aid in lieu thereof." If there were "compelling political reasons for meeting this request in some respect," the JCS suggested limiting it to defensive arms, especially in early-warning and detection systems. For more details, cf. Deputy Assistant Secretary of Defense for International Security Affairs John A. Dabney letter to

Deputy Undersecretary of State for Political Affairs Raymond Hare, June 14, 1960, *FRUS*, 1958–60, Vol. 13, pp. 336–37.

39. Memcon: JFK meeting with Ben-Gurion, May 30, 1961, NSF, Box 118, Israel, General, JFKL.

40. Talbot seems not to have counted 1956, when Israel struck first.

41. Talbot memo to Rusk, Nov. 22, 1961, *FRUS*, 1961–63, Vol. 17, pp. 342–44.

42. For one early Israeli bid for a security guarantee, cf. memorandum for the record: Komer luncheon with Gazit, April 30, 1962, NSF, Box 427, Komer Papers, Israel 1961–1963, White House Memoranda, JFKL.

43. Peres, p. 94.

44. Bundy letter to Talbot, April 3, 1962, Department of Defense Files (DODF), Records of the Secretary of Defense, Office of the Assistant Secretary of Defense for International Security Affairs (OASD-ISA), Box 89, Israel 1962, NA.

45. Acting JCS Chairman G. H. Decker memo to Defense Secretary Robert McNamara, April 5, 1962, DODF, OASD-ISA, Box 89, Israel 1962, NA.

46. Bundy letter to George McGhee, DODF, OASD-ISA, Box 89, Israel 1962, NA.

47. Memcon: Strong meeting with Peres and Gazit, May 23, 1962, DODF, OASD-ISA, Box 89, Israel 1962, NA.

48. Bundy memo to Gilpatric, May 5, 1962, DODF, OASD-ISA, Box 89, Israel 1962, NA.

49. Feldman message to McGeorge Bundy (in Kaysen memo to Bundy), May 18, 1962, NSF, Box 118, Israel General, JFKL.

50. Bundy memo to Talbot, May 28, 1962, NSF, Box 428, Robert W. Komer Papers, Israel, Security (Missile), Development Sale of Hawks, JFKL.

51. Memcon: McGhee and Talbot meeting with Peres, Harman, and Gazit, May 21, 1962, DOSF, Central Decimal File 1960–63, Box 2059, File 784A.5612, NA.

52. Memcon: Talbot meeting with Peres, Harman, and Gazit, May 21, 1962, DOSF, Central Decimal File 1960–63, Box 2059, File 784A.5612, NA.

53. Memcon: Strong meeting with Peres and Gazit, May 23, 1962, DODF, OASD-ISA, Box 89, Israel 1962, NA.

54. Bundy memo to Talbot, May 23, 1962, DODF, OASD-ISA, Box 89, Israel 1962, NA; italics mine.

55. Ibid.

56. Ibid.

57. Rusk telegram to various embassies, May 23, 1962, NSF, Box 428, Komer Papers, Israel, Security (Missile), Development Sale of Hawks, JFKL.

58. Talbot memo to Rusk, June 7, 1962, *FRUS*, 1961–63, Vol. 17, pp. 710–18.

59. Rusk memo to Talbot, June 10, 1962, *FRUS*, 1961–63, Vol. 17, p. 719.

60. Barbour telegram to Rusk, June 8, 1962, NSF, Box 118A, Israel General, JFKL.

61. "Athens Chiefs of Mission Conference: A Summary," DOSF, NEA Files, NEA/Israeli-Arab Affairs (IAI), Middle East General 1962–66, Box 1, Athens Chiefs of Missions Conference, NA.

62. Summary Notes on First Plenary Session, Athens Chiefs of Missions Conference, June 12, 1962, DOSF, NEA Files, NEA/IAI, Middle East General 1962–66, Box 1, Athens Chiefs of Missions Conference, NA.

63. Talbot telegram to Deputy Assistant Secretary of State for NEA James Grant, June 15, 1962, NSF, Box 428, Komer Papers, Israel, Security (Missiles), Development Sale of Hawks, 1962–1963, JFKL.

64. Grant memo to Rusk, June 17, 1962, DOSF, NEA Files, Records of the Director 1958–63, Box 6, Hawk Missiles, NA.

65. Komer memo to Bundy, June 18, 1962, NSF, Box 428, Komer Papers, Israel, Security (Missile), Development Sale of Hawks, JFKL.

66. Ben-Gurion letter to JFK, June 24, 1962, POF, Box 119A, Israel, Security 1961–1963, JFKL.

67. Talbot memo to Rusk, July 9, 1962, *FRUS*, 1961–63, Vol. 18, pp. 2–7.

68. JCS Chairman L. L. Lemnitzer memo to McNamara, Sept. 11, 1962, DODF, OASD-ISA, Box 89, Israel 1962, NA.

69. Bundy letter to Grant, July 16, 1962, NSF, Box 428, Komer Papers, Israel, Security (Missiles), Development Sale of Hawks, 1962–1963, JFKL.

70. Hilsman to Ball, July 23, 1962, RG 330, Records of the Office of the Secretary of Defense, ASD-ISA, Box 68, File 471.6 July 1962, NA.

71. Rusk memo to JFK, Aug. 7, 1962, NSF, Box 427, Komer Papers, Israel 1961–1963, JFKL.

72. Talbot memo to Feldman, Aug. 9, 1962, NSF, Box 118A, Israel, General, JFKL. While the big-ticket item was the Johnson mission, the State Department also had a longer wish list; it hoped to get Israel to surrender its nettlesome claim to sovereignty over the Sea of Galilee, to show restraint in its reprisals against Syrian shelling, and to stop the U.N. push for the so-called Brazzaville resolution, which called for direct negotiations between Israelis and Arabs.

73. Talbot memo to Feldman, Aug. 9, 1962, NSF, Box 118A, Israel, General, JFKL.

74. Feldman memo to JFK, Aug. 10, 1962, *FRUS*, 1961–63, Vol. 18, p. 53.

75. The Johnson plan: Considerations for the United States, in Rusk memo to JFK, Aug. 7, 1962, NSF, Box 118A, Israel General, JFKL.

76. United Nations Preference Questionnaire, undated 1962, NSF, Box 118A, Israel, General, JFKL.

77. Feldman memo to JFK, Aug. 10, 1962, NSF, Box 427, Komer Papers, Israel 1961–1963, JFKL.

78. Could the linkage have been a poison pill? Was State actually trying to sink the Hawk sale by tying it to the foundering Johnson plan? It would have been a shrewd bureaucratic maneuver, but the documentary record shows a State Department that still hoped that the Johnson plan might fly. It is also hard to imagine Rusk throwing his friend Johnson over the side so cavalierly. NEA seems to have been sincerely supporting the Johnson mission rather than using it as an anchor to drag the Hawks down.

79. Notes of White House conference on Johnson plan, Aug. 14, 1962, *FRUS*, 1961–63, Vol. 18, pp. 54–58.

80. Notes of meeting, Aug. 14, 1962, *FRUS*, 1961–63, Vol. 18, pp. 59–60.

81. JFK letter to Ben-Gurion, Aug. 15, 1962, NSF, Box 427, Komer Papers, Israel 1961–1963, JFKL.

82. Rusk telegram to Middle East embassies, Aug. 22, 1962, NSF, Box 118A, Israel General, JFKL.

83. Ball memo to Tel Aviv, Aug. 16, 1962, NSF, Box 118A, Israel General, JFKL.

84. Feldman telegram to JFK, Rusk, and Grant, Aug. 19, 1962, DOSF, Central Decimal File, Box 2059, File 784A.5612, NA.

85. Steven L. Spiegel, *The Other Arab-Israeli Conflict: Making America's Middle East Policy, from Truman to Reagan* (Chicago: University of Chicago Press, 1985), p. 113.

86. FM to Washington Embassy, August 20, 1962, MH 3377/7, ISA.

87. Rusk telegram to Feldman, Aug. 20, 1962, DOSF, Central Decimal File, Box 2059, File 784A.5612, NA.

88. Grant telegram to Strong in Cairo, Aug. 21, 1962, NSF, Box 118A, Israel General, JFKL.

89. Feldman telegram to JFK, Rusk, and Grant, Aug. 21, 1962, NSF, Box 118A, Israel, General, JFKL.

90. Tel Aviv Deputy Chief of Mission N. Spencer Barnes telegram to State, Aug. 22, 1962, NSF, Box 118A, Israel, General, JFKL.

91. Memcon: Feldman visit to Israel, Aug. 24, 1962, *FRUS*, 1961–63, Vol. 18, pp. 73–74.

92. Rusk telegram to Badeau and Strong, Aug. 22, 1962, NSF, Box 118A, Israel, General, JFKL.

93. Badeau telegram to JFK, Rusk, and Grant, Aug. 24, 1962, NSF, Box 427, Komer Papers, Israel 1961–1963, JFKL.

94. Grant telegram to Strong in Cairo, Aug. 21, 1962, NSF, Box 118A, Israel General, JFKL.

95. Badeau telegram to JFK, Rusk, and Grant, Aug. 24, 1962, NSF, Box 427, Komer Papers, Israel 1961–1963, JFKL.

96. Ben-Gurion letter to JFK, Aug. 20, 1962, NSF, Box 119, Country Files, Israel, General, JFKL.

97. On JFK's taping system, cf. Ernest R. May and Philip D. Zelikow, eds., *The Kennedy Tapes: Inside the White House During the Cuban Missile Crisis* (Cambridge: Belknap Press of Harvard University Press, 1997), pp. x–xii.

98. Tape 17, Aug. 27, 1962, 5 P.M., POF, Presidential Recording Collection, JFKL. I had an advance opportunity to listen to the tape through the kind assistance of the Presidential Recordings Project at the University of Virginia's Miller Center of Public Affairs. A transcript of the tape, prepared by a Miller Center team under the supervision of Timothy Naftali, is included in the Miller Center's splendid volumes of Kennedy tape transcriptions; cf. Timothy Naftali, Ernest R. May, and Philip D. Zelikow, eds., *The Presidential Recordings: John F. Kennedy — The Great Crises, Volumes 1–3* (New York: W. W. Norton, 2001).

99. Komer memo to Deputy National Security Adviser Carl Kaysen, Sept. 22, 1962, *FRUS*, 1961–63, Vol. 18, p. 122.

100. Memcon: Feldman dinner with Meir, Harman, Philip Klutznick of USUN, and Abraham Feinberg of Israel Bonds, Sept. 20, 1962, NSF, Box 119, Country Files, Israel, General, JFKL.

101. Feldman memo to JFK, Sept. 25, 1962, POF, Box 63, Staff Memoranda, Myer Feldman 1962, JFKL.

102. "Part of the problem," Kaysen wrote Kennedy, "is Mike Feldman's tendency to take only the Israeli side of the problem into account; hence the need for turning dealings with the Israelis over to the Secretary of State for the time being" (Kaysen to JFK, Sept. 23, 1962, POF, Box 119A, Israel Security 1961–63, JFKL); "Of course," Komer noted later, "I deliberately have *not* clued Mike on this" (Komer memo to Bundy, Dec. 5, 1962, POF, Box 119A, Israel Security 1961–63, JFKL).

103. Lyon telegram to Rusk, Sept. 15, 1962, NSF, Box 119, Country Files, Israel, General, JFKL.

104. Scope Paper, President's Meeting with Israel Foreign Minister: Briefing Materials, Dec. 21, 1962, NSF, Box 119, Country Files, Israel, General, JFKL.

105. Komer memo to JFK, Dec. 5, 1962, NSF, Box 119, Country Files, Israel, General, JFKL.

106. Spiegel, p. 115.

107. The quote is cited in Barbour telegram to Rusk, Jan. 24, 1963, NSF, Box 119, Country Files, Israel, General, JFKL. On the Palm Beach meeting, cf. memcon: JFK meeting with Meir, Dec. 27, 1962 , NSF, Box 119, Israel, General, JFKL.

108. Badeau telegram to Rusk, Sept. 17, 1962, DOSF, Central Decimal File 1960–63, Box 2059, File 784A.5612, NA.

109. Komer memo to Bundy, Sept. 14, 1962, *FRUS*, 1961–63, Vol. 18, pp. 96–97.

110. Bundy memo to JFK, Sept. 16, 1962, NSF, Box 427, Komer Papers, Israel 1961–63, White House Memoranda, JFKL.

111. Ball telegram to Badeau, Sept. 26, 1962, NSF, Box 119, Country Files, Israel, General, JFKL. While Strong had told Nasser that the Hawk sale was coming, the Egyptian president technically was informed, not consulted.

112. Memcon: Talbot meeting with Kamel, Sept. 26, 1962, DODF, Office of the Assistant Secretary of Defense for International Security Affairs (OASD-ISA), Box 89, Israel 1962, NA.

113. Memcon: Seelye meeting with Faysal, Sept. 26, 1962, DODF, OASD-ISA, Box 89, Israel 1962, NA.

114. Hart telegram to Rusk, Oct. 6, 1962, DOSF, Central Decimal File 1960–63, Box 2059, File 784A.5612, NA.

115. Badeau telegram to Rusk, Sept. 27, 1962, NSF, Box 119, Country Files, Israel, General, JFKL.

116. Lewis telegram to Rusk, Sept. 27, 1962, DOSF, Central Decimal File 1960–63, Box 2059, File 784A.5612, NA. Another copy of the document—in NSF, Box 119, Country Files, Israel, General, JFKL—is a classic of transparent (and transparently silly) sanitization.

117. U.S. Information Service Public Affairs Officer Vincent Joyce to USIA Washington, Oct. 2, 1962, DOSF, Central Decimal File 1960–63, Box 2059, File 784A.5612, NA.

118. Badeau telegram to Rusk, Sept. 28, 1962, DOSF, Central Decimal File 1960–63, Box 2059, File 784A.5612, NA.

119. Meyer telegram to Rusk, Sept. 28, 1962, DOSF, Central Decimal File 1960–63, Box 2059, File 784A.5612, NA.

120. Meyer telegram to Rusk, Sept. 28, 1962, NSF, Box 428, Komer Papers, Israel, Security (Missile), Development Sale of Hawks, JFKL.

121. Meyer telegram to Rusk, Sept. 30, 1962, NSF, Box 119, Country Files, Israel, General, JFKL.

122. Melbourne telegram to Rusk, NSF, Box 119, Country Files, Israel, General, JFKL.

123. Knight telegram to Rusk, Sept. 28, 1962, NSF, Box 428, Komer Papers, Israel, Security (Missile), Development Sale of Hawks, JFKL.

124. Mak telegram to Rusk, Oct. 1, 1962, NSF, Box 119, Country Files, Israel, General, JFKL.

125. Ball telegram to Badeau, Sept. 29, 1962, NSF, Box 428, Komer Papers, Israel, Security (Missile), Development Sale of Hawks, JFKL.

126. Prohme telegram to State, Oct. 1, 1962, NSF, Box 119, Country Files, Israel, General, JFKL.

127. Badeau telegram to Rusk, Oct. 16, 1962, NSF, Box 428, Komer Papers, Israel, Security (Missile), Development Sale of Hawks, JFKL.

128. Badeau telegram to Rusk, Sept. 29, 1962, NSF, Box 428, Komer Papers, Israel, Security (Missile), Development Sale of Hawks, JFKL.

129. For a detailed comparison of the capabilities of the Hawk and Bloodhound, which tends to bear out the Israeli assertion that the former was the superior missile, cf. Director of Developments Allen Hulse to Bundy, Aug. 24, 1962, DODF, RG 330, Records of the Office of the Secretary of Defense, Office of the Assistant Secretary of Defense for International Security Affairs, Box 68, File 471.6 August 1962, NA.

130. "Offer of S.A.G.W. to Israel: Anglo-American Discussions," Sept. 1962, FO 371/164353, PRO.

131. "Missiles for Israel," Sept. 3, 1962, FO 371/164348, PRO.

132. Background brief, "Surface-to-air Guided Weapons for Israel," Jan. 24, 1962, FO 371/164344, PRO; Air Ministry Paper on 'Israel's Air Defence System,' undated 1962, FO 371/164345, PRO.

133. Record of Profumo meeting with Peres, Feb. 14, 1962, FO 371/164345, PRO.

134. Minutes: Smart meeting with Newsom, Feb. 15, 1962, FO 371/164345, PRO.

135. Speares to Leonard Figg of FO Eastern Department, June 6, 1962, FO 371/164346, PRO.

136. Foreign Office to Washington, June 14, 1962, FO 371/164346, PRO.

137. Record of Macmillan conversation with Rusk, June 24, 1962, PRO 371/164346, PRO.

138. British Embassy Minister Viscount Samuel Hood to FO, Aug. 17, 1962, FO 371/164347, PRO.

139. London to Rusk, Aug. 18, 1962, NSF, Box 118A, Israel, General, JFKL.

140. Hood to FO, Aug. 19, 1962, FO 371/164347, PRO.

141. Bundy memo to JFK, Aug. 19, 1962, NSF, Box 118A, Israel, General, JFKL.

142. Hood to FO, Aug. 19, 1962, FO 371/164347, PRO.

143. FO to Washington, Aug. 19, 1962, FO 371/164347, PRO.

144. Home to Macmillan, Sept. 5, 1962, FO 371/164349, PRO.

145. Macmillan to Home, Sept. 5, 1962, FO 371/164349, PRO.

146. "Rift in Anglo–U.S. Missiles Pact," *Sunday Telegraph*, Sept. 30, 1962.

147. Cabinet conclusions, Oct. 4, 1962, 10:30 A.M., CAB 128/36, PRO. By late October, British regional ambassadors had begun approaching Arab governments about SAM sales; cf. Knight telegram to Rusk, Oct. 24, 1962, NSF, Box 428, Komer Papers, Israel, Security (Missile), Development Sale of Hawks, JFKL.

148. Bundy memo to JFK, Aug. 19, 1962, NSF, Box 118A, Israel, General, JFKL.

149. Reported in Barbour to State, "Israel's Security," Oct. 5, 1962, NSF, Box 119, Country Files, Israel, General, JFKL.

150. Talbot to Rusk, Oct. 19, 1962, DOSF, Central Decimal File 1960–63, Box 2059, File 784A.5612, NA.

151. McGhee to Talbot, Oct. 26, 1962, DOSF, Central Decimal File 1960–63, Box 2059, File 784A.5612, NA.

152. Memcon: JFK meeting with Meir in Palm Beach, Dec. 27, 1962 , NSF, Box 119, Israel, General, JFKL.

153. Tel Aviv embassy to State, May 1, 1963, NSF, Box 119, Country Files, Israel, General, JFKL.

154. "Costs of Hawk Equipment and Missiles," NSF, Box 428, Komer Papers, Israel, Security (Missiles), Development Sale of Hawks, 1962–1963, JFKL.

155. DoD notes on Peres visit, March 26, 1963 and April 9, 1963, NSF, Box 428, Komer Papers, Israel, Security (Missile), Development Sale of Hawks, JFKL.

156. C. L. Sulzberger, "Foreign Affairs: The Music Goes Round and Round," *The New York Times*, Nov. 18, 1963.

157. Komer memo to Bundy, Feb. 13, 1963, NSF, Box 427, Komer Papers, Israel 1961–63, White House Memoranda, JFKL.

158. Ben-Gurion letter to JFK, April 26, 1963, NSF, Box 119, Country Files, Israel, General, JFKL.

159. Memcon: Talbot meeting with Harman, Oct. 3, 1963, NSF, Box 428, Komer Papers, Israel, Security (Missile), Development Sale of Hawks, JFKL.

160. Rusk telegram to Barbour, Oct. 16, 1962, NSF, Box 428, Komer Papers, U.S.–Israel Talks, UAR Missile Capability, JFKL.

161. "List of DoD Officials General Rabin Is Seeing," NSF, Box 428, Komer Papers, U.S.–Israel Talks, UAR Missile Capability, JFKL.

162. Talbot telegram to Middle East ambassadors, Nov. 13, 1963, NSF, Box 428, Komer Papers, U.S.–Israel Talks, UAR Missile Capability, JFKL.

163. Memo for the record: Komer meeting with Rabin, Nov. 18, 1963, NSF, Box 428, Komer Papers, Israel, U.S.–Israeli Talks re: UAR Missile Capability, JFKL.

164. Memorandum for the Record, Nov. 18, 1962, Komer meeting with Rabin, NSF, Box 428, Komer Papers, U.S.–Israel Talks, UAR Missile Capability, JFKL.

165. Memcon: Bundy and Komer meeting with Harman, Jan. 10, 1964, *FRUS*, 1964–68, Vol. 18, Arab-Israeli Dispute 1964–1967, pp. 11–15.

166. Memcon: Rusk and Talbot meeting with Harman, Jan. 3, 1964, *FRUS*, 1964–68, Vol. 18, Arab-Israeli Dispute 1964–1967, pp. 3–6.

167. Spiegel, pp. 131–35.

CHAPTER SIX : The Delicate Matter

1. Richard Reeves, *President Kennedy: Profile of Power* (New York: Touchstone, 1994), pp.29–33.

2. ACDA paper, "US Position for a Test Ban," Feb. 26, 1963, DOSF, NEA Files, NEA/IAI, Near East Arms Initiative 1963–64, Box 1, Near East Arms, NA.

3. Author conversation, Phillips Talbot, May 29, 2001, New York.

4. For a sharp CIA assessment, cf. "Radiological Warfare in the Middle East," April 18, 1963, DOSF, NEA Files, NEA/IAI, Near East Arms Initiative, Box 1, Near East Arms.

5. On the album *That Was the Year That Was*, Lehrer caught the Middle Eastern nuclear dynamic reasonably well:

> Egypt's gonna get one, too
> Just to use on you-know-who.
> So Israel's getting tense
> Wants one in self-defense
> "The Lord's our shepherd," says the psalm
> But just in case, we better get a bomb.

6. Komer memo, undated, 1964, DOSF, NEA Files, NEA/IAI, Near East Arms Initiative, Box 1, Background papers vis-à-vis 2nd McCloy probe w/Nasser 09-64, NA.

7. Stephen E. Palmer, Jr. letter to H. Earl Russell, Jr., Oct. 18, 1963, DOSF, NEA Files, Records of the Israel-Lebanon Desk 1954–65, Box 8, Correspondence with Israel 1963, NA.

8. Nevertheless, NEA remained nervous that the Israel lobby would use the upcoming 1964 campaigns as leverage to win a security guarantee and to wreck the Nasser initiative; cf. Grant memo to Rusk, May 11, 1963, DOSF, NEA Files, NEA/IAI, Near East Arms Initiative, Box 1, Near East Arms.

9. Mike Feldman's staff memoranda to Kennedy, for instance, contain not one mention of Dimona; cf. POF, Box 63, Staff Memoranda, Myer Feldman, JFKL.

10. Evan Thomas, *Robert Kennedy: His Life* (New York: Simon & Schuster, 2000), p. 172.

11. Memcon: Suggested Guidance for Chairman McCone's use in "Meet the Press" interview, Dec. 17, 1960, USNNP, 1945–1991, NSA; and Avner Cohen, *Israel and the Bomb* (New York: Columbia University Press, 1998), pp. 88–89. For a fuller, fascinating treatment of France's role in the creation of Dimona, cf. Cohen, pp. 58–75.

12. "Summary of Additional Recent Information on Israeli Atomic Energy Program," Jan. 17, 1961, *FRUS*, 1961–63, Vol. 17, pp. 5–6.

13. "Franco-Israeli Nuclear Collaboration," Central Intelligence Bulletin, April 27, 1961, NSF, Box 119A, Israel, Ben-Gurion Visit, JFKL.

14. Ibid., p. 60.

15. "The French-Israeli Relationship," CIA Report, POF, Box 119A, Israel, Security, David Ben-Gurion 1/1961–5/1961, JFKL.

16. Barbour telegram to State, May 28, 1962, Kennedy File, Ben-Gurion Archives. Among the 23 luxury villas being built to house the French Dimona workers was one bought by an Israeli journalist, whom Barbour reported might have gotten his house by blackmailing Peres with threats to run stories about the reactor.

17. Rusk memo to JFK, Jan. 30, 1961, USNNP, NSA; cf. also State Department circular, Dec. 22, 1960, USNNP, NSA.

18. While a research reactor could also be used to generate plutonium, a one-megawatt reactor such as Nahal Soreq could only have done so very slowly.

19. Cohen, p. 82.

20. Rusk memo to JFK, Jan. 30, 1961, USNNP, NSA.

21. Memcon: Jones meeting with Senators Gore, Hickenlooper, Fulbright, Carlson, and Sparkman, Jan. 9, 1961, *FRUS*, 1961–63, Vol. 17, pp. 1–3; also cf. Cohen, p. 85.

22. Reid telegram to Herter, Nov. 29, 1960, USNNP, NSA. Heavy water is a moderator and coolant used in nuclear fission.

23. Memcon: "Israeli Atomic Energy Program" (names of participants censored), Dec. 1, 1960, USNNP, NSA.

24. "Chronology of Israel Assurances of Peaceful Uses of Atomic Energy and Related Events," March 19, 1964, DOSF, NEA Files, NEA/IAI, Near East Arms Initiative, Box 1, Talbot in Spring 1964, NA; Cohen, p. 87.

25. "Summary of Additional Recent Information on Israeli Atomic Energy Program," Jan. 17, 1961, *FRUS*, 1961–63, Vol. 17, pp. 5–6.

26. Ibid., p. 88.

27. Assistant Secretary of State for Congressional Relations Macomber letter to Ramey, Jan. 19, 1961, *FRUS*, 1961–63, Vol. 17, pp. 4–5.

28. Memcon: Suggested Guidance for Chairman McCone's use in "Meet the Press" interview, Dec. 17, 1960, USNNP, NSA.

29. Reid telegram to Herter, Dec. 18, 1960, USNNP, NSA.

30. Transcript, "Meet the Press," Dec. 18, 1960, USNNP, NSA.

31. Cohen, p. 89.

32. McClintock telegram to Herter, Dec. 27, 1960, USNNP, NSA.

33. Michael Bar-Zohar, *Ben-Gurion: A Biography* (New York: Adama Books, 1986), p. 271.

34. Houghton telegram to Herter, Dec. 19, 1960, USNNP, NSA.

35. "Summary of Additional Recent Information on Israeli Atomic Energy Program," Jan. 17, 1961, *FRUS*, 1961–63, Vol. 17, pp. 5–6.

36. State Department circular, Dec. 22, 1960, USNNP, NSA.

37. "Summary of Additional Recent Information on Israeli Atomic Energy Program," Jan. 17, 1961, *FRUS*, 1961–63, Vol. 17, pp. 5–6.

38. Herter telegram to regional embassies, Dec. 22, 1960, USNNP, NSA.

39. Reid telegram to Herter, Dec. 22, 1960, USNNP, NSA.

40. "Franco-Israeli Nuclear Collaboration," Central Intelligence Bulletin, April 27, 1961, NSF, Box 119A, Israel, Ben-Gurion Visit, JFKL.

41. "Chronology of Israel Assurances of Peaceful Uses of Atomic Energy and Related Events."

42. Executive Sessions of the Senate Foreign Relations Committee, Volume XIII, Part 1, 87th Congress, First Session, Jan. 6, 1961 (Washington: GPO, 1984).

43. Memcon: Jones meeting with Senators Gore, Hickenlooper, Fulbright, Carlson, and Sparkman, Jan. 9, 1961, *FRUS*, 1961–63, Vol. 17, pp. 1–3.

44. Cohen, p. 96.

45. Ibid., p. 93.

46. Assistant Secretary of State for Congressional Relations Macomber letter to Ramey, Jan. 19, 1961, *FRUS*, 1961–63, Vol. 17, pp. 4–5.

47. On Dayan and Peres, cf. Barnes airgram to State, June 2, 1961, NSF, Box 119, Israel, General, JFKL.

48. Rusk memo to JFK, Jan. 30, 1961, POF, Box 119A, Israel, Security, JFKL. The appended chronology remains censored.

49. Memcon: Jones meeting with Harman, Feb. 3, 1961, *FRUS*, 1961–63, Vol. 17, pp. 13–15, fn 1.

50. "Chronology of Israel Assurances of Peaceful Uses of Atomic Energy and Related Events."

51. Memcon: JFK meeting with Reid, Jan. 31, 1961, *FRUS*, 1961–63, Vol. 17, pp. 10–11.

52. Seymour Hersh has reported that McCone authorized both U-2 overflights of Dimona and spying missions to infiltrate the compound; Seymour M. Hersh, *The Samson Option: Israel's Nuclear Arsenal and American Foreign Policy* (New York: Random House, 1991), pp. 106–7. There is no evidence of such efforts in the available documents, which, of course, hardly rules out their existence.

53. CIA Information Report, Jan. 18, 1961, POF, Box 119A, Israel, Security, David Ben-Gurion, JFKL. The document's text has not been sanitized, but the identity of the appraiser has been blacked out—a flagrant abuse of the federal government's censorship powers, which are clearly used here not to preserve legitimate national security secrecy but to prevent embarrassment.

54. Memcon: US-UK talks on the Middle East, Feb. 13, 1961, *FRUS*, 1961–63, Vol. 17, pp. 20–21.

55. JFK dictation, conversation with Ogden Reid, Jan. 31, 1961, POF, Box 119A, Israel, General, JFKL.

56. Memcon: Jones meeting with Harman, Feb. 3, 1961, POF, Box 119A, Israel, General, JFKL.

57. Memcon: Bundy meeting with Harman, Feb. 16, 1961, NSF, Box 118, Israel, General, JFKL.

58. Memcon: US-UK talks on the Middle East, Feb. 13, 1961, *FRUS*, 1961–63, Vol. 17, pp. 20–21.

59. Rusk memo to JFK, March 3, 1961, POF, Box 119A, Israel, General, JFKL.

60. Memcon: Jones meeting with Harman, March 28, 1961, NSF, Box 118, Israel, General, JFKL.

61. Cf., for instance, State Executive Secretariat Director Walter J. Stoessel, Jr., to Brig. Gen. Andrew J. Goodpaster, Feb. 3, 1961, NSF, Box 118, Israel, General, JFKL.

62. Memcon: Jones meeting with Harman, April 10, 1961, *FRUS*, 1961–63, Vol. 17, pp. 79–80.

63. Rusk memo to JFK, May 5, 1961, NSF, Box 118, Israel, General, JFKL.

64. Bundy memo to JFK, May 11, 1961, NSF, Box 118, Israel, General, JFKL.

65. Battle memo to Bundy, May 18, 1961, NSF, Box 118, Israel, General, JFKL.

66. Memcon: Rusk meeting with Harman, April 13, 1961, *FRUS*, 1961–63, Vol. 17, p. 81.

67. The most detailed account of their inspection is found in Battle memo to Bundy, May 26, 1961, NSF, Box 118, Israel, General, JFKL.

68. "Chronology of Israel Assurances of Peaceful Uses of Atomic Energy and Related Events."

69. Cohen, p. 104.

70. Feldman memo to JFK, May 26, 1961, POF, Box 119A, Israel, Security, JFKL.

71. Bundy memo to JFK, May 29, 1961, *FRUS*, 1961–63, Vol. 17, pp. 132–33.

72. Bar-Zohar, p. 273.

73. "Chronology of Israel Assurances of Peaceful Uses of Atomic Energy and Related Events."

74. Memcon: JFK meeting with Ben-Gurion, May 30, 1961, NSF, Box 118, Israel, General, JFKL.

75. "The Atomic Reactor," Ben-Gurion meeting with JFK, May 30, 1961, MH 3294/28, ISA. Unless otherwise footnoted, this discussion is based upon the American memcon. The two accounts largely jibe. The Israeli version does call the two countries "very close friends" rather than just "close friends," and it renders JFK's opening salvo as, "But a woman should not only be virtuous, she should appear to be virtuous."

76. "The Atomic Reactor," May 30, 1961, MH 3294/28, ISA.

77. The Israeli version has Ben-Gurion's reply as, "You are free to do what you like with it. On the contrary, we are interested in your doing so."

78. This exchange is drawn from the Israeli minutes.

79. For these aspects of the Waldorf meeting, cf. the discussions in chapters III and V of this book.

80. Bar-Zohar, p. 273.

81. Fulbright letter to Bowles, May 29, 1961, USNNP, NSA.

82. Memcon: Talbot meeting with Arab ambassadors, June 2, 1961, NSF, Box 119A, Israel, Ben-Gurion Visit, JFKL.

83. Memcon: Talbot meeting with Harman, June 22, 1961, NSF, Box 118, Israel, General, JFKL.

84. The complaint was sometimes rendered in more anatomically vivid language.

85. JCS paper, JCSM-523-61, Aug. 1961, FRUS, 1961–63, Vol. 17, pp. 216–21.

86. Rusk letter to Gilpatric, Aug. 30, 1961, DOSF, Central Decimal File, 1960–63, 784A.5611/7-761, NA.

87. Acting Assistant Secretary of State for NEA Armin Meyer memo to Deputy Undersecretary of State for Political Affairs U. Alexis Johnson, Oct. 19, 1961, FRUS, 1961–63, Vol. 17, p. 313.

88. For instance, cf. Talbot memo to Rusk, June 7, 1962, FRUS, 1961–63, Vol. 17, p. 714.

89. Talbot memo to Rusk, Nov. 22, 1961, FRUS, 1961–63, Vol. 17, p. 344.

90. Douglas Little, "The Making of a Special Relationship: The United States and Israel, 1957–68," *International Journal of Middle East Studies*, No. 25 (1993), pp. 563–85.

91. Cohen, p. 174.

92. Hersh, p. 109.

93. Hersh wrote without access to much of the documentary record; and while Feldman and Komer's latter-day reminiscences are important data, they are probably not as reliable as contemporaneous sources.

94. For a concurring opinion, cf. Michael B. Oren, *Six Days of War: June 1967 and the Making of the Modern Middle East* (New York: Oxford University Press, 2002), p. 16.

95. Ibid., p. 176.

96. Lord Hood to Foreign Office, Aug. 14, 1962, FO 371/170579, PRO.

97. Shaw telegram to State, Aug. 18, 1962, JFK collection, BGA; Brubeck memo to Bundy, Sept. 21, 1962, NSF, Box 119, Israel, General, JFKL; "Chronology of Israel Assurances of Peaceful Uses of Atomic Energy and Related Events."

98. Brubeck memo to Bundy, Sept. 21, 1962, NSF, Box 119, Israel, General, JFKL.

99. "Chronology of Israel Assurances of Peaceful Uses of Atomic Energy and Related Events."

100. Rusk telegram to regional embassies, Oct. 31, 1962, USNNP, NSA.

101. Ormsby Gore to Foreign Office, Oct. 24, 1962, FO 371/170579, PRO.

102. State Department scope paper, Dec. 21, 1962, NSF, Box 119, Israel, General, JFKL.

103. Memcon: JFK meeting with Meir, Dec. 27, 1962, NSF, Box 119, Israel, General, JFKL.

104. Komer memo to JFK, Dec. 22, 1962, NSF, Box 119, Israel, General, JFKL.

105. Brubeck memo to Bundy, Dec. 21, 1962, "President's Meeting with Israel Foreign Minister: Briefing Materials," NSF, Box 119, Israel, General, JFKL.

106. Barbour OH, May 22, 1981, p. 21, JFKL.

107. Golda Meir, *My Life* (London: Futura, 1978), pp. 258–59. Meir also reports, not entirely convincingly, that Kennedy responded to her discussion of Israel's existential perils by taking her hand, looking into her eyes, and saying, "I understand, Mrs. Meir. Don't worry. *Nothing* will happen to Israel."

108. The charge is mentioned in "Introductory Remarks by Phillips Talbot," Nov. 12, 1963, NSF, Box 428, Komer Papers, U.S.–Israel Talks on UAR Missile Capability, JFKL. In fact, U.S. intelligence analyses concluded that Nasser did not have much of a nuclear arms program, and Ben-Gurion himself later backed away from charges that Egypt was anywhere near shouting distance of getting the bomb.

109. Cohen, p. 115.

110. Author interview with Zaki Shalom, Ben-Gurion University, July 24, 2001, Sdeh Boqer.

111. "Franco-Israeli Nuclear Collaboration," Central Intelligence Bulletin, April 27, 1961, NSF, Box 119A, Israel, Ben-Gurion Visit, JFKL.

112. NIE 30-63, Jan. 23, 1963, *FRUS*, 1961–63, Vol. 18, pp. 317–18.

113. Defense Intelligence Agency assessment, "Missile Potential of the UAR," Jan. 24, 1963, *FRUS*, 1961–63, Vol. 18, pp. 318–20.

114. CIA Board of National Estimates Chairman Sherman Kent memo to DCI McCone, March 6, 1963, NSF, Box 119, Israel, General, JFKL.

115. Komer memo to JFK, Feb. 9, 1963, *FRUS*, 1961–63, Vol. 18, pp. 345–46.

116. Komer memo to JFK, March 22, 1963, *FRUS*, 1961–63, Vol. 18, pp. 432–33.

117. NSAM No. 231, March 26, 1963, NSF, Box 427, Israel, Nuclear Energy Program 1963, White House Memoranda, JFKL.

118. Rusk telegram to Barbour, March 27, 1963, DOSF, Central Foreign Policy File, 1963, Box 3727, DEF ISR, NA.

119. "Chronology of Israel Assurances of Peaceful Uses of Atomic Energy and Related Events."

120. Barbour to Rusk, April 3, 1963, DOSF, Central Foreign Policy File, 1963, Box 3727, DEF ISR, NA.

121. Ball telegram to Barbour, April 4, 1963, *FRUS*, 1961–63, Vol. 18, pp. 449–50.

122. As Peres recalls, he ran into the British Labour Party leader, Harold Wilson, on his way into the Oval Office, and a grinning Kennedy listened raptly as Wilson gave "a long and salacious account of the Profumo Affair." Cf. Shimon Peres, *Battling for Peace: Memoirs* (London: Weidenfeld & Nicolson, 1995), p. 258.

123. Memcon: Feldman phone call with Talbot, April 5, 1963, NSF, Box 119A, Israel, General, JFKL.

124. Peres, p. 258.

125. Cohen, pp. 118–19. The Israeli minutes of the JFK-Peres meeting are available on the National Security Archive's website. For another translation of the same minutes, cf. Matti Golan, *Shimon Peres: A Biography* (New York: St. Martin's Press, 1982), p. 118.

126. Ben-Gurion letter to JFK, April 26, 1963, POF, Box 119A, Israel, Security, JFKL.

127. Cohen, p. 120.

128. JFK letter to Ben-Gurion, May 4, 1963, MH 3377/9, ISA. Kennedy rejected the idea of a joint U.S.–Soviet declaration affirming the Middle East's present borders and declined Ben-Gurion's offer to meet in person again.

129. Barbour telegram to Rusk, May 5, 1963, NSF, Box 119, Israel, General, JFKL.

130. Grant memo to Rusk, May 11, 1963, *FRUS*, 1961–63, Vol. 18, pp. 526–27.

131. Komer's irritation was heightened by the fact that he had spent several days in Egypt that spring—and the visit had included a trip to Nasser's Inschass reactor. Alas, the documentary record of his trip is tantalizingly thin. We know that during a trip to the Indian subcontinent, Komer dropped by Egypt for at least three days, beginning on April 10; that he advised Badeau that a mysterious "personal matter" was indeed "a potential problem"; that he flew to the Aswan High Dam; that he met with various dignitaries, including Nasser; and that he later sent on some American coffee as a gift for Cairo Governor Salah Dessouki's wife, who loved the stuff. More dramatically, *Ma'ariv* ran a front-page story on May 8 claiming that Kennedy had sent Komer to investigate Israeli charges that Nasser was using German scientists to try to get the bomb. An angry Komer fired off a memo to Feldman, accusing him of leaking. Calling the story a "complete fabrication," Komer accused the Israelis of "seeking to destroy our (as well as my) credibility with the UAR" by painting him as Jerusalem's errand-boy. He had told only Bundy, Talbot, Strong, and Feldman about seeing the Egyptian reactor, Komer complained. "Mac - though Mike denies this to the skies it is a fact that I mentioned my Inchass visit to him only 4–5 days ago, and then boom!" he scrawled to Bundy. "Can't we keep Mike out of the Arab side at least? I'm worried." Komer would get his wish; Feldman was increasingly cut out of the nuclear loop. Cf. Komer letter to Cairo Governor Salah Dessouki, March 28, 1963, NSF, Box 446, Komer Papers, UAR 1/63–11/63, White House Memoranda, JFKL. Komer letter to Badeau, April 23, 1963, NSF, Box 446, Komer Papers, UAR 1/63–11/63, White House Memoranda, JFKL. Dessouki letter to William R. Polk of Policy Planning, April 23, 1963, NSF, Box 446, Komer Papers, UAR 1/63–11/63, JFKL. Komer letter to William Boswell at the U.S. embassy in Cairo, July 25, 1963, NSF, Box 446, Komer Papers, UAR 1/63–11/63, White House Memoranda, JFKL. Barbour telegram to Rusk, May 8, 1963, NSF, Box 119, Israel, General, JFKL. Komer to Feldman (Bundy's copy), May 9, 1963, NSF, Box 119, Israel, General, JFKL.

Komer was not even the unlikeliest American visitor to Cairo that spring; in June, Richard Nixon—now a private citizen after failed bids for president in 1960 and California governor in 1962—also turned up. Along with his wife, Pat, the former vice president wandered through Cairo's Khan al-Khalili bazaar, admired the pyramids at Giza and the Temple of Karnak at Luxor, met with Nasser, and even pronounced himself impressed after being flown in Nasser's private Ilyushin jet to see the dam at Aswan that the Eisenhower administration had so fatefully declined to fund. Taken together with Henry Cabot Lodge's 1961 trip, Nixon's jaunt meant that, oddly, the entire 1960 GOP ticket visited Egypt during Kennedy's presidency. Only Nixon could go to Cairo. Memcon: Nixon meeting with Nasser, in Badeau telegram to Rusk, June 26, 1963, NSF, Box 169, UAR General 6/63–8/63, JFKL. For Nixon's schedule, cf. Embassy Counselor for Political Affairs Donald C. Bergus memo to Rusk, July 3, 1963, NSF, Box 169, UAR General 6/63–8/63, JFKL.

132. Memcon: Feldman lunch with Harman (Komer's copy), May 6, 1963, NSF, Box 119, Israel, General, JFKL.

133. Rusk telegram to Barbour, May 10, 1963, NSF, Box 119, Israel, General, JFKL.

134. *The Kennedy Presidential Press Conferences* (New York: Earl M. Coleman, 1978), pp. 497–98.

135. *FRUS*, 1961–63, Vol. 18, p. 528.

136. Discussions on sending PM's letter to Kennedy on 8.5, MH 3377/9, ISA.

137. Brubeck memo to Bundy, May 14, 1963, DOSF, NEA Files, Records of the Israel-Lebanon Affairs Desk, 1954–1965, Box 9, White House Correspondence 1963, NA; Cohen, pp. 122–23.

138. Talbot memo to Rusk, May 14, 1963, POF, Box 119A, Israel, Security, JFKL.

139. Talbot did not mention the Hawk sale.

140. Harman to FM, May 16, 1963, MH 3377/9, ISA.

141. Memo for the record: Komer meeting with Gazit, May 14, 1963, NSF, Box 119, Israel, General, JFKL.

142. Komer memo to JFK, May 16, 1963, POF, Box 119A, Israel, Security, JFKL.

143. Barbour telegram to Rusk, May 15, 1963 [two sections], NSF, Box 119, Israel, General, JFKL.

144. Rusk telegram to Barbour, May 16, 1963, NSF, Box 119, Israel, General, JFKL.

145. JFK letter to Ben-Gurion, May 18, 1963, POF, Box 119A, Israel, Security, JFKL; italics mine.

146. The paragraph was thought so sensitive that the U.S. government kept it classified for nearly 40 years. For the censored version of Kennedy's letter, cf. *FRUS*, 1961–63, Vol. 18, pp. 543–44. The *FRUS* volume was published in 1995.

147. Cohen, p. 129.

148. "Chronology of Israel Assurances of Peaceful Uses of Atomic Energy and Related Events."

149. Barbour telegram to Rusk, May 27, 1963, NSF, Box 119, Israel, General, JFKL.

150. Ben-Gurion letter to JFK, May 27, 1963, NSF, Box 119, Israel, General, JFKL; italics mine.

151. Brubeck memo to Bundy, May 29, 1963, NSF, Box 119, Israel, General, JFKL.

152. Komer memo to Bundy, May 29, 1963, NSF, Box 119, Israel, General, JFKL.

153. Brubeck memo to Bundy, June 12, 1963, NSF, Box 427, Komer Files, Israel, Nuclear Energy Program 1963, JFKL.

154. For the science, cf. Richard L. Garwin and Georges Charpak, *Megawatts and Megatons: A Turning Point in the Nuclear Age?* (New York: Knopf, 2001), p. 315.

155. JFK letter to Ben-Gurion, June 15, 1963, POF, Box 119A, Israel, Security, JFKL; italics mine.

156. Barbour telegram to Rusk, April 27, 1963, NSF, Box 125, Jordan, General, JFKL.

157. Cohen, p. 135. Both Sapir and Galili had thought Ben-Gurion's drive to get the bomb wrongheaded.

158. Author interview with Zaki Shalom, Ben-Gurion University, July 24, 2001, Sdeh Boqer. Shalom is at work on a major new study of Israel's atomic program.

159. Hersh, p.117.

160. Barbour telegram to Rusk, June 16, 1963, 5:47 P.M., NSF, Box 119A, Israel, General, JFKL.

161. Author interview with Shabtai Teveth, July 30, 2001, Tel Aviv.

162. The best account of the Lavon affair is Shabtai Teveth, *Ben-Gurion's Spy: The Story of the Political Scandal That Shaped Modern Israel* (New York: Columbia University Press, 1996).

163. Barbour telegram to Rusk, June 16, 1963, 5:15 P.M., NSF, Box 119A, Israel, General, JFKL.

164. JFK letter to Eshkol, July 4, 1963, MH 3377/9, ISA; italics mine. Another copy is found in POF, Box 119A, Israel, Security, JFKL. A censored version, omitting the threat, is reprinted in *FRUS*, 1961–63, Vol. 18, pp. 624–25.

165. Barbour telegram to Rusk, July 17, 1963, NSF, Box 119A, Israel, General, JFKL.

166. "Chronology of Israel Assurances of Peaceful Uses of Atomic Energy and Related Events."

167. Talbot memo to Rusk, May 14, 1963, DOSF, NEA Files, NEA/IAI, Near East Arms Initiative, Box 1, ME General, NA.

168. State memo, "Background Report for NSAM No. 231," April 3, 1963, DOSF, NEA Files, NEA/IAI, Near East Arms Initiative, Box 1, Near East Arms, NA.

169. Ball telegram to London, May 23, 1963, NSF, Box 169A, United Arab Republic, UAR-Israel Arms Limitation, JFKL.

170. Special National Intelligence Estimate 30-2-63, May 8, 1963, *FRUS*, 1961–63, Vol. 18, pp. 517–18.

171. Badeau telegram to Rusk, July 24, 1962, DOSF, Central Decimal File, Box 2076, File 786B.5612/9-2462, NA.

172. Tel Aviv Embassy First Secretary William Lockling to State Department, Aug. 3, 1962, DOSF, Central Decimal File, Box 2076, File 786B.561/3-2860, NA.

173. CIA Assistant Director, Scientific Intelligence memo to McCone, Jan. 17, 1963, NSF, Box 446, Komer Papers, UAR, Missiles 1963, JFKL.

174. Komer memo to JFK, March 22, 1963, NSF, Box 119, Israel, General, JFKL.

175. CIA Assistant Director, Scientific Intelligence memo to CIA Deputy Director/ Intelligence, Jan. 8, 1963, NSF, Box 428, Komer Papers, Israel, Security (Missile), Development of Sale of Hawks, JFKL.

176. Polk memo to Grant, "Scope of 'Phase I' of the U.S. Initiative," April 15, 1963, NSF, Box 437, Komer Papers, Middle East, CANE 1961–63, JFKL.

177. JFK letter to Nasser, May 27, 1963, NSF, Box 169A, United Arab Republic, UAR-Israel Arms Limitation, JFKL.

178. Walter Isaacson and Evan Thomas, *The Wise Men: Six Friends and the World They Made* (New York: Touchstone, 1988), p. 730. McCloy used the opportunity to urge JFK to protect Big Oil from the Justice Department's antitrust watchdogs to let it compete with the newly founded OPEC cartel. The president obligingly called his brother on the spot.

179. Talbot memo to Rusk, June 4, 1963, DOSF, NEA Files, NEA/IAI, Near East Arms Initiative, Box 1, Authority to Consider Steps for NEA Arms Limitations, NA.

180. Ball telegram to London, May 23, 1963, NSF, Box 169A, United Arab Republic, UAR-Israel Arms Limitation, JFKL.

181. Komer memo to JFK, May 31, 1963, POF, Box 119A, Israel, Security, JFKL.

182. Komer memo to McCloy, June 19, 1963, NSF, Box 169A, United Arab Republic, UAR-Israel Arms Limitation, JFKL.

183. Komer memo to JFK, June 14, 1963, NSF, Box 437, Komer Papers, Middle East, CANE 1961–63, White House Memoranda, JFKL.

184. Memorandum for the Record: President's Meeting on McCloy Exercise, June 15, 1963, NSF, Box 169A, United Arab Republic, UAR-Israel Arms Limitation, JFKL.

185. Komer memo to JFK, July 19, 1963, NSF, Box 427, Israel, Nuclear Energy Program 1963, White House Memoranda, JFKL.

186. Nasser letter to JFK, June 7, 1963, NSF, Box 169A, United Arab Republic, UAR-Israel Arms Limitation, JFKL.

187. Rusk telegram to Eilts, June 21, 1963, NSF, Box 169A, United Arab Republic, UAR-Israel Arms Limitation, JFKL.

188. Rusk telegram to Badeau, June 15, 1963, NSF, Box 169A, United Arab Republic, UAR-Israel Arms Limitation, JFKL.

189. McCloy telegram to State, June 28, 1963, NSF, Box 169A, United Arab Republic, UAR-Israel Arms Limitation, JFKL.

190. "The Use of Poison Gas in Yemen by Egyptian Armed Forces," undated, 1963, NSF, Box 428, Komer Papers, Israel, U.S.–Israeli Talks re: UAR Missile Capability, JFKL.

191. Badeau telegram to Rusk, June 27, 1963, NSF, Box 169A, United Arab Republic, UAR-Israel Arms Limitation, JFKL.

192. Komer memo to Bundy, July 15, 1963, *FRUS*, 1961–63, Vol. 18, p. 643, fn8.

193. McCloy telegram to State, June 30, 1963, NSF, Box 169A, United Arab Republic, UAR-Israel Arms Limitation, JFKL.

194. Badeau telegram to Rusk, July 1, NSF, Box 169A, United Arab Republic, UAR-Israel Arms Limitation, JFKL.

195. Komer memo to JFK, July 3, 1963, NSF, Box 169A, United Arab Republic, UAR-Israel Arms Limitation, JFKL.

196. Rusk telegram to Badeau, July 7, 1963, NSF, Box 169A, United Arab Republic, UAR-Israel Arms Limitation, JFKL.

197. Unsigned (presumably Komer) telegram to Badeau, July 11, 1963, NSF, Box 437, Komer Papers, Middle East, CANE 1961–63, White House Memoranda, JFKL.

198. Badeau telegram to Rusk, July 11, 1963, NSF, Box 169A, United Arab Republic, UAR-Israel Arms Limitation, JFKL.

199. Komer memo to JFK, July 12, 1963, NSF, Box 169A, United Arab Republic, UAR-Israel Arms Limitation, JFKL.

200. "Chronological Summary of the Arms Probe with Nasser and Related Events," Aug. 25, 1964, DOSF, NEA Files, NEA/IAI, Near East Arms Initiative, Box 1, Background papers vis-à-vis 2nd McCloy probe w/Nasser 09-64, NA.

201. Talbot memo to Rusk, July 11, 1963, DOSF, NEA Files, NEA/IAI, Near East Arms Initiative, Box 1, Background papers vis-à-vis 2nd McCloy probe w/Nasser 09-64, NA.

202. Memcon: JFK meeting on McCloy mission, July 23, 1963, DOSF, NEA Files, NEA/IAI, Near East Arms Limitation Initiative, Box 1, Background papers vis-a-vis 2nd McCloy probe w/Nasser 09-64, NA.

203. That assessment implicitly paid a considerable compliment to Israel's nuclear program, including its ability to procure materials, amass expertise, and test the device.

204. "Chronological Summary of the Arms Probe with Nasser and Related Events."

205. Barbour telegram to Rusk, July 15, 1963, NSF, Box 119A, Israel, General, JFKL.

206. Komer memo to JFK, July 19, 1963, NSF, Box 427, Israel, Nuclear Energy Program 1963, White House Memoranda, JFKL.

207. JCS memo to McNamara, Aug. 7, 1963, *FRUS*, 1961–63, Vol. 18, pp. 667–69.

208. Deputy Assistant Secretary of Defense for ISA Frank Sloan letter to Grant, Aug. 22, 1963, NSF, Box 119A, Israel, General, JFKL.

209. Komer memo to JFK, July 23, 1963, NSF, Box 169A, United Arab Republic, UAR-Israel Arms Limitation, JFKL. Italicized portions are underlined in original.

210. Barnes telegram to Rusk, Aug. 23, 1963, NSF, Box 119A, Israel, General, JFKL.

211. Barnes telegram to Rusk, Aug. 30, 1963, NSF, Box 119A, Israel, General, JFKL.

212. Barbour telegram to Rusk, Aug. 8, 1963, NSF, Box 119A, Israel, General, JFKL.

213. Eshkol letter to JFK, Aug. 19, 1963, NSF, Box 119A, Israel, General, JFKL.

214. Barbour telegram to Rusk, Aug. 19, 1963, NSF, Box 119A, Israel, General, JFKL.

215. Barbour telegram to Rusk, Aug. 28, 1963, NSF, Box 119A, Israel, General, JFKL.

216. Ball memo to JFK, Aug. 23, 1963, NSF, Box 119A, Israel, General, JFKL.

217. Komer memo to JFK, Aug. 23, 1963, NSF, Box 119A, Israel, General, JFKL.

218. JFK letter to Eshkol, Aug. 26, 1963, MH 3377/10, ISA. Another copy is found in POF, Box 119A, Israel, Security, JFKL.

219. Bundy memo to Rusk, Aug. 23, 1963, NSF, Box 119A, Israel, General, JFKL.

220. Barbour to Rusk, Aug. 28, 1963, NSF, Box 119A, Israel, General, JFKL.

221. Barbour telegram to Rusk, Aug. 8, 1963, NSF, Box 427, Komer Papers, Israel Nuclear Energy Program 1963, JFKL.

222. Nasser speech at Port Said (U.S. translation from *al-Ahram* text), Aug. 11, 1963, DOSF, NEA Files, NEA/IAI, Near East Arms Initiative, Box 1, Background papers vis-à-vis 2nd McCloy probe w/Nasser 09-64, NA.

223. Rusk memo to JFK, Sept. 10, 1963, DOSF, NEA Files, NEA/IAI, Near East Arms Initiative, Box 1, ENAC-CANE, NA; Komer memo to JFK, Sept. 9, 1963, NSF, Box 437, Komer Papers, Middle East, CANE 1961–63, White House Memoranda, JFKL.

224. JFK letter to Nasser, Sept. 12, 1963, NSF, Box 169A, United Arab Republic, UAR-Israel Arms Limitation, JFKL.

225. Badeau telegram to Rusk, Oct. 8, 1963, NSF, Box 169A, United Arab Republic, UAR-Israel Arms Limitation, JFKL.

226. "Chronological Summary of the Arms Probe with Nasser and Related Events."

227. Memcon: Rusk meeting with Meir, Sept. 30, 1963, *FRUS*, 1961–63, Vol. 18, pp. 717–19.

228. When told by Meir that Israel was thinking of procuring new European tanks, Rusk—hardly an RMA (Revolution in Military Affairs) man—astonishingly told her that American "military authorities" thought that tanks were well on their way to obsolescence since individual soldiers could now destroy them.

229. JFK letter to Eshkol, Oct. 2, 1963, MH 3377/10, ISA. Another copy is found in POF, Box 119A, Israel, Security, JFKL.

230. Rusk telegram to Barbour, Oct. 16, 1963, DOSF, Central Foreign Policy File, 1963, Box 3727, DEF-ISR, NA.

231. Eshkol letter to JFK, Nov. 4, 1963, NSF, Box 119A, Israel, General, JFKL; State Department Executive Secretary Read memo to Bundy, Nov. 9, 1963, DOSF, NEA Files, Records of the Israel-Lebanon Affairs Desk, 1954–1963, Box 9, White House Correspondence 1963, NA.

232. Barbour telegram to Rusk, Nov. 4, 1963, NSF, Box 119A, Israel, General, JFKL.

233. "Schedule for U.S.–Israeli Talks," Nov. 12, 1963, NSF, Box 428, Komer Papers, U.S.–Israel Talks on UAR Missile Capability, JFKL.

234. Memo for the record: Komer lunch with Gazit, Nov. 21, 1963, Box 119A, Israel, General, JFKL.

CONCLUSION: A Time to Cut Bait

1. Tel Aviv to Figg, Nov. 22, 1963, FO 371/170579, PRO.

2. Barbour telegram to Rusk, Nov. 18, 1963, NSF, Box 119A, Israel, General, JFKL.

3. Harman to Eban, Nov. 5, 1963, MH 3377/10, ISA.

4. Chronology of Key Events, November 1963, DOSF, NEA Files, Records of the Israel-Lebanon Desk 1954-65, Box 8, Correspondence with Israel 1963, NA.

5. Badeau telegram to Rusk, Nov. 22, 1963, NSF, Box 169, UAR General, JFKL.

6. Counselor for Political Affairs Donald C. Bergus airgram to State, Dec. 9, 1963, NSF, Box 430, Komer Papers, Kennedy, Reactions to Death, Misc., JFKL.

7. Mohamed H. Heikal, *The Cairo Documents: The Inside Story of Nasser and His Relationship with World Leaders, Rebels, and Statesmen* (Garden City, NY: Doubleday, 1973), pp. 223–24.

8. Bergus airgram to State, Dec. 9, 1963, NSF, Box 430, Komer Papers, Kennedy, Reactions to Death, Misc., JFKL.

9. Heikal, p. 224.

10. Bergus telegram to State, Dec. 18, 1963, SF, Box 430, Komer Papers, Kennedy, Reactions to Death, Misc., JFKL.

11. Bergus airgram to State, Dec. 9, 1963, NSF, Box 430, Komer Papers, Kennedy, Reactions to Death, Misc., JFKL.

12. Minister-Counselor Stuart Rockwell to State, Jan. 23, 1964, NSF, Box 430, Komer Papers, Kennedy, Reactions to Death, Misc., JFKL.

13. Consul Charles Henebry to State, Dec. 1, 1963, NSF, Box 430, Komer Papers, Kennedy, Reactions to Death, Misc., JFKL.

14. Meyer to State, Nov. 25, 1963, NSF, Box 430, Komer Papers, Kennedy, Reactions to Death, Misc., JFKL.

15. Second Secretary Brooks Wrampelmeier to State, Dec. 6, 1963, NSF, Box 430, Komer Papers, Kennedy, Reactions to Death, Misc., JFKL.

16. Taiz to State, Nov. 26, 1963, NSF, Box 430, Komer Papers, Kennedy, Reactions to Death, Misc., JFKL.

17. Counselor John F. Root to State, Nov. 30, 1964, NSF, Box 430, Komer Papers, Kennedy, Reactions to Death, Misc., JFKL.

18. Counselor Nicholas G. Thacher to State, Dec. 13, 1963, NSF, Box 430, Komer Papers, Kennedy, Reactions to Death, Misc., JFKL.

19. Root to State, Nov. 30, 1964, NSF, Box 430, Komer Papers, Kennedy, Reactions to Death, Misc., JFKL.

20. *Le Peuple* (Algiers), Nov. 23, 1963, page A1.

21. Henebry to State, Dec. 1, 1963, NSF, Box 430, Komer Papers, Kennedy, Reactions to Death, Misc., JFKL.

22. Meyer telegram to Rusk, Nov. 25, 1963, NSF, Box 430, Komer Papers, Kennedy, Reactions to Death, Misc., JFKL.

23. Wrampelmeier to State, Dec. 6, 1963, NSF, Box 430, Komer Papers, Kennedy, Reactions to Death, Misc., JFKL.

24. Hart OH, p. 62, JFKL.

25. Wrampelmeier to State, Dec. 6, 1963, NSF, Box 430, Komer Papers, Kennedy, Reactions to Death, Misc., JFKL.

26. Barbour OH, May 22, 1981, p. 33, JFKL.

27. Ben-Gurion diary, Nov. 22, 1963, BGA.

28. Ben-Gurion diary, Nov. 23, 1963, BGA.

29. Barbour telegram to Rusk, Nov. 25, 1963, NSF, Box 430, Komer Papers, Kennedy, Reactions to Death, Misc., JFKL.

30. For a reflection on the murder of both leaders, cf. Barbie Zelizer, "The Past in Our Present: The Assassinations of Yitzhak Rabin and John F. Kennedy," in Yoram Peri, ed., *The Assassination of Yitzhak Rabin* (Stanford: Stanford University Press, 2000). On the assassination of Rabin, cf. Michael Karpin and Ina Friedman, *Murder in the Name of God: The Plot to Kill Yitzhak Rabin* (London: Granta Books, 1998) and David Horovitz, ed., *Shalom, Friend: The Life and Legacy of Yitzhak Rabin* (New York: Newmarket Books, 1996).

31. Dan Kurzman, *Soldier of Peace: The Life of Yitzhak Rabin* (New York: Harper-Collins, 1998), p. 195. Kurzman, relying on latterly written memoirs, has the Rabins back in Israel when they hear about the assassination—which would have required considerable hustle to get from Oklahoma to an airport large enough to have a flight back to Tel Aviv before Lydda Airport closed for the Sabbath.

32. "List of DoD Officials General Rabin Is Seeing," undated Nov. 1963, NSF, Box 428, Komer Papers, Israel, U.S.–Israeli Talks re: UAR Missile Capability, JFKL.

33. Barbour OH, May 22, 1981, p. 33, JFKL.

34. Barbour telegram to Rusk, Nov. 25, 1963, NSF, Box 430, Komer Papers, Kennedy, Reactions to Death, Misc., JFKL.

35. Golda Meir, *My Life* (London: Futura, 1978), p. 261.

36. Ibid., p. 259.

37. Phillips Talbot OH, Dec. 5, 1964, JFKL, pp. 69–70.

38. Edward Tivnan, *The Lobby: Jewish Political Power and American Foreign Policy* (New York: Simon & Schuster, 1988), p. 67.

39. Shimon Peres, *Battling for Peace: A Memoir* (New York: Random House, 1995), pp. 224–25.

40. David Halberstam, *The Unfinished Odyssey of Robert Kennedy* (New York: Random House, 1968), p. 78.

41. Douglas Little, "The Making of a Special Relationship: The United States and Israel, 1957–68," *International Journal of Middle East Studies*, No. 25 (1993), p. 575.

42. Daniel Pipes, *The Hidden Hand: Middle East Fears of Conspiracy* (New York: St. Martin's Press, 1996), p. 38.

43. Komer to Bundy, Dec. 10, 1963, NSF, Box 428, Komer Papers, Israel, U.S.–Israel Talks re: UAR Missile Capability, JFKL.

44. William B. Quandt, *Decade of Decisions: American Policy Toward the Arab-Israeli Conflict 1967–1976* (Berkeley: University of California Press, 1977), p. 67.

45. Author conversation with Leslie H. Gelb, October 15, 2001, New York.

46. Talbot memo to Rusk, Feb. 21, 1964, DOSF, NEA Files, NEA/IAI, Near East Arms Initiative, Box 1, ENAC-CANE, NA.

47. Komer memo to Talbot, Feb. 21, 1964, DOSF, NEA Files, NEA/IAI, Near East Arms Initiative, Box 1, ENAC-CANE, NA.

48. Komer memo to Jernegan, March 12, 1964, DOSF, NEA Files, NEA/IAI, Near East Arms Initiative, Box 1, ENAC-CANE, NA.

49. "Scenario with Eshkol," undated, 1963, DOSF, NEA Files, NEA/IAI, Near East Arms Initiative, Box 1, ENAC-CANE, NA.

50. Avner Cohen, *Israel and the Bomb* (New York: Columbia University Press, 1998), pp. 177–86.

51. Ball circular to regional embassies, June 28, 1966, USNNP, NSA.

52. Cohen, p. 1.

53. Joseph Sisco memo to Rogers, March 7, 1969, USNNP, NSA.

54. Rogers telegram to Tel Aviv, April 10, 1969, USNNP, NSA.

55. Little, p. 578.

56. Zach Levey, *Israel and the Western Powers, 1952–60* (Chapel Hill: University of North Carolina Press, 1997), p. 99.

Bibliography

A Note on Sources

This work is based primarily upon documents. To reconstruct the story of the Kennedy administration's Middle East policy-making, I have relied upon contemporaneous memoranda, cable traffic, minutes, and other primary sources that provided the best available picture of the events chronicled herein. The skeleton of the book comes from the rich documentary record found in the John F. Kennedy Library, the U.S. National Archives, and published documents on the period, including the invaluable *Foreign Relations of the United States* series known affectionately to diplomatic historians as *FRUS*; it has been fleshed out with archival material from the Israel State Archives, the British Public Record Office, the David Ben-Gurion Archives, and the National Security Archive, as well as taped White House conversations provided by the University of Virginia's Miller Center of Public Affairs.

Even so, that picture remains incomplete. I chose to focus on U.S. decision making toward Israel and Egypt rather than on Israeli or Egyptian decision making toward the United States because we simply lack the documents to tell the latter stories properly. The Egyptian state that Nasser helped build remains too authoritarian to provide true access to its papers—which in any event would necessarily be incomplete and suspect. For its part, a democratic but embattled Israel continues to withhold key national security documents, including papers on issues such as Dimona and the Hawks. As such, my portraits of Nasser, Ben-Gurion, and Eshkol often draw upon secondary sources or portrayals of their actions read back through U.S. documents. I have taken pains to ensure that my renderings of their behavior and motives are convincing, careful, and accurate; but being definitive takes documents.

Similarly, many U.S. sources related to Dimona and arms sales to Israel remain censored, even four decades later. I am sure that among them lie genuine state secrets that, if revealed, would harm U.S. national security. But many of the withheld documents would do much to give the republic a fuller picture of its diplomatic history and nothing to endanger its citizenry. Alas, the deck is stacked against the historian; granting Freedom of Information Act or mandatory review requests means running significant bureaucratic risks, while denying them risks only the ire of a researcher—and the American public's ability to understand how it has been represented. After completing this book, I am more convinced than ever of the necessity for greater access to the people's papers and more skeptical than ever of the chances of getting it.

I have supplemented the documentary base with secondary scholarship, memoirs, oral histories, and some interviews. In particular, I have extensively consulted the useful oral history collection at the JFK Library, which features interviews conducted relatively close to the events they describe—something that I found often made them more reliable than later interviews. But I have usually chosen to rely upon a document, however musty, over a recollection, however polished. Memoirs and after-the-fact reconstructions can be deeply useful to historians, but their veracity must be constantly evaluated to compensate for the inevitable self-editing of memory.

As for secondary sources, the scholarship of John Lewis Gaddis, Robert Dallek, William Appleman Williams, Melvyn P. Leffler, Walter LaFeber, Barton J. Bernstein, Akira Iriye, Warren F. Kimball, Ernest R. May, and others have created an impressive literature on the history of American foreign policy. This study also falls on the shelf alongside a small but growing literature on U.S.–Israel relations. I am honored to be able to acknowledge debts of intellectual gratitude to Nadav Safran's *Israel: The Embattled Ally*; Howard M. Sachar's *A History of Israel*; William B. Quandt's *Decade of Decisions* and *Peace Process*; a series of thoughtful, elegant articles by Douglas Little; Mordechai Gazit's important 1983 study *President Kennedy's Policy Toward the Arab States and Israel: Analysis and Documents*, which still holds up remarkably well; Peter Grose's *Israel in the Mind of America*; and the tour de force of archival excavation that makes up Avner Cohen's *Israel and the Bomb*. In particular, I admire Steven L. Spiegel's *The Other Arab-Israeli Conflict*, with its superb chapters on almost every administration ever to manage the issue, and David Schoenbaum's *The United States and the State of Israel*, which remains both the best one-volume survey of the special relationship and the wittiest. On questions related to Egypt, Nasser, and the wider Middle East, I have been particularly influenced by such disparate scholars as Albert Hourani, Malcolm H. Kerr, Fouad Ajami, Roy Mottahedeh, Avi Shlaim, Keith Kyle, Mark Tessler, Itamar Rabinovich, Shlomo Avineri, Abraham Ben-Zvi, Benny Morris, and Anita Shapira. This list could be far longer; all historians write alone, and yet none of us do.

Archives

John F. Kennedy Library, Boston, MA (JFKL)
    National Security Files (NSF)
    President's Office Files (POF)
    White House Central Subject Files (WHCSF)
    Oral Histories (OH)
National Archives II, College Park, MD (NA)
    Department of State Files (DOSF)
    State Department Bureau of Near East Affairs Files (NEA)
    Department of Defense Files (DODF)
National Security Archive, Washington, DC (NSA)
    U.S. Nuclear Nonproliferation Project (USNNP)
Presidential Recordings Project, Miller Center of Public Affairs, University of Virginia, Charlottesville, VA
Israel State Archives, Jerusalem, Israel (ISA)
    Foreign Ministry Files (MH)
Ben-Gurion Archives, Sdeh Boqer, Israel (BGA)
Public Records Office, Kew, London, United Kingdom (PRO)
    Foreign Office Files (FO)

Collected Documents

Foreign Relations of the United States, Near East, 1961–63, Vols. *17, 18* (Washington, DC: Department of State, 1995).
The Kennedy Presidential Press Conferences (New York: Earl M. Coleman Enterprises, 1978).
John F. Kennedy on Israel, Zionism and Jewish Issues (New York: Herzl Press for the Zionist Organization of America, 1965).
Documents on Foreign Relations of the State of Israel, 1960 (Jerusalem: Israel State Archives, 1998).
Timothy Naftali, Ernest R. May, and Philip D. Zelikow, eds., *The Presidential Recordings: John F. Kennedy—The Great Crises, Volumes 1–3* (New York: W. W. Norton, 2001).

Interviews
(excluding JFKL oral histories cited in notes)

Zaki Shalom
Theodore C. Sorensen
Phillips Talbot
Shabtai Teveth
Harris Wofford

Memoirs and Secondary Sources

Dean Acheson, *Present at the Creation: My Years in the State Department* (New York: W.W. Norton, 1969).
Fouad Ajami, *The Arab Predicament: Arab Political Thought and Practice Since 1967* (Cambridge: Cambridge University Press, 1981).
Ahmed Noman Kassim Almadhagi, *Yemen and the United States: A Study of a Small Power and Super-State Relationship 1962–1994* (London: I. B. Tauris, 1996).
Isaac Alteras, *Eisenhower and Israel: U.S.–Israeli Relations, 1953–1960* (Gainesville: University Press of Florida, 1993).
Hannah Arendt, *Eichmann in Jerusalem: A Report on the Banality of Evil* (New York: Penguin Books, 1977).
Shlomo Avineri, *The Making of Modern Zionism: The Intellectual Origins of the Jewish State* (New York: Basic Books, 1981).
John S. Badeau, *The American Approach to the Arab World* (New York: Council on Foreign Relations, 1968).
———. *The Middle East Remembered* (Washington: Middle East Institute, 1983).
Kenneth Ray Bain, *The March to Zion: United States Policy and the Founding of Israel* (College Station: Texas A&M University Press, 1979).
Yaacov Bar-Siman-Tov, "The United States and Israel since 1948: A 'Special Relationship'?" *Diplomatic History,* Vol. 22, No. 2 (Spring 1998).
Michael Bar-Zohar, *Ben-Gurion: A Biography* (New York: Adama Books, 1986).
Warren Bass and Derek Chollet, "The Triage of Dayton," *Foreign Affairs,* Vol. 77, No. 5 (September/October 1998), pp. 95–108.

Abraham Ben-Zvi, *Decade of Transition: Eisenhower, Kennedy, and the Origins of the American-Israeli Alliance* (New York: Columbia University Press, 1998).

Sir Isaiah Berlin, *Personal Impressions* (London: Pimlico, 1998).

Kai Bird, *The Color of Truth: McGeorge and William Bundy, Brothers in Arms: A Biography* (New York: Simon & Schuster, 1998).

Paul F. Boller, Jr., *Presidential Anecdotes* (New York: Oxford University Press, 1981).

Chester Bowles, *Promises to Keep: My Years in Public Life 1941–1969* (New York: Harper & Row, 1971).

Benjamin C. Bradlee, *Conversations with Kennedy* (New York: W.W. Norton, 1975).

Taylor Branch, *Parting the Waters: America in the King Years 1954–63* (New York: Touchstone, 1989).

Alan Brinkley, *Liberalism and Its Discontents* (Cambridge: Harvard University Press, 1998).

Richard W. Bulliet, *Islam: The View from the Edge* (New York: Columbia University Press, 1994).

Clark Clifford with Richard Holbrooke, *Counsel to the President: A Memoir* (New York: Random House, 1991).

Andrew and Leslie Cockburn, *Dangerous Liaison: The Inside Story of the U.S.–Israeli Covert Relationship* (New York: HarperCollins, 1991).

Avner Cohen, *Israel and the Bomb* (New York: Columbia University Press, 1998).

Michael J. Cohen, *Palestine and the Great Powers, 1945–1948* (Princeton: Princeton University Press, 1982).

———. *Truman and Israel* (Berkeley: University of California Press, 1990).

John Milton Cooper, Jr., *The Warrior and the Priest: Woodrow Wilson and Theodore Roosevelt* (Cambridge: The Belknap Press of Harvard University Press, 1983).

Robert Dallek, *Franklin D. Roosevelt and American Foreign Policy, 1932–1945* (New York: Oxford University Press, 1995).

Robert A. Divine, "The Cold War and the Election of 1948," *The Journal of American History*, Vol. 59, Issue 1 (June 1972).

———. *Eisenhower and the Cold War* (New York: Oxford University Press, 1981).

Robert Donovan, *Crisis and Conflict: The Presidency of Harry S. Truman, 1945–1948* (New York: W.W. Norton, 1977).

Abba Eban, *Personal Witness: Israel Through My Eyes* (New York: G. P. Putnam's Sons, 1992).

Dwight D. Eisenhower, *Waging Peace, 1956–61* (Garden City, NY: Doubleday, 1965).

Yaron Ezrahi, *Rubber Bullets: Power and Conscience in Modern Israel* (New York: Farrar, Straus and Giroux, 1997).

Robert H. Ferrell, ed., *The Eisenhower Diaries* (New York: Norton, 1981).

Steven Z. Freiberger, *Dawn Over Suez: The Rise of American Power in the Middle East, 1953–1957* (Chicago: Ivan R. Dee, 1992).

David Fromkin, *A Peace to End All Peace: The Fall of the Ottoman Empire and the Creation of the Modern Middle East* (New York: Avon Books, 1989).

Aleksandr Fursenko and Timothy Naftali, *"One Hell of a Gamble": Khrushchev, Castro, and Kennedy 1958–1964* (New York: W.W. Norton, 1997).

John Lewis Gaddis, *Strategies of Containment: A Critical Appraisal of Postwar American National Security Policy* (New York: Oxford University Press, 1982).

———. *The United States and the Origins of the Cold War, 1941–1947* (New York: Columbia University Press, 1972).

———. *We Now Know: Rethinking Cold War History* (New York: Oxford University Press, 1997).

Zvi Ganin, *Truman, American Jewry, and Israel, 1945–1948* (New York: Holmes & Meier, 1979).

Richard L. Garwin and Georges Charpak, *Megawatts and Megatons: A Turning Point in the Nuclear Age?* (New York: Knopf, 2001).

F. Gregory Gause III, *Saudi-Yemeni Relations: Domestic Structures and Foreign Influence* (New York: Columbia University Press, 1990).

Mordechai Gazit, *President Kennedy's Policy Toward the Arab States and Israel: Analysis and Documents* (Tel Aviv: Shiloah Center for Middle Eastern and African Studies, 1983).

Fawaz A. Gerges, *The Superpowers and the Middle East: Regional and International Politics, 1955–1967* (Boulder: Westview Press, 1994).

Galia Golan, *Soviet Policies in the Middle East from World War Two to Gorbachev* (Cambridge: Cambridge University Press, 1990).

Matti Golan, *Shimon Peres: A Biography* (New York: St. Martin's Press, 1982).

James M. Goldgeier, *Not Whether But When: The U.S. Decision to Enlarge NATO* (Washington: Brookings Institution Press, 1999).

Peter Grose, *Israel in the Mind of America* (New York: Knopf, 1984).

Fred I. Greenstein, *The Hidden-Hand Presidency: Eisenhower as Leader* (New York: Basic Books, 1982).

Ernest Gruening, *Many Battles: The Autobiography of Ernest Gruening* (New York: Liveright, 1973).

Peter L. Hahn, "Special Relationships," *Diplomatic History*, Vol. 22, No. 2 (Spring 1998).

———. "Suez," *Reviews in American History*, Vol. 20, No. 4 (Dec. 1992).

———. *The United States, Great Britain, and Egypt, 1945–1956: Strategy and Diplomacy in the Early Cold War* (Chapel Hill: University of North Carolina Press, 1991).

David Halberstam, *The Best and the Brightest* (New York: Ballantine, 1992).

———. *The Unfinished Odyssey of Robert Kennedy* (New York: Random House, 1968).

Alonzo L. Hamby, *Man of the People: A Life of Harry S. Truman* (New York: Oxford University Press, 1995).

Robert E. Harkavy, "Pariah States and Nuclear Proliferation," *International Organization*, Vol. 35, No. 1 (Winter 1981).

Mohamed Hassanein Heikal, *The Cairo Documents: The Inside Story of Nasser and His Relationship with World Leaders, Rebels, and Statesmen* (Garden City, NY: Doubleday, 1973).

———. *Cutting the Lion's Tail: Suez Through Egyptian Eyes* (London: Andre Deutsch, 1986).

Seymour M. Hersh, *The Samson Option: Israel's Nuclear Arsenal and American Foreign Policy* (New York: Random House, 1991).

Arthur Hertzberg, ed., *The Zionist Idea: A Historical Analysis and Reader* (New York: Atheneum, 1973).

Chaim Herzog, *The Arab-Israeli Wars: War and Peace in the Middle East from the War of Independence through Lebanon* (New York: Vintage Books, 1984).

George C. Herring, *America's Longest War: The United States and Vietnam, 1950–1975* (New York: John Wiley & Sons, 1979).

Roger Hilsman, *To Move a Nation: The Politics of Foreign Policy in the Administration of John F. Kennedy* (Garden City, NY: Doubleday, 1967).

E. J. Hobsbawm, *Nations and Nationalism since 1780: Programme, Myth, Reality* (Cambridge: Cambridge University Press, 1990).

Townsend Hoopes, *The Devil and John Foster Dulles* (Boston: Atlantic Monthly Press, 1973).

David Horovitz, ed., *Shalom, Friend: The Life and Legacy of Yitzhak Rabin* (New York: Newmarket Books, 1996).

Albert Hourani, *A History of the Arab Peoples* (Cambridge: Harvard University Press, 1991).

———. *Arabic Thought in the Liberal Age 1798–1939* (London: Oxford University Press, 1962).

J. C. Hurewitz, *The Struggle for Palestine* (New York: W.W. Norton & Company, Inc., 1950).

Stephen D. Isaacs, *Jews and American Politics* (Garden City, NY: Doubleday, 1974).

Walter Isaacson, *Kissinger: A Biography* (New York: Simon & Schuster, 1992).

Walter Isaacson and Evan Thomas, *The Wise Men: Six Friends and the World They Made* (New York: Touchstone, 1988).

Godfrey Jansen, *Why Robert Kennedy Was Killed: The Story of Two Victims* (New York: The Third Press, 1970).

Lyndon B. Johnson, *The Vantage Point: Perspectives of the Presidency 1963–1969* (New York: Holt, Rinehart and Winston, 1971).

Manfred Jonas, *Isolationism in America 1935–1941* (Ithaca: Cornell University Press, 1972).

Robert D. Kaplan, *The Arabists: The Romance of an American Elite* (New York: The Free Press, 1995).

Zachary Karabell, *The Last Campaign: How Harry Truman Won the 1948 Election* (New York: Knopf, 2000).

Michael Karpin and Ina Friedman, *Murder in the Name of God: The Plot to Kill Yitzhak Rabin* (London: Granta Books, 1998).

I. L. Kenen, *Israel's Defense Line: Her Friends and Foes in Washington* (Buffalo: Prometheus Books, 1981).

David M. Kennedy, *Freedom from Fear: The American People in Depression and War, 1929–1945* (New York: Oxford University Press, 1999).

John F. Kennedy, *Profiles in Courage* (New York: Perennial Classics, 2000).

Malcolm H. Kerr, *The Arab Cold War: Gamal 'Abd al-Nasser and His Rivals, 1958–1970* (London: Oxford University Press, 1981).

Rashid Khalidi, *Palestinian Identity: The Construction of Modern National Consciousness* (New York: Columbia University Press, 1997).

Warren F. Kimball, *The Juggler: Franklin Roosevelt as Wartime Statesman* (Princeton: Princeton University Press, 1991).

Baruch Kimmerling and Joel S. Migdal, *Palestinians: The Making of a People* (Cambridge: Harvard University Press, 1994).

Henry A. Kissinger, *Diplomacy* (New York: Simon & Schuster, 1994).

William Klaber and Philip H. Melanson, *Shadow Play: The Murder of Robert F. Kennedy, the Trial of Sirhan Sirhan, and the Failure of American Justice* (New York: St. Martin's Press, 1997).

Thomas J. Knock, *To End All Wars: Woodrow Wilson and the Quest for a New World Order* (Princeton: Princeton University Press, 1995).

Dan Kurzman, *Ben-Gurion: Prophet of Fire* (New York: Simon and Schuster, 1983).

Keith Kyle, *Suez* (New York: St. Martin's Press, 1991).

Jean Lacouture, *Nasser* (Paris: Éditions du Seuil, 1971).

Walter LaFeber, *America, Russia, and the Cold War 1945–1966* (New York: John Wiley and Sons, Inc., 1967).

Walter Laqueur, *A History of Zionism* (New York: Schocken Books, 1989).

Walter Laqueur and Barry Rubin, eds., *The Israel-Arab Reader: A Documentary History of the Middle East Conflict* (New York: Penguin, 1987).

Melvyn P. Leffler, *A Preponderance of Power: National Security, the Truman Administration, and the Cold War* (Stanford: Stanford University Press, 1992).

George Lenczowski, *American Presidents and the Middle East* (Durham: Duke University Press, 1990).

David W. Lesch, ed., *The Middle East and the United States* (New York: Westview Press, 1996).

Zach Levey, *Israel and the Western Powers, 1952–60* (Chapel Hill: University of North Carolina Press, 1997).

N. Gordon Levin, Jr., *Woodrow Wilson and World Politics: America's Response to War and Revolution* (New York: Oxford University Press, 1968).

James M. Lindsay, "The New Apathy," *Foreign Affairs*, Vol. 79, No. 5 (September/October 2000).

George Liska, *The New Statecraft: Foreign Aid in American Foreign Policy* (Chicago: University of Chicago Press, 1960).

Douglas Little, "From Even-Handed to Empty-Handed: Seeking Order in the Middle East," in Thomas G. Paterson, ed., *Kennedy's Quest for Victory: American Foreign Policy, 1961–1963* (New York: Oxford University Press, 1989).

———. "The Making of a Special Relationship: The United States and Israel, 1957–68," *International Journal of Middle East Studies*, No. 25 (1993).

Wm. Roger Louis and Roger Owen, eds., *Suez 1956: The Crisis and its Consequences* (Oxford: Clarendon Press, 1991).

John Lukacs, *The Duel: The Eighty-Day Struggle Between Churchill and Hitler* (New Haven: Yale University Press, 1990).

Harold Macmillan, *At the End of the Day, 1961–1963* (New York: Harper & Row, 1973).

David Makovsky, *Making Peace with the PLO: The Rabin Government's Road to the Oslo Accord* (Boulder: Westview Press, 1996).

William Manchester, *The Death of a President* (New York: Harper & Row, 1967).

Philip Mattar, *The Mufti of Jerusalem: Al-Hajj Amin al-Husayni and the Palestinian National Movement* (New York: Columbia University Press, 1988).

Ernest R. May and Philip D. Zelikow, eds., *The Kennedy Tapes: Inside the White House During the Cuban Missile Crisis* (Cambridge: Belknap Press of Harvard University Press, 1997).

David McCullough, *Truman* (New York: Touchstone, 1992).

Christopher J. McMullen, *Resolution of the Yemen Crisis, 1963: A Case Study in Mediation* (Washington: Georgetown School of Foreign Service, 1980).

Robert S. McNamara, *The Essence of Security: Reflections in Office* (New York: Harper & Row, 1968).

Golda Meir, *My Life* (London: Futura, 1978).

Yossi Melman and Dan Raviv, *Friends in Deed: Inside the U.S.–Israel Alliance* (New York: Hyperion, 1994).

Dan E. Moldea, *The Killing of Robert F. Kennedy* (New York: W. W. Norton, 1995).

Elizabeth Monroe, *Britain's Moment in the Middle East 1914–1971* (London: Chatto & Windus, 1981).

Benny Morris, *The Birth of the Palestinian Refugee Problem, 1947–1949* (Cambridge: Cambridge University Press, 1989).

Donald Neff, *Warriors at Suez: Eisenhower Takes America into the Middle East* (New York: Simon & Schuster, 1981).

Anthony Nutting, *Nasser* (New York: E.P. Dutton, 1972).

———. *No End of a Lesson: The Story of Suez* (New York: Clarkson N. Potter, Inc., 1967).

Michael B. Oren, *Six Days of War: June 1967 and the Making of the Modern Middle East* (New York: Oxford University Press, 2002).

Conor Cruise O'Brien, *The Siege: The Saga of Israel and Zionism* (New York: Simon & Schuster, 1986).

Herbert S. Parmet, *JFK: The Presidency of John F. Kennedy* (New York: Dial Press, 1983).

———. *Eisenhower and the American Crusades* (New York: Macmillan, 1972).

Thomas G. Paterson, ed., *Kennedy's Quest for Victory: American Foreign Policy, 1961–1963* (New York: Oxford University Press, 1989).

Richard B. Parker, *The Politics of Miscalculation in the Middle East* (Bloomington: Indiana University Press, 1993).

Shimon Peres, *Battling for Peace: Memoirs* (London: Weidenfeld & Nicolson, 1995).

———. *David's Sling* (New York: Random House, 1970).

Yoram Peri, ed., *The Assassination of Yitzhak Rabin* (Stanford: Stanford University Press, 2000).

Bradford Perkins, "Reluctant Midwife: America and the Birth of Israel," *Reviews in American History*, Vol. 9, No. 1 (March 1981).

Amos Perlmutter, Michael I. Handel, and Uri Bar-Joseph, *Two Minutes Over Baghdad* (London: Vallentine Mitchell, 1982).

Daniel Pipes, *The Hidden Hand: Middle East Fears of Conspiracy* (New York: St. Martin's Press, 1996).

Forrest C. Pogue, *George C. Marshall: Statesman, 1945–1959* (New York: Penguin, 1989).

Kenneth M. Pollack, *The Threatening Storm: The Case for Invading Iraq* (New York: Random House, 2002).

Ronald W. Pruessen, *John Foster Dulles: The Road to Power* (New York: The Free Press, 1982).

William B. Quandt, *Decade of Decisions: American Policy Toward the Arab-Israeli Conflict 1967–1976* (Berkeley: University of California Press, 1977).

———. *Peace Process: American Diplomacy and the Arab-Israeli Conflict Since 1967* (Washington, DC: The Brookings Institution and University of California Press, 1993).

Itamar Rabinovich, *The Road Not Taken: Early Arab-Israeli Negotiations* (Oxford: Oxford University Press, 1991).

———. *The War for Lebanon, 1970–1985* (Ithaca: Cornell University Press, 1989).

Richard Reeves, *President Kennedy: Profile of Power* (New York: Touchstone, 1993).

Bernard Reich, ed., *An Historical Encyclopedia of the Arab-Israeli Conflict* (Westport: Greenwood Press, 1996).

———. *Quest for Peace: United States–Israel Relations and the Arab-Israeli Conflict* (New Brunswick, NJ: Transaction Books, 1977).

Jehuda Reinharz, *Chaim Weizmann: The Making of a Statesman* (New York: Oxford University Press, 1993).

David Reynolds, *One World Divisible: A Global History Since 1945* (New York: Norton, 2000).

Gideon Rose, "Democracy Promotion and American Foreign Policy," *International Security*, Vol. 25, No. 3 (Winter 2000/01).

Walt W. Rostow, *A Diffusion of Power: An Essay in Recent History* (New York: Macmillan, 1972).

Dean Rusk, *As I Saw It* (New York: W.W. Norton, 1990).

Howard M. Sachar, *A History of Israel: From the Rise of Zionism to Our Time* (New York: Knopf, 1989).

———. *A History of Israel, Volume II: From the Aftermath of the Yom Kippur War* (Oxford: Oxford University Press, 1987).

———. *A History of the Jews in America* (New York: Vintage Books, 1992).

Anwar el-Sadat, *In Search of Identity: An Autobiography* (New York: Harper & Row, 1979).

Nadav Safran, *Israel: The Embattled Ally* (Cambridge: Belknap Press of Harvard University Press, 1981).

———. *Saudi Arabia: The Ceaseless Quest for Security* (Ithaca: Cornell University Press, 1988).

Edward Said, *Orientalism* (New York: Vintage Books, 1979).

Pierre Salinger, *With Kennedy* (Garden City, NY: Doubleday, 1966).

Arthur M. Schlesinger, Jr., *A Thousand Days: John F. Kennedy in the White House* (Boston: Houghton Mifflin, 1965).

———. *Robert Kennedy and His Times* (New York: Ballantine, 1978).

Dana Adams Schmidt, *Yemen: The Unknown War* (New York: Holt, Rinehart and Winston, 1968).

David Schoenbaum, "More Special Than Others," *Diplomatic History*, Vol. 22, No. 2 (Spring 1998).

———. *The United States and the State of Israel* (New York: Oxford University Press, 1993).

Patrick Seale, *Asad of Syria: The Struggle for the Middle East* (Berkeley: University of California Press, 1988).

Zaki Shalom, *The Superpowers, Israel and the Future of Jordan 1960–1963: The Perils of the Pro-Nasser Policy* (Portland, OR: Sussex Academic Press, 1999).

Anita Shapira, *Land and Power: The Zionist Resort to Force, 1881–1948* (New York: Oxford University Press, 1992).

Avi Shlaim, *The Iron Wall: Israel and the Arab World* (New York: Norton, 2000).

Gary G. Sick, *All Fall Down: America's Tragic Encounter with Iran* (New York: Penguin Books, 1988).

Theodore C. Sorensen, *Kennedy* (New York: Bantam, 1966).

John Snetsinger, *Truman, the Jewish Vote, and the Creation of Israel* (Stanford: Hoover Institution Press, 1974).

Steven L. Spiegel, *The Other Arab-Israeli Conflict: Making America's Middle East Policy, from Truman to Reagan* (Chicago: University of Chicago Press, 1985).

William Stivers, *America's Confrontation with Revolutionary Change in the Middle East, 1948–83* (London: Macmillan, 1986).

Ray Takeyh, *The Origins of the Eisenhower Doctrine: The US, Britain and Nasser's Egypt, 1953–57* (New York: St. Martin's Press, 2000).

Yael Tamir, *Liberal Nationalism* (Princeton: Princeton University Press, 1993).

Mark Tessler, *A History of the Israeli-Palestinian Conflict* (Bloomington: Indiana University Press, 1994).

Shabtai Teveth, *Ben-Gurion and the Palestinian Arabs: From Peace to War* (New York: Oxford University Press, 1985).

———. *Ben-Gurion's Spy: The Story of the Political Scandal That Shaped Modern Israel* (New York: Columbia University Press, 1996).

———. *Ben-Gurion: The Burning Ground 1886–1948* (Boston: Houghton Mifflin Company, 1987).

Evan Thomas, *Robert Kennedy: His Life* (New York: Simon & Schuster, 2000).

Edward Tivnan, *The Lobby: Jewish Political Power and American Foreign Policy* (New York: Simon & Schuster, 1988).

Selwyn Ilan Troen and Moshe Shemesh, *The Suez-Sinai Crisis, 1956: Retrospective and Reappraisal* (New York: Columbia University Press, 1990).

Harry S. Truman, *Memoirs, Volume Two: Years of Trial and Hope* (Garden City, NY: Doubleday, 1956).

Melvin I. Urofsky, "America and Israel: Trying to Find the Straight Path," *Reviews in American History*, Vol. 3, No. 3 (Sept. 1975).

Stephen M. Walt, *The Origins of Alliances* (Ithaca: Cornell University Press, 1987).

Edward Weintal and Charles Bartlett, *Facing the Brink: An Intimate Study of Crisis Diplomacy* (New York: Charles Scribner's Sons, 1967).

Theodore H. White, *The Making of the President* 1960 (New York: Atheneum Publishers, 1961).

William Appleman Williams, *The Tragedy of American Diplomacy* (Cleveland: World Publishing Company, 1959).

Garry Wills, *Nixon Agonistes: The Crisis of the Self-Made Man* (Boston: Houghton Mifflin Company, 1970).

———. *The Kennedy Imprisonment* (Toronto: Little, Brown, 1981).

Acknowledgments

O N THE WHITE HOUSE lawn on September 13, 1993, Yitzhak Rabin growled, "It's not so easy." He meant something rather grander than this enterprise, but the point still holds. It is one thing to pledge oneself to support any friend; it is quite another to support a friend writing a book. As such, I have unsurprisingly racked up a lengthy series of debts of gratitude.

In Columbia University's history department, my adviser, Richard W. Bulliet, offered expert supervision, encouraged good writing, demanded hard thinking, and even tolerated the scandalous absence of camels from this work. Michael Stanislawski was a consistent source of intellectual challenge and encouragement. Alan Brinkley, Gary Sick, and Lisa Anderson offered careful, close readings that helped me—and this book—enormously. I also owe large intellectual debts to other Columbia professors, including Warren Zimmermann, Richard Betts, Anders Stephanson, Reeva Simon, and, finally, Simon Schama, who tried to teach me how to write history beyond the academy.

The principal funding for my doctorate at Columbia came from the Wexner Foundation, which provided the nicest imaginable way to get through grad school. Leslie and Abigail Wexner's generosity is a model of civic leadership. I am deeply grateful to Bob Chazan for his imperturbable wisdom, steady support, and dry wit; to Rabbi Maurice Corson for hatching and implementing a particularly inspired idea; to Elka Abrahamson, Andy Koren, and Cindy Chazan for their unflagging encouragement (and the bribe of lunch at Tabla); to Karen Collum and the rest of the foundation's classy staff; and to the foundation's president, the incomparable Larry Moses, who is always not only the savviest person in the room but also the menschiest. Thanks, too, to my many fellow fellows who either encouraged or put up with me.

Major funding for the writing and research of this book came from the Miller Center of Public Affairs at the University of Virginia, an admirable bastion of support for research on the modern presidency. My warm thanks to Philip Zelikow (a fellow Hawk-sale aficionado), Brian Balogh, and the rest of the center's staff. Tim Naftali commented thoughtfully on several sections and generously let me listen to the new Kennedy tapes—virtually the ultimate historical source.

The Israel research herein was conducted while I was a junior research associate at the Moshe Dayan Center for Middle East and African Studies at Tel Aviv University. I am particularly grateful to the Dayan Center's past and present directors, Martin Kramer and Asher Susser, and to Tel Aviv University's president, Itamar Rabinovich. The center's staff helped get me past the Israeli bureaucracy, which is no mean feat; Dan Zisenwine gave splendid counsel throughout. Finally, my time at the Dayan Center would have been impossible without Anita Shapira, who is an exemplar of scholarship, integrity, and friendship.

Other funding was generously provided by the Memorial Foundation for Jewish Culture and the Center for Israel and Jewish Studies at Columbia. Their support was invaluable.

At the archives, I am grateful to the staffs of the John F. Kennedy Library in Dorchester, Massachusetts; the National Archives II in College Park, Maryland; the National Security Archive in Washington, DC; the Public Records Office in Kew Gardens, London; the Israel State Archives in Jerusalem; and the David Ben-Gurion Archive in Sdeh Boqer. Ed Barnes guided me through the (to put it charitably) idiosyncratically organized holdings of the National Archives. Stephen Plotkin of the Kennedy Library, who has suffered for years with Kennedy's handwriting, helped me decipher the scrawl of JFK's 1951 travel journal. Hana Pinshow at Midreshet Sdeh Boqer led me through another penmanship nightmare, Ben-Gurion's diary.

Avi Shlaim of St. Antony's College, Oxford, has encouraged me and this project ever since he offhandedly suggested, "Why don't you do Kennedy?" From JFK's staff, Ted Sorensen and Phil Talbot offered their insights and memories. In Israel, Shabtai Teveth took the time to discuss Ben-Gurion, and Zaki Shalom shared his observations about Dimona.

I am particularly grateful to Marc Israel and Abbey Frank of Washington, DC; Rahle Issroff of St. John's Wood, London; Basil and Noga Porter of Omer, Israel; Betty and Bernie Hirshowitz of Haifa, Israel; and the redoubtable Browns of JFK's birthplace, Brookline, Massachusetts, for their extraordinary and much-abused hospitality.

This project (or, at least, its author) has been informed over the years by a wonderful series of mentors, colleagues, and friends. At *Foreign Affairs*, a formidable group of people taught me about world politics, sharp prose, and grace under deadline pressure. Jim Hoge and Fareed Zakaria were exemplary mentors, splendid bosses, and captains of a ship I was proud to help crew. Trish Dorff was the first to bring me aboard, and she, Joe O'Keefe, and Kirk Krauetler gave me an exceptional apprenticeship in the craft of editing. I also had the great good fortune to work with two other dream teams of associate editors: Will Dobson, Alice Phillips, Jacob Kramer, Jonathan Tepperman, and Helen Fessenden, as well as the eagle-eyed Amy Rowe and Traci Nagle. Deborah Millan, and Rosemary Hartman were wonderful friends. I am also deeply grateful to David Kellogg for all his help over the years, and to a terrific series of interns, especially Tarek Masoud, Brianna Avery, and Roshna Balasubramanian.

At the Council on Foreign Relations, Les Gelb gave me a nonpareil opportunity to think through the implications of a second day that will live in infamy. Warm thanks, as well, to a great group of friends and colleagues, including Mike Peters, Lisa Shields, Rachel Bronson, Scott Lasensky, Ken Pollack, Calvin Sims, Larry Korb, Jan Murray, Dick Murphy, Henry Siegman, Adam Segal, Jim Goldgeier, Julia Sweig, Arthur Helton, Anne Luzzatto, Joy Drucker, Bernie Gwertzman, and many, many more. Jeremy Marwell generously and patiently helped ensure my nuclear science was right. Above all, I'm eternally in debt to my own questioning-and-answering team, the "axis of good"—Blake Eskin, Sarah Bright, Kate Julian, Shabnam Faruki, Stephanie Shemin, Dafna Hochman, Jeremy Weinberg, Aidrian O'Connor, and Ann Tappert. They dealt in what we know and don't know, but I'd be remiss if they didn't know how much it meant to me to get to work with them.

I am especially indebted to my outlandishly erudite literary agent, Peter Matson, for not only believing that this was a book but for making it one.

At Oxford University Press, I was overwhelmingly lucky to get Tim Bartlett as my editor, who seems never to have been told that masterful book editing is a dying art; this book is vastly better for what, with apologies to *West Wing* fans, I think of as the Bartlett administration. Peter Ginna left me no doubt that Oxford was the right press for this book. My warm thanks, too, to Sara Leopold, Rob Tempio, Catherine Humphries, Saskia Cornes of Sterling Lord Literistic, and many more.

David Makovsky was my first boss in journalism and taught me an embarrassingly large proportion of what I know about the Middle East peace process; he has been both a mentor and a stalwart friend. The magnificent, principled, and much-missed philanthropist behind the Dorot Foundation, the late Joy Ungerleider-Mayerson, remains an inspiration. Warren Christopher has been wonderfully gracious. For their insights on the Middle East over the years, I am particularly grateful to Fouad Ajami, Bart Gellman,

Rob Danin, Dan Byman, Gideon Rose, Rob Satloff, Neal Levy, Wylie Thomas, Ken Stein, Guillermo Christensen, Stan Moskowitz, and my old Rehavia neighbor, Hirsh Goodman, who leaked me a precious copy of the still-unsigned Oslo accord in August 1993.

At Columbia Graduate School of Journalism, David Krajicek subjected my prose to a devastating onslaught, for which I offer lasting gratitude and the hope he will never do it again. Steve Isaacs taught us Flaubert; Leonard Doyle was followed by ferrets; Dick Blood was, well, Dick Blood; the late Irv Horowitz taught me that there are two types of people; and Jim Carey rode herd on a vastly less grandiose thesis. Sam Freedman always believed that this was a book. I trust that this will allay their collective suspicion that I lacked the staying power for a sustained reporting job. At Queen's University, I learned much from Gerald Tulchinsky, Geoffrey Smith, and many others. Duff Crerar, wherever he may be, first made academic history seem thrilling.

Many thanks, too, to a series of splendid editors: David Shipley, Barry Gewen, and Caroline Rand Herron of the *New York Times*; Bob Berger and Cherry Gee of the *Los Angeles Times*; Peter Beinart and Chuck Lane of *The New Republic*; Brian Duffy of *U.S. News & World Report*; Eva Friede of *The Montreal Gazette*; Jeff Barak of *The Jerusalem Post*; and David Horovitz, Sharon Ashley, and Gershom Gorenberg of *The Jerusalem Report*.

On a more personal level, I owe a deep debt to the other two Musketeers of my dissertation group, David Greenberg and Sharon Musher, for cheerful friendship, academic strategizing, superb comments, and loyalty straight out of Dumas. They both endured many early chapters, and right before his wedding, David somehow read the entire final manuscript, providing an editing tour de force that dramatically improved this book. (Needless to say, all errors contained herein are entirely their fault.)

Wexner Class VIII provided a wonderful sense of fellowship, taught me everything I know about Habermas, and gave me such magnificent friends as Aaron Panken, Shaul Kelner, Lauren Eichler Berkun, Angela Warnick Buchdahl, Robin Axelrod, Alyssa Gray, Caron Blau Rothstein, Eve Rudin Weiner, and Dov Weiss. A lugheaded thank you to Emily Bazelon, Marina Fineman, Bruce Goldberger, Jay Michaelson, Tanya Schlam, Aleeza Strubel, and Adam Shear. In Toronto, my special thanks to Paul Beard, Laz Klein, Stuart Shapiro, Ian Solomon, Ari Finkelstein, Eric Moses, Rob Funk, Mike Allibon, Angus McMurtry, and the rest of the Queen's and Hebrew University crews.

And my abiding gratitude to all of the following, all of whom should know why they're here but shouldn't miss the chance to let me remind them: Wendy Cracower, David Sloane, Beth Berkowitz, Shira Deener,

Josh Feinberg, Derek Chollet, Tara Bahrampour, Rachel Beck, Jennifer Buksbaum, Lance Gould, Meera Somasundaram, Adam Entous, John Pitman, Ilene Prusher, Tess Reisgies Stevenson, Gillian Judge, Raquel Ukeles, Amy Sandgrund, Aren Gottlieb, Sari Levinson Raskin, Adam Raskin, Rachel Goldberg, Heidi Winig, Greg Harris, Amy Jo Ravin, Eric Brown, Eric Morrow, Debbie Weinstein, Elissa Schwartz, Andy Sandler, Elana Behar, Risa Kaufman, Judith Shapero, Rebecca Starr, Reva Nelson, Lynn Harris, Jill Rackmill, Esther Sperber, Lisa Messinger, Pam Ely, Dani Eisenstadt, Rachel Kirsner Schneider, Amy Tirk Seigle, Heather Hostetter, Ron Krebs, Rob Genter, Chris Copazolla, Michael Miller, Marina Rustow, Josh Mitnick, and Julie Zuckerman—as well as four more teachers, Ihor Pelech, Levi Lauer, Zvi Wolff, and Judy Klitsner. And Dena, sweetie.

Finally, my most elemental debt is to my family; they were not supporting a friend, but their support has been cherished nonetheless. My love to my outstanding parents, Karen and Arthur, and also to Martin and Lyn; Cathy, Jonny, and young Thomas; Gina and Jeffy; Stan, Lisa, Kai, Barb, and Davin; Leone and Hazel; Janine, Robyn, Steven, Lori, Yossi, Talia, and Trevor; my Israeli relatives, Hirshowitzes of all ages; the extended family around the globe; and Gary, Jack to my Bobby and Bobby to my Jack. This work is dedicated to my grandparents: Gert and Nate Basserabie and Joe (Chona) Bobrow, who did not live to see it finished, and Bess Bobrow, who proudly did. I hope the whole family will take lasting satisfaction from these pages.

They are also dedicated to the memory of Yitzhak Rabin; I am from a generation that remembers where they were when Rabin was shot, not when Kennedy was. God forbid I get over either. "If I had not been angry about that," Orwell wrote, "I should never have written the book."

And as JFK put it, in his inimitable Boston tones, we do these things "not because they are easy, but because they are hard."

—WB
New York City
January 2003

Credits

JFK in Egypt, John F. Kennedy Library
JFK in Mandate Palestine, John F. Kennedy Library
RFK in Jerusalem, John F. Kennedy Library

Ben-Gurion and JFK in 1951, Israeli Government Press Office (Fritz Cohen)
Palm Beach meeting of JFK and Meir, John F. Kennedy Library

Talbot and Ben-Gurion, Israeli Government Press Office
Feldman and Eban, Israeli Government Press Office (Moshe Milner)
Barbour presenting creditials, Israeli Government Press Office (Moshe Pridan)

Nasser on the cover of *Time*, courtesy *Time*
JFK and Kamel, John F. Kennedy Library

King Saud's arrival, John F. Kennedy Library
JFK and Faysal, John F. Kennedy Library
JFK and LeMay, John F. Kennedy Library

Peres and Rabin, Israeli Government Press Office (Moshe Pridan)
Hawk battery, Israeli Government Press Office (Moshe Pridan)

Nahal Soreq reactor, Israeli Government Press Office (Fritz Cohen)
Dimona reactor, data available from U.S. Geological Survey, EROS Data Center, Sioux
Falls, S.D.

JFK's last press conference, John F. Kennedy Library
Eshkol signing condolence book, Israeli Government Press Office (Moshe Pridan)
Yad Kennedy dedication, Israeli Government Press Office (Moshe Pridan)

Index